Antisocial Behavior and Mental Health Problems

Explanatory Factors in Childhood and Adolescence

Antisocial Behavior and Mental Health Problems

Explanatory Factors in Childhood and Adolescence

Rolf Loeber
University of Pittsburgh

David P. Farrington
University of Cambridge

Magda Stouthamer-Loeber
University of Pittsburgh

Welmoet B. Van Kammen
University of Pittsburgh

LEA LAWRENCE ERLBAUM ASSOCIATES, PUBLISHERS
1998   Mahwah, New Jersey   London

Lawrence Erlbaum Associates, Inc., Publishers
10 Industrial Avenue
Mahwah, NJ 07430

Cover design by Kathryn Houghtaling Lacey

Library of Congress Cataloging-in-Publication Data

Antisocial behavior and mental health problems : explanatory factors in childhood and adolescence / Rolf Loeber ... [et al.].
     p.   cm.
  Includes bibliographical references (p.   ) and index
  ISBN 0-8058-2956-3 (hardcover : alk. paper)
  1.   Problem youth—Pennsylvania—Pittsburgh—Longitudinal studies. 2.   Problem children—Pennsylvania—Pittsburgh—Longitudinal studies.
  RJ506.P63A57 1998   97–38123
  618.92'89—dc21   CIP

Printed in the United States of America
10 9 8 7 6 5 4 3 2 1

Contents

Preface

If undertaking longitudinal studies on the development of problem behavior is one major and daunting task, publishing books about such studies is quite another. This volume reports results obtained in the Pittsburgh Youth Study, whose first assessments were carried out in 1987–1988 on three samples of boys ($N = 1,517$) and, which, we are happy to say, is still going strong with regular assessments of two out of the three samples ($N = 1,009$) of boys and their families. On perusal of this volume, readers might ask why this report focuses primarily on only the first two assessments of this rich data set. The answer is that, early on, we decided to write about the basic elements of the study, how it was started, how the samples were selected, what measurements were administered, and what the "baseline" behaviors were of the boys in the three samples. We found that this task alone easily produced a book-length manuscript, and that the results were extremely interesting in and of themselves. Second, unfortunately we encountered several delays in publishing this volume. To paraphrase Britton (1835):

> Had we been less scrupulous, and influenced more by the pressing emergencies of the moment, and the entreaties and complaints of friends and correspondents, than the desire of satisfying our own minds . . ., we would certainly have finished the work two or three years ago. (p. v)

We are now in the process of writing a second volume reporting on results obtained with longitudinal data over 10 data waves. Also, we already published a good number of analyses in scientific articles and chapters using longitudinal data over more data waves, which are occasionally referred to in the present report. Among these publications is a volume on the art of executing this complex study and retaining a very high percentage of the participants over many repeated assessments (see Stouthamer-Loeber, & Van Kammen, 1995).

The present volume provides the key background and specific information on which most of the later longitudinal analyses rest.

In the preparation of this volume, we are greatly indebted to several individuals who worked on this project, have given advice, or sponsored it. First, we owe much to the efforts of the data collection team, particularly, the numerous interviewers and their supervisors, Dianne Miller and Rosemary Constanzo. Also, we are greatly indebted to the data management team, especially Barbara Kumer and Matthew Cronin, and secretarial staff, particularly Celia Nourse Eatman, Susan Jones, and more recently JoAnn Fraser, who assisted with the preparation of this book. In the early stages of the research, we benefitted greatly from collaboration with Anthony Costello. We also received valued advice from our advisory board, consisting of Alfred Blumstein, Dante Cicchetti, Malcolm Klein, Lloyd Ohlin, and Lee Robins. Moreover, we received valued support and advice from a number of other longitudinal researchers, including Pat Cohen, Marc Le Blanc, Joan McCord, and Richard E. Tremblay. Also, in the preparatory stages of the study, we were inspired by the advice and collaboration with the two "sister" studies, the Denver Youth Study, and the Rochester Youth Development Study, and their principal investigators, David Huizinga and Terence Thornberry, and their colleagues. We are also grateful to Joseph Daugardas for facilitating access to the juvenile court records of the Pittsburgh boys.

Finally, the study would never have gotten underway without the encouragement and sponsorship of the Office of Juvenile Justice and Delinquency Prevention, United States Department of Justice. Particularly, we are extremely grateful to Pam Swain and Barbara Tatem Kelley for initiating the program of research, and to Donnie Le Boeuf, Irving Slott, and in more recent years, James C. Howell, for their valuable support and assistance. More recently the support for the study and for the completion of this volume has been primarily forthcoming from the National Institute of Mental Health, and we are particularly grateful to John Richters and Peter Jensen for their support. Points of view or opinions in this document are those of the authors and do not necessarily represent the official position or policies of the United States Department of Justice or the National Institute of Mental Health.

We have found that the Pittsburgh Youth Study is an extremely exciting adventure. We hope that the present volume will convey some of that excitement to readers, and that it will whet their appetite for follow-up publications in future years.

1

Introduction: Juvenile Delinquency, Substance Use, Sexual Behavior, and Mental Health Problems

Juvenile problem behaviors affect us all. Multitudes of parents are confronted by their child's stealing, early sexual behavior, serious substance use, or prolonged depressed moods. At home, parents may see endless harangues and quarrels in which children and their siblings may become participants as well as victims. Parents are often afraid that their child will not outgrow serious problem behavior and might become chronically delinquent, addicted to alcohol or drugs, or mentally unstable. Teachers find their main mandate in the classroom thwarted by students who disrupt academic courses, bully fellow students, bring weapons into the school, or simply become chronically truant.

Outside of the family and the school, the impact of juveniles' problem behavior on society is colossal. Huge numbers of delinquent youth are incarcerated in detention centers and large numbers of youth with substance use and mental health problems are brought to detoxification centers and assessed and treated by mental health professionals (American Psychiatric Association, 1994; Burns, 1991). In addition, many youth damage their health by the consumption of harmful substances suffer from serious anxiety, depression, withdrawal, and commit suicide.

Another major area of concern is youths' emulation of adult behaviors, including drinking alcoholic beverages, driving cars, having sexual intercourse, or staying out late. Adolescents' increasing demands for independence in these areas may clash with the interests of and protection offered by parents. Often parents and their children disagree about the timing of children's independence from their parents; to some extent, conflict around this theme can be considered normal. However, a minority of youth presses to become more independent at what is generally considered to be a premature age.

Epidemiological surveys have provided key information about the prevalence and degree of seriousness at different ages of a wide array of child problem behaviors in such domains as delinquency (Glueck & Glueck, 1950; Magnusson, 1988; West, 1982; West & Farrington, 1973, 1977), substance use (Kandel, Yamaguchi, & Chen, 1992; Pulkkinen, 1988; White, 1988), early sexual behavior (e.g., Jessor & Jessor, 1977), and mental health problems (e.g., Cohen & Brook, 1987). Because the prevalence of these problems changes dramatically between childhood and adulthood, cumulative prevalence curves help document when changes in prevalence accelerates or slows down. However, such curves do not demonstrate the cessation of deviance.

Problem behaviors should not be seen as inevitable, as is evident from historic variations in the level of juvenile problem behavior. We are convinced about the necessity to document the extent of problem behaviors in current generations of youth. This we can accomplish by studying developmental sequences of problems, thereby establishing continuity among behaviors over different periods of children's lives. A further improvement will take place by identifying critical precursors that explain why some youth and not others engage in serious delinquency, substance use or early sexual behavior or suffer from mental health problems.

Knowledge of the extent and changes of these problem behaviors is important for several reasons. In general, interventions and health planning can be difficult when the extent of the problems and their course over time are unclear. Also, understanding which risk and protective factors apply to which problem behaviors, and whether particular risk and protective factors can best explain some but not other problem behaviors, is essential for the formulation of theories that form the basis of interventions.

CONTINUITY AND DEVELOPMENT

Continuity

Evidence about the continuity of problem behaviors has been mounting (Blumstein, Cohen, Roth, & Visher, 1986; Caspi, Moffitt, Newman & Silva, 1996; Loeber, 1982; Pulkkinen & Hurme, 1984; Sampson & Laub, 1993). Male aggressive and delinquent behavior is often highly stable over several decades (Loeber & Stouthamer-Loeber, 1987; Olweus, 1979). Also, numerous studies have linked early physical aggression to later violence (Farrington, 1991), early tobacco consumption to later drug use (Ellickson, 1992), and early depressed mood to later clinical depression (Kovacs, Paulauskas, Gatsonis, & Richards, 1988). Similar findings apply to conduct disorder. For instance, in a study of clinic-referred boys, Lahey (1995) showed that 87.7% of the boys with a diagnosis of conduct disorder continued to qualify for a diagnosis of conduct disorder in the next 3 years. Similarly, Farrington (1992a) found that 76% of males convicted between ages 10 and 16 were reconvicted between ages 17 and 24. Although such stability is in evidence within the same category of behavior over time, it is essential to broaden the inquiry about continuity by studying a wider range of related behaviors. For example, in the domain of disruptive behavior, Farrington (1991) analyzed the continuity of behavior from ages 8–10 to age 32 in the Cambridge Study in Delinquent Development. More than twice as many of the most disruptive males at ages 8–10 were convicted for a violent offense by age 32 as the remaining, less disruptive boys at ages 8–10.

In the area of substance use, studies have shown moderate levels of stability over time (Maddahian, 1985), but such stability depends on the age at which the use is first measured and the type of substance. As to mental health problems, in many studies, the stability coefficients for externalizing problems are substantially higher than those for internalizing problems (Achenbach, 1985; Capaldi, 1992).

The stability of behavior is often difficult to gauge prospectively. However, looking back over individuals' lives, it is often more apparent which types of behaviors in an individual's life are stable or not. Loeber and Stouthamer-Loeber (1987) reviewed prospective and retrospective studies and concluded that, when viewed retrospectively, the majority of adult chronic offenders had acted in a disruptive manner during their elementary school years. This high degree of stability, as Robins and Ratcliff (1979) and Zeitlin (1986) pointed out, implies that serious antisocial behavior rarely emerges *de novo* in adulthood and instead typically begins much earlier in life.

Thus, there is considerable evidence for the continuity of problem behavior. However, looking prospectively, continuity is far from perfect and, therefore, predictions from early problem behavior to later problem behavior are usually not high. Moreover, continuity is usually not limited to the stability of the same behaviors over time. Also important is heterotypic continuity (i.e., the continuity among different problem behaviors over time). Often heterotypic continuity occurs primarily because new problem symptoms are added to existing ones, gradually leading to a diversification of problem behavior (Loeber, 1988).

Development

Many problem behaviors in childhood and adolescence can be considered age normative, in that they occur more often at certain age periods than others. For example, separation anxiety early in life and highly oppositional behavior later are both common (Loeber & Hay, 1994). Therefore, in several ways, numerous problem behaviors can be thought of as developmentally normal at some ages. However, there are at least three criteria to use in judging whether problem behaviors are deviant. First, child problem behaviors can be considered deviant when they persist during periods in which most youth have outgrown such behaviors. An example is the persistence of highly oppositional behavior during the elementary school-age period. Second, a problem behavior is deviant if it results in a high degree of impairment (e.g., when the withdrawn behavior is so serious that affected children refuse to go to school and suffer in their academic performance, or when substance use seriously affects personal relationships). Third, problem behaviors are deviant when they result in harm to others. Examples are violence and theft of others' property.

A critical issue in the study of children's behavior is our lack of knowledge about how best to (a) discriminate prospectively between those youngsters who will outgrow their early problem behaviors and those who will not, (b) discriminate between youth who will become impaired in functioning because of their problem behavior and those who will not, and (c) differentiate between those youth whose infliction of harm is transitory and those who are on the road to persistence in these behaviors.

In recent decades, researchers have started to look beyond prediction and have focused on deviancy processes that take place during the interval between the occurrence of a predictor and an outcome (Loeber & Le Blanc, 1990). There are several reasons why this question is critical. The development of delinquency, substance use, early sexual behavior, and mental health problems often takes place gradually over time, with some behavior problems starting earlier than others but most taking years to reach a serious level. This is illustrated hypothetically in Fig. 1.1. We are learning more about the ordering of the development of problem behaviors from childhood to adolescence, both about development within particular domains (Belson, 1975; Loeber et al., 1993; Robins & Wish, 1977; Yamaguchi & Kandel, 1984) and about parallel development between domains (Caron & Rutter, 1991; Loeber & Keenan, 1994; Nottelmann & Jensen,

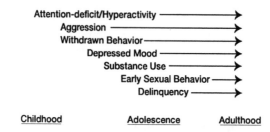

FIG. 1.1. A schematic representation of the developmental sequence of mental health problems, substance use, and delinquency from childhood to adulthood.

1995). The latter, often discussed in terms of comorbidity, helps us better understand which youth are most at risk to develop, for example, both disruptive behaviors and mood problems.

The preceding discussion illustrates several points. First, predictions are far from perfect, indicating that we are not yet able to predict adequately which youth are most at risk for later serious maladjustment. Second, a proportion of youth shows highly stable problem behavior over time. Third, processes leading to serious deviant behavior usually are incremental and take years to become apparent and in full bloom. Fourth, some youth are more at risk than others to develop comorbid conditions. Fifth, youth who desist or improve overtime are an important group to study.

A SINGLE PROBLEM THEORY OR THEORIES OF DISTINCT PROBLEMS?

Researchers have not been in agreement about whether to consider all juvenile problem behaviors as sufficiently similar to be covered by a single construct (e.g., Jessor, Donovan, & Costa, 1991; Jessor & Jessor, 1977; Kaplan, 1980; Loeber, 1988; Osgood, Johnston, O'Malley, & Bachman, 1988). Whether data fit a single problem theory or different theories for different problem behaviors at different ages can be evaluated according to several criteria, of which we want to stress: (a) strength of the interrelations among problem behaviors, (b) age shifts in problem behaviors, (c) specific and general explanatory factors, and (d) shifts in explanatory factors with age. We briefly address the importance of each of these criteria.

Interrelations Among Problem Behaviors

Evidence for a single underlying problem behavior, with several manifestations, can best be justified when the manifestations are highly correlated. However, when the intercorrelations are very different, this provides some evidence that there may be several underlying problem entities. Based on the intercorrelations among problem behaviors, some researchers have advocated a single general deviance or problem construct (e.g., Jessor, Donovan, & Costa, 1991; Jessor & Jessor, 1977; Kaplan, 1980; Patterson, Reid, & Dishion, 1992; Robins, 1966), whereas others found support for a distinction between delinquency and substance use (Gilmore et al., 1991; Loeber, 1988; Tildesley, Hops, Ary, & Andrews, 1995; White & Labouvie, 1994). Most of these studies did not include measures of internalizing problems (such as depressed mood) and therefore do not show to what extent internalizing problems correlate more highly with either delinquency or substance use.

There is a consensus in psychological studies that factor analytic studies have revealed separate factors for externalizing and internalizing child problems (Achenbach, 1985; Achenbach, Conners, Quay, Verhulst & Howell, 1989). However, some researchers have made a distinction within externalizing problems, such as between covert (or concealing) and overt (or confrontive) problem behaviors (e.g., Frick et al., 1993; Loeber, 1988; Loeber & Schmaling, 1985a). Within the domain of externalizing problems, some studies support factorial distinctions between oppositional behaviors and conduct problems (e.g., Achenbach et al., 1989; Achenbach & Edelbrock, 1979; Frick et al., 1991), and between these disruptive behaviors and hyperactive/inattention problems (Hinshaw, 1987). Likewise, diagnostic systems of pathology in childhood and adolescence have made distinctions among such diagnoses as oppositional defiant disorder, conduct disorder, and attention-deficit hyperactivity disorder (ADHD). In contrast, sociological investigators have tended to ignore attention deficit and hyperactivity as possible components of a general problem syndrome.

Moreover, practically all investigations of problem syndromes have been limited to adolescents. Consequently, little is known about syndrome patterns for elementary school-age children (but see Achenbach et al., 1989; Achenbach & Edelbrock, 1979; Frick et al., 1991). Problem behavior in this age group is particularly of interest because of the emergence of early onset delinquents who often become later chronic, diversified offenders (Farrington, Loeber, & Van Kammen, 1990).

One of the untested assumptions of a single problem theory is that behavior problems of one kind are interchangeable with behavior problems of another kind. However, there is increasing evidence that some categories of problem behaviors are not interchangeable. For example, Loeber et al. (1993) found that physical fighting enhanced the probability of boys' onset of covert conduct problems, but that the onset of covert conduct problems did not enhance the probability of physical fighting. As another example, attention deficit and hyperactivity are implicated in the onset of delinquency or conduct problems (Farrington et al., 1990; Loeber et al. 1995), but delinquency or conduct problems are not known to affect the onset of attention deficit or hyperactivity. Thus, several types of problem behavior are not equivalent or interchangeable and their interaction may be asymmetrical, in that one problem behavior may influence another but the reverse may not apply (White, 1990). This type of evidence lends more support for a multiproblem than a single-problem syndrome theory.

Finally, a single-problem theory usually does not question the course and degree that juveniles develop multiple-problem behaviors. On the one hand, there is no doubt that groups of individuals with specific problem behaviors emerge over time (e.g., delinquents with no substance use problems and nondelinquent substance abusers). On the other hand, there is a consensus that groups of multiproblem youth develop as well (Loeber, 1988). For example, many aggressive youth may eventually display both violent and property crime in adulthood and may become heavy substance abusers. When a single-problem theory is applied to both single- and multi-problem youth, it becomes impossible to discover why some individuals' deviancy becomes varied, whereas others' deviance remains limited to a single domain.

Age Shifts in Problem Behavior

One of the most characteristic features of problem behavior during childhood and adolescence is that manifestations change. The change pattern varies in terms of severity, frequency, variety, and onset (Cohen et al., 1993; Loeber, 1982). In general, with age, the severity, frequency, and variety of problem behaviors increase. This happens as new problem behaviors emerge: The onset of novel problem behaviors occurs while, as a rule, old problem behaviors are retained (Kandel, 1975; Loeber, 1988).

In addition, the strength of relationships among different domains of behavior problems may change with age. For example, Osgood et al. (1988) reported that, with age, both criminal behavior and heavy alcohol use become less associated with general deviance. A problem theory should predict the temporal sequencing of behavior problems and changes in strength of association between different types of problem behavior with age, and which youth are at particular risk of advancing to multiple and serious problem behaviors.

Specific and General Explanatory Factors

There is increasing evidence that different problem behaviors are associated with distinct explanatory factors. This is also reflected in distinct diagnoses applicable to mental disorders occurring in childhood and adolescence (American Psychiatric Association, 1987). For example, the etiology of attention-deficit/hyperactivity is very different from the etiology of conduct problems, particularly in terms of age of onset (attention-deficit and hyperactivity starting earlier), correlates, and explanatory factors (Farrington, Loeber & Van Kammen, 1990; Hinshaw, 1987; Loeber, Brinthaupt, & Green, 1990; Loeber, Green, Lahey, Christ, & Frick, 1992). Likewise, Brook, Whiteman, and Cohen (1995) demonstrated that the correlates of drug use and aggression only partly overlapped. Thus, the correlates of several types of problem behaviors are not equivalent or interchangeable. Furthermore, aggression and theft were found to have only partly overlapping correlates in at least one study (Loeber & Schmaling, 1985b).

The issue of specific versus general explanatory factors is particularly pertinent to the development of multiproblem boys. We know too little to what extent explanatory factors associated with the development of single deviant outcomes also apply to the development of multiple deviant outcomes.

Age Shifts in Explanatory Factors

A final criterion for evaluating a problem theory is to examine the extent that explanatory factors at one age are the same as those at another age, or whether there are explanatory factors that emerge as children mature. Examples are explanatory factors in the realm of peer and school influences, which do not clearly apply to the preschool period, or unemployment, which does not apply to childhood or most of adolescence. In our eyes, the best theories of problem behavior need to take into account that explanatory factors may change with age and that such changes need to be incorporated in the theory.

In summary, we see more grounds for making distinctions among categories of problem behaviors than for merging them all into one single-problem category. Among those reasons, we stressed differential interrelationships among problem behaviors, age shifts in problem behavior, specific and general explanatory factors, and age shifts in explanatory factors. For these reasons, this volume separately treats different general and specific categories of problem behaviors. It distinguishes among delinquency, substance use, and early sexual behavior. However, we are also interested in disruptive behaviors that do not necessarily qualify as delinquent acts, but often are developmental precursors to such acts. Here we focus on attention-deficit/hyperactivity, physical aggression, and covert behavior. In addition, we are interested in internalizing problems, particularly shy/withdrawn behavior and depressed mood. Although some of these distinctions are more supported in the empirical literature than others, the present investigation takes seriously the issue of distinctiveness.

THE DEARTH OF RELEVANT EXPLANATIONS

We see a need to examine a multiproblem group of boys and contrast them with boys who have single types of problems. However, investigators have usually worked within each domain of delinquency, substance use, early sexual behavior, or externalizing and internalizing mental health problems rather than across several domains. There are several reasons why explanations across different domains are needed. First, a considerable proportion of juveniles show more than one type of problem behavior. However, the extent of such comorbidity is still poorly understood (Caron & Rutter, 1991; Loeber & Keenan, 1994). Second, relatively little is known about the pattern of explanatory factors that apply to multiproblem youth. Also, it remains to be seen to what extent explanations of the behavior of youth with few problems still apply once youth with multiple-problem behaviors are accounted for.

Thus, we need to know both the nature of explanatory variables that can account for youth manifesting specific problem behaviors and the nature of explanatory variables that cut across different domains of problem behavior. Prior longitudinal research has rarely addressed these issues. Information about explanatory factors that are associated with different types of problem behaviors is potentially highly relevant for interventions because a reduction in the impact of such risk factors may lead to an improvement in multiple deviant outcomes.

Multivariate Models of Distal and Proximal Influences

Because the explanation of child problem behavior is multifaceted and not determined by a single explanatory factor, multivariate techniques of analysis have been increasingly used. Typically, these analyses examine which variables account for most of the variance when other factors are taken into account. Also, characteristically, investigators usually have used nonhierarchical analyses in which all variables, irrespective of their nature, have an equal chance of entering into the equation.

We see several reasons why such a strategy is not optimal. First, such an approach is usually atheoretical. As a result, variables from different spheres and mechanisms of influences (e.g., neighborhood crime and parental disciplinary method) compete for entry into the equation. Along with the work of Bronfenbrenner (1979) and others (Dishion, French, & Patterson, 1995; Jessor, Donovan, & Costa, 1991; Roff & Wirt, 1984; Sampson & Laub, 1993), we propose (Fig. 1.2) that the most immediate influences affecting child problem behavior are other child characteristics (such as attention deficit, hyperactivity, and lack of guilt feelings). Second in order of influence are social factors, particularly parent variables, and third in order are macrovariables (socioeconomic, demographic, and neighborhood factors).

We would add that, more often than not, distal influences on child behavior appear to be mediated through the most proximal layer of influences. An

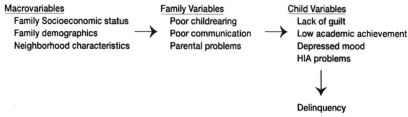

FIG. 1.2. Schematic representation of the major sources of influence on child behavior.

example of such a thesis is that, although neighborhoods may influence child problem behaviors directly, most of their influence can be accounted for through their influence on parents. There is a surprising theoretical consensus among several neighborhood researchers (Simcha-Fagan & Schwartz, 1986; Gottfredson, McNeil, & Gottfredson, 1991) and longitudinal researchers (Farrington, 1994; Rutter, 1981a) that neighborhoods exercise indirect effects on delinquency through their effects on families and individuals. Explicitly, the neighborhood context influences methods of childrearing, methods of childrearing influence the extent to which children build up internal inhibitions against deviant behavior, and these internal inhibitions reduce the likelihood of children engaging in delinquent acts. Although plausible, there are few studies that have empirically demonstrated such a hierarchy of influences (see e.g., Robins, 1966; Rutter, 1978). We propose to use a hierarchical regression method to investigate this hierarchy.

In the social sciences, it is not always easy to make clear-cut distinctions between dependent and independent variables, and confounds pose a threat to the validity of any analysis. For instance, is it reasonable to use children's reports of delinquent activities of their peers (as the independent variable) as a predictor of the youth's own delinquent involvement (the dependent variable)? Although some researchers have maintained that these two constructs are distinct (e.g., Elliott, Huizinga, & Ageton, 1985), we are cautious about assuming this. Instead, we would argue that, because juveniles commit crimes in the company of their peers more often than not (Reiss & Farrington, 1991), the use of the youth's report of his delinquent peers may be measuring the same underlying construct as the youth's own delinquency. In other words, because offenses are mainly committed with others, delinquent boys will usually, as a consequence, have delinquent peers. This is just one example of confounds introduced by the lack of distinction between independent and dependent variables (see also Amdur, 1989). This is addressed further in chapter 5.

The usual multivariate analyses used by researchers in the social sciences are directed at identifying the statistically most optimal combination of presumed explanatory variables in predicting an outcome. Although justifiable in many respects, we argue that this is not sufficient because interaction effects among independent variables usually are not investigated. Interaction effects need to be examined because a given independent variable may have an effect only in the presence of another variable that acts as a catalyst, or it may be less potent in the presence of another variable (e.g., when the other variable acts as a protective factor). Also, the effect of two variables in combination may be much greater than the sum of their separate effects.

WHY ANOTHER LONGITUDINAL STUDY?

The multivariate analyses reported in this volume concern the first two waves of our longitudinal investigation—the Pittsburgh Youth Study—complemented by a follow-up over 6 years in the juvenile court records. In this research, we owe much to an array of prospective longitudinal studies that have been undertaken and, in many cases, are continuing. Many of these classic studies are summarized in Table 1.1. We used the following criteria for inclusion in the list: a sample size of several hundred at least, a large number of different types of variables measured (e.g., individual and family factors), a longitudinal design with publications reporting on data spanning at least 5 years, prospectively chosen general, preferably representative population samples, more than one personal contact with participants (as opposed to data from records), and measures of offending, substance use, early sexual behavior, or mental health problems. Space does not allow a more detailed discussion of the merits of each study, but we wanted to list them to place our own study in context (for previous reviews of longitudinal surveys, see Farrington, 1979, 1988). The studies differ in their design, participant selection, and number and types of assessments. There are, of course, more recently mounted ongoing longitudinal studies not listed in Table 1.1 because the long-term follow-ups have not yet come to fruition. Also, some famous studies did not have more than one personal contact with participants (e.g., Shannon, 1988; Tracy, Wolfgang, & Figlio, 1985, 1990; Wolfgang, Thornberry, & Figlio, 1987).

Design

Some prior research projects are retrospective, in that data collection was limited to participants' recall of events in the distant past (e.g., Lewis, Shanok, Grant, & Ritvo, 1983). This design may be justified in studying rare outcomes such as homicide, where a retrospective case-control study may be needed, but

TABLE 1.1
Classic Longitudinal Studies on Delinquency, Substance Use,
Sexual Behavior, and Mental Health Problems.

Principal Investigators	Sample	Typical Recent Publication
Brunswick (U.S.)	668 African American males ages 12–17 living in Harlem in 1967–1968. Followed up to ages 26–31. Focus on substance use.	Brunswick (1984)
Cairns (U.S.)	Follow-up of 695 boys and girls in 4th and 7th grades, started in 1981. Assessments included the children, parents, grandparents, and other caregivers. Since then, followed up at yearly intervals with a high degree of subject cooperation. Focus on aggression, school dropouts, and gender differences.	Cairns and Cairns (1994)
Cohen & Brook (U.S.)	Random sample of 975 children living in upper New York State ages 1–10 in 1975. Psychiatric evaluations including each child and mother. Follow-up interviews of children in 1983 and 1985–1986.	Cohen et al. (1993)
Douglas and Wadsworth (U.K.)	5,362 children selected from legitimate single births in England, Scotland, and Wales in 1 week of March 1946. Followed up in criminal records to age 21. Mainly medical and school data collected, but samples interviewed at ages 26, 36, and 43.	Wadsworth (1991)
Elliott and Huizinga (U.S.)	Nationally representative sample of 1,725 adolescents ages 11–17 years old in 1976. Interviewed in 5 successive years (1977–1981) and again in 1984, 1987, 1990, and 1993. Arrest records collected.	Elliott (1994)
Eron and Huesmann (U.S.)	875 eight-year-old children in a semirural setting of New York State first assessed in 1960. Focus on aggressive problem behavior. Follow-up interviews 10 years and 22 years later.	Eron and Huesmann (1990)
Fergusson (New Zealand)	1,265 children born in Christchurch in 1977. Studied at birth, 4 months, 1 year, and annually up to age 15. Data from mother, child, and teacher, including self-reported delinquency and substance use.	Fergusson et al. (1994)
S. Glueck and E. Glueck (U.S.)	500 male delinquents in Massachusetts correctional schools in 1939–1944, and 500 matched nondelinquents. Contacted at average ages of 14, 25, and 31. Nondelinquents followed up to age 47 by Vaillant. Original data reanalyzed by Sampson and Laub.	Glueck and Glueck (1968) Sampson and Laub (1993)
Hawkins and Catalano (U.S.)	All 919 fifth-grade students in 18 elementary schools in Seattle in the Fall of 1985. Some of sample had been studied since first grade and had been exposed to an experimental school intervention. Annual follow-up interviews to 1993.	Peterson, Hawkins, Abbott, & Catalano (1994)
Huizinga, Elliott, and Weiher (U.S.)	Probability sampling of households produced 1,500 children in high risk neighborhoods of Denver, Colorado, of boys and girls, ages 7, 9, 11, 13, and 15 years old in 1988. Follow-up at almost yearly intervals and still ongoing.	Huizinga (1995)
Janson and Wikström (Sweden)	All 15,117 children born in Stockholm in 1953 and living in Stockholm in 1963. Tested in schools in 1966. Subsample of mothers interviewed in 1968. Followed up in police records to 1983.	Wikström (1990)
Jessor (U.S.)	A sample of 1,126 high school students (Grades 7–9) first assessed in 1969 (average age 14) and a sample of 497 freshman college students first assessed in 1970 (average age 19). Self-reports of problem behavior and substance use. Follow-up to 1981.	Jessor et al. (1991)

Principal Investigators	Sample	Typical Recent Publication
Kandel (U.S.)	8,206 adolescents from a representative secondary school sample (Grades 10–11) in New York State. Completed self-report substance use questionnaires in the fall of 1971 and then half a year later; 5,574 parents responded to questionnaires. Adult follow-ups of a subsample in 1980, 1984, and 1990 (N = 1,160).	Kandel et al. (1992)
Kellam and Ensminger (U.S.)	Sample of 1,242 first graders in an African American Chicago neighborhood (Woodlawn) first assessed in 1966–1967. Focus on shy and aggressive behaviors and substance use. Reassessed in 1975–1976. Followed up by Ensminger and McCord in 1993.	Ensminger, Kellam, & Rubin (1983); McCord & Ensminger, in press
Le Blanc and Fréchette (Canada)	(1) Representative sample of 3,070 French-speaking Montreal adolescents. Completed self-report questionnaires in 1974 at ages 12–16 and again in 1976. (2) 470 male delinquents seen at age 15 in 1974 and again at ages 17 and 22. All followed up in criminal records to age 25. Male samples interviewed at age 32.	Le Blanc (1994); Le Blanc & Fréchette (1989)
Loeber and Lahey (U.S.)	Sample of 177 clinic referred boys, who were 7–12 years old at the beginning of the study (1987–1988). Yearly follow-up with diagnostic assessments, and many other measurements. Currently still being followed-up.	Loeber, Green, Keenan, & Lahey (1995)
Magnusson and Stattin (Sweden)	All 1,027 children (age 10) in Orebro in 1965. Followed up at ages 13 and 15. Followed up in criminal records to age 30. Two other cohorts born in 1950 and 1952 also followed up.	Klinteberg, Andersson, Magnusson, & Stattin (1993)
McCord and McCord (U.S.)	All 650 boys (average age 10) nominated as difficult or average by Cambridge and Somerville (Massachusetts) schools in 1937–1939. Experimental group visited by counselors for average of 5 years. Followed up in 1975–1980 by mail questionnaires and interviews and in criminal records.	J. McCord (1991)
Miller and Kolvin (U.K.)	All 1,142 children born in Newcastle in May–June 1947. Children and families contacted at least once a year up to age 15 and finally at age 22. Children followed up in criminal records to ages 32–33. Subsample (N = 266) interviewed at ages 32–33. Original sample, their spouses, and their children followed up in criminal records to 1994.	Kolvin, Miller, Scott, Gatzanis, and Fleeting (1990)
Patterson (U.S.)	Follow-up of 206 fourth-grade boys in Eugene, Oregon, first assessed in 1984 and followed up at yearly intervals with intensive assessments every other year. Also follow-up in juvenile court records.	Capaldi and Patterson (1994); Stoolmiller (1994)
Pulkkinen (Finland)	All 369 children ages 8–9 in Jyvaskyla in 1968 completing peer, teacher, and self-ratings. Followed up at ages 14, 20, and 26 with questionnaires and to age 26 in criminal records.	Pulkkinen and Pitkanen (1993)
Robins (U.S.)	(1) 524 children treated in St. Louis child guidance clinic in 1924–1929 and 100 public school children. Interviewed more than 30 years later. (2) 235 African-American males born in St. Louis in 1930–1934 and located in elementary school records. Interviewed in 1965–1966.	Robins (1979)
Rutter and Quinton (U.K.)	(1) All 1,689 ten-year-old children in Inner London borough attending state schools in 1970. (2) All 1,279 ten-year-old children on the Isle of Wight attending state schools in 1964. Both samples retested at age 14. Inner London children followed up to age 25 in criminal records.	Rutter (1981b)
Schwartzman (Canada)	All 324 French-Canadian first graders (age 7) in Montreal were assessed by peers and self-reports in 1978. Followed up at ages 10 and 14 when self-reported delinquency was measured.	Tremblay et al. (1992)

Principal Investigators	Sample	Typical Recent Publication
Silva and Moffitt (New Zealand)	All 1,037 children born in 1972–1973 in Dunedin first assessed at age 3 and followed up to age 18. Biannual evaluations on health, psychological, educational, and family factors. Self-reported delinquency measured at ages 13, 15, and 18. Police records collected up to the 18th birthday.	Moffitt, Silva, Lynam, & Henry (1994)
Thornberry, Lizotte, and Krohn (U.S.)	All 1,000 seventh and eighth graders were first assessed in 1988, disproportionally sampled from high-crime neighborhoods. Three quarters are male. Initial assessments were carried out at half-yearly intervals. Subsequent assessments were carried out yearly and are still ongoing.	Thornberry, Lizotte, Krohn, Farnworth, & Jang (1994)
Tremblay (Canada)	All 1,161 kindergarten boys in Montreal assessed by teachers and followed up to age 12. Subsamples of disruptive boys were part of prevention experiment.	Tremblay, et al. (1992)
Verhulst (Netherlands)	All 2,600 children ages 4–16 from Zuid-Holland, first assessed in 1983, followed up at 2-year intervals over 8 years. Assessment of mental health functioning by mothers and self-reports.	Ferdinand & Verhulst (1994)
Werner (U.S.)	All 698 children tracked from birth in Kauai, Hawaii, in 1955. Interviewed at ages 10, 18, and 32. Health, education, and police records collected.	Werner & Smith (1982, 1992)
West & Farrington (U.K.)	All 411 boys ages 8–9 in 1961–1962; all those of that age in six London schools. Boys contacted about every 2–3 years up to age 32. Families contacted every year while boy at school. Boys and all biological relatives searched in criminal records up to 1994.	Farrington (1995)
White and Labouvie (U.S.)	Stratified random sample of 1,380 twelve-, fifteen-, and eighteen-year-olds first assessed in 1979–1981 in New Jersey and reassessed 3 and 6 years later. Focus on substance use.	White and Labouvie (1994)

it may result in retrospective bias (Radke-Yarrow, Campbell, & Burton, 1968). Also, such studies have the disadvantage of not reliably connecting past explanatory factors to child problem behavior. Therefore, the best longitudinal studies involve the prospective collection of data. However, this means that the duration of such studies may need to be quite long and that results may only be forthcoming after years or decades of data collection. Remarkably, the use of the accelerated longitudinal design (Bell, 1953, 1954), which is meant to shorten longitudinal studies (Farrington, Ohlin, & Wilson, 1986; Tonry, Ohlin & Farrington, 1991), has been very limited. In such a design, the age period of interest is carved up into several segments (age ranges). For example, a multiple cohort sample may be formed with the youngest cohort of participants being followed for, say, 4 years. The next cohort, 3 years older than the youngest cohort, is started at the same time as the youngest cohort and is also followed for 4 years. Several more older cohorts can be added in the same fashion, thereby covering a large total age range in a relatively brief time. One of the advantages of the multiple cohort design is that, after 4 years, there will be an overlap among the different cohorts, which allows the linking of the different cohorts and the replication of results. Replication of findings in longitudinal studies is crucial to preclude spurious findings. The main disadvantage with the accelerated longitudinal design is that within-individual change cannot be tracked over long time periods from childhood to adulthood. Also, there are technical problems in linking up the different cohorts.

Selection of Participants

The studies listed in Table 1.1 vary enormously as to the age, type, and representativeness of the participants included. (The sample size listed in Table 1.1 is the original sample size.) Most of the studies concerned adolescent populations, with few studies starting in the elementary school-age period (e.g., Eron, Huesmann, Dubow, Romanoff, & Yarmel, 1987) and even fewer in first grade (e.g., Kellam, Ensminger, & Simon, 1980). For most studies, it is difficult to discern whether an age period was selected by investigators for reasons other than convenience. Under the best of circumstances, this critical choice should be based on knowledge of the risk period for pathology, with a sufficiently wide window to cover the typical period of onset, worsening, and improvement in problem behavior. Many of the problems of concern here—delinquency, substance use, early sexual behavior, and mental health problems—take years and possibly even decades to emerge. However, studies that covered childhood, adolescence, and early adulthood were in the minority.

Almost invariably, studies did not use a screening method to enhance the likelihood of capturing those youth most at risk for serious pathology later. This point is especially important because a low base rate of those most seriously affected poses a threat to the usefulness of prospective longitudinal studies. Another problem is the choice of samples that are highly selective and non-representative (e.g., some studies did not allow the examination of factors affecting juveniles from ethnic minorities, but others did). Although analyses may produce intriguing results, the representativeness of the findings is often in question. It should be noted that, as in the Pittsburgh Youth Study, screening to increase the size of the high-risk group of participants can be used in conjunction with a representative sample. This strategy has the dual advantages of drawing conclusions about the population by weighting the screened results (e.g., Stouthamer-Loeber, Loeber, & Thomas, 1992) while maximizing the yield of pathological outcomes. In summary, the best longitudinal studies focus on large representative samples with sufficient numbers of the highest risk participants. The sample size should be sufficiently large to allow replication of findings for different ethnic (or gender) categories.

Frequency of Assessments

Another criterion to evaluate longitudinal studies is the frequency of assessments completed. Not uncommonly, studies have only two assessments—one baseline assessment and a single follow-up—often separated by many years. By necessity, such studies shed more light on outcomes over time than on the developmental processes of maturation and psychopathology. If we want to understand developmental processes better, we need to measure both child behavior and explanatory factors repeatedly and regularly within the time frame that they are most likely to emerge. It is only then that we can determine the age of onset of problem behaviors, and detect when the worsening and amelioration of such behaviors over time take place. Only repeated assessments can also illustrate the extent that explanatory variables change or stay constant over time and how they may affect children differently at one period compared with other periods of development. Ideally, explanatory variables should be measured at the time they exert their causal influence, but sometimes they may have continuing causal effects.

The interval between assessments should not result in blank, *white-out* periods, (i.e., segments of children's lives in which informants could not recall critical events or segments of development excluded from the assessments). We found that, at least initially, half-yearly rather than yearly assessments were desirable to better capture the rapidity of change in children's lives.

Baseline Measure of Past Behavior

Longitudinal studies did not always capture much of the past history of participants or their families prior to the first assessment. This lack of historical baseline data usually makes it impossible to ascertain whether the onset of any problem behavior noted in subsequent assessments is truly a first occurrence or merely a reoccurrence of the behavior. We believe that it is essential to be able to trace the onset and sequencing of different manifestations of problem behavior. Only a retrospective review of these behaviors at the first assessment allows investigators to create a baseline against which to judge subsequent changes in child behavior. It goes without saying that a retrospective baseline review of past onsets of problem behavior can best be accomplished when based on information from multiple rather than single informants. Also, distortions of historical development are less pronounced the fewer the number of years the development is supposed to cover.

Inclusion and Exclusion of Domains of Problem Behaviors

Studies listed in Table 1.1 vary in their inclusion and exclusion of problem behavior domains. Many of the studies concentrated on delinquency or substance use, but relatively few have focused on child mental health problems as well (e.g., Elliott, Huizinga, & Menard, 1989; Fergusson, Hopwood, & Lynskey, 1994). Others concentrated on mental health problems only (e.g., Cohen & Brook, 1987).

There are several reasons why an extended rather than a narrow range of domains of problem behavior is fruitful in longitudinal studies. First, the chances are that, at some time in their development, children will experience problems in several domains of functioning. Thus, it is not uncommon for conduct problem youth to start to abuse substances or become depressed, or for depressed youngsters to become delinquent. The second reason is that the determination of a negative outcome in, for example, adulthood, when restricted to a single domain, often misses individuals who are not functioning in other domains. For example, although some seriously deprived youth may not eventually become antisocial in adulthood, they often are isolated and socially impaired (Farrington, Gallagher, Morley, St. Ledger, & West, 1988). Also, it is important to document comorbid conditions and identify multiply deviant individuals who may be responsible for many of the findings in each domain. Thus, longitudinal studies should focus on multiple domains of functioning so that the interactions between different domains can be traced and outcomes across domains can be evaluated.

The Variety of Potential Explanatory Variables

Each domain of functioning may be explained not only by a set of common variables but also by a set of distinct explanatory variables. Studies vary as to what factors their investigators thought were desirable or possible to include for measurement. We argue that the best longitudinal studies are those that tap a wide variety of potential explanatory variables. This makes it possible to investigate the relative importance of all variables and the extent to which each is important independently of others. Preferably, the choice of such variables should allow investigators to evaluate not only their single most preferred theory but an array of theories. It is only by the careful evaluation of different theories that we can hope to generate new knowledge and come to a better integration of different theories.

Attrition

One of the major threats to the validity of findings in longitudinal studies is attrition or loss of participants, as increasing numbers may refuse to participate in later assessments or may not be located at follow-up. Several of the existing studies have had low attrition rates (e.g., Farrington & West, 1990; Robins, 1966). Studies have shown that attrition usually is not random, but takes a disproportionate toll of those participants who are most at risk (e.g., Farrington, Gallagher, Morley, St. Ledger, & West, 1990) and most essential to the topic of investigation. As a consequence, selective attrition can affect prevalence estimates of child problem behavior and may also reduce the strength of or change the relationship between explanatory variables and child problem behaviors. Also, the omission of the most deviant participants at follow-up makes it more difficult for longitudinal studies to document which sequence of behaviors is most likely to lead to serious outcomes. Thus, the best longitudinal studies are the ones in which great efforts are made and strict procedures are consistently implemented to reduce the probability of participant attrition (Stouthamer-Loeber, Van Kammen, & Loeber, 1992).

Multiple Informants

Typically, longitudinal studies have obtained information from several informants—usually the youth, a parent, teacher, or peer (e.g., Ensminger, Kellam, & Rubin, 1983; Fergusson et al., 1994; Glueck & Glueck, 1968; McCord, 1991; West & Farrington, 1973). Likewise, we decided to collect information about juveniles from the youth and from their parents and teachers. There are several compelling reasons for this data-collection strategy. First, juveniles are not necessarily the best informants about certain areas of functioning, such as hyperactivity and oppositional behavior (Loeber, Green, & Lahey, 1990; Loeber, Green, Lahey, & Stouthamer-Loeber, 1989). Second, a proportion of juveniles may not report to an interviewer the extent of their problem behavior, such as the severity of their delinquency. The reasons for this may include the participants' failing to recall the behavior or intentionally concealing the information. To reduce such false negatives, information should be obtained from parents and teachers about these and other problem behaviors. To strengthen the validity of such measures as delinquency, researchers might use *best estimate* procedures, in which the data from different informants are pooled (Patterson & Stouthamer-Loeber, 1984; Rutter, Tizard, & Whitmore, 1970).

A third reason to use multiple informants is that problematic behavior in childhood and adolescence may be shown in some but not other settings. For example, some youth may show highly oppositional behavior in the home only and others in the school only, whereas a third group show it in both settings. Only the use of multiple informants can help substantiate the extent that problem behavior is situationally specific or occurs across different settings.

The inclusion of peers as another group of informants about the behavior of study children should also be considered. Although the information provided by peers often has high validity (Asher & Coie, 1990; Dodge, Coie, & Brakke, 1982; Eron et al., 1987), there are major impediments to collecting data from peers. In large community studies, the participants usually are distributed over a large number of classrooms in numerous schools. This makes it prohibitive to obtain permission from the parents of the peers in each of these classrooms to participate in a study. Peer participation is further complicated in longitudinal follow-up studies when participants move to other classrooms and schools, necessitating researchers to get permission from the parents of new sets of peers in new settings.

A more common and more feasible expansion of sources in large studies is to obtain information from official records, such as the records on juvenile offending lodged in juvenile courts or child welfare agencies. Official records—when complemented by other sources of information from the youth, his parent, and his teacher—maximize the validity of measurement and strengthen the explanation of delinquency, substance use, early sexual behavior, and mental health problems compared with the use of a single source.

Dichotomization of Variables

There are several advantages of using dichotomized scores rather than continuous variables. First, results with dichotomous variables are much more meaningful and encourage a focus on individuals in addition to variables. Also, because many of the variables of concern are nonlinearly distributed, it is undesirable to rely on product–moment correlations (which presume a normal distribution and a linear relationship). As is demonstrated here, the relationship between independent and dependent variables is often nonlinear. For example, the age of the mother at the boy's birth was associated with a high prevalence of delinquency for young (teenage) mothers, but was not linearly related to delinquency above age 20. These kinds of nonlinear relationships (e.g., teenage mothers as a risk factor) are usually better captured by dichotomization than by continuous variables, although nonlinear correlations can be calculated. Also, the study and understanding of interaction effects are greatly facilitated by the dichotomization of variables compared with the use of continuous variables.

However, dichotomization of variables has often been criticized because it leads to a lower measured association (correlation) between variables. Although we do not dispute this point, we later demonstrate (chap. 5) that the actual loss is not large and that the relative importance of the variables is not significantly changed by dichotomization (except where the changes are meaningful, as in the case of teenage mothers). In summary, we consider that the advantages of dichotomization outweigh its disadvantages, although we also checked that the results with dichotomous variables were similar to those obtained with continuous variables.

THE PITTSBURGH YOUTH STUDY

We started the Pittsburgh Youth Study in 1987. The aim was to examine delinquency, substance use, early sexual behavior, and mental health problems in an inner city community sample of over 1,500 boys from childhood to adulthood (see chap. 2 for the details of data collection). Our research initially took place under the aegis of the Program on the Causes and Correlates of Delinquency, sponsored by the Office of Juvenile Justice and Delinquency Prevention. Two other research projects were launched under this program—one in Rochester, New York (Terence Thornberry, principal investigator), and the other in Denver, Colorado (David Huizinga, principal investigator). Many of the measurement instruments used by the three projects were the same to permit replication of results.

Our study can be typified as an accelerated longitudinal design (Bell, 1953, 1954) with three samples of boys. The youngest sample was first studied at age 7 (Grade 1), the middle sample at age 10 (Grade 4), and the oldest sample at age 13 (Grade 7). Although this book concentrates on the first two assessments in this study, subsequent follow-ups have been conducted and are still continuing, now sponsored by the National Institute of Mental Health.

The Metropolitan Area of Study

Pittsburgh is largely a blue-collar city formerly dominated by the steel industry. Because this industry has all but disappeared, Pittsburgh has gone through a period of high unemployment. No new major industry has replaced the steel industry. Instead, Pittsburgh has become a city of corporate headquarters, with the largest industry being the universities and their associated hospitals. A survey ranking of 286 metropolitan areas in the United States (Levine, 1988) shows that the city ranked 143rd in terms of alcoholism (with first being the lowest), 66th in terms of crime, 142nd for suicide, and 25th for divorces.

In 1990, the Pittsburgh metropolitan area had about 2,243,000 inhabitants and the City of Pittsburgh (the inner city where the study is located) had about 370,000 citizens (Hoffman, 1991). Table 1.2 lists some demographic characteristics for the latter area and provides comparable national data. It shows that Pittsburgh has a stable population. Most of the inhabitants were born in the state, and there is only a small proportion of people with a non-American background. In addition, only 2% of the population is not fluent in English. These characteristics make Pittsburgh ideally suited as a location for a prospective longitudinal study.

The median family income in Pittsburgh is somewhat lower than in the United States as a whole, which is also reflected in the larger percentage of

TABLE 1.2
Census data for the City of Pittsburgh and the U.S. in 1990
(U.S. Department of Commerce, 1990)

Variable	Pittsburgh (%)	United States (%)
Born in state of residence	80.1	61.8
Foreign born	4.6	8.0
Linguistically isolated	2.0	3.2
Median family income 1989	$27,484	$35,225
Persons below poverty level	21.4	13.1
Unemployment rate (of those in labor force)	9.1	6.3
African American	25.8	12.1

persons living below the poverty level and a higher unemployment rate. About one quarter of the population is African American, with the remainder, except for 2.1%, being Caucasian.

At the start of the study in 1987, the public schools in Pittsburgh had an enrollment of 40,038 boys and girls, with approximately 1,300–1,700 boys enrolled in each of the elementary school grades. Of all the children in the City of Pittsburgh, 72% attended public schools in 1990.

The 1990 FBI crime statistics show that the Crime Index rate for the City of Pittsburgh was 8,760 crimes per 100,000 inhabitants. This was higher than the national rate of 5,820. The Pittsburgh rate was somewhat below the average (10,200) of cities of similar size (i.e., those with a population of between 250,000 and 499,999).

With regard to juvenile delinquency, comparisons are difficult to make because states have different lower and upper limits for juvenile court criminal jurisdiction and may or may not include status offenses (e.g., in Pennsylvania, status offenses are excluded). In 1991, the national rate of juvenile court dispositions per 1,000 youth at risk was estimated to be 51.3 for nonstatus offenses, which compares with a rate of 47.4 for Allegheny County of which the City of Pittsburgh is a part (National Center for Juvenile Justice, 1994). Data were not available to make comparisons with cities of similar size for disposition as well as arrest rates.

A survey by Louis Harris and Associates (1986) of 200 households in Pittsburgh in the period just before the study started showed that 68% of the respondents thought that problems affecting children had become worse since the time that they themselves grew up. Specifically, 71% thought that crime had become worse and 48% noted the worsening of family life. Opinions about conditions of children were backed up by concrete handicaps (e.g., one in five children was not covered by medical insurance). Twelve percent of the parents had a child with learning disabilities, 6% had a child who had trouble with the law, and 1% had a child with substance use problems. Overall, 37% of the parents interviewed had a child with one or more of these problems.

The survey also highlighted difficulties that parents experienced in raising children: 63% thought that it was important for one parent not to work until the children were in school, and 54% advocated strict discipline for their children. At the same time, 54% of the parents said that it was difficult to obtain day care, and a similar percentage found that after-school care was a problem.

AIMS OF THIS BOOK

The main aim of this volume is to address the following questions:

1. What is the prevalence and age of onset of delinquency, substance use, and early sexual behavior for three samples of boys at ages 7, 11, and 14? What are the average mental health problems for these ages? How strong are the relationships among these problem behaviors in each of the samples?

2. Which variables best explain individual differences among the boys in their manifestations of delinquency, substance use, early sexual behavior, and mental health problems? To what extent do explanatory factors vary with age? How accurately can boys with different outcomes be identified by risk scores based on hierarchical multiple regressions?

3. To what extent are explanatory factors that are associated with one outcome also associated with other outcomes? Are explanatory factors that are especially characteristic of a multiproblem group of boys (who display many different problem behaviors) different from explanatory factors associated with boys with few problems?

4. Do the results fit a general theory of juvenile problem behaviors or is a differentiated theory more applicable?

To answer these questions, this volume is organized as follows.

We first describe the data-collection procedures, including the basic format of the study, sample selection, and participant retention (chap. 2). We then summarize the data-measurement procedures, instrumentation, and data-reduction methods (chap. 3). Chapter 4 presents the prevalence of delinquency, substance use, early sexual behavior, and mental health problems for the boys in the three samples over two points in time.

The next set of chapters presents data showing explanatory factors and correlates of delinquency (chap. 5), substance use (chap. 6), early sexual behavior (chap. 7), and mental health problems, including attention-deficit/hyperactivity and conduct problems (chap. 8), physical aggression and covert problem behaviors (chap. 9), and depressed mood and shy/withdrawn behaviors (chap. 10). These chapters also discuss the interrelationships among delinquency, substance use, early sexual behavior, and mental health problems. Methodological issues relevant to the analyses are discussed in the Methodological Appendix.

Chapter 11 integrates the findings from the preceding chapters and addresses the question that explanatory factors best account for a range of juvenile problem behavior. This chapter also focuses on multiproblem boys and examines the extent to which explanatory factors accounting for this group also apply to boys with few problem behaviors. Finally, chapter 12 presents a summary and conclusions.

2

Data-Collection Procedures

RESEARCH DESIGN

The design of the Pittsburgh Youth Study aimed at following up urban boys who were in Grades 1, 4, and 7 in Pittsburgh public schools at the outset of the study (called the *youngest, middle,* and *oldest samples*). Out of an enrollment of 1,631, 1,432, and 1,419 male students in the spring of 1987 and 1988 in Grades 1, 4, and 7, respectively, we randomly selected in the fall of 1987 and 1988 about 1,100 boys in each of the three grades (1,165, 1,146, and 1,125 in Grades 1, 4, and 7, respectively) to be contacted. This number was chosen on the advice of the school district research department, expecting a 75% participation rate. The participant acquisition phase was spread over 2 school years. One third of the boys, called *Cohort 1* (247, 249, and 247 in the youngest, middle, and oldest samples, respectively) were recruited and interviewed in the spring of 1987 for the screening assessment. The remaining two thirds of the participants, called *Cohort 2* (602, 619, and 609 in the youngest, middle, and oldest samples, respectively), were recruited and interviewed in the spring of 1988. The participation rate of boys and their parents was 84.7% of the eligible subjects (see Table 2.1).

The first assessment (described later) allowed us to screen the boys for their antisocial behavior. This allowed us to reduce the sample for follow-up to about 500 boys in Cohorts 1 and 2 combined (503, 508, and 506) in each of the three samples, which were reassessed 6 months after the initial assessment. The current report covers the screening and first follow-up data waves for both cohorts. Boys at follow-up were, on average, in second, fifth, and eighth grades, respectively. Later assessments fall outside the scope of this book. Table 2.2 summarizes the design and number of participants at screening and follow-up.

Data collection in each data wave consisted of information gathered from three informants: the boy, his caregiver (usually the mother), and his teacher. In addition, information was collected from school records and juvenile court records.

ACQUISITION OF PARTICIPANTS FOR THE SCREENING ASSESSMENT

All potential participants were male students in the City of Pittsburgh public schools, in which 72% of all students residing within the city limits were enrolled. Although no figures could be obtained on the differences between public school students and private or parochial school students, it is a reasonable assumption that those students not enrolled in public schools were more likely to be Caucasian and of higher socioeconomic status (SES) than the public school students.

TABLE 2.1
Participant Acquisition

	Sample						
Variable	Youngest		Middle		Oldest		Total
Boys enrolled in grades	1,631		1,432		1,419		4,482
Cohort	C1	C2	C1	C2	C1	C2	
Names released to interviewers	381	784	376	770	373	752	3,436
Ineligible	11	30	5	18	7	11	82
Moved out of town	10	12	10	15	10	25	82
Not found in school catchment area	13	8	21	10	4	6	62
Released to interviewers but withdrawn:							
No attempt to contact	40	6	20	6	20	5	97
Contacted and agreed	8	4	16	5	12	5	50
Some contact, no refusal	8	7	6	6	8	6	30
Inappropriate interviews	2	0	3	1	4	1	11
Refusal	43	111	46	91	64	94	449
Interviewed	247	602	249	619	247	609	2,573
Percentage Interviewed	84.6		86.3		83.9		84.7
Selected for follow-up (see text for details)	503		508		506		1,517

TABLE 2.2
The Screening and Follow-Up Assessments

Assessment	Grade	N
Cohort 1		
Screening (Spring 1987)	1	247
	4	249
	7	247
Follow-up (Fall 1987)	2	149
	5	152
	8	151
Cohort 2		
Screening (Spring 1988)	1	602
	4	619
	7	609
Follow-up (Fall 1988)	2	354
	5	356
	8	355
Total		
Screening	1	849
	4	868
	7	856
Follow-up	2	503
	5	508
	8	506

School Selection

The study had been discussed, in an early stage of preparation, with Pittsburgh public school administrators. Hence, when we finally needed formal approval, all officials were thoroughly acquainted with the plan and gave their full cooperation to the study. However, the proviso was that individual principals could refuse to let their schools participate in the study.

Because extensive cooperation from school principals and teachers was required for school data collection, we decided to make our first unit of selection the schools. At the time of the inception of the study, there were 47 elementary schools and 14 middle schools in the city of Pittsburgh. The plan was to acquire, in 2 consecutive years, a random selection of male students in Grades 1, 4, and 7. Therefore, the schools were divided into two groups. In the first year of participant acquisition (Cohort 1 participants), 18 elementary and 6 middle schools were selected, spread throughout the city of Pittsburgh. All of the schools that were approached agreed to participate. Obtaining cooperation from each school required visiting each principal and meeting with the teachers in each school. In the second year of participant acquisition (Cohort 2 participants), the aim was to include the remaining 29 elementary schools and 8 middle schools. However, 4 of the 29 elementary schools targeted for Cohort 2 refused to participate. In addition, to have enough seventh-grade participants available, one randomly selected middle school from the Cohort 1 schools was asked to participate again.

The school selection procedure left us with several questions to be answered. First, because schools were selected over 2 years, it was necessary to ascertain that schools were comparable in the 2 consecutive years. Fortunately, the catchment areas for the schools had not changed and no new schools had been opened, nor had any schools been closed. In addition, school enrollment, the percentage of students who were African American or Caucasian, and average achievement scores were not different for the 2 years of school selection. Therefore, we concluded that year of school selection did not introduce any particular bias.

The second question dealt with whether the refusal of 4 out of the 47 elementary schools to participate affected the potential first- and fourth-grade participant pool with respect to geographic coverage, ethnic composition, and average achievement test scores. The four refusing schools were spread out geographically. One school was on the outskirts of the city, one was in a relatively well-to-do neighborhood, and two were in poor housing project areas. However, the remaining schools represented well the variety of schools in the district and encompassed 92.1% and 92.5% of the target population for first and fourth graders, respectively. The loss of the four schools slightly reduced the number of potential African American participants—from 56.5% for all first graders in the district to 54.9% for all first graders in the participating schools, and from 54% for fourth graders district wide to 52.2% for fourth graders in the participating schools. No difference was found in average achievement scores.

The third question that needed to be addressed was how the use in both years of the same randomly selected middle school affected the potential sample. Because middle schools did not have a local catchment area, but drew students from a number of areas spread out over the city, the re-use of the middle school did not greatly alter the geographic coverage of the potential sample. Also, although the percentage of African American seventh graders in the school district was 54.6%, the addition to Cohort 2 of the previously selected middle school changed the percentage of potential African American participants only slightly, to 55.2% in the combined Cohorts 1 and 2. The average achievement score was not affected. In conclusion, the pool of potential participants for the two cohorts combined was not significantly different from all first-, fourth-, and seventh-grade male students in the city of Pittsburgh.

Participant Acquisition

The staff of the Board of Public Education provided us with the names and addresses of all eligible first-, fourth-, and seventh-grade boys in participating schools. Excluded were students in classes for severely mentally or physically handicapped children. Only one child per family was allowed to enroll in the study. Within each grade, boys were randomly selected and their parents were sent a letter briefly explaining the study and announcing that an interviewer would contact them.

Interviewers were sent out to the residences of the families to gain their cooperation. Telephone contacts were discouraged in this phase because they generate a lower participation rate than do face-to-face contacts (Frey, 1983). At the first contact, the interviewer explained the purpose of the study in general and the assessment in particular. Usually a time was then set for a subsequent visit to interview the boy in private and to have the caregiver complete some questionnaires. Before the interview commenced, the caregiver and child were asked to sign consent forms for their participation in the study. The interview with the boy lasted 45 minutes to 1 hour, during which time the caregiver completed a questionnaire. All interviews were conducted within three and a half months in the spring of 1987 and 1988; they required 25 interviewers in 1987 and 50 in 1988. Families were paid $12.50 per interview, and seventh-grade boys received an additional $5.

The person designated as the main caregiver was the natural, step, or adoptive mother in 91.1% of the cases. The main caregiver was the grandmother or father, in 3% and 5.6% of the cases, respectively. The remainder of the children lived with other relatives or foster parents. For ease of exposition, the main caregiver is called the *parent* and is treated as female.

Interviewers were selected to be able to read well, have good interpersonal skills, and be streetwise. The minimum educational requirement was a high school diploma. We selected females for the initial interview, because caregivers may be suspicious of unknown males who wish to enter their homes. The pool of interviewers contained both Whites and African Americans. Because the school district did not release information on ethnic background of students, we could not match the ethnicity of interviewers with that of potential participants.

Interviewers were trained in groups over 2 weeks. Training consisted of learning to obtain cooperation and handle the paperwork and consent forms, as well as the administration of the interview. In addition, interviewers were taught how to deal with reluctant families and find families that did not reside at their recorded address. The confidentiality of the information gained was stressed. Details about interviewer selection and training methods as they have developed in the Pittsburgh Youth Study can be found in Stouthamer-Loeber and Van Kammen (1995).

Participation in the Screening Assessment

We received a computer file from the school district with the names and
addresses of all male students in the selected grades. Unfortunately this file had
its shortcomings. There is always a gap between changes that occur in individual schools' enrollment and the central computer files. In addition, we found
out that the file contained a small number of errors.

The details of the participant acquisition are shown in Table 2.1. Of the 4,482
names and addresses of first-, fourth-, and seventh-grade boys obtained from
the Board of Public Education, a random selection of 3,452 names was released
to the interviewers. The release of names was done gradually to force interviewers to solve the more difficult cases before they received new names. At
the end of the interview period, 2,584 boys had been interviewed, of whom 11
proved to be ineligible because a student was female or enrolled in a nontargeted
grade. This resulted in samples of 849 first graders, 868 fourth graders, and 856
seventh graders. Four hundred and sixty-five families refused to participate.
The remaining 403 names, released to interviewers, included a number of
ineligible children ($N = 82$) such as girls, children in wrong grades, those who
had moved out of participating schools, and more than one qualifying child per
family, such as twins, or brothers in more than one of the three targeted grades.
The ineligibility of these 82 subjects was noticed before an interview was set up.

Another 82 names were ineligible because the children were found to have
left the city. In addition, 62 children could not be located, even with the active
help of the schools, most likely because their parents had deliberately provided
false addresses to enroll children in particular schools (in which case these
children would have been ineligible, if found). This was particularly the case
for the youngest and middle samples who were in elementary schools where
the catchment areas were much smaller than in middle schools, from which the
oldest sample was drawn.

Because of our inexperience in large-scale data collection in a short time
span, we had released too many names to interviewers at the end of the
data-collection phase, particularly in our first year of data collection. Thus, at
the close of the interview phase, 177 families, whose names had been released
late in the interview phase, remained uninterviewed. Of these, 50 (28%) had
already agreed to participate. However, they could not be interviewed within
the available time frame and were not needed to reach the target sample size of
750 in the first year of participant acquisition and 1,800 in the second year.
Some contact had been made with 30 of the remaining 127 families; those
contacts ranged from leaving a message if they had not been found at home to
actually talking with a person at the address. However, the contacts had not
progressed to the point of either a firm date for an interview before the closing
date of the participant acquisition wave. It is reasonable to assume that these

177 families did not constitute a group that was different from the remainder of the sample with regard to their refusal rate. Late releases that had become refusals were not counted in the 177 names, but were counted in the refusal total. Hence, the percentage of refusals is slightly over-estimated.

The overall cooperation rate (Table 2.2) has been calculated as the number of completed eligible interviews divided by the number of completed eligible interviews plus the number of refusals, yielding a rate of 82.9% for Cohort 1 and 85.6% for Cohort 2. The slight increase probably reflected interviewers' improved skills in persuading participants to cooperate. The overall participation rate was 84.7% for the combined cohorts. The cooperation rate varied slightly across grades: 84.6% for the youngest sample, 86.3% for the middle sample, and 83.5% for the oldest sample.

The cooperation rate in the current study compares favorably with that of other longitudinal studies on antisocial child behavior. A review of such studies by Capaldi and Patterson (1987) showed a range of participation rates from 52% to 100%, with a median of 75%. In most of the reviewed studies, however, only the permission of one person (e.g., the parent) was requested, whereas in our study either the parent or the boy could refuse.

Teacher Cooperation in the Screening Assessment

For each participating boy, a teacher was requested to complete a questionnaire. The school district administration did not allow us to pay teachers. Therefore, it was very important to keep contacts with the schools positive; we took several steps to make the collaboration of the schools more rewarding for school personnel. Principals were visited first and the data-collection procedure was discussed with them. At that point, a letter was sent to the teachers letting them know that a study involving students from their school was in progress and that we would be in touch with them at a later point. When we were ready to bring the booklets to the school, an appointment was set up with the teachers in which the study was explained, the booklets were distributed, and a date was set to pick up the booklets. All teachers, principals, and secretaries who had been vital to the data collection and tracking of participants, received thank-you letters at the end of each data phase. In addition, school libraries received a donation of $1 per completed questionnaire. We also delivered a flowering plant to the administrative office of each school at the beginning of the school year, starting with the follow-up assessment for Cohort 2. This process was labor intensive, but paid off in terms of the school personnel's cooperation.

Few teachers actually refused to complete the questionnaires. Rather, some teachers failed to complete the booklets before the deadline, despite reminders and encouragement. Also, some children had moved to a different school after they had been interviewed and we were not always able to contact the new school before the end of the school year. This resulted in a 95.8% completion rate for teacher assessments in the screening phase.

Characteristics of the Screening Sample

Our goal was to draw a representative sample of male students from Grades 1, 4, and 7. Thus, a question of concern was whether the participants in the screening assessment were representative of the school population from which they had been drawn. We could only investigate this by comparing our sample with aggregate data obtained from the school district. Table 2.3 shows the ethnic composition and California Achievement Test (CAT) results for reading in the screening sample. It also shows the district-wide percentage of African American students and CAT reading scores in the grades; averaged over the 2 years of acquisition.

The percentage of African American participants in the screening sample for each of the grades was close to the percentage of African American students in Pittsburgh public schools (Pittsburgh Public Schools, 1986, 1987). Similarly, the percentages of participants in the screening sample scoring over the 50th percentile on the CAT reading test were not significantly different from the figures obtained for the representative grades.

Table 2.4 shows some characteristics of the screening samples. The majority of the boys lived in households with their natural mother (92.3%), whereas there was a natural father present for only 43.8% of the boys. In 42.3% of the households, there was no natural or acting father. About one fifth (21.6%) of the natural or acting mothers living with the child had not completed high school, whereas 10% had a college degree. For natural or acting fathers living with the child, 19.5% had not completed high school and 15.7% had a college degree. Thus, the screening sample was disadvantaged in terms of family cohesion and parental education.

TABLE 2.3
Ethnic Representativeness and CAT Reading Scores
of Participants in the Screening Assessment

	Sample					
	Youngest		Middle		Oldest	
Variable	Study %	School %	Study %	School %	Study %	School %
African American	56.4	56.5	54.1	54.0	55.8	54.6
>50th percentile CAT reading score	54.5	56.5	40.7	40.9	37.9	36.7

TABLE 2.4
Characteristics of the Screening Sample

	Sample		
Characteristic	*Youngest*	*Middle*	*Oldest*
Grade	1	4	7
Number of participants	849	868	856
Average age	6.9	10.2	13.2
% Living with natural mother	94.2	91.7	90.9
% Living with natural father	45.0	45.6	40.8
% Not living with (acting) father	43.9	39.5	43.5
% (Acting) mother not completed high school	21.2	20.8	22.9
% (Acting) mother with college degree	9.0	9.7	11.3
% (Acting) father not completed high school	16.8	17.8	24.0
% (Acting) father with college degree	14.5	14.5	18.0

PARTICIPANT SELECTION CRITERIA FOR THE FOLLOW-UP

Given that only a small proportion of males eventually become serious repeat offenders, we created an enriched sample for follow-up to increase the likelihood of potential chronic offenders eventually appearing at numbers sufficiently large for statistical analyses. The initial assessment served to provide screening information, which allowed us to increase in the follow-up sample the number of boys thought to be at risk for chronic offending. However, we did not want a sample consisting solely of such boys, but also wanted boys who were not apparently at risk to serve as a group from which boys with a late onset of problem behaviors could emerge. In addition, the inclusion of low-risk participants allowed us to estimate population statistics by weighting the sample back to the original population.

A risk score was constructed of antisocial, delinquent-like acts. The choice of this risk score was governed by prior research, showing that early conduct problems and early forms of delinquency are among the best predictors of later delinquency (Loeber & Dishion, 1983; Loeber & Stouthamer-Loeber, 1987). The risk score included information from the youth's self-report and from ratings by the parent and teacher. It consisted of the following behaviors: attack, run away, set fires, steal from places other than the home, truancy, vandalism, steal from car, robbery, steal bicycle, shoplift, steal car, attack with weapon, gang fight, hit/hurt teacher, hit/hurt parent, joyride, burglary, arrested, liquor use, sniff glue, and marijuana use. Whenever possible, the information was extracted from lifetime questions in addition to behavior that took place in the past half year.

The first step in the creation of the risk score was to form a *best estimate* of the presence of a behavior by scoring a behavior as present when at least one of the informants reported it. The exception was that aggressive problem behaviors from the youth's self-report were not included because of studies showing that children, compared with adults, are not always the best reporters on their own aggression (Loeber, Green, & Lahey, 1990; Loeber, Green, Lahey, & Stouthamer-Loeber, 1989). A cutoff score identifying as nearly as possible the most antisocial third of the sample was designed (a score of more than one antisocial behavior was used for the youngest sample, a score of more than two for the middle sample, and a score of more than three for the oldest sample). Hence, high-risk participants were those who scored in the upper 30th percentile for their grade on the resulting risk score. About 250 participants in each sample were randomly selected from the high-risk group, whereas about 250 were randomly selected from the low-risk group.

Data Collection for the Follow-Up Assessment

The follow-up assessment occurred 6 months after the screening assessment. The data collection at follow-up consisted of an interview with the boy, an interview with the main caregiver, questionnaires completed by the caregiver, a questionnaire completed by the teacher, and school record data. Caregivers and boys were each paid $15 for their participation.

Every effort was made to maximize participant cooperation and to reduce participant attrition. About 10% of the participants moved to a different address within 6 months. To always know the participants' whereabouts, we put the following procedures in place.

First, seven times a year, mail went out to the families. Envelopes with an address correction request were used. In this way, we received new addresses for families that had moved and had informed the post office. Search procedures were instigated for those families whose mail was undeliverable. We learned to put both the first and last names of the child and caregiver on the envelope, because the household could be known by one or the other name. In every item of correspondence, we asked families to let us know of changes in address or telephone.

Second, every 6 months, participants provided the names, addresses, and telephone numbers of a relative and friend who would always know the family's whereabouts. The address update was written as a permission form that could be sent to the person from whom we were requesting information. In addition to the persons mentioned in the address update, neighbors—when asked by an interviewer—often knew a family's new address.

Third, all participating families gave permission to schools to release the address of the family to the Pittsburgh Youth Study. Because we could almost always trace the school where the child was in attendance (through the previous school, which had to send on the student's permanent record), this proved an effective way to track families, providing that schools cooperated. Finally, whenever families could not be found, we used an organization that, for a small fee made it their business to track people.

At the follow-up assessment, nine families had moved out of state, and another 24 families lived outside Pittsburgh but within the state of Pennsylvania. Several options were pursued to interview families that lived outside driving distance. For families that had a telephone and were very cooperative, the interview was completed in several telephone calls, whereas questionnaires were sent by mail for completion. For other families, an interviewer was hired locally. This required extensive written training notes and several telephone calls to ensure that the interviewer understood the interview well.

When a family refused to participate, an experienced interviewer visited the family again after several weeks. This procedure reduced participant loss by one third. Not all refusals were recontacted. A small proportion of the persons who refused made it clear that they did not wish to be recontacted. However, more important was the time factor. The assessment phases had narrow time frames and, because a few weeks had to elapse between the original refusal and the recontacting, it was not always possible to recontact all refusals within the assessment period.

Participation Rate at Follow-Up

Participation rates across the three samples were 94.9% and 94.0% for Cohorts 1 and 2, respectively. However, it was possible to replace refusals at follow-up ($N = 88$) by participants matched on risk from the larger pool of participants who had participated in the screening assessment. Hence, the target number of 1,517 youngsters were re-assessed. Table 2.5 shows the final sample composition for the follow-up study. In the follow-up, teachers completed questionnaires on 92.2% of the participants who were screened. Sixty-seven students had moved to schools other than Pittsburgh public schools, which doubled the number of schools that needed to be contacted to obtain teacher questionnaires.

TABLE 2.5
Number of Participants in the Follow-Up Assessment

Group	Sample		
	Youngest	Middle	Oldest
High risk	256	259	257
Low risk	247	249	249
Total	503	508	506

Sample Characteristics at Follow-Up

The percentage of African American participants in the follow-up sample was not significantly different from the percentage of African American students in Pittsburgh public schools (see Table 2.6). Also, the follow-up sample had similar CAT reading scores to those obtained in Pittsburgh public schools. Looking back to Table 2.3, the screening procedure did not significantly alter these aspects of the sample.

Other characteristics of the samples were also not greatly affected by the screening procedure (see Table 2.7). Almost all the boys in the follow-up samples lived in households with their natural mothers (92.6%), whereas only 37.8% of the boys lived with their natural fathers. In 43.6% of the households, there was no natual or acting father. About one fifth (18.5%) of the natural or acting mothers living with the child had not completed high school, whereas 6.4% had a college degree. For natural or acting fathers living with the child, 17.3% had not completed high school and 11.4% had a college degree. These figures are not greatly different from those shown in Table 2.4.

TABLE 2.6
Ethnic Representativeness and CAT Reading Scores of Participants in the Follow-Up Assessment.

| | Sample | | | | | |
| | Youngest | | Middle | | Oldest | |
Variable	Study %	School %	Study %	School %	Study %	School %
African American	57.3	56.5	55.8	54.0	57.5	54.6
>50th percentile CAT reading score	55.2	56.5	37.6	40.9	36.5	36.7

TABLE 2.7
Characteristics of the Follow-Up Sample

| | Sample | | |
Characteristic	Youngest	Middle	Oldest
Average age	7.4	10.7	13.8
% Living with natural mother	94.0	90.9	93.0
% Living with natural father	38.5	40.7	34.1
% Not living with (acting) father	45.3	40.5	45.1
% (Acting) mother not completed high school	16.9	18.7	19.8
% (Acting) mother with college degree	6.3	5.7	7.1
% (Acting) father not completed high school	15.4	16.6	19.9
% (Acting) father with college degree	12.4	11.4	10.4

PROCEDURES TO COMBAT INCOMPLETENESS OF DATA AND MINIMIZE ERRORS

To ensure that the data were as complete and correct as possible, several procedures were instituted. Interviewers were trained to check all booklets, including the questionnaires completed by the caregivers, for completeness before they left the home of the family they had interviewed. As soon as possible after the interview had been completed, they were required to edit the interview and questionnaire booklets carefully to ensure that no information was missing and that all answers were in the required format. After the interview materials were handed in to the supervisor, all booklets and forms were checked for completeness and correctness by the office staff. Only if the booklets were found to be complete and correct was payment to the interviewer authorized. If material was incorrect or missing, the booklets went back to the interviewer to obtain additional information for completion by telephone or by paying another visit to the family.

Interviewers were told during training that a number of their families would be contacted by their supervisors to ensure that the interviews were actually done and that the interviewers were courteous. About 10% of the families interviewed, chosen at random, were called by the supervisors and asked a number of factual questions. The answers were then compared to those on the actual interview schedule. Interviewers knew that they would be fired immediately if they were found to have fabricated data. This did not prove to be necessary, however.

All data was double entered and verified. After the data had been entered, the files were checked for impossible values. In addition, a number of cross-checks, especially focusing on more factual demographic information, were carried out to ensure consistency across the data set. The effectiveness of all data-collection and data-management procedures depended, to a large extent, on our ability to handle a large volume of data within a short period of time. Problems had to be spotted and rectified immediately at every step of the data-collection and data-management process to guarantee the high quality of the data collected.

To interview 3,000 individuals (1,500 children and 1,500 parents) and obtain 1,500 teacher ratings within three-and-a-half months for each assessment, we developed an interlocking computerized data-management system to keep track of the status of each interview, the performance of the interviewers, and the payment of interviewers and participants. This allowed us to take immediate action if problems arose. For example, at any given time, each interviewer was allowed to work on no more than 10 cases. Thus, they could not simply interview the easy cases and postpone working on the more difficult ones. The tracking system kept a record of how long cases were outstanding and flagged the cases that were in the hands of the interviewers for more than 4 weeks. If interviewers held onto too many overdue interviews, they had to complete these before they were given new cases to contact. For further details of our data-collection and data-management procedures, see Stouthamer-Loeber and Van Kammen (1995).

3

Measurement Instruments and Constructs

This chapter reviews first the measurement instruments and then describes the data-reduction procedures leading to the definition of key constructs. Because many constructs contain items from more than one measure, constructs are discussed after all measures have been described. Measures and constructs derive from two assessments: (a) the screening assessment (S), administered in the spring of 1987 for Cohort 1 and in the spring of 1988 for Cohort 2; and (b) the follow-up, followed for each cohort 6 months later. The follow-up was more extensive. From now on, the two cohorts will not be discussed separately, but will be combined. Official records of offending were searched in the Juvenile Court of Allegheny County in Pittsburgh. They covered up to the date of the follow-up for participants living in that county and, prospectively, for about 6 years subsequent to the follow-up assessment.

The following terms are used: *Parent* is used to describe the person who responded to the interview and concerns the individual who claimed to have the principal responsibility for looking after the boy in the household. For simplicity of exposition, we refer to the parent using the female gender. The terms *mother* and *father* are used to denote the female and male parents, respectively, so they include operative as well as biological parents.

We used existing measures as much as possible. However, a large number of measures had to be developed or adjusted in language suitable for an urban, generally lower socioeconomic class sample. Some of these new measures were derived from earlier work at the Oregon Social Learning Center. We are much indebted to the input from staff there. In addition, several measures resulted from the collaboration among investigators of the Program of Research on the

Causes and Correlates of Delinquency (Terence P. Thornberry, Alan J. Lizotte, Margaret Farnworth, Susan B. Stern, David Huizinga, Finn Esbensen, and Delbert S. Elliott).

MEASUREMENT INSTRUMENTS AT THE SCREENING ASSESSMENT

In the screening interview, the boy's parent and teacher provided information on antisocial behavior and psychopathology, as well as social and academic competence. The parent also provided basic demographic information. The boys completed self-reports of antisocial behavior, delinquency, and substance use, with some variations to make measures suitable for youngsters of different ages. The boys in the oldest sample also gave information on other behavioral problems and social and academic competence.

Although some instruments had originally been designed for self-administration (e.g., the Youth Self-Report; Achenbach & Edelbrock, 1987), we assumed that the reading skills of many participants were limited. Therefore, all interviews were verbally administered to the boys. For all boys, the interviewer discussed the time frame of the previous 6 months for these and other measures before the questions were asked, and personal events as well as dates (e.g., Christmas, the beginning of school) were used to help delineate the appropriate time period.

Oldest Sample

Seventh graders were administered a 40-item Self-Reported Delinquency Scale (SRD) and a 16-item Substance Use Scale based on the National Youth Survey developed by Elliott and his colleagues, (Elliott, Huizinga, & Ageton, 1985), which has been evaluated extensively. For each delinquency or drug item, the boys were asked whether they had ever engaged in the behavior and, if so, how often they had done it in the previous 6 months. The lifetime questions used a *yes–no* format, whereas for the questions pertaining to the previous 6 months, the number of times that the event had occurred was recorded (see Table 4.1 in chap. 4 for a listing of the items in these questionnaires). In addition, the boys were administered the 112-item Youth Self-Report (YSR; Achenbach & Edelbrock, 1987), which measures child behavior problems as well as social and academic competence. Nine items were added to this scale to increase the overlap with the parent and teacher form of the Child Behavior Checklist and to cover covert antisocial behaviors. The answer format was *not true, somewhat or sometimes true,* and *very true or often true.* The time frame was the previous 6 months.

Youngest and Middle Sample

The self-reported delinquency questionnaire used with the seventh-grade boys was judged to be too difficult to understand for first and fourth graders and not all items applied to this younger age group. Therefore, a new 33-item Self-Reported Antisocial Behavior Scale (SRA) was developed, which included six items on substance use (Loeber, Stouthamer-Loeber, Van Kammen, & Farrington, 1989). Another rationale for not using the SRD and Substance Use Scale for these age groups was that a number of the behaviors in these scales were age-inappropriate, or would have an exceedingly low base rate for early elementary school-age boys. Examples of such SRD items were: being drunk in a public place, lying about one's age to get into a movie or to buy alcohol, using checks illegally, and committing rape.

Other changes had to do with making the items more specific and hence easier to understand for younger children. An example of this was theft, which, in the SRD, was categorized according to value. However, in the SRA, theft was split into theft in different locations without specifying the value. Another example in the SRD was hitting to hurt without specifying the victim, which was changed in the SRA to hitting specific victims such as teachers, parents, students, or siblings.

Thus, the SRA was shorter and used, at times, wording slightly different from the SRD (e.g., taking something that does not belong to you on the SRA vs. stealing on the SRD). In addition, certain items were repeated, specifying different situations or persons to make the content less abstract (this was done for damage, stealing, and hitting). An abbreviated listing of the SRA items can be found in Table A4.1 in chapter 4.

In the case of some items, we doubted whether young boys understood the meaning of the question. Therefore, a series of questions preceded those items to ascertain whether the boy knew their meaning. First, the interviewer would read a sentence containing the behavior and ask the boy whether he knew what that meant. If he said yes, he was asked to give an example. If the boy did not understand the behavior or had difficulty giving an example, the interviewer gave an example and then asked the boy again to give an example. If he still could not produce an example that indicated that he understood what the behavior meant, the question was skipped. Exceptions to this procedure were the items for smoking marijuana and sniffing glue, for which no explanation was provided by the interviewer to the boy. The explanation of these two behaviors was withheld for ethical reasons to avoid any possibility of raising the boy's curiosity about those acts. As with the scale for the oldest boys, information about the previous 6 months and lifetime was collected. For the lifetime questions, the answer format was *yes–no*; for the 6-months questions, the answer format was *never, once or twice,* and *more often* because exact frequency estimates were thought to be beyond the scope of most young boys.

Parent

The parent completed a demographic questionnaire on the entire family. In addition, an extended version of the Child Behavior Checklist (Extended CBCL) was administered (Achenbach, 1978; Achenbach & Edelbrock, 1979, 1983). The CBCL is a 112-item questionnaire covering a wide range of child behavior problems such as anxiety, depression, compulsions, oppositional behaviors, hyperactivity, and delinquency. It has been widely used and has adequate test–retest reliability (Achenbach & Edelbrock, 1983). However, specific delinquent behaviors and concealing antisocial behaviors (e.g., various forms of dishonesty and minor forms of property infraction) were underrepresented in this scale. Therefore, 88 items were added to cover concealing antisocial behaviors and most of the behaviors from the SRD. The time frame for the Extended CBCL was the previous 6 months. The answer format was *not true, somewhat or sometimes true*, and *very true or often true*. In addition, 21 lifetime questions for discrete antisocial items with a *yes–no* answer format formed the basis for a lifetime scale.

Teacher

Teachers completed an extended version of the Teacher Report Form (Extended TRF), which is complementary to the CBCL (Edelbrock & Achenbach, 1984). Twenty-three delinquent and concealing antisocial behavior items were added to this scale to increase its comparability with the child and parent reports. Both the TRF and the parent CBCL had a 6-months time frame.

MEASUREMENT INSTRUMENTS
AT FOLLOW-UP

Whereas the screening assessment covered mostly antisocial and delinquent behaviors of the participants and demographic characteristics of the families, the follow-up interview was more extensive. The main measurement domains covered by the constructs are shown in Table 3.1.

Because adults and youngsters often perceive the same events differently, care was taken to collect as much information about each topic from more than one informant. For example, both the parent and boy provided information about the parents' supervision of the boy. Although only one parent was interviewed, the boy was asked about, for example, the parenting practices of both parents or parent figures if present in the home. The time frame was the previous 6 months unless otherwise noted. The measures are discussed by domain, although certain measures cover information from more than one domain.

TABLE 3.1
Main Measurement Domains in the Follow-up

Child	Family	Other
Delinquency	Discipline	Peer delinquency
Substance use	Supervision	Peer substance use
Psychopathology and	Involvement	Prosocial peers/friends
conduct problems	Positive parenting	Demographics/SES
Sexual behavior	Communication	Neighborhood
Injuries	Attitudes	
Attitudes	Relationships	
Competence	Mother's stress	
	Parent psychopathology	

INFORMATION ON THE CHILD

Delinquency

For the boys in the oldest sample, the SRD was repeated; for the boys in the youngest sample, the SRA was used. For the middle sample of boys, the SRD was administered for the first time, replacing the SRA administered at screening.[1] In addition, the Extended CBCL (administered to the parent), the Extended TRF, as well as, for the oldest sample of boys, the YSR, contained delinquency items.

With regard to official delinquency, Juvenile Court Records in Allegheny County were searched and coded for offense date, offense category, and disposition according to the format developed by Weinrott (1975) and further improved by Maguin (1994). The coding system follows the definitions of crimes in the FBI Uniform Crime Reports and corresponds with the computerized format used by the National Center for Juvenile Justice. Coding of the offense committed was based on the behavioral description found in the police contact report and/or in the petition.

Substance Use

For the boys in the oldest sample, the Substance Use Scale was repeated; for the boys in the youngest sample, the SRA was used, which contained items on substance use. For the middle sample of boys, the Substance Use Scale was administered for the first time at follow-up, replacing the SRA administered at screening.

---

[1] For the middle sample, the life time questions concerning self-reported delinquency and substance use were repeated at follow-up because of the new instruments used in that data wave.

Psychopathology and Conduct Problems

The Revised Diagnostic Interview Schedule for Children (DISC–P); (Costello, Edelbrock, Kalas, Kessler, & Klaric, 1982; Costello, Edelbrock, & Costello, 1985) was administered to the parent. This was developed as a measure of child psychopathology to be administered by lay interviewers in epidemiological surveys. It covers most forms of child psychopathology contained in *Diagnostic and Statistical Manual of Mental Disorders* (3rd ed. [DSM–III]; American Psychiatric Association, 1982) and *DSM–III–R* (American Psychiatric Association, 1987), as well as the age at which the problem behaviors were first noted. Not covered were anxiety and relatively rare disorders such as psychosis.

Because parents or teachers are usually not good judges of children's depression, the boys were administered the Recent Mood and Feelings Questionnaire (MFQ). This 13-item scale, developed by Angold and associates (Angold et al., 1995; Costello & Angold, 1988; Messer et al., 1995), is a measure of children's depressed mood. The time frame is the previous 2 weeks.

The Extended CBCL, administered to the parent, as well as the Extended TRF, and, for the boys in the oldest sample, the YSR, are also measures of child psychopathology and conduct problems.

Attitudes

A Perception of Antisocial Behavior Scale, consisting of 20 items (18 items for the youngest sample), measured the boys' attitudes toward antisocial and rule-breaking behaviors. The Attitude Toward Delinquent Behavior Scale, a 15-item scale (12 items for the youngest sample), developed by the Boulder group, measured boys' attitudes toward behaviors in the SRD and the Substance Use Scale. The oldest and middle samples were also administered the Likelihood of Being Caught Scale. This 11-item scale measures boys' perceptions of the likelihood of their being caught for specific delinquent acts and their perception of what happens when they are caught by the police.

Sexual Behavior

Only the boys in the oldest sample were given the Sexual Activity Scale. Questions for this scale were developed by the Boulder group to assess youngsters' sexual involvement.

Physical Health

A Family Health Questionnaire, administered to the parent, contains five questions about any accidents and injuries experienced by the child.

Competence

The CBCL, TRF, and, for the oldest sample, the YSR contain information on competence with regard to the child's involvement in sports and other social activities, as well as academic competence. In addition, California Achievement Test (CTB; McGraw-Hill, 1979, 1980) results on reading, language, and mathematics were collected from the schools for the years of the two assessments.

INFORMATION ON THE FAMILY

Discipline

The Discipline Scale assessed the boy's perception of his mother's and father's discipline methods (eight items for each). The scale evolved from previous pilot work at the Oregon Social Learning Center. The middle and oldest sample boys were also asked about the persistence and consistency with which discipline was applied. Parents were administered a parallel version to the questionnaire given to the middle and oldest samples but reported only on themselves. Family members of seriously antisocial children are often afraid of them. As a consequence, such children are left to do as they wish. The 11-item Countercontrol Scale is an attempt to measure the extent to which the boy may be in control of the family and the extent that the parent avoids disciplining him to minimize escalation in antisocial child behavior.

Supervision/Involvement

Parents and boys were administered versions of the Supervision/Involvement Scale. The 43 questions in this scale concern the parents' knowledge of the boy's whereabouts; the amount of joint discussions, planning, and activities; and the amount of time that the boy is unsupervised. The boy reported on his mother and father, whereas the parent only reported on her knowledge of and interaction with the child. The scale is based on our literature review of family factors related to delinquency (Loeber & Stouthamer-Loeber, 1986), on previous pilot work, on Moos' Family Environment Scale (Moos & Moos, 1975), and Skinner, Steinhauer, and Santa-Barbara's (1983) Family Assessment measure.

Positive Parenting

The Positive Parenting Scale was administered to the boys and parents. It consists of the boy's perception of his mother's and father's frequency of responding in a variety of positive ways to his behavior (10 items for each). The parent only reports on her own positive responding.

Communication

The Revised Parent–Adolescent Communication Form was administered to the boys in the middle and oldest samples and to the parents of all samples. This scale, based on Barnes and Olson (1982), Moos and Moos (1975), and Skinner, Steinhauer, and Santa-Barbara (1983), measures the quality of parent–child communication and display of affect. The child version contains separate questions for mothers and fathers (77 items), whereas the parent only reports on her behavior.

Parent Attitudes

The Perception of Child Problem Behavior Scale was administered to the parent. This scale consists of 20 evaluative (approving or disapproving) statements about child problem behaviors ranging from aggression to covert conduct problems to substance use.

Relationships

Boys and parents were given the Child's Relationship with Parent/Siblings Scale (Stouthamer-Loeber, 1991). This scale has 15 items on the boy's perception of his relationship with his mother, and 15 items on the boy's perception of his relationship with his father. Separate questions concern the boy's relationship to other children in the home. Each parent reported on her own relationship with the child, as well as how well the child got along with the other parent or children in the household.

Relations with Partner

A short, eight-item version (Sharpley & Cross, 1982) of the Dyadic Adjustment Scale (Spanier, 1976) was used. This scale measures agreement with a partner about important areas of the relationship, the amount of time spent together, and how satisfying the relationship is.

Parental Stress

The Perceived Stress Scale was administered to the parent. This 14-item scale, constructed by D. Cicchetti (personal communication, 1987), asks about perceived stress and the parent's ability to cope with the stress.

Parental Pathology

The Family Health Questionnaire contained questions about help sought for mental problems of the parent(s) and absent biological parents.

DEMOGRAPHIC AND NEIGHBORHOOD INFORMATION

Demographics

The Demographic Questionnaire used at screening was expanded to collect extensive information from the parent on the child's household. The information collected included names, aliases, birthdates, place of birth, ethnicity, education, work, and marital status of the parent(s). Information was also collected on other persons who might take care of the child. In addition, information was collected on absent and present siblings and other children and adults in the household. Demographic questions were asked about absent biological parents as well as the amount of contact the participant had with the absent biological parent(s). The Financial Information Questionnaire was administered to collect information on the number of wage earners per family, public assistance, total income, and housing.

Neighborhood—Census Data.   We used the 1980 U.S. Census data at the Census tract level. The participant's address was linked to a Census tract so that Census tract information could be attached to individual participants. Examples of Census tract variables are: median age, percent of female headed households, percent of African Americans, percent of adults who graduated from high school, % owner occupied houses, % of families below the poverty level, and stability of residence. The Neighborhood Scale, developed by Huizinga and Colleagues in Boulder, measures the parent's perceived quality of the neighborhood with 17 items covering prostitution, assaults, breaking and entering, and so on.

INFORMATION ON PEERS

Peer Delinquency

A Peer Delinquency Scale was administered to the boy. It contained 15 items (12 for the youngest sample) that corresponded to a number of items on the SRD and Substance Use Scale. Like these scales, it was developed by the Boulder group; it measures the proportion of the boy's peers who engage in delinquent acts or substance use. In addition, both the boys and their parents were given the Parents and Peers Scale. This measure, developed by the Boulder group, consists of 11 items measuring the number and nature of the boy's friendships, the extent to which his parent(s) approve of these friendships, and the behaviors that friends engaged in that caused parents to disapprove of his friends.

Prosocial Peers

Boys were also given the Conventional Activities of Peers Scale. This is an eight-item measure of peers' involvement in conventional activities based on work by the Boulder group.

Friends

Information on the number of the boy's friends and the frequency of his contact with them is contained in the Parents and Peers Scale, which is administered to both the parent and the boy.

RELIABILITY OF THE INTERVIEW PROCEDURES

Interviewers can contribute two types of errors to the data. First, they may not be trained well enough and may not follow the instructions. Second, they may intentionally make up data, particularly in the case where some information had been missed during the interview and the interviewer is required to recontact the family. With regard to reducing the first source of error, thorough interviewer training and practice was mandatory. In addition, early in each phase, interviewers were accompanied at least twice by senior staff members to be observed. The staff members also recorded the answers for later comparison with the interviewer's questionnaire. Further, at each phase, at least 10% of the interviewed families were called by office staff to re-ask some questions that interviewers had missed during the interview and that needed to be retrieved later. Interviewers were aware of the extensive checking procedures and, so far, we have not lost any data because of interviewer incompetence or dishonesty.

GENERAL STRATEGY FOR DATA REDUCTION

The data from the 1987 and 1988 cohorts were combined into one data set so that data on about 500 participants were available for each of the three (youngest, middle, and oldest) samples. The constructs were made from several questionnaire items to optimize psychometric quality and reduce nonconstruct-related variance (Wiggins, 1973). Also, each construct needed to be meaningful to lay people as well as professionals so that the results of analyses could be communicated clearly. The latter requirement implied that the items included had to be reasonably homogeneous. In general, constructs were created from items that had face validity and were intercorrelated. The next step was to calculate Cronbach's (1951) alpha (α) to measure the internal consistency of the construct. Alpha was not calculated for constructs consisting of less than five items; instead, average intercorrelations are presented. If there was no reason to expect high intercorrelations because of different base rates but the items conceptually belonged to the same domain, the items were combined into constructs without calculating alphas. This was the case for constructs made up of delinquency or drug items (e.g., shoplifting items of low value may not correlate with burglary, but nevertheless may be combined in a delinquency score). When Cronbach's alphas have been calculated, they are listed by sample, with Y denoting the youngest sample and M and O denoting the middle and oldest samples, respectively.

If possible, a construct was formed using information from different informants (the boy, parent, and teacher). This strategy of multiple informants makes it possible to: (a) measure behaviors occurring in different settings such as the home or the school, and (b) use a *best estimate* strategy to establish whether the behavior was present within the measurement time frame. For example, if the boy reported that he had never set fires but the parent reported that he had, then the construct *firesetting* needed to reflect that at least one informant reported the behavior. For some constructs concerning activities in the family home only the boy's and the parent's information was used, whereas for a number of school behaviors the boy's and teacher's information formed the basis for a construct.

Unless specifically stated, the constructs refer to behaviors over the previous 6 months or to current behaviors or attitudes. Constructs in the domains of the boy's delinquency, substance use, and antisocial and internalizing behaviors combined items measured at screening and follow-up to ascertain lifetime behavior prevalence rates at follow-up and strengthen construct validity. Coding of items was reversed, when necessary, so that a higher score denoted a more negative (antisocial or undesirable) value for those variables for which this was appropriate.

For many analyses, variables were dichotomized, separating the 25% of the participants with the most negative values from the remaining 75%. This had the advantage of achieving comparability and removing skewed distributions. Other reasons for dichotomization are discussed in chapter 5 and the Methodological Appendix.

CHILD BEHAVIOR CONSTRUCTS

Delinquency

Table 3.2 summarizes the different constructs concerning boys' delinquency.

High Risk. This variable indicates the high-risk boys according to the screening procedure. A risk score was constructed of serious antisocial, delinquent-like acts based on the information provided by the boy, his parent, and his teacher at the screening assessment. This risk score consisted of the following behaviors: attack, run away, set fires, steal from places other than the home, truancy, vandalism, steal from car, robbery, steal bicycle, shoplift, steal car, attack with a weapon, gang fight, hit/hurt teacher, hit/hurt parent, joyride, burglary, arrested, liquor use, sniff glue, and marijuana use. Whenever possible, the information was extracted from lifetime questions in addition to behavior (that) took place in the past half year.

High-risk participants were those who scored in the upper 3rd percentile for their grade on the resulting risk score. As explained previously the risk score varied somewhat for each of the three samples; a criterion score of more than one serious behavior was used for the youngest sample, a score of more than two for the middle sample, and a score of more than three for the oldest sample.

Police and Court Contacts. The following constructs were obtained from the juvenile court records:

TABLE 3.2
Constructs Pertaining to Boys' Delinquency

Domain	Specific Constructs
Risk status	High risk
Official records of deliquency	Past court referral
	Future court referral
Self-report	Age of first self-reported police contact
	Prevalence self-reported delinquency
	Frequency of self-reported delinquency
	Prevalence self-reported theft
	Frequency of self-reported theft
	Prevalence self-reported vandalism
	Frequency of self-reported vandalism
	Prevalence of self-reported fraud
	Frequency of self-reported fraud
	Prevalence self-reported violence
	Frequency of self-reported violence
Classification	General delinquency classification
	Theft seriousness classification
	Violence seriousness classification
	Age of onset of self-reported delinquency (by level)

Past Referrals. This refers to the presence of a record in the Juvenile Court of Allegheny County, Pittsburgh, of a delinquent act committed by a participant by the time of the follow-up. This excluded information on boys in the youngest sample because none of them had reached the age of 10, which is the age of criminal responsibility in Pennsylvania.

Future Referrals. This refers to the presence of a record in the Juvenile Court of Allegheny County, Pittsburgh, for a delinquent act committed by a participant during the interval of about 6 years between the follow-up assessment and the search of court records in 1994.

Prevalence and Frequency of Self-Reported Delinquency. The various constructs concerning the prevalence and frequency of self-reported delinquency use information from screening and follow-up. Each covers 6 months, as well as the lifetime information collected at screening and, (for the middle sample) at follow-up as well. As mentioned before, the SRA was administered to the youngest sample at screening and follow-up and to the middle sample at screening. The SRD was administered to the oldest sample at screening and at follow-up and to the middle sample at follow-up. Prevalence was calculated for all three samples for 6 months at screening, 6 months at follow-up, one year (combining the two 6-month periods at screening and follow-up), and for lifetime at follow-up. However, the prevalence for violence and fraud could not be derived from the SRA due to the limited number of items that qualified as delinquent behavior in each of these areas. Thus, prevalence constructs are lacking for violence and fraud for the youngest sample and for the middle sample at screening. Frequency constructs applied only to the oldest sample for the 6 months up to screening and follow-up, and they were combined into a 1-year frequency. Frequency was also available for the middle sample for 6 months at follow-up. The SRA had only categorical answers that did not make it possible to calculate exact frequencies.

Age of First Self-Reported Police Contact. This is based on the boy's self-reported age at first contact with the police for delinquent acts other than for minor traffic offenses, as measured at follow-up. This construct was made for the middle and oldest samples only.

Prevalence of Self-Reported Delinquency. This construct provides an overall prevalence score for self-reported delinquency, using 24 items from the SRD or 15 items from the SRA, covering theft, violence, vandalism, and fraud. Status offenses such as truancy or running away, are not included in this scale.

Frequency of Self-Reported Delinquency. This score includes the 24 items from the SRD that were used in the previous construct.

Prevalence of Self-Reported Theft. Ten SRD or eight SRA theft items form the basis for this construct, ranging from minor theft of items worth less than $5 to breaking and entering (and, for the SRD, car theft).

Frequency of Self-Reported Theft. This construct includes the 10 items from the SRD that were used in the previous construct.

Prevalence of Self-Reported Vandalism. This construct combines destruction or defacement and firesetting. The SRD contains two items and the SRA contains five items on vandalism.

Frequency of Self-Reported Vandalism. This score includes the two items from the SRD that were used in the previous construct.

Prevalence of Self-Reported Fraud. The fraud construct consists of four SRD questions pertaining to avoiding payment, selling things for more than they are worth, and the illegal use of checks or credit cards. The SRA has only one item on fraud and, as a consequence, no separate construct was made from the SRA.

Frequency of Self-Reported Fraud. This score includes the four items from the SRD that were used in the previous construct.

Prevalence of Self-Reported Violence. The violence construct includes the more serious forms of violence, not just hitting someone or having a fight. The six SRD items cover behaviors such as attack with a weapon or with the idea of seriously hurting or killing another person, carrying a weapon, gang fights, and forced sex. Only one SRA item qualified for this scale (carrying a weapon) and, as a consequence, no separate construct was made from the SRA.

Frequency of Self-Reported Violence. This construct includes the six items from the SRD that were used in the previous construct.

Delinquency Seriousness Classification. The delinquency classification places a boy in the category of the most serious behavior ever committed. The information is derived from the parent (CBCL, Lifetime Scale), teacher (TRF), and from the boy (SRA or SRD and, for the oldest sample, the YSR) at screening and follow-up. To classify delinquent behaviors according to seriousness, the severity ratings developed by Wolfgang, Figlio, Tracy, and Singer (1985) were used. Most behaviors were represented by more than one question and more than one respondent. The constructs were made first from the screening and follow-up data separately and then combined to form the final construct. Three related classifications were developed: General Delinquency Seriousness Classification, based on all delinquent items; Theft Seriousness Classification, based on theft items; and a Violence Seriousness Classification, based on violence items. The asterixed behaviors in each of the classifications listed next did not occur in the SRA and, therefore, do not apply to the youngest sample at screening and follow-up and to the middle sample at screening. In each of the classifications, a value of zero was assigned to those nondelinquent participants who did not qualify for any level.

General Delinquency Seriousness Classification (lifetime and previous year). Delinquent acts were classified in the following manner: Level 1 Delinquency: No delinquency or minor delinquency at home, such as stealing minor amounts of money from a parent's purse or minor vandalism. Level 2 Delinquency: Minor delinquency outside of the home, including minor forms of theft, such as shoplifting and stealing something worth less than $5, and vandalism and minor fraud, such as not paying for a bus ride. Level 3 Delinquency: Moderately serious delinquency, such as any theft of $5 or over, gang fighting, carrying weapons, and joyriding. Level 4 Delinquency: Serious delinquency, such as *car theft, breaking and entering, strongarming, *attack to seriously hurt or kill, *forced sex, or selling drugs.

Theft Seriousness Classification (lifetime). Four levels of theft seriousness were formed, consisting of the following items: Minor Theft at Home. Minor Theft Outside the Home: *Theft of something worth less than $5, shoplifting, theft outside of the home, or theft at school. Moderate Theft: *Theft of something worth $5 or more, theft of a bicycle, theft from a car, picking pockets, fencing, or joyriding. Serious Theft: *Car theft or breaking and entering.

Violence Seriousness Classification (lifetime). The following behaviors formed the three levels of violence seriousness: Minor Violence: Gang fighting or carrying a weapon. Moderate Violence: Strongarming. Serious Violence: *Attack to seriously hurt or kill.

Age of Onset. The age of onset constructs follow the layout of the General Delinquency Seriousness construct, but are based on self-reported delinquency only. The self-reported seriousness categories are slightly different from the Delinquency Classification, which was based on both self-report and parent and teacher reports. The self-reported delinquency seriousness has three levels: (a) minor delinquency (e.g., firesetting, shoplifting, damage property), (b) moderate delinquency (steal items worth $5 or more, steal from car, joyriding), and (c) serious delinquency (e.g., breaking and entering, strongarming, forced sex). The levels are based on the seriousness of delinquent acts ever committed by the time of the follow-up. An age of onset is calculated for each of the three delinquency seriousness levels as well as for delinquency at any level. These constructs were only created for the middle and oldest samples, because, for the youngest sample, being only 7 years old, onsets are relatively infrequent and the range of age of onset would be narrow.

Substance Use

Table 3.3 shows the main domains for substance use—that is, use and exposure to drugs. For the self-reported alcohol items, cases where the boy reported consuming beer, wine, or hard liquor (e.g., at a festive occasion) with the permission of his parent(s) were excluded.

TABLE 3.3
Constructs Pertaining to Boys' Substance Use

Domain	Specific Constructs
Use	Parent report of boy's smoking
	Parent–teacher report of boy's substance use
	Frequency of tobacco use
	Frequency of alcohol use
	Frequency of hard liquor use
	Frequency of marijuana use
	Substance use classification
	Age of onset of substance use
	Age of onset of substance use classification score
Exposure	Exposure to drugs

Parent Report of Boy's Smoking (previous year). This construct concerns the parent's report of the boy having smoked either during the 6 months prior to the screening or 6 months prior to follow-up (one question each).

Parent–Teacher Report of the Boy's Substance Use (lifetime). This construct consists of six parent questions (CBCL) and one teacher question (TRF) administered at screening as well as follow-up. The questions cover the adults' knowledge of the boy's tobacco, alcohol, and drug use, as well as their suspicions of his drinking or use of substances. At screening, the parent was also asked about the boy's lifetime use of drugs and alcohol. A confirmatory answer to any of these questions resulted in a positive score on this construct.

Adults' Report of the Boy's Substance Use Excluding Smoking (lifetime). This construct consists of five parent questions (CBCL) and one teacher question (TRF) administered at screening as well as follow-up. They cover the adults' knowledge of the boy's alcohol and drug use as well as their suspicions of his drinking or use of substances. At screening, the parent was also asked about the boy's lifetime use of drugs and alcohol. A confirmatory answer to any of these questions resulted in a positive score on this construct. Unlike the previous construct, this construct excludes reports of smoking.

Frequency of Tobacco Use (previous year). This construct combined the boy's self-reported frequencies of the use of tobacco at screening and follow-up. Because the youngest and middle samples reported categorical frequencies of substance use at screening, this score could only be computed for the oldest sample.

Frequency of Alcohol Use (previous year). This construct combined the boy's self-reported frequencies of the use of beer, wine, and hard liquor (except drinking alcohol at festive occasions with parental knowledge) at screening and follow-up. Because the youngest and middle samples reported categorical frequencies of substance use at screening, this score could only be computed for the oldest sample.

Frequency of Liquor Use (previous year). This construct combined the boy's self-reported frequencies of the use of hard liquor (except drinking alcohol at festive occasions with parental knowledge) at screening and follow-up. Because the youngest and middle samples reported categorical frequencies of substance use in screening, this score could only be computed for the oldest sample.

Frequency of Marijuana Use (previous year). This construct combined the boy's self-reported frequencies of the use of marijuana at screening and follow-up. Because the youngest and middle samples reported categorical frequencies of substance use in screening, this score could only be computed for the oldest sample.

Substance Use Classification Score (lifetime). This score reflects the boy's self-reported involvement in smoking, drinking beer, wine, and hard liquor (except drinking alcohol at festive occasions with parental knowledge); and use of marijuana and other drugs such as LSD and barbiturates (middle and oldest samples only). For the youngest sample, this involved 5 questions, and for the middle and oldest samples a maximum of 19 questions. The Substance Use Classification Score was computed in the following way: All boys who had never used any substances received a score of 0, boys who, at the time of follow-up, had ever consumed either beer or wine received a score of 1, and boys who had smoked at least once in their life received a score of 2. A score of 3 was given to participants who had used hard liquor and 4 to participants who had smoked marijuana. For the middle and oldest samples, a score of 5 was given to participants who had used other drugs such as cocaine, LSD, barbiturates, and so on. Boys were given the highest score that they had achieved.

Age of Onset of Substance Use (at follow-up). The age of onset construct (middle and oldest samples) was based on the boy's report at follow-up of the age he first started to use any substance. This involved any report of smoking; drinking beer, wine, or hard liquor; or use of marijuana or other drugs such as cocaine, LSD and barbiturates.

Age of Onset of Substance Use Classification Score (at follow-up and previous year). The age of onset for participants who had reached the different levels of substance use (middle and oldest samples) was computed for all boys reaching a score of 1 and 2 combined (smoking, or the use of beer or wine) and for all boys reaching a score of 3 (the use of liquor). Again, the ages of onset for drinking alcohol at festive occasions with parental knowledge were excluded. For the oldest sample, an age of onset was also computed for those boys reaching a score of 4 (the use of marijuana).

Exposure to Drugs (previous 6 months). This construct is based on two questions asking if the boy has been offered any drugs or had seen others getting or buying drugs in the neighborhood. These questions were asked of the middle and oldest samples at follow-up. A confirmatory answer to any of these questions resulted in a positive score on this construct.

Psychopathology and Conduct Problems

Table 3.4 summarizes the principal constructs in the domain of boys' psychopathology: conduct disorder, oppositional defiant disorder, and ADHD diagnoses, as well as conduct problems, oppositional behavior, and ADHD symptom scores. It also summarizes the disruptive problem behaviors and internalizing problems.

Any DSM–III–R Disruptive Behavior Diagnosis (previous 6 months). This construct represents the prevalence of boys qualifying for a diagnosis of

TABLE 3.4
Constructs Pertaining to Boys' Psychopathology and Conduct Problems

Domain	Specific Constructs
Disruptive behavior	Disruptive behavior disorder diagnosis
	Conduct disorder diagnosis
	Conduct problems symptom score
	Oppositional defiance disorder diagnosis
	Oppositional behavior symptom score
	ADHD
	High ADHD score
	HIA problems
Other disruptive problem behaviors	Nonphysical aggression
	Physical aggression
	Cruel to people
	Truant
	Covert behavior
	Lack of guilt
	Suspended
	Runs away
Depression/anxiety	Depressed mood
	Anxiety
	Shy/withdrawn

disruptive behavior disorder. Qualifying boys have at least one of the following diagnoses: ADHD, oppositional defiant disorder, or conduct disorder.

Conduct Disorder Diagnosis (CD) (previous 6 months). The *DSM–III–R* definition of CD is a disturbance of at least 6 months duration, during which at least 3 of a list of 13 behaviors apply.

Conduct Problems Symptom Score (previous 6 months). This construct is based on the DISC questions used in the diagnosis of CD. The behaviors range from frequent lying to status offenses and delinquent acts. Twenty-five questions in the DISC cover 13 conduct problems. The values of the answers, ranging from *never* (0) to *sometimes* (1) and *often* (2), were added and range from zero to 50.[2]

---

[2]The psychiatric definition of *conduct problems* partly overlaps with the legal definition of *delinquency*. We considered whether to pare down the conduct problem list to the nondelinquent items only. Although attractive in that such a construct would not overlap with delinquency, the disadvantage was that it would yield a construct that would not be very meaningful for psychiatrists. Therefore, we opted for a construct of conduct problems based on the full list of symptoms of conduct disorder.

Oppositional Defiant Disorder Diagnosis (ODD) (previous 6 months). To meet the *DSM–III–R* criterion for a diagnosis of ODD, the disturbance has to last at least 6 months during which at least five of a list of nine behaviors are present. The behaviors are of a nondelinquent nature and range from losing one's temper to arguing and blaming others. ODD is not diagnosed if the criteria for CD are present.

Oppositional Behavior Symptom Score (previous 6 months). This construct is based on the DISC questions used in the diagnosis of Oppositional Defiant Disorder. Thirteen questions in the DISC cover nine oppositional defiant behaviors. Symptoms were scored as described for the Conduct Problem Symptom Score, with a range of 0 to 50.

Attention-Deficit Hyperactivity Disorder (ADHD) Diagnosis (previous 6 months). To meet the *DSM–III–R* criterion for ADHD, the disturbance has to last at least 6 months, during which at least 8 of a list of 14 behaviors are present. The disturbance should have an onset before age 7. The DISC contains 28 questions concerning ADHD.

ADHD Score (previous 6 months). The 28 DISC questions to the mother, covering 14 behaviors used in the diagnosis of ADHD make up this construct of ADHD symptom score (called here *ADHD Score*). Symptoms were scored as described for the Conduct Problem Symptom Score, with a range of 0 to 50. The behaviors fall under the broad categories of *restlessness* or *hyperactivity*, *attention deficit*, and *impulsivity*.

Hyperactivity-Impulsivity-Attention Problems (HIA problems) (previous year). This construct is made up of 14 behaviors represented by 50 ratings by parents and teachers on hyperactivity, impulsive behaviors, and attention problems. It is called *HIA problems*. Examples are *does not finish jobs* or *impatient*. The 14 behaviors were measured at screening and at follow-up by both parent (CBCL) and teacher (TRF). An endorsement of *sometimes* or *often* by any informant at either screening or follow-up resulted in a positive count for that behavior [α (Y) = .82; α (M) = .84; α (O) = .85, where Y = youngest sample, M = middle sample, and O = oldest sample].

Nonphysical Aggression (lifetime). This construct summarizes the boys' mainly verbally aggressive behaviors, such as bragging, being explosive, swearing, and disturbing others. The construct is based on questions from screening, including the lifetime assessment, and follow-up using information from the parent (CBCL) and teacher (TRF). An endorsement of *sometimes* or *often* by any informant at either screening or follow-up resulted in a positive count for that behavior. The behaviors were represented by 25 questions [α (Y) = .90; α (M) = .92; α (O) = .91].

Physical Aggression (lifetime). This construct summarizes the boys' physical aggression based on screening, including the lifetime assessment, and follow-up using information from the parent (CBCL) and teacher (TRF). An endorsement of *sometimes* or *often* by any informant at either screening or follow-up resulted in a positive count for that behavior. The behaviors were represented by seven questions, such as *starts physical fights* and *hits teacher*, [α (Y) = .70; α (M) = .69; α (O) = .66].

Cruel to People (previous year). The construct of cruelty to people is based on one CBCL question for the parent and one TRF question for the teacher, administered both at screening and follow-up. The values of the four questions were added. The questions refer to cruelty, bullying, or meanness to others.

Truant (lifetime). This construct represents the lifetime estimate of whether a boy has been truant based on the boy's (SRA/SRD, and oldest sample YSR), the parent's (CBCL), and the teacher's (TRF) reports at screening and follow-up.

Covert Behavior (previous year). This score combines the *z*-scored values of the *concealing behavior*, *untrustworthy*, and *manipulates* constructs, which were made in the following manner:

- *Concealing Behavior*. This construct refers to the extent to which the boy makes himself unaccountable to adults as measured at screening and follow-up. The construct consists of five behaviors represented by 18 questions—12 for the parent (CBCL), 2 for the teacher (TRF), and 4 for the boy (YSR, oldest sample only). Example questions are: *stays out late at night, does not come straight home from school and you do not know where he is, and refuses to explain where he has been.* An endorsement of sometimes or often by any informant at either screening or follow-up resulted in a positive count for that behavior [α (Y) = .61; α (M) = .65; α (O) = .64].

- *Untrustworthy*. This construct is based on seven behaviors relating to the untrustworthiness of the boy's behavior measured at screening and follow-up through parent (CBCL), teacher (TRF), and participant (YSR, only oldest sample) information. An endorsement of *sometimes* or *often* by any informant at either screening or follow-up resulted in a positive count for that behavior. The seven behaviors were represented for the youngest and middle samples by 20 questions and for the oldest sample by 22 questions. Examples of questions are: *does not keep promises, says he is one place when he is somewhere else,* and *when confronted about his behavior is a fast or a smooth talker* [α (Y) = .79; α (M) = .79; α (O) = .81].

- *Manipulates*. This construct is based on five behaviors measured at screening and follow-up through the parent (CBCL) and teacher (TRF). An endorsement of *sometimes* or *often* by any informant at either screening or follow-up resulted in a positive count for that behavior. The five behaviors were represented by 16 questions. The construct summarizes how these adults perceive the boy as manipulative. Example questions are: *acts sneakily, manipulates people,* and *tells nasty things about others behind their backs* [α (Y) = .63; α (M) = .66; α (O) = .67].

Lack of Guilt (previous year). This construct concerns the lack of guilt displayed by the boy measured by one question from the parent (CBCL) and one question from the teacher (TRF), both at screening and follow-up. The values of the four questions were added.

Suspended (lifetime). This construct represents whether the boy was ever suspended from school, usually for misbehavior. The information was based on five questions for the youngest sample and four questions for the middle and oldest samples from the parent (CBCL) and boy (SRA/SRD).

Runs Away (lifetime). This construct is based on questions from the parent (CBCL) and the boy (SRA/SRD) at screening and follow-up to assess whether the boy had ever run away from home during his lifetime. The behavior is represented by five questions for the youngest and middle samples. The oldest sample has two additional questions (YSR).

Depressed Mood (previous 2 weeks). This construct is the total score of the 13 items on the Recent Mood and Feelings Questionnaire at follow-up. The questions cover the symptoms necessary for making a diagnosis of major depression according to *DSM–III–R* criteria [α (Y) = .80; α (M) = .82; α (O) = .84].

Anxiety (previous year). This construct is a measure of the boy's anxiety problems and combines information from the caregivers (CBCL) and teacher (TRF) at screening or follow-up. An endorsement of *sometimes* or *often* by either the caregiver or the teacher at either assessment resulted in a positive count for an item. The construct consists of nine items, covering such behaviors as *clings to adults or too dependent, fears certain animals, situations or places other than school*, and *nervous, highly strung, or tense* [α (Y) = .69; α (M) = .65; α (O) = .69].

Shy/Withdrawn (previous year). This construct is similar to the *anxiety* construct and combines information from the caregiver (CBCL) and teacher (TRF) at screening and follow-up. The construct consists of seven items concerning such behaviors as *likes to be alone, refuses to talk, shy,* and *gets teased* [α (Y) = .57; α (M) = .61; α (O) = .57].

Sexual Behavior

The constructs concerning sexual behavior (Table 3.5) were measured for the oldest sample only.

Age of First Sex. This is based on a single question asking at what age the boy first had sexual intercourse with a female.

Had Sex. This is based on a single question asking whether the boy had ever had sexual intercourse with a female.

Frequency of Heterosexual Sex (previous 6 months). This was based on a single question about the frequency of sexual intercourse with a female at follow-up.

Multiple Partners (previous 6 months). This was based on a single question about the number of female sexual partners at follow-up.

Injuries

Frequency of Injuries. This construct consists of five questions about the boy's physical injuries such as severe cuts, burns, or head injuries.

Attitudes

Table 3.6 summarizes the different constructs measuring boys' attitudes toward delinquency, substance use, and problem behaviors.

Positive Attitude to Problem Behavior (at follow-up). This construct is based on questions at follow-up from the Perception of Antisocial Behavior Scale, tapping the boy's opinion about whether it is right to engage in various problem behaviors, such as driving a car before the age of 16, smoking, or using fists to resolve a conflict. For the youngest sample, 15 items make up this construct, compared with 18 items for the middle and oldest samples [α (Y) = .76; α (M) = .77; α (O) = .84].

Positive Attitude to Delinquency (at follow-up). This construct captures the boy's opinion at follow-up of how wrong he judges a number of delinquent acts

TABLE 3.5
Constructs Pertaining to the Boys' Sexual Behavior

Construct
Age of first sexual intercourse
Had sexual intercourse
Frequency of heterosexual sex
Multiple partners

TABLE 3.6
Constructs Pertaining to Boys' Attitudes

Constructs
Favorable to problem behavior
Favorable to delinquency
Unlikely to be caught
Favorable to substance use

(9 questions for the youngest sample and 11 for the middle and oldest samples) from the Attitude Toward Delinquent Behavior Scale, scored on a five-point scale [α (Y) = .82; α (M) = .83; α (O) = .87].

Unlikely to be Caught (at follow-up). This construct was measured for the middle and oldest samples only and consisted of 10 questions from a scale with the same name administered at follow-up. It asked how likely the boy thought it was that he would be caught by the police if he engaged in specific delinquent acts [α (M) = .91; α (O) = .89].

Positive Attitude to Substance Use (at follow-up). This construct captures the boy's opinion at follow-up about whether it is wrong to consume various kinds of substances (for the youngest sample: drinking alcohol, using marijuana, or sniffing glue; for the middle and oldest samples: sell hard drugs; use alcohol, marijuana, or hard drugs), scored on a five-point scale in the Attitude Toward Delinquent Behavior Scale [α (Y) = .66; α (M) = .84; α (O) = .80].

Competence

Table 3.7 summarizes the constructs referring to the boy's competence in four areas: achievement, school, organizations, and jobs.

Low Achievement (Parent, Boy, Teacher) (previous year). This construct combines judgments of parents (CBCL), teachers (TRF), and boys (YSR, only in the oldest sample) on how well the boy performs in a maximum of seven academic subjects. The information was collected at screening and at follow-up. Each academic subject is rated on a four-point scale from *failing* to *above average*. Teacher ratings were made on a five-point scale. Before combining with the other scores, the two extreme scale points at the high end were combined. The ratings of all academic subjects by all informants at both assessments were averaged to arrive at a final score [average intercorrelations: (Y) = .56; (M) = .62; (O) = .49].

TABLE 3.7
Constructs Referring to the Boys' Competence

Domain	Specific Constructs
Achievement	Low achievement (parent, boy, teacher)
	Low achievement (CAT)
School	Low school motivation
	Negative attitude to school
Organizations	Low organizational participation
	Low religiosity
Jobs	Low jobs/chores involvement

California Achievement Test Scores for 1988, and 1989. Total reading, language, and math percentile scores from the California Achievement Test were obtained for the boys who attended Pittsburgh public schools at follow-up. If boys were tested more than once in an academic year, the scores were averaged. The variable *Low Achievement* (CAT) combines the three scores.

Low School Motivation (previous year). At screening and follow-up, teachers reported on a seven-point scale how hard the participant was working. The ratings of the two different teachers at screening and follow-up were averaged to form this construct. The two ratings correlated: (Y) = .54; (M) = .58; (O) = .46.

Negative Attitude to School (at follow-up). This construct consists of seven items (eight items for the oldest sample) tapping the boy's attitude and behavior in school at follow-up, such as *Do you try hard in school?, Do you think homework is a waste of time?,* and *Do you care what teachers think of you?* [α (Y) = .46; α (M) = .48; α (O) = .63].

Low Organizational Participation (previous year). This construct uses information from the parent (CBCL) from screening and follow-up on the number of organizations, clubs, and teams the boy belongs to and how active he is in these organizations. For the oldest sample, boys also provided this information in the YSR. The constructs from the different assessments (and, for the oldest sample, from different respondents) were averaged [average intercorrelations: (Y) = .62; (M) = .45; (O) = .52].

Low Religiosity (at follow-up). This construct is based on the youngest and middle samples on two questions at follow-up about the boy's preference and behavior in participating in religious services. For the oldest sample, three questions were combined, which were slightly differently worded than for the other samples.

Low Jobs/Chores Involvement (previous year). This construct uses information from the parent (CBCL) from screening and follow-up on the number of jobs and chores the boy has and how well he performs those. For the oldest sample, boys also provided this information in the YSR. The constructs from the different assessments (and, for the oldest sample, from different respondents) were averaged [average intercorrelations: (Y) = .45; (M) = .41; (O) = .29].

Family Constructs

Family Functioning.   Several domains of family functioning were translated into constructs covering the following domains: parents' discipline and supervision of the boy, their involvement with the boy, their positive parenting, parent–child communication, parents' tolerance of deviant child behavior, and the boy's relationships with his parents. The term *parent* is only used when the sex of the informant was not of material importance, allowing the inclusion of a maximum number of participants. Table 3.8 summarizes the specific constructs representing each of the domains.

Discipline.

- *Discipline Not Persistent* (previous 6 months). For the middle and oldest samples, this construct combines four items from the parents' report of her persistence in disciplining and five items from the boy's report on the same behavior [α (M) = .55; α (O) = .59]. For the youngest sample, only the parent's report was available [α (Y) = .48]. The questions address the degree to which the parent persisted with a disciplinary action and were scored on a three-point frequency scale. An example of a question in the boy's report is: *If your mother asks you to do something and you don't do it right away, does your mother give up trying to get you to do it?*.

TABLE 3.8
Family Functioning Constructs

Domain	Specific constructs
Discipline	Discipline not persistent
	Counter control
	Physical punishment
	Disagree on discipline
Supervision	Poor supervision
	No set time home
Involvement	Low family talk
	Low family activities
	Don't enjoy boy
	Boy not involved
Positive parenting	Low parental reinforcement
Communication	Poor parent–child communication
Attitude	Parent antisocial attitude
Relationships	Poor relation with parents
	Poor relation with siblings
	Not close to mother/father
	Unhappy parents
	Low marital involvement
	Low marital agreement
Mother's stress	High parental stress
Parent pathology	Father behavior problems
	Parent substance use problems
	Parent anxious/depressed

- *Countercontrol* (previous 6 months). This construct summarizes 11 items of the parent's report concerning whether the boy's behavior became worse when punished. Examples are: *If you punish your son, does his behavior get worse?*, and *Do you think that your son will take it out on other children if you try to make him obey you?* [α (Y) = .78; α (M) = .78; α (O) = .81].
- *Physical Punishment* (Combined, previous 6 months). This combined parent and child construct tapped whether the parent slapped or spanked the boy.
- *Disagree on Discipline* (combined, previous 6 months). Two questions for the parent and one question for the boy (middle and oldest samples) tapped the extent to which the parent and her partner agreed on how to bring up the boy.

Supervision.

- *Poor Supervision* (combined, previous 6 months). This construct is based on the boy's report and the parent's report, each covered by four questions. An example for the boy is: *Do your parent(s) know who you are with when you are away from home?* [α (Y) = .63; α (M) = .64; α (O) = .75].
- *No Set Time Home* (previous 6 months). This construct is based on the parent's and the boy's answers to three questions each about whether there is a set time for the boy to be home on school or weekend nights and whether the parent would know if the boy did not come home in time [α (Y) = .57; α (M) = .49; α (O) = .70].

Involvement.

- *Low Family Talk* (combined, previous 6 months). This construct combines four questions from the parent and five questions from the boy about the parent's talking with the boy about his activities, scored on a four-point scale, ranging from *More than a month ago*, to *Yesterday/today*. Examples of questions are: *When was the last time that you discussed with your son his plans for the coming day?* and *In the previous six months, about how often have you talked with your son about what he had actually done during the day?* [α (Y) = .69; α (M) = .76; α (O) = .82].
- *Low Family Activities* (combined, previous 6 months). This construct is based on eight questions to the parent and six questions to the boy at follow-up about the amount of time that the parent spent with the child. Examples of questions are: *How often do you have a friendly chat with your mom/dad?* and *How often do you help your mom/dad?* [α (Y) = .68; α (M) = .73; α (O) = .77].

- *Don't Enjoy Boy* (previous 6 months). This is based on a single question inquiring from the parent how enjoyable the time is that she spends on activities with the boy.
- *Boy Not Involved* (combined, previous 6 months). This construct is based on four questions to the parent and four questions to the boy about the degree that he is involved in family activities, such as planning family activities and joining family members on outings [α (Y) = .61; α (M) = .62; α (O) = .73].

Positive Parenting.

- *Low Reinforcement* (combined, previous 6 months). This construct is based on the parent's and the boy's information about the frequency of the parent's positive behaviors toward the boy, measured with nine items in the parent questionnaire and seven items in the child questionnaire. Items refer to the parent saying something nice to the child, and giving a special privilege or reward [α (Y) = .70; α (M) = .72; α (O) = .75].

Communication.

- *Poor Communication* (combined, previous 6 months). This construct combines information from the parent and the boy on the Revised Parent–Adolescent Communication Form. It taps on a three-point frequency scale how often the boy (28 items) and the parent (30 items) communicate directly or indirectly about emotions, disagreements, and problems. Examples for the boy are: *Do you tell your mother/father about your personal problems?* and *If your mother/father is angry with you, do you hear about it from someone else?* The constructs in this form only apply to the middle and oldest samples, because the youngest boys were too young to be given the instrument. We had information about parent–child communication in the youngest sample from the parent only, but did not include it in the analyses because of concerns about its comparability with data from the other two samples.

Attitudes.

- *Parent Antisocial Attitude* (at follow-up). This is a summary construct encompassing 18 questions about the parent's attitude to antisocial behaviors of the boy, such as whether it is all right to yell, argue, and fight; be truant; and choose one's own friends even if they are undesirable [α (Y) = .58; α (M) = .69; α (O) = .67].

Relationships.

- *Poor Relation with Parents* (combined, previous 6 months). This construct consists of 13 items tapping how often the boy perceived the relationship to his parent in positive or negative terms, with 16 items of the parent's report on her relationship with the boy. Examples of questions for the boy are: *How often have you thought your mother/father bugged you a lot? and How often have you liked being your mother/father's child?* and for the parent: *How often have you thought your child was a good child?* and *How often have you wished he would just leave you alone?* [α (Y) = .73; α (M) = .78; α (O) = .84].
- *Poor Relation with Siblings* (previous 6 months). This is a construct combining parent's and boy's information at follow-up about how well he gets along with siblings in the family, measured on a three-point scale for the boy's information and on a five-point scale for the parent's information. The number of items varies by participant depending on the number of siblings. Items were z scored to combine parent and child information.
- *Not Close to Mother/Father* (at follow-up). This construct consists of two questions asking the boy whether he thinks that his mother/father feels close to him and how close he feels to his mother/father. The construct only exists for the middle and oldest samples. A boy is considered not close to his mother/father if he is not close to either one of his parents.
- *Unhappy Parents* (at follow-up). This is a summary evaluation by the parent of how she rates the degree of happiness (on a five-point scale) in her relationship with her partner.
- *Low Marital Involvement* (at follow-up). This construct is based on three questions to the parent pertaining to how often the parent and her partner talk or work together on a project [α (Y) = .78; α (M) = .81; α (O) = .78].
- *Low Marital Agreement* (at follow-up). This construct consists of three questions to the parent tapping the degree that the parent and her partner agree about goals, beliefs, time spent together, and what they want out of life [α (Y) = .82; α (M) = .81; α (O) = .85].

Mother's Stress.

- *High Parental Stress* (previous month). The 14 items of the Perceived Stress Scale, administered at follow-up to the parent, form the basis for the *high parental stress* construct. The items measure the mother's perceived stress and her perceived ability to handle problems. Examples are: *Have you found that you could not cope with all of the things you had to do?* and *You felt nervous and stressed?* The time frame is 1 month [α (Y) = .83; α (M) = .83; α (O) = .83].

Parent Psychopathology.

- *Parental Pathology* (lifetime). The parents were asked at follow-up whether they or, if one or both biological parents were currently not living with the child, these absent parents had ever sought help for mental problems. In addition, the parents were asked if the child's biological mother/father suffered mental problems. The mother was considered pathological if she had sought help or indicated that she had suffered from the problem(s). In the case that the female caregiver was not the biological mother, the variable was scored pathological if either the caregiver or the biological mother fell into this category. The same held for the pathology of the fathers. Two more subconstructs were made for parents : anxiety/depression, and substance use problems. In addition, a subconstruct was made for father behavior problems.
- *Parent Substance Use Problems.* Combines information on whether either absent or present father or mother has ever had substance use problems (i.e., alcohol or drug problems).
- *Parent Anxious/Depressed.* Combines information on whether either absent or present father or mother has ever had problems with anxiety, including depression and suicide.
- *Father Behavior Problems.* This concerned those fathers (either living in the house or absent) for whom the respondent reported that the father has or had *behavior problems.*

Demographic and Neighborhood Constructs

Demographics. Table 3.9 summarizes the main constructs relating to demographic characteristics of boys and their families.

Boy.

- *Old for Grade* (at follow-up). The age of the boy at the time of the follow-up interview was determined by calculating the interval in days between the date of the interview and the boy's date of birth, divided by 365.25. The cutoff for *Old for grade* was 7.8, 11, and 14 years of age for the youngest, middle and oldest samples, respectively. This variable identified age-inappropriate boys who had probably been held back for failing a grade.
- *African American.* Information on the boy's ethnicity was obtained from the parent at screening. Participants were classified as White ($N = 652$, which included 11 Asians) or African American ($N = 865$, which included 23 of mixed race, 4 Hispanics, and 1 American Indian).

TABLE 3.9
Demographics

Domain	Specific Constructs
Boy	Old for grade
	African American
Parent	Young mother
	Young father
	Teenage mother
	Poorly educated mother
	Poorly educated father
	Low socioeconomic status (SES)
	Unemployed mother
	Unemployed father
Family	Large family
	Family on welfare
	Broken family
Residence	Small house
	Poor housing

Parent.

- *Young Mother/Father* (at follow-up). These constructs cover the age of the parents in the home at the time of the follow-up interview. Mothers were considered young if they were less than 27, 30, and 33 years of age for the youngest, middle, and oldest samples, respectively. Fathers were considered young if they were less than 30, 32, and 35 years of age for the youngest, middle, and oldest samples, respectively.
- *Teenage Mother.* This dichotomized construct divides mothers into those who were less than 20 years of age at the boy's birth and those who were 20 years of age or older.
- *Poorly Educated Mother/Father* (lifetime). The total years of schooling of female and male parents in the home was assessed at follow-up. Parents who had not reached Grade 12 were considered to be poorly educated.
- *Low Socioeconomic Status (SES)* (at follow-up). Using the Hollingshead (1975) index of social status, the parents' socioeconomic scores are computed by multiplying the scale value for occupational prestige by a weight of five and the scale value for educational level by a weight of three. If the family had two parents in the family, the highest score was selected.
- *Unemployed Mother/Father* (previous year). The total number of weeks of unemployment in the year prior to follow-up was calculated for both parents of the boy. For the time period that parents were homemakers, they were not considered unemployed.

Family.

- *Large Family.* This construct is based on information at follow-up from the child about how many other children live with him in the family. Boys living with three or more siblings (not necessarily biological) were considered to have a large family.
- *Family on Welfare* (previous year). This construct is scored positive if anyone in the boy's household was on welfare during the year prior to follow-up.
- *Broken Family* (parent's report at follow-up). Based on the parent's report at follow-up, this construct classifies the boy's living condition as: living with both biological parents or not living with both biological parents.

Residence.

- *Small House* (at follow-up). This construct covers the total number of rooms in the boy's residence including bathrooms and kitchens as reported by the parent at follow-up. Residences with less than six rooms were considered small.
- *Poor Housing* (at follow-up). This construct covers the assessment by the interviewer of the condition of the house that the boy lived in at the time of the follow-up interview. The total score was based on eight questions covering the structural condition of the house, visible signs of peeling paint and plaster, and cleanliness inside the house [α (Y) = .82; α (M) = .80; α (O) = .82].

Neighborhood Constructs

Table 3.10 summarizes the principal constructs describing the neighborhood in which the boy and his family lived, either from census information or from the parent's or interviewer's point of view.

Bad Neighborhood, Census. Tract information from the 1980 U.S. Census was linked to each boy based on the address where he resided at follow-up. The construct included three domains of Census information: (a) family income,

TABLE 3.10
Neighborhood Constructs

Domain	Specific Constructs
Census tract	Bad neighborhood, census
Perception	Bad neighborhood, parent

with three items concerning median family income (rank ordered with lowest income receiving the highest rank and, subsequently, expressed as a percentile), percentage of persons in the labor force who were unemployed in 1979, and percentage of families below the poverty level; (b) juveniles, represented by one item concerning the percentage of persons who are between the ages of 10 and 14; (c) family composition, with two items concerning the percentage of families with children under the age of 18 headed by a female with no husband present and the percentage of persons age 15 and over who are separated or divorced. For each of the items, the boy received a positive score if the percentage for that item was in the top 25%. For the domains with multiple items, the scores were summed and dichotomized. Next, the three domains were combined into a Bad Neighborhood rating based on a score of more than one out of a possible score of three (top 25%). Thus, a positive score on the total construct indicated that the boy came from a neighborhood with handicaps in at least one of the three areas (family income, presence of juveniles, or family composition).

Bad Neighborhood, Parent (at follow-up). This is an overall appraisal by the parent of the quality of the neighborhood where she lives on 17 items, including unemployment, abandoned houses, racial strife, winos and junkies, and various forms of delinquency [α (Y) = .95; α (M) = .95; α (O) = .95].

Peer Behavior Constructs

Table 3.11 summarizes the ways that peer influences are measured through the parent's and boy's report's. Of prime concern are the peers' antisocial acts, substance use, and nonconventional behaviors. Another set of constructs concern the boy's friendships.

Delinquency.

- *Peer Delinquency* (previous 6 months). This construct for the middle and oldest samples summarizes the proportion of friends who engage in 11 different forms of delinquency (scaled on a five-point scale). The types of delinquency correspond to the items from the SRD. Examples of questions are: *How many of them (i.e., friends) have gone into or tried to go into a building to steal something?* and . . . *attacked someone with a weapon with the idea of seriously hurting that person?* [α (M) = .84; α (O) = .90]. For the youngest sample, the construct is based on nine items and asks for the proportion of friends who engaged in the behavior, scaled on a three-point scale [α (Y) = .79].

TABLE 3.11
Constructs Pertaining to Boys' peers

Domain	Specific Constructs
Delinquency	Peer delinquency
	Offends alone
Substance use	Peer substance use
Prosocial peers	Nonconventional peers
Friends	Few friends
	Bad friends
	Poor relation with peers

- *Offends Alone* (previous 6 months). This construct is based on a question for each of the delinquent acts reported by the boy at the time of the follow-up assessment. It asks whether, for the most serious or most costly act, the boy was alone or with someone else when committing the act. The construct was available only for the middle and oldest samples because of the nature of the assessment instruments.
- *Peer Substance Use* (previous 6 months). This construct, for the middle and oldest samples, consists of four items concerning the proportion of friends who use alcohol or drugs or sell drugs. Examples of questions are: *How many of them (i.e., friends) used marijuana or hashish?* and . . . *sold hard drugs such as heroin, cocaine, or LSD?* [α (M) = .51; α (O) = .68].
- *Nonconventional Peers* (previous 6 months). This construct is based on the proportion of peers who engage in eight different conventional activities, such as being involved in athletics, obeying school rules, and participating in activities with the participant's family [α (Y) = .68; α (M) = .71; α (O) = .77].

Friends.

- *Few Friends* (previous 6 months). This is a combined construct based on the parent's and boy's information about how many close or special friends the boy has.
- *Bad friends* (previous 6 months). This combined variable, based on the parent's and boy's report's, summarizes information on the boy's associating with bad friends (five items for the boy and parent, respectively). Examples of questions for the boy are: *Are there any children in your group of friends of whom your parents disapproved?* and *Did any of the kids in your group of friends do things that your parents don't want you to do?* [α (Y) .61; α (M) .72; α (O) .75].

- *Poor Relation With Peers* (previous year). This construct is based on the teacher's report of how well the boy gets along with other children, scaled on a three-point scale assessed at screening and follow-up. We hope that readers have stayed with us during this necessarily long and complex chapter, because it contains information that is essential for understanding many of the later chapters.

4

Prevalence, Frequency, and Onset

This chapter summarizes the prevalence of the main outcome variables considered in this book (e.g., delinquency, substance use, mental health problems, and sexual intercourse), and examines differences in prevalence among the three age samples. In addition, it reviews the prevalence of the diagnoses of disruptive behavior disorders (attention deficit hyperactivity disorder [ADHD], oppositional defiant disorder, and conduct disorder). It also examines whether the average scores on various continuous behavioral indicators change with age. The following disruptive scores are considered: a high ADHD score, conduct problems, and physical aggression. It also examine's internalizing problems such as shy/withdrawn behavior, depressive mood, and anxious/fearful behavior.

We were particularly interested in the extent to which the prevalence and frequency (when available) of problem behaviors in the Pittsburgh boys compares with prevalence and frequency in other samples. We also wanted to know the extent that problem behaviors emerge during the elementary school years. This period has often been neglected in prior studies.

DELINQUENCY

Young Boys' Understanding of Delinquency Questions

A first step in the delinquency analyses was to ascertain, for the youngest and middle samples, the percentage of boys who did not understand the delinquency questions asked in the Self-Reported Antisocial Behavior Scale (SRA) at screening. The results, not weighted for the sampling procedure, are presented in Table 4.1. They show that the majority of the boys in each sample were able to respond to the question asked. For example, 85.1% of the boys in the youngest sample understood the question about damaging things on purpose, compared with 97.9% in the middle sample.

In order to make prevalence estimates, the boys who did not understand the question were considered not to have engaged in the behavior. However, because there is a possibility that some of those who did not understand the question had engaged in the behavior, this is a minimum estimate. If we assume that the maximum prevalence of the behavior among those who did not understand the question would be the same as the prevalence for those who did understand it, we can establish an upper limit for the prevalence of the entire sample. In most cases, the maximum to minimum range established was quite narrow (i.e., within one percentage point). However, the range was larger for those questions where a sizable number of children did not understand the question. For the youngest sample, the following behaviors fell into this category: smoking marijuana (prevalence range .4%–1.4%) and sniffing glue (2.8% to 7.4%). For the middle sample, only sniffing glue had a relatively wide range (2.8%–5.6%).

Prevalence of Delinquency Seriousness Levels

The following tables show the weighted rather than the raw prevalence of problem behaviors. Whereas the *raw prevalence* refers to the prevalence based on the enriched sample of 1,517 boys selected for follow-up, the *weighted prevalence* involves the application of a weighting formula to estimate the prevalence of the behaviors for the sample of 2,573 boys assessed at screening, which was considered a random sample of the school population from which it was drawn.[1]

Table 4.2 shows the weighted prevalence of the seriousness levels of delinquency based on the combined reports of the boys, their caregivers and teachers. The meaning of these levels was described in chapter 3 and is only briefly summarized here. Level 1 consists of no delinquency or minor delinquency only at home. Level 2 concerns minor delinquency outside of the home. Level 3 pertains to moderately serious delinquency, such as theft over $5, gang fighting, and joyriding. Level 4 delinquency (serious delinquency) consists of

---

[1]The weights used were:

	High-risk group	Low-risk group
Youngest sample	.7979	1.2084
Middle sample	.6868	1.3254
Oldest sample	.6485	1.3626

TABLE 4.1
Percentage of Boys in the Youngest and Middle Samples Who Understood
Certain Delinquency Questions in the Screening Assessment

	Sample	
Deliquency Question	Youngest	Middle
Damage on purpose	85.1	97.9
Steal bicycle	91.3	98.5
Cheat on school tests	92.0	99.7
Hit someone	98.8	99.6
Skip school	75.0	99.6
Avoid paying	81.0	95.5

TABLE 4.2
Weighted Prevalence of Highest Lifetime Level of Seriousnes of Delinquency
Reached (%), Together With Percent of Boys at Each Level Who
Showed Delinquency at Each Lower Level

Sample	Weighted Prevalence	% Boys with Minor Delinquency Outside the Home*	% Boys with Moderate Delinquency*
Youngest			
No delinquency or minor delinquency at home	44.3		
Minor delinquency outside the home	30.4		
Moderately serious delinquency	16.4	62.5	
Serious delinquency	8.8	77.3	33.3
Middle			
No delinquency or minor delinquency at home	25.9		
Minor delinquency outside the home	32.5		
Moderately serious delinquency	19.7	82.7	
Serious delinquency	21.9	94.6	62.5
Oldest			
No delinquency or minor delinquency at home	24.0		
Minor delinquency outside the home	22.4		
Moderately serious delinquency	24.9	80.0	
Serious delinquency	28.7	93.0	77.5

* Percentage shows the boys at each level who also show delinquency at a lower level.

acts such as car theft, breaking and entering, and forced sex. Boys are placed
in the most serious level they have reached at the time of the last measurement
(i.e., follow-up). As expected, the percentage of nondelinquent boys decreased
with age: from 44.3% in the youngest sample to 25.9% in the middle sample.
However, there was only a very slight decrease to 24% in the oldest sample.

How are boys distributed across the seriousness levels? Table 4.2 shows that, for the youngest sample, 30.4% had committed minor delinquency, 16.4% moderately serious delinquency, and 8.8% serious delinquency. Slightly more boys in the middle sample had reached minor delinquency (32.5%), whereas about the same proportion had reached either moderately serious or serious delinquency (19.7% and 21.7%, respectively). In the oldest sample, however, about the same proportion of boys had reached each of the three levels of delinquency (22.4%, 24.9%, and 28.7%, respectively). This pattern across samples reflects that the prevalence of serious delinquency more than tripled with age (i.e., from 8.8% in the youngest sample to 21.9% in the middle sample and 28.7% in the oldest sample).

It has been postulated elsewhere that delinquency develops from less to more serious behavior and that almost all of those who have advanced to higher levels of seriousness will have manifested delinquency of a lower seriousness level (Loeber & Le Blanc, 1990). Although we do not address the longitudinal data in this volume, Table 4.2 shows the percentage of boys at the higher levels of seriousness who also manifested delinquency at a lower level. For example, about three quarters (77.3%) of the seriously delinquent boys in the youngest sample also manifested minor delinquency outside of the home and 33.3% manifested moderately serious delinquency. Thus, the hypothesized association only partly applied to this sample. However, as shown, the association improved with age and was best for the oldest sample.

More specifically, 93.0% of the most seriously delinquent boys also showed minor delinquency outside of the home, and three quarters (77.4%) also showed moderately serious delinquency. Thus, most of the seriously delinquent boys also displayed less serious forms of delinquency. Although the findings presented are not longitudinal, they conform to a hypothesized order of development. Elsewhere, using slightly different categories of delinquency and pre-delinquent problem behaviors and longitudinal data over six data waves, we have shown that the majority of individuals who progress to serious levels indeed first pass through levels of delinquency of lower seriousness (Loeber, Keenan, & Zhang, 1997; Loeber, DeLatnatre et al., in press; Loeber, Wung et al., 1993).

Age at Onset of Delinquency

At what age periods do different levels of seriousness of delinquency first emerge? Data are presented for the middle and oldest boys only because the youngest boys were not deemed old enough to accurately answer questions about the age of onset of delinquent acts. The upper age of onset is restricted to age 10 for the middle sample and age 12 for the oldest sample, because these were the highest ages reached by all in each of the samples. Rather than report on the age at onset of each specific form of delinquency, this chapter reports on the age of onset of different self-reported seriousness levels of delinquency.

Figure 4.1 shows that, for the middle sample, the number of boys who had an onset of any form of delinquency gradually increased from age 5 to age 7 and accelerated between ages 7 and 10. Turning to the category of minor delinquency, a similar pattern is shown in Fig. 4.1. The curve for moderate delinquency shows an onset that was later than that for minor delinquency and started to accelerate after age 7. The onset of serious delinquency tended to be later than that of moderate delinquency. Thus, a sequential pattern of onsets is suggested, with the less serious forms of delinquency occurring first and the most serious forms occurring last. The more serious the delinquency level, the fewer boys experienced an onset on that level.

The analyses were repeated for the oldest sample (Fig. 4.2). The results for the sequential ordering of the onsets of increasingly serious forms of delinquency were replicated. In terms of the earliest ages at onset, the results for the oldest sample are similar to those reported for the middle sample: minor delinquency started at age 5 and moderate delinquency started at ages 5 to 6 and accelerated between ages 10 and 12. Serious delinquency also had an early onset in a small proportion of boys then gradually increased at ages 6 to 7, and accelerated between ages 11 and 12. It should be kept in mind that the data in both Figs. 4.1 and 4.2 are censored on the right-hand side.

One of the main rationales for the plotting of ages of onsets of different seriousness levels of delinquency is to understand when risk and causal factors affecting different levels of delinquency seem to operate. As shown in Figs. 4.1 and 4.2, the prime time for the emergence of minor and moderate forms of

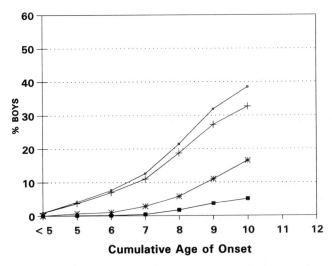

FIG. 4.1. Cumulative age of onset for levels of delinquency (middle sample).

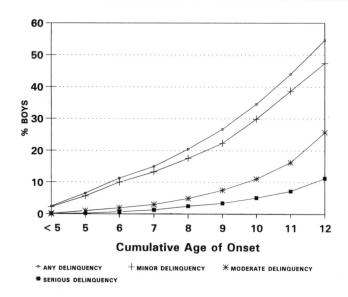

FIG. 4.2. Cumulative age of onset for levels of delinquency (oldest sample).

delinquency is in the elementary school age period, whereas it seems likely that the middle school period is the most crucial time for the emergence of more serious forms of delinquent acts.

Prevalence of Different Forms of Delinquency

Table 4.3 shows the prevalence of various types of delinquency—namely, theft, violence, vandalism, and fraud. The prevalence of specific delinquent acts is shown in Appendix 4.1. It should be noted that the Self-Reported Antisocial Behavior Scale (SRA) was used for the youngest boys and for the screening assessment of the middle sample. For the rest, the Self-Reported Delinquency Scale (SRD) was used. Although the two instruments overlap, they set some limits to the comparability of the data across the three samples.

As shown in Table 4.3, the lifetime prevalence of theft was 28.1% for boys in the youngest sample; 32.2% had committed vandalism. About half (51.2%) had committed some type of delinquent act (not shown in Table 4.3). The lifetime prevalence of theft and vandalism for boys in the middle sample was substantially higher (56.8% and 55.5%) than for the boys in the youngest sample (28.1% and 32.2%), suggesting that delinquency increased substantially between Grades 1 and 4.

How much did the prevalence of delinquency increase from the middle to the oldest samples? To investigate this, we considered only those delinquent

TABLE 4.3
Weighted Prevalence of Types of Delinquency (%) at Follow-Up

| | Sample | | | | | |
| | Youngest* | | Middle** | | Oldest | |
Delinquency Type	Lifetime	Past Year	Lifetime	Past Year	Lifetime	Past Year
Theft	28.1	20.6	56.8	36.8	64.0	31.8
Violence	—	—	24.1	—	35.5	29.4
Vandalism	32.2	24.0	55.5	37.6	26.4	19.1
Fraud	—	—	22.3	—	38.2	30.3
More than one	28.7	20.5	22.2	—	48.5	42.9

*Data waves using SRA.

**SRA was used at the screening assessment only; remaining data waves consisted of SRD.

—, Estimate could not be computed.

acts that were measured across at least two samples with either the SRA or SRD. As shown in Table 4.3, two thirds (64%) in the oldest sample had engaged in some form of theft during their lifetime, compared with 56.8% of the boys in the middle sample and 28.1% of the boys in the youngest sample. As to violence and fraud, the lifetime prevalence for boys in the oldest sample was 35.5% and 38.2%, respectively, compared with 24.1% and 22.3% in the middle sample. There was an increase in the variety in the type of delinquency with age, as is shown by 48.5% of the boys in the oldest sample having displayed more than one form of delinquency, compared with 28.7% of the boys in the youngest sample and 22.2% of the boys in the middle sample. Thus, boys' delinquency increased in prevalence and was more varied in the older compared with the younger boys.

Table 4.3 also shows the past-year prevalence of delinquency (i.e., summed over the two half-year assessments at screening and follow-up). Not surprisingly, the one-year prevalence for the youngest boys was more similar to their lifetime prevalence than for the oldest boys. When we compare the samples, Table 4.3 shows that the past-year prevalence of theft and vandalism substantially increased from the youngest to the middle sample, but then decreased (especially for vandalism) from the middle to the oldest sample.

Prevalence of Specific Delinquent Acts

The past year prevalence of specific delinquent acts are listed in Table A4.1 in the appendix. Only a few of the findings are highlighted here. In the youngest sample, already 11.9% of the boys had taken money from home during their lifetime and 7.9% over the past year. Similar proportions had engaged in shoplifting (10.2% and 7.2%). Surprisingly, 11.2% had carried a hidden weapon over the past year, which was about the same in the middle sample

(12.1%) but almost doubled in the oldest sample (22.7%). The lifetime prevalence of gang fighting was 7.9% in the middle sample, compared with 16.9% in the oldest sample. Finally, the lifetime prevalence of selling worthless goods tripled from the middle to the oldest samples (from 6.8% to 18.4%). In all, these and other figures shown in Table A4.1 illustrate the increasing prevalence of specific acts from middle childhood through early adolescence.

Frequency of Delinquent Acts

From middle childhood to adolescence, the frequency of delinquent acts also increased. These results are detailed in Table A4.2 in the appendix for the middle and oldest samples and are based on the boys' self-reports only (boys in the youngest sample were not asked the frequency questions). Because the frequency questions were part of the SRD, which was administered for the first time to the boys in the middle sample at follow-up, only 6-month frequency measures could be computed for that sample. To present comparable data for the oldest sample, Table A4.2 only lists 6-month frequency rates at follow-up. These rates were not normally distributed. For that reason, the mean, median, and standard deviation were computed for those boys who had engaged in the particular behavior. Also, for certain categories of delinquent acts (e.g., selling drugs, strongarming), the number of individuals who admitted engaging in the acts was small. For that reason, we only present the frequency estimates when at least 10 boys in a sample had displayed the behavior. In general, boys' median frequency of engaging in delinquent acts in a 6-month period was similar for those in the middle and oldest samples. For instance, the median frequency was 2.0 for such acts as theft of items worth less than $5, carrying weapon, avoid paying for things, and joyriding. Whereas none of the boys in the middle sample had stolen a car, 12 boys in the oldest sample were known to have done this, with a median frequency of two times over the past 6 months.

What is the degree of overall increase in the frequency of delinquent acts from ages 11 to 14? Comparing the mean rate of all delinquent acts for the middle and oldest samples, the results show that the active delinquent boys in the middle sample averaged 8.2 acts in 6 months, compared with a mean of 13.6 for the boys in the oldest sample—a relative increase of 65%.

Relationships Among Delinquency Seriousness, Frequency, and Variety of Offending

To what extent are the levels of seriousness of delinquency reached (lifetime), frequency of commission of delinquent acts (past year), and variety of types of delinquent acts (theft, violence, vandalism, fraud; past year) intercorrelated? It should be kept in mind that the seriousness of delinquency was measured only on a four-point scale, so we would not expect high correlations with such a restriction of range. However, the correlations between delinquency seriousness and variety were relatively stable with age (i.e., about .60 for the three samples; .58, .59, and .65, respectively; $p < .001$). In contrast, the correlation between delinquency seriousness and frequency was low for the middle and oldest samples (.26 and .30, respectively), but the correlation between frequency and variety was higher (.56 and .50; $p < .001$ for each sample).

SUBSTANCE USE

Young Boys' Understanding of Substance Use Questions

Several questions in the SRA administered to the boys in the youngest and middle samples at screening pertained to substance use. We first established whether young boys were able to understand the questions on substance use. The results show that boys in the youngest sample, compared with boys in the middle sample, were less able to understand the question on marijuana use (24.5% and 81.1%, respectively, understood the question). Because boys in both samples poorly understood the question concerning sniffing glue (18.3% and 35.7%, respectively), this substance will not be analyzed further. As discussed earlier, we estimated the extent that misunderstanding of the questions affected the prevalence estimate. For first graders, the prevalence of marijuana use ranged from .4% (if all the boys who did not understand the question were considered not having used marijuana) to 1.4% (i.e., marijuana reporting boys irrespective of whether they understood the question).

Prevalence of Substance Use

Substance use was classified in five categories: (a) beer or wine, (b) tobacco, (c) hard liquor, (d) marijuana use, and (e) other drug use. The ordering of substances was based on two criteria: prevalence and age at onset, with Category (a) substances being the most prevalent compared with Category (e) being the least prevalent and the other categories falling in between. In addition, the onset of Category (a) substance use was the earliest and higher categories emerged in the numeric order specified.

Boys were assigned to one of these categories (or placed in the no use group) on the basis of the highest lifetime level of substance use they had reached at follow-up. Boys' use of a substance such as wine or beer at special occasions, such as birthdays and religious festivities with parental permission, was excluded. Table 4.4 shows that the percentage of boys not having used any substance during their lifetime decreased from 84.4% in the youngest sample to 63% in the middle sample to 25.9% in the oldest sample. Table 4.4 also shows the prevalence of various levels of substance use reached in the three age samples.

The percentage of boys who had reached beer or wine as their highest use level at the time of the follow-up more than doubled between the youngest and middle samples (9.3%–25.2%) and further increased to 32.5% in the oldest sample. The percentage of boys who had reached tobacco as their highest was 4.9% for the youngest sample, increasing to 7.5% for the middle sample and further increasing by a factor of three for the oldest sample (22.7%). The percentage of boys who had reached the level of liquor use in the youngest sample was 1.0%, which tripled in the middle sample (3.3%) and more than doubled again in the oldest sample (8.1%). Not surprisingly, the percentage of boys who had reached the marijuana use level was low in the middle sample (.8%) and much higher in the oldest sample (8.6%). The percentage of boys in the other drug use level in the oldest sample amounted to 2.2%.

Table 4.4 also shows the past-year prevalence of substance use level reached at follow-up. Most of the age trends in these figures mirror the lifetime results: The use of minor substances such as beer and wine showed the largest increase from middle to late childhood, whereas the use of higher level substances increased particularly between late childhood and adolescence.

Age of Onset of Substance Use

We asked the boys at what age they first consumed a particular substance. Figure 4.3 shows that the percentage of boys in the middle sample who had used beer or wine increased linearly between the age of 6 and 10, whereas the

TABLE 4.4
Weighted Prevalence of Highest Level of Substance Use (%) Reached at Follow-Up

| | Sample | | | | | |
| | Youngest | | Middle | | Oldest | |
Level of Substance Use	Lifetime	Past Year	Lifetime	Past Year	Lifetime	Past Year
None	84.4	90.9	63.0	77.8	25.9	44.3
Beer or wine	9.3	4.2	25.2	15.8	32.5	31.8
Tobacco	4.9	4.1	7.5	4.3	22.7	10.8
Liquor	1.0	0.6	3.3	1.5	8.1	5.2
Marijuana	0.4	0.2	0.8	0.5	8.6	6.1
Other Drugs	—	—	0.1	0.1	2.2	1.8

—, Questions concerning other drugs were not asked of the youngest sample.

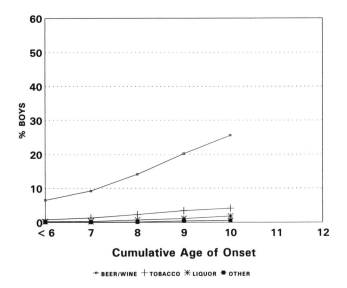

FIG. 4.3. Cumulative age of onset of levels of substance use (middle sample).

use of tobacco increased at a lower rate during that period. The onset of liquor use occurred later and was almost absent over this age range. The onset of marijuana and other drugs was also very rare. Figure 4.4 shows the cumulative percentage of boys with an onset of substance use at each age for the oldest sample covering the age range 6 to 12. The onset of beer or wine use increased linearly between ages 6 and 9 and accelerated after age 9. The onset of tobacco, liquor, and marijuana (combined here with other drugs) also increased linearly during that period, but at less steep rates. Again, it should be kept in mind that the curves shown in Figs. 4.3 and 4.4 are right hand censored. In both samples, the age of onset data show the magnitude of the onset of substance use during the elementary school-age period. For instance, by age 12, nearly half of the boys had initiated drinking beer or wine without parental knowledge.

Frequency of Substance Use

It can be countered that many of the youngsters who use one or another substance do so infrequently and only as part of a ritual of experimentation. We were not able to measure frequency of use in the youngest sample, but the results for the two older samples are shown in Table A4.3 in the appendix to this chapter. In the middle sample, the median number of cigarettes smoked in the past half year by those boys who smoked was 2.0 with a mean of 40.1. Consumption increased substantially between ages 11 and 14, to a median of

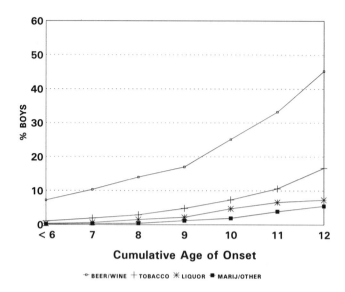

FIG. 4.4. Cumulative age of onset of levels of substance use (oldest sample).

182 for the oldest sample (mean 173.5). However, this is only about one cigarette per day. The frequency of wine drinking did not increase much with age, but this was not the case for beer drinking, which increased from a mean of 2.4 times in the middle sample to a mean of 6.8 in the oldest sample.

The frequency in one category of substance use (e.g., beer or wine) may depend on whether an individual has penetrated into higher levels of substance use. We would expect that penetration to more serious substance use is associated with higher frequency of use in lower levels. Data presented in Table A4.4 in the appendix only partially supported this. For example, the median frequency of beer or wine use was 2.0 for those who did not engage in other forms of substance use, but tripled to 6.0 for those who had advanced to marijuana or other drugs. However, no such increases were observed for tobacco or liquor use.

SEXUAL INTERCOURSE

Questions about sexual behavior were only asked of the boys in the oldest sample because they were considered inappropriate for the vast majority of younger boys and we were concerned about negative reactions to these questions from their parents. At the time of the follow-up, 44.2% of the oldest boys had reported sexual intercourse when they were on average 13.2 years old.

Figure 4.5 shows the age of onset curve, indicating that the onset of first intercourse linearly increased between ages 6 and 9, (to about 8%) after which it accelerated to about 28% by age 12. Only a few boys claimed to have had sexual intercourse prior to age 6, and it is not clear whether intercourse was actively initiated by the child or by another person. It should be noted that adolescents' recall of age of first sexual intercourse is not always consistent (Alexander, Somerfield, Ensminger, Johnson, & Kim, 1993).

MENTAL HEALTH PROBLEMS

A proportion of children face mental health problems. Some of these may occur independently from delinquency and substance use, and knowledge about them is important in their own right. Other mental health problems not only co-occur with delinquency, but may also influence its course (Farrington et al., 1990; Mannuzza, Klein, Bessler, Malloy, & LaPadula, 1993). We first discuss the results of a psychiatric diagnostic assessment of the boys and then review the results of rating scales on a variety of mental health problems.

The Prevalence of Psychiatric Diagnoses

We first examined the prevalence of diagnoses of disruptive behavior disorders (ADHD, oppositional defiant disorder, and conduct disorder) according to

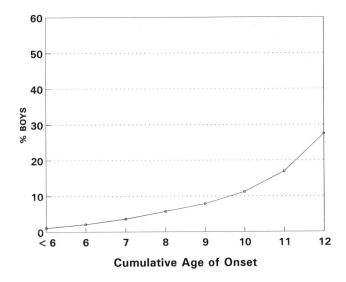

FIG. 4.5. Age of onset of sexual intercourse (oldest sample).

TABLE 4.5
Weighted Prevalence (%) of *DSM–III–R* Disruptive Behavior Disorders

Disorder	Sample		
	Youngest	Middle	Oldest
Any disruptive behavior disorder	20.1	17.8	18.8
ADHD	15.2	10.5	7.6
Oppositional defiant disorder	2.2	4.8	5.0
Conduct disorder	5.6	5.4	8.3

DSM–III–R (American Psychiatric Association, 1987). Table 4.5 shows the weighted prevalence of these disorders in each of the samples.[2] The prevalence of any disruptive disorder remained about the same from the youngest to the oldest samples at about one fifth of the boys. However, the apparent stability disguises different age trends for different disorders. There was a decrease in the prevalence of ADHD with age, which was as high as 15.2% in the youngest sample, but decreased to 10.5% in the middle sample and 7.6% in the oldest sample. In contrast, the prevalence of oppositional defiant disorder increased slightly, particularly between ages 7 and 11 (from 2.2% to 4.8% in the youngest and middle samples, respectively, and to 5.0% in the oldest sample). Finally, the prevalence of conduct disorder also increased with age, but particularly in adolescence (i.e., from about 5% at ages 7 and 11 to over 8% at age 13).

Average Levels of Mental Health Problems

We now turn to continuously measured variables of disruptive behavior, which are not captured in our delinquency measures, including physical aggression, oppositional defiant behavior (based on the symptom score for oppositional defiant disorder), conduct problems (based on the symptom score for conduct disorder), and ADHD score (based on the symptom score for ADHD). The question is to what extent there are differences in the means of these scores among samples, which might indicate age trends.

---

[2]The figures in this table vary somewhat from those reported in our earlier analyses (Stouthamer-Loeber, Loeber, & Thomas, 1992) because the earlier published data were based on parent report only, whereas the information in Table 4.5 for conduct disorder was based on parent and child information. As a consequence, more boys qualified for conduct disorder, therefore reducing the percentage of boys with oppositional defiant disorder. In addition, improved criteria were used for the age of onset information on ADHD in Table 4.5 (only one symptom had to qualify for the age of onset criterion, instead of all symptoms in the former computations).

The mean physical aggression score was the same across the three samples [$F(2,1327) = 1.07$, n.s.]. Boys' average oppositional defiant score significantly increased with age— averages of 9.7, 10.9, and 11.4, for the three samples [$F(2,1250) = 3.76$, $p = .024$]. There was also a trend for the conduct problem score to increase with age, particularly between the youngest and middle samples but not surprisingly, between the middle and oldest samples [$F(2,727) = 2.83$, $p = .06$]. However, recall that the conduct problem score was based on information from the parent only and is likely to underestimate the actual prevalence and age trend of conduct problems (Loeber, Green, Lahey, & Stouthamer-Loeber, 1989). In contrast, the average ADHD score decreased with age [$F(2,1384) = 3.40$, $p = .034$].

Finally, turning to internalizing problems, Table 4.6 shows that the average shy/withdrawn score increased with age [$F(2,1482) = 4.74$, $p = .009$], but that there was a substantial decrease in the depressed mood score—averages 7.44, 5.99, and 4.01, for the three samples [$F(2,1248) = 62.55$, $p < .001$]. The average anxious/fearful score also decreased with age—from 3.85 in the youngest sample to 3.63 in the middle sample and 3.28 in the oldest sample [$F(2,1406) = 9.62$, $p < .001$].

In summary, we observed distinct age trends in the prevalence of the behaviors with average oppositional defiant behavior scores, conduct problems, and shy/withdrawn behavior increasing with age. In contrast, average scores on ADHD and depressed mood decreased with age, whereas the average physical aggression score remained the same across the three age samples.

CONCLUSION

There is little doubt that a segment of boys in each of the three samples experienced delinquency, substance use, mental health problems, and sexual

TABLE 4.6
Average Problem Scores Across the Samples

| | Sample | | |
Score	Youngest	Middle	Oldest
Physical aggression score	3.08	3.22	3.10
Oppositional defiant symptom score*	9.72	10.88	11.43
Conduct disorder symptom score*	4.76	5.57	5.59
ADHD score*	12.81	12.35	11.20
Shy/withdrawn behavior score	4.08	4.31	4.40
Depressed mood score	7.44	5.99	4.01
Anxious/fearful score	3.85	3.63	3.28

*Scores range from 0 to 50.

intercourse at a relatively early age. We now briefly compare our findings with those from other studies.

Delinquency

There are no studies using exactly the same delinquency seriousness scale as ours for comparison of the life-time prevalence of different seriousness levels of delinquency. However, we collaborated with the two companion studies in Denver, Colorado (The Denver Youth Survey), and in Rochester, New York (The Rochester Youth Development Study) using different indices of delinquency. The findings across the three studies show remarkable agreement in the prevalence of delinquency (Huizinga, Loeber, & Thornberry, 1993; Thornberry, Huizinga, & Loeber, 1995).

Also, numerous studies have documented that the prevalence of delinquency increases with age (see e.g., Farrington, 1990), but few studies have investigated whether there is a concomitant increase in the frequency of delinquency (Loeber & Snyder, 1990). In our study, the mean frequency of offending doubled between ages 10–11 and 13–14 to an average of 13.6 acts per half year (or 27.1 acts per year).

Few studies have used a lifetime seriousness classification of delinquency as we did. An exception is the birth cohort study by Wadsworth (1979), but that study did not have multiple informants to ensure that the ascertainment of delinquency was sufficiently comprehensive. Instead, it relied on official records of law-breaking only. We had extensive self-reported delinquency data.

What is truly new in the results that we presented in this chapter is the information about delinquency from middle childhood to early adolescence, which, with the exception of the Denver Youth Survey (Huizinga et al., 1993), cannot be found in other studies. It is clear that law breaking is already practiced by a substantial proportion of elementary school-age boys. Considering what is known about early onset as a risk factor for chronicity of offending (Loeber, 1982; Farrington et al., 1990), this group of boys should be of greatest concern to officials of the courts, mental health professionals, teachers, and parents.

Substance Use

The prevalence data on substance use, especially for the older boys, can be compared with that in other studies. However, few studies have examined substance use in elementary school-age populations. Even for the older age groups, comparisons are often problematic because many studies did not report prevalence figures by age and separately for male participants. For example, the observed past-year prevalence of marijuana use in our study for the oldest sample was 6.1%, which compared with that of eighth graders in the Monitoring the Future study (for 1991–1992), but this study included both boys and girls as participants (Johnston, O'Malley, & Bachman, 1993). The lifetime prevalence of marijuana use in the middle and oldest samples in our study (0.8% and 8.6%) was much lower than in a comparable sample of 7th and 10th graders (14% and 44%) in California and Oregon (Ellickson, Hays, & Bell, 1992), and a sample of 12- and 15-year-old males from New Jersey (2% and 24%–38%, respectively; White & Labouvie, 1994). Similarly, the lifetime prevalence of tobacco and alcohol use was higher in the Ellickson study (Ellickson et al., 1992), but more variable in the White and Labouvie (1994) study, compared with the figures for our middle and oldest samples. Finally, the 1-year prevalence of marijuana use in the Pittsburgh sample was lower than in the companion studies in Denver and Rochester (Huizinga et al., 1993).

Our findings on the increase of substance use with age parallel those reported by several researchers (e.g., Huizinga et al., 1993; White & Labouvie, 1994). The difference is that elementary school-age boys were rarely included in studies (an exception is the Denver Youth Survey). Our data, especially regarding the age of onset curves for different forms of substance use (Figs. 4.3 and 4.4), clearly show the importance of the elementary school-age period for the initiation of use of various substances (see Van Kammen, Loeber, & Stouthamer-Loeber, 1991).

Mental Health Problems

Turning to mental health problems, our findings based on *DSM–III–R* diagnoses are unusual because of the scarcity of epidemiological studies using that version of the *DSM*. The prevalence of any disruptive behavior disorder was relatively high: about one in five boys in all three samples. The following comparisons with other population studies should be viewed with some caution because they used different versions of *DSM*.

The percentage of boys in the middle and oldest samples who qualified for oppositional defiant disorder (about 5%) was generally lower than that found in other studies (e.g., Bird et al., 1988; Velez, Johnson, & Cohen, 1989). Only in the New Zealand Dunedin study (Anderson et al., 1987), was a comparable prevalence found (5.7%). In contrast, for our youngest sample, the prevalence of oppositional defiant disorder was low (2.2%). Comparison with other studies is not possible due to the unavailability of diagnostic data for that age group (Nottelmann & Jensen, 1995).

As to conduct disorder, the prevalence for the youngest sample (5.6%) and middle sample (5.4%) compares well with the 4- to 11-year-old boys (6.5%) in the Ontario Health Study, although that study derived the diagnosis from rating scales rather than from a psychiatric interview (Offord, Alder, & Boyle, 1986). For the oldest sample, the prevalence at age 14 (8.3%) was in the same range as for the 12- to 16-year-olds in that study (10.4%). Likewise, for the older sample, the results concur with findings in Puerto Rico (Velez et al., 1989).

Turning to ADHD, the prevalence in the youngest sample (15.2%) compares with the 11.9% for the 9- to 12-year-old age group in the Velez et al. (1989) study. However, several other studies have reported lower prevalence rates of the disorder at a young age (e.g., Offord, Sullivan, Allen & Abrams, 1979).

We found a substantial decrease in the prevalence of ADHD between the first and seventh grades—a finding that is also evident from cross-sectional studies (e.g., Offord et al., 1987) and longitudinal clinic studies (e.g., Hart, Lahey, Loeber, Applegate, & Frick, 1995). In contrast, we found an increase in the prevalence of oppositional defiant disorder (especially between ages 7 and 11) and conduct disorder (especially between ages 11 and 14).

Analyses of continuous symptom scores showed a decrease in ADHD score with age and increases in oppositional defiant behavior and conduct problems with age. In addition, we found an increase in the average level of shy/withdrawn behaviors with age across the three samples and a decrease in depressed mood. The latter was recently investigated by Angold et al. (1995) using extended longitudinal follow-up data in the three samples, which further confirmed the decrease in depressed mood with age especially from middle childhood to early adolescence.

The findings underscore important age-related changes in mental health problems. Our conclusions on other mental health-related problems are difficult to compare with those of other studies because of a lack of common instruments. It would have been useful in our study to measure the impairment resulting from mental health problems, but unfortunately this was not included in the measurement instruments.

Sexual Behavior

That 44.2% of the boys in the oldest sample (mean age 13.8) had reported sexual intercourse is somewhat higher than the proportion reported in the 1989 Secondary High School Student Health Risk Survey (33.5%), the 1990 Youth Risk Behavior Survey (35.0%) for students below the age of 15 (Holtzman, Lowry, Kann, Collins, & Kolbe, 1994), a representative sample of 8th- to 10th graders (Udry, 1988), and a City of New York sample of African American and Puerto Rican adolescents (Brook, Balka, Abernathy, & Hamburg, 1994). In our study, the onset curve of sexual intercourse gradually increased between the ages of 6 and 9, but then accelerated. This is substantially earlier than documented in a sample of males studied by Devine, Long, and Forehand (1993), in which onset only accelerated after age 12.

The Unfolding of Problem Behaviors

The onset data on delinquency, substance use, mental health problems, and sexual intercourse can be compared directly. Because it was most complete for the oldest sample, it is best to compare onset curves for that sample (Figs. 4.2, 4.4, and 4.5). The onset of minor delinquency occurred first, followed by the onset of beer or wine. This was followed in turn by the onset of sexual intercourse, followed by the onset of moderately serious delinquency. Next in line was the onset of tobacco use, followed by the onset of serious delinquency and marijuana use/other drugs.

The results confirm findings in several studies showing that the onset of minor disruptive and minor delinquent behavior precedes the onset of more serious conduct problems and more serious forms of delinquency (Belson, 1975; Hinshaw, Lahey, & Hart, 1993; Loeber, Green, Lahey, Christ, & Frick, 1992; Robins, 1986). However, the crucial test is whether conclusions drawn from age of onset graphs also apply to the within-subject order of onset of diverse problem behaviors. We examined this in a separate study, and found that, in general, boys who progressed to the more serious delinquent acts did so in an orderly fashion by advancing from minor problem behaviors to moderately serious acts and, eventually, to serious problem behaviors (Loeber et al., 1993, 1995, 1997).

Also, the cross-sectional results presented in this chapter on the onset of delinquency and substance use agree with earlier findings by Elliott, Huizinga, and Menard (1989). They showed that the onset of minor delinquency almost always came first, followed by the onset of alcohol use. Alcohol use was followed by marijuana use, which preceded index offenses (although the order between alcohol use and index offenses was not the same for all participants). Thus, although there are some minor variations, there is considerable congruence between the present findings on the order of onset of problem behaviors and the order found in other studies.

APPENDIX

The following tables show the prevalence and frequency of specific delinquent behaviors and the frequency of different types of substance use reported by boys in each of the three samples.

TABLE A4.1
Weighted Prevalence of Specific Delinquent Acts (%)

	Sample					
	Youngest*		Middle		Oldest	
Delinquent Act	Lifetime	Past Year	Lifetime	Past Year	Lifetime	Past Year
Take money from home	11.9	7.9	—	—	—	—
Other than money at home	10.0	6.8	—	—	—	—
Take things from school	6.4	5.3	—	—	—	—
Steal <$5	—	—	9.2	—	26.3	14.9
Steal $5–$50	—	—	1.1	—	9.5	5.1
Steal >$50	—	—	0.7	—	7.7	5.1
Break and enter	4.8	2.9	4.2	3.1	10.0	5.2
Shoplift	10.2	7.2	20.9	10.2	34.8	18.6
Pickpocket	1.4	1.4	2.3	1.9	3.9	3.2
Steal from car	2.4	1.9	4.3	2.0	8.4	6.5
Joyride	—	—	1.3	—	5.1	4.6
Steal car	—	—	0.4	—	4.6	3.5
Steal bike	3.4	2.3	—	—	—	—
Fence	—	—	1.8	—	12.5	10.2
Carried weapon	11.6	11.2	14.4	12.1	25.5	22.7
Attack with weapon/kill	—	—	3.7	—	8.0	6.2
Strongarm	—	—	0.4	—	1.4	1.3
Gang fight	—	—	7.9	—	16.9	12.1
Damage, destroy	—	—	13.4	—	24.0	17.9
in home	20.4	14.0	—	—	—	—
in school	4.4	3.7	—	—	—	—
anywhere else	10.8	7.7	—	—	—	—
Write, use spray paint	8.2	7.0	—	—	—	—
Set fire	6.4	5.0	6.5	3.5	6.7	3.2
Avoid paying	8.0	5.1	14.4	11.7	27.6	22.0
Illegal checks	—	—	0.1	—	1.8	1.6
Illegal credit	—	—	0.1	—	2.1	1.3
Sell worthless goods	—	—	6.8	—	18.4	10.4
Hurt for sex	—	—	0.0	—	0.0	0.0
Forced sex	—	—	0.0	—	1.1	1.1
Sold marijuana	—	—	0.0	—	2.4	2.0
Sold hard drugs	—	—	0.0	—	0.5	0.4

*Data waves using SRA; remaining data waves consisted of SRD.

—, Data not available because of the differences in items between SRA and SRD.

94

TABLE A4.2
Six-Months Frequency of Specific Delinquent Acts At Follow-Up*

Delinquent Act	Sample							
	Middle				Oldest			
	N	Mean	Median	SD	N	Mean	Median	SD
Steal <$5	21	3.2	2.0	4.43	38	2.9	2.0	5.30
Steal $5–$50	4	—	—	—	11	1.7	1.0	1.24
Steal >$50	1	—	—	—	11	1.8	1.0	1.02
Break and enter	8	—	—	—	10	2.6	2.0	1.81
Shoplift	21	3.0	1.0	4.14	53	2.6	1.0	2.84
Pickpocket	2	—	—	—	6	—	—	—
Steal from car	8	—	—	—	22	3.9	1.0	12.17
Joyride	5	—	—	—	18	4.0	2.0	5.79
Steal car	0	—	—	—	12	6.0	2.0	16.69
Fence	5	—	—	—	26	8.9	1.0	21.82
Carry weapon	49	7.3	2.0	22.67	73	12.2	2.0	33.47
Attack with weapon/kill	13	3.1	2.0	4.46	13	3.0	1.0	5.54
Strongarm	1	—	—	—	1	—	—	—
Gang fight	24	1.8	1.0	1.42	34	2.5	1.0	4.17
Damage, destroy	46	3.2	1.0	5.25	48	4.8	1.0	20.99
Set fire	11	1.7	1.0	1.09	5	—	—	—
Avoid paying	38	5.2	2.0	10.38	63	4.1	2.0	7.38
Illegal checks	0	—	—	—	6	—	—	—
Illegal credit cards	1	—	—	—	2	—	—	—
Sell worthless goods	21	6.1	1.0	18.54	37	2.8	1.0	4.73
Hurt for sex	0	—	—	—	0	—	—	—
Forced sex	0	—	—	—	2	—	—	—
Sold marijuana	0	—	—	—	6	—	—	—
Sold hard drugs	0	—	—	—	2	—	—	—
Total	144	8.23	3.00	26.05	184	13.56	4.0	39.58

*Univariate statistics are computed on active delinquents only.

—, Computation not applicable because of low N.

TABLE A4.3
Six-Month Frequency of Substance Use at Follow-Up*

	Sample					
	Middle			Oldest		
Substance Use	N	Mean	Median	N	Mean	Median
Beer	65	2.4	1.0	150	6.8	2.0
Wine	15	2.2	1.0	38	1.8	1.0
Tobacco	14	40.1	2.0	86	173.5	182.0
Hard liquor	4	**	**	20	3.6	1.0
Marijuana	2	**	**	28	14.7	2.0
Other	0	—	—	4	**	**

*Univariate statistics are computed on active substance users only.
**N too small to compute univariate statistics.

TABLE A4.4
Frequency of Substance Use in Middle and Oldest Samples

	Beer or Wine		Tobacco		Liquor		Marijuana/ Other Drugs	
Frequency of	Mean	Median	Mean	Median	Mean	Median	Mean	Median
Beer or wine	3.5	2.0	4.4	2.0	10.2	5.0	19.6	6.0
Tobacco			130.5	182.0	209.0	182.0	200.8	182.0
Liquor					3.2	2.0	4.3	2.0
Marijuana/ other drugs							10.6	2.0

5

Explanatory Factors for Delinquency

This chapter shows which explanatory variables are related to boys' delinquency and how these variables vary with age. To validate our measure of delinquency, we first show the interrelationship between the delinquency seriousness scale (described in chap. 3) and official records of juvenile court petitions for offenses. We then explain our dichotomization of the delinquency seriousness scale and how we narrowed down the array of potential explanatory variables by distinguishing these from variables more likely to be correlates of delinquency. All the analyses from now on are based on unweighted data; the equivalence of weighted and unweighted results is investigated in the Methodological Appendix. Also discussed in this appendix is whether dichotomized variables lead to similar findings as continuous variables. Additionally, we consider whether the explanatory variables for delinquency are similar at different ages.

The chapter also reports multiple regression analyses to examine which explanatory variables best explain delinquency while controlling for other variables. For ease of exposition, we will often refer to "predictors," while realizing that our analyses are essentially correlational. There are several options for such analyses. One is to consider all variables as having potentially simultaneous effects, irrespective of whether they might directly or indirectly affect child behavior. Under that schema, such diverse variables as parenting practices, child characteristics, and neighborhood factors would all have an equal chance of being entered in the equation irrespective of whether they directly affect child behavior or mostly operate indirectly through other factors (such as childrearing), which in turn might affect child behavior more directly. In subsequent chapters, we use the same conceptual paradigm to explain a variety of outcomes other than delinquency.

As mentioned in chapter 1 (Fig. 1.2), we decided to organize the multiple regression analyses according to a conceptual framework in which potentially direct and indirect influences are hierarchically structured. For that reason, we used a hierarchical strategy for the analysis of delinquency (and other problems reviewed in later chapters), in which we first enter the block of child variables into the equation, then the block of family variables, and last the demographic, neighborhood, and socioeconomic variables.

MEASUREMENT OF DELINQUENCY

Table 5.1 shows the delinquency classification used in this book for offenses committed during a boy's lifetime up to the follow-up interview (note that this unweighted prevalence is slightly different from the weighted prevalence reported in chap. 4). *Serious delinquency* includes burglary, car theft, robbery, attacking to hurt, forced sex, and selling drugs; *moderate delinquency* includes joyriding, theft over $5, carrying weapons, and gang fights; *minor delinquency* includes shoplifting, theft of $5 or less, vandalism, and minor fraud; and *no delinquency* includes minor stealing at home (for details, see chap. 3). As expected, the seriousness of delinquency increased with age. For example, the percentage of serious delinquents increased from 10.1% in the youngest sample to 27.6% in the middle sample and 36.6% in the oldest sample. Conversely, the percentage of nondelinquents decreased from 39.4% in the youngest sample to 20.1% in the middle sample and 17.6% in the oldest sample. For these reasons, and those explained in the Methodological Appendix, we separately analyzed the results of the three samples instead of merging the data across the samples.

DELINQUENCY CLASSIFICATION VERSUS JUVENILE COURT PETITIONS

Allegheny County Juvenile Court records (paper files) were searched to try to locate records of offenses by each boy between his 10th and 18th birthdays. The City of Pittsburgh covers the inner city population and is surrounded by Allegheny County.

Detected juvenile offenders in Allegheny County may be referred to the Juvenile Court by the police or other agencies (e.g., the school board). The intake officer (in the probation department) reviews all cases and almost always meets with the alleged offender, the family, and the victim. The intake officer may dismiss or withdraw the case because of doubts about whether the offender is in fact guilty, doubts about whether there is sufficient evidence to prove that

TABLE 5.1
Delinquency Classification, Unweighted Prevalence

	Sample					
	Youngest		Middle		Oldest	
Delinquency	N	(%)	N	(%)	N	(%)
None	198	(39.4)	102	(20.1)	89	(17.6)
Minor	165	(32.8)	153	(30.1)	98	(19.4)
Moderate	89	(17.7)	113	(22.2)	134	(26.5)
Serious	51	(10.1)	140	(27.6)	185	(36.6)
Total	503	(100)	508	(100)	506	(100)

the offender is guilty, or for procedural reasons such as the victim not turning up. The intake officer may divert the offender (e.g., by giving a warning or requiring informal probation) if the case is minor or the offender is young and criminally inexperienced. If the intake officer believes that there is sufficient evidence of a serious offense, the case will be petitioned to the Juvenile Court. We have only counted petitioned cases. Therefore, our recorded juvenile offenders are relatively serious cases where there is convincing evidence of guilt.

Offense types were classified according to the FBI Uniform Crime Report system. *Index violence* includes homicide, forcible rape, robbery, and aggravated assault. *Index property* includes burglary, larceny, motor vehicle theft, and arson. Together, index violence and index property comprise *index offenses*. *Nonindex delinquency* includes simple assault, forgery, fraud, embezzlement, receiving stolen property, weapons offenses, vandalism, sex offenses (e.g., prostitution and statutory rape), drug offenses, malicious mischief, disorderly conduct, criminal conspiracy, threats and endangering, involuntary deviate sexual intercourse (homosexual rape), indecent assault, indecent exposure, and spousal sexual assault. Our *delinquency* category includes index and nonindex offenses. We have excluded minor offenses such as liquor law violations, drunkenness, traffic offenses, violations of ordinances (e.g., cruelty to animals, vagrancy), and status offenses.

The first date of occurrence of each offense type was coded. It was classified as occurring before or after the date of the follow-up assessment. Table 5.2 shows the prevalence of Juvenile Court petitions for each offense type in the middle and oldest samples. The youngest sample was not included in these analyses because of the low prevalence of petitions (only 26 boys) up to the latest Juvenile Court data collection in May 1994. The median age of the oldest sample at follow-up was 13.8 and they were at risk of Juvenile Court petitions for 4.2 years up to the 18th birthday (which they had all passed). The median age of the middle sample at follow-up was 10.6 and they were at risk for a median time of 5.8 years up to May 1994.

TABLE 5.2
Prevalence % of Court Petitions for Delinquency

Variable	Ever* %	Before Follow-up %	After Follow-up %
Middle sample	(N = 495)	(N = 501)	(N = 485)
Delinquency	29.7	2.0	28.2
Index offense	22.2	1.2	21.4
Index violence	11.9	0.4	11.8
Index property	18.2	1.2	17.3
Oldest sample	(N = 457)	(N = 468)	(N = 396)
Delinquency	44.6	12.8	36.4
Index offense	34.1	10.5	27.0
Index violence	14.7	3.2	13.2
Index property	28.1	8.5	22.2

*Up to May 1994 for the middle sample (median age 16.4) and up to the 18th birthday for the oldest sample. The follow-up was the first assessment half a year after screening.

Table 5.2 shows that, up to the follow-up assessment, only 2% of the middle sample had a Juvenile Court petition for delinquency, compared with 12.8% of the oldest sample. In calculating these percentages, cases with no consent forms or incomplete records (7 in the middle sample and 38 in the oldest sample) were excluded. The percentage with Juvenile Court petitions for index offenses up to the follow-up assessment was 1.2% in the middle sample and 10.5% in the oldest sample. Table 5.2 also shows the prevalence of petitions for index violence and index property offenses.

Up to May 1994 29.7% of the middle sample had a Juvenile Court petition for delinquency and 22.2% for an index offense. Up to the 18th birthday for the oldest sample, 44.6% had a Juvenile Court petition for delinquency and 34.1% for an index offense. In calculating these percentages, cases with no Juvenile Court petitions who lived outside Allegheny County for the majority of the time between the follow-up assessment and assessment E just two years later (6 in the middle sample and 11 in the oldest sample) were excluded. Generally, juveniles who live in Allegheny County are processed by the Allegheny County Juvenile Court even if they commit offenses outside Allegheny County (unless they commit offenses outside Pennsylvania).

After the follow-up assessment, 28.2% of the middle sample who had no previous petition record were petitioned for delinquency and the corresponding figure for the oldest sample was 36.4%. In calculating these percentages, we excluded boys with any petition record for any offense before the follow-up assessment (10 in the middle sample and 61 in the oldest sample) so that our analyses of petitions after the follow-up assessment would be truly predictive. After the follow-up assessment 21.4% of boys in the middle sample (with no petition for any offense before the follow-up assessment) were petitioned for an index offense, compared with 27% of boys in the oldest sample.

The prevalence figures in Table 5.2 are higher than for all boys in public schools in the City of Pittsburgh because of oversampling of high-risk boys in the follow-up sample for the follow-up assessment. It is easy to re-weight the follow-up sample to provide estimates for the City of Pittsburgh public school population. When this was done, the cumulative prevalence of Juvenile Court petitions for delinquency up to May 1994 came to 25.6% for the middle sample (up to a median age of 16.4, remember) and 39% for the oldest sample (up to the 18th birthday). The weighted cumulative prevalence of Juvenile Court petitions for index offenses came to 19% for the middle sample and 28.4% for the oldest sample. Generally, weighted and unweighted data produce different prevalence estimates but similar correlations among variables (see section 5.3). Because our interest in this section is to study the validity of delinquency seriousness scales rather than reporting the prevalence of Juvenile Court petitions, we use unweighted data here.

Table 5.3 shows that the combined delinquency seriousness scale had concurrent validity in relation to past Juvenile Court petitions. In the oldest sample, 20.9% of those in the serious delinquent category had a petition for

TABLE 5.3
Combined Delinquency Seriousness Scale at Follow-Up
as a Predictor of Juvenile Court Petitions

| Variable | Delinquency Seriousness | | | | χ^2 | p |
	None %	Minor %	Moderate %	Serious%		
Middle sample						
% Petitions after follow-up	(100)	(147)	(108)	(130)		
Delinquency	10.0	12.2	36.1	53.8	80.3	.0001
Index offense	8.0	8.8	27.8	40.8	56.0	.0001
Index violence	5.0	4.8	12.0	24.6	32.1	.0001
Index property	6.0	6.8	23.1	33.1	45.4	.0001
Oldest sample						
% Petitions up to follow-up	(80)	(90)	(126)	(172)		
Delinquency	6.3	3.3	12.7	20.9	20.5	.0001
Index offense	3.8	2.2	8.7	19.2	24.7	.0001
Index violence	0.0	0.0	4.0	5.8	9.6	.022
Index property	3.8	2.2	5.6	16.3	21.6	.0001
% Petitions after follow-up	(73)	(84)	(107)	(132)		
Delinquency	15.1	23.8	35.5	56.8	43.9	.0001
Index offense	8.2	16.7	29.9	41.7	32.5	.0001
Index violence	2.7	8.4	12.3	22.7	19.2	.0001
Index property	6.8	13.1	26.2	33.3	24.4	.0001

Note. *p* values are two-tailed. Follow-up was first assessment one-half year after screening.

delinquency, compared with 12.7% of moderate delinquents, 3.3% of minor delinquents, and 6.3% of nondelinquents [X^2 (3) = 20.5, p < .0001]. The combined scale was also concurrently related to petitions for index offenses.

The combined scale also had predictive validity in relation to Juvenile Court petitions. In the middle sample of previously nonpetitioned boys, 53.8% of serious delinquents were petitioned for delinquency in the future, compared with 36.1% of moderate delinquents, 12.2% of minor delinquents, and 10% of nondelinquents [X^2 (3) = 80.3, p<.0001]. Of the serious delinquents, 40.8% were petitioned for index offenses, 24.6% for index violence, and 33.1% for index property offenses.

In the oldest sample of previously nonpetitioned boys, 56.8% of serious delinquents were petitioned for delinquency up to the 18th birthday, compared with 35.5% of moderate delinquents, 23.8% of minor delinquents, and 15.1% of nondelinquents [X^2 (3) = 43.9, p<.0001]. Of the serious delinquents, 41.7% were petitioned for index offenses, 22.7% for index violence, and 33.3% for index property offenses. (For more measures of concurrent and predictive validity, using ROC curves, see Farrington et al., 1996).

There is some evidence that self-reported delinquency is more valid for Whites than for African Americans in the United States. For example, Hindelang, Hirschi, and Weis (1981) found that African Americans were less likely to admit their recorded offenses than Whites. This may be because African Americans are more likely to conceal or forget their delinquent acts or because more of those who are recorded are in fact innocent. We did not expect our delinquency seriousness classification to be differentially valid by ethnicity because it was derived from reports by teachers and parents as well as from the boys. However, we did investigate concurrent and predictive validity separately for Whites and African Americans.

Table 5.4 shows that the combined delinquency seriousness scale had concurrent and predictive validity for both ethnic groups. For example, in the oldest sample, the proportion that was petitioned in the past for delinquency increased from 4.7% of nondelinquents to 22.6% of serious delinquents for Whites, and from 8.1% to 20.2% for African Americans. Concurrent validity was higher for Whites.

In the middle sample, the proportion petitioned in the future for delinquency increased from 4.8% of nondelinquents to 34.2% of serious delinquents for Whites and from 18.4% to 62% for African Americans. The chi-squared values were higher in this case for African Americans. In the oldest sample, the proportion petitioned in the future for delinquency increased from 10.3% of nondelinquents to 46.3% of serious delinquents for Whites and from 20.6% to 61.5% for African Americans. Again, the chi-squared values were higher for African Americans.

Within each category of delinquency seriousness, African Americans were always more likely to be petitioned in the future but not always more likely to be petitioned in the past. These differences could be caused by biases in police

TABLE 5.4
Combined Delinquency Seriousness Scale at A as a Predictor
of Juvenile Court Petitions, Controlling for Ethnicity

Variable		Delinquency Seriousness				x^2	p
		None %	Minor %	Moderate %	Serious %		
Middle sample							
% Petitions after follow-up							
Delinquency	(W)	4.8	8.8	24.0	34.2	20.5	.0001
	(AA)	18.4	15.2	46.6	62.0	47.5	.0001
Index offense	(W)	3.2	4.4	16.0	26.3	17.8	.0005
	(AA)	15.8	12.7	37.9	46.7	28.8	.0001
Oldest sample							
% Petitions up to follow-up							
Delinquency	(W)	4.7	2.5	6.3	22.6	14.9	.002
	(AA)	8.1	4.0	19.4	20.2	9.4	.025
Index offense	(W)	2.3	2.5	4.7	18.9	13.7	.003
	(AA)	5.4	2.0	12.9	19.3	11.7	.009
% Petitions after follow-up							
Delinquency	(W)	10.3	18.9	26.3	46.3	14.9	.002
	(AA)	20.6	27.7	46.0	61.5	24.0	.0001
Index offense	(W)	2.6	13.5	21.1	34.1	14.1	.003
	(AA)	14.7	19.1	40.0	45.1	16.1	.001

Note. W = White; AA = African American. p values are two-tailed. Follow-up was first assessed half a year after screening.

and court processing. However, if so, it is surprising that they are not clearly seen in the past data. Perhaps a more plausible explanation is that the developmental course of delinquency is quicker or more intense for African Americans than for Whites. In other words, although Whites and African Americans in the same delinquency seriousness category at follow-up may be equivalent, the delinquency of the African Americans may quickly become more frequent and more serious. Longitudinal data collected in the Pittsburgh Youth Study might be used in the future to test this hypothesis.

DICHOTOMIZED MEASURES OF DELINQUENCY

For the next analyses, we dichotomized the delinquency seriousness scores (and the scores on explanatory factors and correlates). As we show in detail in the

Methodological Appendix, we justified such dichotomization on the following grounds. First, results based on dichotomized data are easy to understand and to communicate to a nontechnical audience. Second, many of the continuous variables are not normally distributed and, indeed, we found nonlinear relationships. Moreover, dichotomization fits the risk factor approach of this book in that the cumulative impact of several risk factors on an outcome, such as delinquency, can be assessed in terms that are easily understood. Likewise, the investigation of interaction effects is greatly enhanced when dichotomized rather than continuous factors are considered. In addition, dichotomization allows us to use odds ratios as an index of strength of association. For example, if the odds ratio for the relationship between poor supervision and delinquency is 2.0, this means that the odds of delinquency (the probability of delinquency as opposed to nondelinquency) is increased by a factor of 2 when poor supervision occurs, compared with supervision that is not poor.

Correlational measures do not always represent well the strength of relationships. For instance, an odds ratio of 2, doubling the risk of delinquency, might correspond to correlation of about .12, which translates into 1.4% of the variance explained. The percentage of variance explained gives a misleadingly low impression of predictive efficiency. Unlike correlational indices, odds ratios are independent of the marginal distributions of variables and are therefore a better indicator of the strength of association among factors, especially when such factors are not normally distributed. Finally and perhaps most important, dichotomized constructs encourage a focus on individuals rather than variables. The percentage of individuals affected is a highly meaningful statistic.

Following these conclusions, we dichotomized the delinquency seriousness score. For the middle and oldest samples, we split the score between moderately serious delinquency and serious delinquency, effectively identifying those boys who had committed the most serious crimes during their lifetime (as far as possible, the upper 25% approximately; $N = 140$ and 185, in the middle and oldest samples, respectively). For the youngest sample, however, few boys (51) had engaged in serious delinquency. For that reason, the split was made between minor delinquency and moderately serious delinquency. Thus, for this group, the procedure identified boys in the youngest sample as *delinquents* who had committed moderate or serious delinquent acts ($N = 140$ or 27.9%).

Types of Delinquent Acts

As explained in chapter 3, the major types of delinquent acts—violence and theft—were also classified according to the seriousness of the acts. *Minor violence* consisted of gang fights and carrying weapons, *moderate violence* consisted of strongarming (robbery), and *serious violence* consisted of attacking to hurt and forced sex. *Minor theft* consisted of shoplifting, theft of $5 or less, theft outside of the home, or theft at school. *Moderate theft* consisted of theft over $5, theft of a bicycle, theft from a car, picking pockets, fencing, or joyriding. *Serious theft* consisted of burglary and car theft. The prevalence of *serious violence* increased from nil in the youngest sample to 24 (4.7%) in the middle sample and 60 (11.9%) in the oldest sample (see Table 5.4). Similarly, the prevalence of *serious theft* increased from 13 (2.6%) in the youngest sample to 45 (8.9%) in the middle sample and 106 (20.9%) in the oldest sample.

Generally, there was a relationship between committing violence and committing theft. For example, Table 5.5 shows that, in the oldest sample, 43.3% of those who had committed serious violence had also committed serious theft, whereas another 38.3% had committed moderate theft. Conversely, 51.4% of nonviolent boys had committed no theft and another 25.7% had only committed minor theft. Similar relationships are also seen in the middle and youngest samples. However, these tables suggest that moderate violence is clearly not worse than minor violence at least in its relationship to theft.

There are some important age trends. When we compare the percentage of boys committing moderate violence (which is comparable across the three samples) who also commit serious theft, this increased from 7.5% in the youngest sample to 11.6% in the middle sample and then tripled to 31.1% in the oldest sample. Also, for seriously violent boys in the middle and oldest samples, there was an increase with age in the percentage who also engaged in serious theft (25%–43.3%).

Moreover, in the oldest sample, the majority of serious delinquents (62.7% of 185) were versatile in committing serious violence and moderate or serious theft (not shown in Table 5.5). However, this was true of only 47.1% of the 140 serious delinquents in the middle sample and only 21.6% of the 51 serious delinquents in the youngest sample. Most of the serious delinquents in the youngest sample (64.7%) committed only violence, as did 45.7% of the serious delinquents in the middle sample. Thus, the co-occurrence of more serious levels of violence and theft increased between childhood and early adolescence, leading to the emergence of a versatile category of offender.

NARROWING DOWN THE EXPLANATORY VARIABLES

For our analyses, we narrowed down the long potential list of explanatory variables on three grounds. First, we deleted those variables that could be assumed to measure some aspect of delinquency or disruptive behavior. Thus, we tried to avoid placing dependent variables on the independent side of the

TABLE 5.5
Interrelation Between Violence and Theft
(Percentage of Boys in Different Theft Categories Given Violence)

*Youngest Sample**

Violence	% None	% Minor	% Moderate	% Serious	Total N
None	67.5	25.8	5.1	1.5	391
Minor	47.2	26.4	20.8	5.6	72
Moderate	42.5	40.0	10.0	7.5	40
Total *N*	315	136	39	13	503

Middle Sample

Violence	% None	% Minor	% Moderate	% Serious	Total N
None	54.2	32.5	9.8	3.4	295
Minor	23.3	44.7	13.6	18.4	103
Moderate	22.1	39.5	26.7	11.6	86
Serious	8.3	37.5	29.2	25.0	24
Total *N*	205	185	73	45	508

Oldest Sample

Violence	% None	% Minor	% Moderate	% Serious	Total N
None	51.4	25.7	11.8	11.0	245
Minor	17.1	27.1	31.4	24.3	140
Moderate	16.4	32.8	19.7	31.1	61
Serious	5.0	13.3	38.3	43.3	60
Total *N*	163	129	108	106	506

*None of the boys in the youngest sample was known to have committed serious violence.

equation. Second, to avoid problems of colinearity, we deleted some variables that were highly intercorrelated with other variables (i.e., phi >.40). Third, when there was a choice between different variables measuring the same construct, we chose the variable that best represented the construct.

The Avoidance of Possible Confounds

In our analyses, we wanted to avoid confounds. For that reason, we aimed to include as explanatory variables only those factors that clearly did not measure antisocial behavior. In contrast, in past studies (Amdur, 1989), one analytic problem has been authors including in their analyses some independent variables that measured aspects of the dependent variable. If two variables measure the same underlying construct, using one as an explanation of the other artifactually increases the amount of variance explained, but this is of little practical significance for the explanation of deviant behavior.

For example, in the explanation of juvenile delinquency, peer delinquency is often seen as an important correlate. The question is to what extent the two are confounded. In our study, three quarters of the serious delinquent acts reported by the boys took place in the company of their peers (75.6% and 74.9% in the middle and oldest samples, respectively). Therefore, asking the boys to report on the extent of their peers' delinquent involvement tends to include a proportion of acts that the peers committed in the company of the boys studied. Although we cannot determine exactly what that proportion is, we consider it imprudent to use boys' reports of their peers' delinquent involvement as an explanatory variable for the boys' own delinquency. Instead, we consider peer delinquency as a correlate of the sample boys' delinquency. Thus, we examine correlates separately from explanatory variables, which are selected to be more independent of the delinquent behavior. Similarly, parents' reports of bad friends were considered correlates of delinquency rather than explanatory variables. The same applied to nonconventional peers, poor peer relationships, peer substance use, and boys' exposure to drugs.

There are several other variables that confounded with the dependent variable of delinquency—namely, positive attitudes to problem behavior, delinquency, or substance use, and the perceived likelihood of getting caught by the police. In addition, associated problem behaviors—such as nonphysical aggression, cruel to people, oppositional behavior, running away, and frequency of injuries—were also considered correlates rather than explanatory variables for delinquency. This also applied to various nonacademic problems associated with school (suspension, truancy, low school motivation, and negative attitude to school).

In contrast, we retained lack of guilt as an explanatory variable because guilt feelings are associated both with externalizing and internalizing problems (Williams & Bybee, 1994). Guilt and misbehavior are logically different constructs. Guilt can act as an inhibitor of misbehavior, just as lack of guilt may promote misbehavior. In that sense, we agree with Baumeister, Stillwell, and Heatherton (1994), who stated that, "guilt helps enforce the communal norms . . . [and] may punish and hence reduce the frequency of interpersonal transgressions so that it makes people less likely to hurt, disappoint, or alienate their partners" (p. 247). Misbehavior is not necessarily linked to a lack of guilt, whereas juvenile delinquency is often necessarily linked to peer delinquency. However, lack of remorse, which is often associated with lack of guilt, is a symptom of antisocial personality disorder (American Psychiatric Association, 1994) and psychopathy (Hare, Hart, & Hampur, 1991).

Some interactions within the family may also reflect the boy's misbehavior, such as parents not consistently disciplining the boy or the boy responding to discipline by escalating problem behavior (here called *countercontrol*). Poor relationships with parents and siblings may often result from the boy's misbehavior. For that reason, they were considered correlates rather than explanatory variables for delinquency. Generally, we aimed to include as explanatory variables only those factors that clearly did not measure antisocial behavior. Some of the variables that we have counted as correlates may in fact be explanatory, but we have erred on the side of caution and excluded some variables as explanatory.

The Avoidance of Colinearity

We deleted from consideration several variables that were highly correlated with other conceptually similar variables (a phi of .40 or higher in at least one sample). For example, the ages of the mother and father at the time of the boy's birth were highly correlated (phi = .53 in the oldest sample). To maximize the number of participants available for analysis, we chose the age of the mother as the independent variable. All variables based on operative fathers had large numbers of missing cases (e.g., 47% missing on this variable in the oldest sample) because of absent fathers' and mothers' lack of knowledge about them. Similarly, we simplified family structure by focusing on broken families (i.e., the boy not living with two biological parents) in preference to other correlated variables like single-parent female-headed households, the mother not married, the father not married, and separation from the biological father. Also, because the education of the mother was highly correlated with the education of the father (calculated by the number of years of schooling; phi = .34 in the oldest sample), we chose to include the education of the mother to maximize the N in the analyses.

In another instance, we decided to use poor communication between parent and child, rather than family activities (i.e., doing things together) or talking about family activities, because all these variables were highly correlated (e.g., poor communication vs. not doing things together; phi = .42 in the oldest sample). Three variables describing the marital state (unhappy parents, low parental agreement, and low parental involvement or time spent together) were also highly intercorrelated (e.g., unhappy parents vs. low agreement; phi = .57 in the oldest sample). We chose to include unhappy parents as the best representative of this cluster.

Representative Constructs

In some instances, we could make a choice between different variables measuring the same construct. For example, boys' depressed mood was measured through self-reports and parent or teacher ratings. We chose the self-reports as our explanatory variable because we assumed that this was the most valid measure of the underlying construct. Sometimes our choice was made to maximize the available N. Thus, we chose mother not close rather than father not close or family not close out of these three correlated variables. In a few instances, we decided not to include a variable such as cruelty to animals because of its low prevalence (e.g., only 9% cruel to animals in the oldest sample).

RISK ATTACHED TO EACH OF THE EXPLANATORY VARIABLES FOR DELINQUENCY

Having reduced the data to a set of 40 potentially important and distinct explanatory variables (listed in Table 5.6), we related these variables to delinquency and calculated the odds ratio for each of the relationships.

Table 5.6 summarizes the association between the explanatory variables and delinquency in each of the three samples. Odds ratios are used to measure strength of relationships and chi-squared to measure significance of relationships. We organized the explanatory variables in three categories: child, family, and macro (socioeconomic, demographic, and neighborhood). Table 5.6 shows that almost all of the child variables increased the risk of delinquency; these results were well replicated across the three samples. The most powerful explanatory variable was lack of guilt (odds ratios: 3.4, 4.7, and 3.5, for the youngest, middle, and oldest samples, respectively), followed by HIA problems (2.1, 1.9, and 2.7, for the samples in the same order), a high ADHD score (2.2, 2.8, and 1.8), old for grade (1.9, 2.7, 2.3), and low achievement (1.3 [n.s.], 3.0, and 1.6). Although depressed mood was related to delinquency in all samples, the odds ratio was highest for boys in the youngest sample (2.6, 1.8, and 1.7).

Turning to the family variables, poor supervision was the best explanatory variable for delinquency, increasing the risk of delinquency by a factor of 2.6 for the oldest sample, but somewhat lower for the other samples (1.9 and 1.5). Next came poor parent-child communication, which increased the risk of delinquency by a factor of 2.4 in the middle sample and 1.5 in the oldest sample. (This was not measured in the youngest sample.) Physical punishment increased the risk of delinquency by a factor of about 2 in each of the three samples. Several other parent variables increased the risk of delinquency, but only for the youngest and middle samples, such as mother's high stress, substance use problems, and anxiety/depression.

Of the socioeconomic factors, family on welfare was associated with the highest risk of delinquency in all three samples (2.1, 2.5, and 2.4), followed by low socioeconomic status (1.5, 2.2, and 1.5). Other variables that increased the risk of delinquency in two out of the three samples were a small house, an unemployed father, and a poorly educated mother.

Among the demographic variables, the most strongly related were a broken family (2.0, 2.9, and 2.8) and African American ethnicity (1.9, 2.5, and 2.3). A young mother (under age 20 at the time of the boy's birth) doubled the risk of delinquency, but only for the middle and oldest samples. Finally, bad neighborhood—either measured through census data or by means of the parent's report—also doubled the risk for delinquency in all three samples.

We undertook several methodological analyses, which are reported in the Methodological Appendix. For example, the appendix examines the extent that explanatory factors were the same for the three samples. The

TABLE 5.6
Odds Ratios for Explanatory Variables for Delinquency

	Sample		
Variable	Youngest	Middle	Oldest
Child			
Lack of guilt (PT)	3.4****	4.7****	3.5****
Old for grade (P)	1.9**	2.7****	2.3****
HIA problems (PT)	2.1**	1.9*	2.7****
High ADHD score (P)	2.2***	2.8****	1.8**
Low achievement (PBT)	1.7*	2.6****	2.6****
Low achievement (CAT)	1.3	3.0****	1.6*
Low organizational participation (PB)	1.5*	1.6*	1.2
Depressed mood (B)	2.6****	1.8**	1.7**
Shy/withdrawn (PT)	1.5*	1.6*	−1.2
Family			
Poor supervision (PB)	1.9**	1.5*	2.6****
Poor communication (PB)	—	2.4****	1.5*
No set time home (PB)	1.0	−1.6	1.5*
Physical punishment (PB)	1.7*	2.0***	1.9**
Boy not involved (PB)	1.6*	1.3	1.8**
Disagree on discipline (PB)	—	2.1*	1.1
Unhappy parents (P)	2.0*	1.5	1.0
High parental stress (P)	1.7**	1.9**	1.2
Parent substance use problems (P)	1.9**	1.6*	1.4
Parent anxiety/depression (P)	1.5*	1.8**	1.3
Father behavior problems (P)	1.6	1.7*	1.5

Table 5.6 (continued)

Variable	Sample		
	Youngest	Middle	Oldest
Macro			
Socioeconomic			
Low SES (P)	1.5*	2.2***	1.5*
Family on welfare (P)	2.1***	2.5****	2.4****
Poor housing (P)	1.2	1.5	1.7*
Small house (P)	1.7*	1.3	1.7*
Unemployed father (P)	2.2*	2.6**	1.6
Unemployed mother (P)	1.3	1.5*	1.1
Poorly educated mother (P)	2.1***	1.4	1.9**
Demographic			
African American (P)	1.9**	2.5****	2.3****
Large family (P)	1.7*	1.2	1.2
Young mother (P)	1.1	1.9**	2.1***
Broken family	2.0**	2.9****	2.8****
Neighborhood			
Bad neighborhood (C)	2.0**	1.8**	2.1***
Bad neighborhood (P)	2.2***	1.8**	2.0***

Note. B = Boy; C = Census; CAT = California Achievement Test; P = Parent; T = Teacher. * $p < .05$. ** $p < .01$. *** $p < .001$. **** $p < .0001$. *p* values are one-tailed based on chi-square with correction for continuity. No significant relationship: anxiety, low jobs/chores involvement, low religiosity, few friends, low reinforcement, boy not close to mother, and parent antisocial attitude. —, Variable not measured due to young age.

results indicate substantial but not complete convergence, justifying our strategy to continue to consider each of the samples separately rather than jointly. We also examined whether the results on explanatory factors were essentially the same for weighted compared with unweighted samples. Analyses spelled out in the appendix show a high correlation between the two, which led us to continue using unweighted data. Likewise, we examined whether variables scored continuously would produce different results from analyses based on dichotomized data. The results are sufficiently similar to justify our choice to proceed with dichotomized variables.

Finally, in the Methodological Appendix we justify our hierarchical, sequential, theoretical model, and analytic strategy. First, we took the most important explanatory factor for delinquency (i.e., lack of guilt) and examined the best explanatory factors for lack of guilt (other than child variables). Of the several factors identified, we found that poor supervision and poor communication were the best explanatory factors for lack of guilt. Taking this a step further, we then explored what were the best explanatory factors for poor supervision and poor communication. The reader is referred to the Methodological Appendix for the results of these analyses, and to Farrington and Loeber (in press) for similar analyses.

In summary, the results of chapter 5 show considerable replication of relationships with explanatory variables across the three samples, but also some potentially important shifts in the effects of explanatory variables with age. Methodological analyses strengthened our justification to use dichotomized and unweighted data, because the results are similar to those obtained with continuous and weighted data.

CORRELATES OF DELINQUENCY

As mentioned, many variables were not included in our list of explanatory variables because we considered them either expressions of an underlying antisocial tendency (e.g., a delinquent attitude), co-occurring with offending (e.g., peer delinquency), or the result of the problem behavior (e.g., being suspended). However, we now review these correlates separately. They are important because they represent a profile of the problem behaviors and conditions associated with delinquency.

Table 5.7 shows the extent that each problem attitude or behavior is associated with an increased risk of delinquency (as expressed by the odds ratio). Of the attitudinal measures, a positive attitude to problem behavior was associated in each of the samples, but most strongly in the oldest sample (2.3, 1.6, and 3.4). Other attitudes, such as a positive attitude to delinquency and a positive attitude to substance use, were relevant for the middle and oldest samples only. As expected, our risk score that was used in selecting the sample for follow-up was strongly related to delinquency (3.8, 7.6, and 8.6).

Not surprisingly, several problem behaviors were highly associated with delinquency in all of the samples, particularly nonphysical aggression, cruelty to people, and oppositional behavior, whereas running away was associated with delinquency in two out of the three samples. Table 5.7 shows that several school variables were highly associated with delinquency, such as being suspended (3.9, 6.2, and 6.5) and truancy (2.7, 3.2, and 6.3). A negative attitude to school and low school motivation were related to delinquency in the middle and oldest samples, with the risk of delinquency increasing especially in the latter (3.0 and 4.4).

It is well known that delinquent youth often have poor relationships with their parents. This was also found for boys in each of the three samples. The delinquents also used more countercontrol to thwart their parents' disciplinary practices, and this was evident especially in the oldest sample. Surprisingly, a boy's poor relationship with his siblings was only related to delinquency in the youngest sample. However, poor peer relations outside of the home were characteristic of delinquent boys in all three samples, increasing the risk substantially (4.4, 5.5, and 4.1). Parents' reports of bad friends and the boys'

Table 5.7
Odds Ratios for Correlates of Delinquency

	Sample		
Correlate	Youngest	Middle	Oldest
Risk status			
High risk	3.8****	7.6****	8.6****
Attitude			
Positive attitude to delinquency (B)	1.3	1.9**	2.2***
Positive attitude to problem behavior (B)	2.3****	1.6*	3.4****
Positive attitude to substance use (B)	1.3	1.6*	1.9**
Unlikely to be caught (B)	—	1.3	1.9**
Behavior			
Nonphysical aggression (PT)	2.8****	8.8****	3.4****
Cruel to people (PT)	4.2****	8.0****	6.8****
Oppositional behavior (P)	2.2***	3.3***	2.0**
Runs away (PB)	2.9****	1.4	2.3****
Frequency injuries	1.7*	−1.1	1.0
School			
Suspended (PB)	3.9****	6.2****	6.5****
Truant (PBT)	2.7****	3.2****	6.3****
Low school motivation (T)	1.4	3.0****	4.4****
Negative attitude to school (B)	1.4	1.6*	2.0***
Family			
Discipline not persistent (PB)	—	1.0	1.7*
Poor relationship with parent (PB)	2.6****	3.1****	1.6*
Counter control (P)	1.5	1.5*	2.1***
Poor relationship with siblings (PB)	1.7*	1.3	1.1
Peers			
Poor relationship with peers (T)	4.4****	5.5****	4.1****
Bad friends (PB)	2.2***	2.4****	2.2***
Peer delinquency (B)	2.2***	4.0****	3.8****
Nonconventional peers (B)	2.0*	−1.1	1.6*
Peer substance use problems (B)	—	2.8****	3.6****
Exposed to drugs (B)	—	2.5****	2.5****

Note. B = Boy; C = Census; P = Parent; T = Teacher. * $p < .05$. ** $p < .01$. *** $p < .001$. **** $p < .0001$. (one-tailed), based on chi-squared with correction for continuity. No significant relationship: Don't enjoy boy. —, Variable not measured in this form, because boy was not considered old enough to respond to the relevant questions.

reports of delinquent peers were consistently related to the boys' delinquency across all three samples. This also applied to peer substance use and the boys' exposure to drugs, which were only measured for the middle and oldest samples.

In summary, significant correlates of delinquency known from other studies are also found in this study. The presence of these other problems was often associated with a considerably increased likelihood of delinquency.

REGRESSION ANALYSES

Because of our empirically derived conceptual scheme, we carried out hierarchical multiple regression analyses to investigate which explanatory variables were independently predictive of delinquency. In the Methodological Appendix we demonstrate that results obtained with Ordinary Least Squares (OLS) Multiple Regression are similar to those obtained with logistic regression. OLS analyses were carried out because of problems of missing data with logistic regression. The child variables were entered in the analyses first, then the family variables and finally the macrovariables. Table 5.8 shows the results of these analyses. The total multiple R amounted to .389 for the youngest sample, .466 for the middle sample, and .419 for the oldest sample. The child variables accounted for most of the variance, whereas demographic, neighborhood, and socio-economic variables accounted for little extra variance.

Although the total amount of variance explained may appear to be modest, recall that we did not include in these analyses possible confounds of the dependent variables; their inclusion would have substantially increased the amount of variance explained. Also, the multiple R is misleadingly low because of the use of dichotomous variables; the explanatory power appears (more realistically) greater when risk measures are used. These analyses are particularly useful in indicating which explanatory variables are important independently of other variables and more attention should be paid to the independently important variables than to the multiple Rs. We have focused on F changes rather than beta weights because beta weights are sensitive to the intercorrelations among the variables in the model (Gordon, 1968).

Table 5.8 shows that, of the child variables, the most important predictor was lack of guilt—a finding that was consistent for each sample. Also, among the next most important predictors were old for grade (all samples) and depressed mood (youngest and oldest samples). In addition, a high ADHD score contributed in the youngest and middle samples and HIA problems in the middle and the oldest samples. Low (academic) achievement only entered for the oldest sample.

Turning to the parent variables, physical punishment predicted delinquency for the middle and oldest samples, whereas poor supervision predicted for the

TABLE 5.8
Hierarchical Multiple Regression for Delinquency

Variable	Multiple R	F Change	p
Youngest sample			
Child			
Lack of guilt	.251	30.81	.0001
Depressed mood	.310	16.89	.0001
Old for grade	.319	2.86	.046
High ADHD score	.326	2.21	.069
Family			
Unhappy parents	.353	5.17	.012
Macro			
Unemployed father	.378	5.23	.012
Bad neighborhood (P)	.389	2.38	.062
Middle sample			
Child			
Lack of guilt	.335	53.90	.0001
Low achievement (CAT)	.382	16.96	.0001
Old for grade	.401	7.61	.003
High ADHD score	.411	4.07	.022
HIA problems	.416	1.95	.081
Low organizational participation	.420	1.70	.096
Family			
Physical punishment	.426	2.89	.045
Parent anxious/depressed	.433	2.89	.045
Macro Variables			
Unemployed father	.447	3.84	.026
African American	.458	3.16	.038
Young mother	.466	2.37	.062
Oldest Sample			
Child Variables			
Lack of guilt	.268	34.48	.0001
Old for grade	.308	11.30	.0004
Depressed mood	.324	4.82	.014
HIA problems	.332	2.60	.054
Low achievement (PBT)	.338	2.12	.073
Family Variables			
Poor supervision	.356	6.41	.006
Physical punishment	.370	4.78	.015
Macro Variables			
Young mother	.391	8.10	.002
Bad neighborhood (C)	.408	6.67	.005
Broken family	.414	2.60	.054
Bad neighborhood (P)	.419	2.02	.078

Note. p values one-tailed. No other variables entered. All weightings positive.
C = Census; CAT = California Achievement Test; P = Parent.

oldest sample only. Parent anxiety/depression entered into the equation only for the middle sample, whereas unhappy parents were most relevant for the youngest sample. Remarkably, no other parent variable predicted delinquency in the youngest sample; other parent variables only entered the equation for children at a later age.

Turning to the macrovariables, young mother, unemployed father, and bad neighborhood were significant predictors in two of the three samples. African American ethnic status was a less consistent predictor (middle sample only). The relative unimportance of ethnicity in relation to delinquency was interesting. We considered carrying out all the analyses separately for African Americans and Whites, but decided that this approach would give too much a priori importance to ethnicity as a variable. We thought it was better to treat ethnicity in the same way as other variables—to allow it to enter the analyses only if it were empirically driven. Similarly, we decided not to investigate all possible interactions with ethnicity, but to allow the analysis of interaction effects to be driven by the data.

In summary, the results indicate good replication of findings across the samples. The most important predictors of delinquency were lack of guilt, the boy old for his grade (indicating low attainment, causing the boy to be held back), a high ADHD score, depressed mood, poor supervision, physical punishment, young mother, unemployed father, and bad neighborhood.

DETECTING INTERACTION EFFECTS

It is important to investigate possible interactions among the explanatory variables. Most multivariate studies do not attempt to do this because it is extremely difficult with continuous variables. As a consequence, it is unclear from such studies to what extent the following types of interactions apply to the data (Farrington, 1994): (a) the joint occurrence of two risk factors is associated with a disproportionately higher prevalence of delinquency than would be obtained if the two factors were merely additive (called an *enhancing interaction effect*); (b) the joint absence of two risk factors is associated with a disproportionately lower prevalence of delinquency than if the two factors were merely additive (called a *suppressing interaction effect*); and (c) the presence of one risk factor has a big effect on delinquency, particularly or only in the absence of the other risk factor (called a *nonlinear interaction effect*).

There are several conditions that should be met before one can speak of an interaction. First, because the systematic investigation of interaction effects usually involves large numbers of comparisons, it is necessary to determine the extent to which the number of observed significant interactions is higher than might be obtained by chance alone. Second, we were interested in finding whether interaction effects could be replicated across the three samples. This means finding a significant effect and examining whether the effect was of the same type in each sample (see the types outlined earlier). Obviously when the particular type of interaction was replicated across two or more samples, this gave us confidence that the interaction effect was meaningful and not due to chance.

Third, the replication of interaction effects may be investigated in a slightly broader context than the exact replication of combinations of particular variables. For example, if poor housing interacts with poor supervision in one sample and with no set time to be home in another sample, this may be considered as a replicated effect if the interaction effects for each sample are of the same type (because poor supervision and no set time to be home are probably measuring similar underlying constructs). Fourth, even if an interaction effect is found, this does not necessarily mean that the interaction effect will be associated with delinquency (or any other outcome) independently of the main effects of other explanatory variables. Interaction effects are more important in multivariate analyses if they are associated with an outcome independently of the main effects.

We limited ourselves to the investigation of two-way interactions because, in our selection procedures, only relatively few significant two-way interactions were identified. Because three-way or higher level interactions are usually only investigated when lower level interactions are present, we could not justify a search for higher level interactions.

We followed two analytic approaches to interactions. In the first approach, we focused on how well interaction effects supplemented the hierarchical regression analyses for the explanatory variables for delinquency. Hence, we only studied interaction effects among independently important explanatory factors. This approach can inform us about which interaction effects significantly contribute to the explanation of delinquency over and above main effects. However, one of the disadvantages of these analyses is that, because the main effects in the multivariate analyses vary somewhat among the three samples, we cannot expect much replication of the interaction effects. Therefore, the second approach focused on all possible interactions (irrespective of the main effects found) and established which of the interactions were replicated across more than one sample and were of the same type.

In the first approach, the independently important variables detected in the regression analyses were studied. Three-way tables were constructed relating each of these variables to delinquency at both levels of each other variable. Recall that the variables were dichotomized, identifying moderate to serious delinquents for the youngest sample and serious delinquents for the middle and oldest samples, whereas all explanatory variables were dichotomized at the upper 25th percentile (as far as possible). Potentially important interaction effects were investigated where the difference between one phi correlation and the other phi correlation was at least .15. This screening device detected all significant interaction effects (and many nonsignificant ones). The exact interaction effect was calculated using logistic regression; Table 5.9 shows the likelihood ratio chi-squared (LRCS) values. Finally, we investigated whether the interaction effects added significantly to the main effects in explaining delinquency in multiple regression analyses. (The interaction term was scored 1 if both risk factors were present or if both risk factors were absent, and 0 otherwise). Because this is a quite stringent test, we include interaction effects that were nearly significant as independent explanatory variables.

Table 5.9 shows the most important interaction effects for delinquency. Overall, the number of significant interactions was considerably higher than would be expected by chance alone. There were 131 possible interaction terms investigated in the three samples. The chance expectation for the number of significant terms (at p = .05, two-tailed) is therefore 6 or 7. Table 5.9 shows that 11 terms were statistically significant (with an LRCS value of 3.84 or greater). Therefore, it might be concluded that four of five of these significant interaction terms are likely to be important. Coincidentally, four interaction terms were significantly associated with delinquency over and above the main effects. We focus on these independently important interaction terms (and three other near-significant interactions) as the most meaningful.

In the youngest sample, there was a significant interaction effect between lack of guilt and ADHD score. Lack of guilt was only associated with delinquency in the absence of a high ADHD score. Conversely, a high ADHD score was only associated with delinquency in the absence of lack of guilt. In the middle sample, low participation in organizations was only associated with delinquency where the father was employed. Conversely, an unemployed father was only associated with delinquency where participation in organizations was not low. Physical punishment was only associated with delinquency where participation in organizations was low. Conversely, low participation in organizations was only associated with delinquency in the presence of physical punishment. Because physical punishment was not associated with delinquency when there was participation in organizations, participation in organizations might be viewed as a protective factor against the effects of physical punishment. A high ADHD score was only associated with delinquency in the absence of HIA problems and vice versa.

In the oldest sample, physical punishment was only associated with delinquency if the neighborhood was not bad. Conversely, a bad neighborhood was only associated with delinquency in the absence of physical punishment. A

Interaction Effects for Delinquency

| | | % Delinquent | | | | | | Regression | |
| | | B = No | | B = Yes | | | | | |
Variable A	Variable B	A = No	A = Yes	A = No	A = Yes	LRCS	p	F change	p
Youngest sample (27.8)									
Lack of guilt	High ADHD score	18.8	57.4	38.7	42.6	10.17	.001	3.62	.059
Middle sample (27.6)									
Low organizational participation	Unemployed father	12.3	33.3	41.0	32.0	6.82	.009	7.13	.008
Low achievement (CAT)	Low participation	17.2	47.9	30.5	40.0	5.42	.020	—	—
High ADHD score	Old for grade	16.0	42.0	39.4	47.2	5.16	.023	—	—
Low organizational participation	Physical punishment	22.5	23.5	28.9	52.5	4.78	.029	5.54	.019
Physical punishment	African American	12.3	31.8	32.7	39.7	4.25	.039	—	—
Low organizational participation	Parent anxiety/depression	19.4	33.6	38.3	34.1	4.05	.044	—	—
Lack of guilt	Unemployed father	11.7	44.2	34.2	45.0	3.77	.052	—	—
High ADHD score	HIA problems	19.0	41.6	44.9	48.9	3.66	.056	2.92	.087
HIA problems	Parent anxiety/depression	21.9	36.2	27.3	63.9	2.77	.096	—	—
Oldest sample (36.6)									
HIA problems	Low achievement (PBT)	27.1	56.0	53.1	55.8	5.19	.023	—	—
Broken family	Bad neighborhood (P)	15.7	39.9	45.2	49.5	4.76	.029	—	—
Physical punishment	Bad neighborhood (P)	27.7	50.0	49.5	46.9	4.59	.032	4.94	.027
HIA problems	Old for grade	24.6	56.4	45.1	55.6	4.05	.044	—	—
Depressed mood	Bad neighborhood (P)	27.5	47.1	49.0	46.4	3.64	.056	—	—
Low achievement (PBT)	Old for grade	25.0	53.8	43.4	54.1	3.32	.68	—	—
Nonbiological parent	Bad neighborhood (C)	17.3	38.5	47.4	49.2	3.25	.071	3.46	.064
Lack of guilt	HIA problems	24.8	54.1	52.9	61.2	3.04	.081	5.05	.025
Low achievement (PBT)	Young mother	24.8	52.6	45.5	55.6	2.90	.089	—	—

Note. LRCS = Likelihood ratio chi-squared. *p* values two-tailed. —, nonsignificant value.

broken family was only associated with delinquency if the neighborhood was not bad. Conversely, a bad neighborhood was associated with delinquency especially where two biological parents were present. Finally, lack of guilt was associated with delinquency only in the absence of HIA problems and vice versa. This largely replicated the significant interaction between lack of guilt and ADHD score in the youngest sample.

Thus, these analyses show divergent results among the three samples and only one near replication in two out of the three samples (lack of guilt and ADHD score, and lack of guilt and HIA problems). Some of this lack of replication may have resulted from the fact that partly different explanatory variables entered the regression analyses for each of the three samples. For that reason, we undertook a second set of interaction analyses by examining all possible interactions, irrespective of the main effects in the hierarchical regression analyses. These analyses were based on 40 explanatory factors in the middle and oldest samples, and on 37 in the youngest sample.

The results show a large number of interaction effects. The observed number of significant effects slightly exceeded the expected number (for the youngest sample, 38 observed vs. 33 expected by chance; for the middle and oldest samples, 48 and 47 observed, respectively, vs. 39 expected by chance). Because the difference between the numbers observed and expected was not very large, we used as an additional criterion—the replication of interaction effects across samples—to identify the most important interactions.

In the middle and oldest samples, there was a replication of the interaction between old for grade and ADHD score, whereas in the youngest and middle samples, there was a replication of the interaction between mother's high stress and parental anxiety. In both instances, one risk factor was associated with delinquency especially in the absence of the other one. Two other, approximately equivalent, replications were found: HIA problems interacted with a small house in the middle sample and with poor housing conditions in the oldest sample. In both instances, HIA problems were related to delinquency for boys not in inadequate housing. Finally, poor housing conditions interacted with poor parenting (i.e., with poor supervision) in the youngest sample and with no set time to be home in the middle sample. In both cases, the joint occurrence of poor housing and poor parenting was associated with a disproportionately high prevalence of delinquency, so that one risk factor was associated with delinquency especially in the presence of the other one. Thus, the second set of analyses led to only a few replicated interaction results and then across only two out of three samples.

Overall, the first and second sets of interaction analyses produced some interesting results, but the yield was rather meager in comparison with the large number of analyses executed. Moreover, the results only marginally add to our understanding of the explanation of boys' delinquency in the three samples.

Therefore, in future chapters, we do not study all possible interaction effects. Instead, we focus on interaction effects among independently important explanatory variables and then only on those interactions that are associated with outcomes significantly over and above the main effects.

However, the interaction effects, are important. Some of the interactions suggested a cumulative effect of different risk factors. Knowledge of such a cumulative effect may help to identify high-risk groups of juveniles (e.g., those youth living in poor housing who are poorly supervised by their parents). Other types of interactions are also important because they may show for which combination of variables participants are unlikely to be at risk for a deviant outcome or where variables have protective effects. We discuss combinations of risk factors in more detail in the next section.

CUMULATIVE EFFECT OF RISK FACTORS ON THE LIKELIHOOD OF DELINQUENCY

The multivariate results showing the independently important explanatory variables for delinquency do not reveal what percentage of boys are delinquent in different risk categories (i.e., possessing different numbers of risk factors). Therefore, each boy was scored according to the number of explanatory factors that he possessed (e.g., out of 11 in the oldest sample identified in Table 5.8). Where a boy was missing on one explanatory factor, his score was expressed as a percentage of the number of measured risk factors and multiplied to make it comparable with that of boys measured on all factors (e.g., expressed as a score out of 11 in the oldest sample). In presenting the results, we divided up the risk scores into five categories, each containing about 100 boys. Where numbers did not permit this, we set the minimum number of boys in a category at about 50. For the youngest sample, the risk of delinquency increased until, at four or more risk factors, 60.3% of the boys were delinquent. The results for the middle and oldest samples show similar increases, reaching a maximum of 60.4% and 69.6% delinquent in the two samples at the level of six or more risk factors.

In all cases, the most risky category showed a disproportionate increase in the percentage of boys who were delinquents. To assess the strength of the association between the risk score and delinquency, the odds ratio was calculated for the highest risk category versus the rest. The results show that the odds ratio was higher for the middle sample (6.5) than for the youngest (5.4) and oldest (5.5) samples, although overall the three odds ratios are quite similar. These odds ratios can be compared with the multiple R's shown in Table 5.8 (.389 for the youngest sample, .466 for the middle sample, and .419 for the oldest sample). Thus, multiple R's of the order of .4 correspond to a 5–6 times increase in the risk of delinquency by the most high-risk boys.

To compare the samples more directly, risk scores were calculated based on the same 12 key explanatory variables for each sample: lack of guilt, old for grade, low achievement (parent, boy, teacher ratings), ADHD score, depressed mood, poor supervision, physical punishment, ethnicity, broken family, SES, family on welfare, and bad neighborhood (parent measure). Figure 5.1 shows the percentage delinquent in resulting risk categories. Once again, there was a disproportionate increase in the percentage delinquent in the most risky category but only in the youngest and middle samples. The percentage delinquent increased more linearly with the risk score in the oldest sample. The percentage delinquent in the most risky category was 3% to 8% lower than in the multiple regression example, whereas the odds ratios ranged from 3.5 to 5.2 (compared with 5.4–6.5 in the multiple regression example and 3.4–4.7 for the best single explanatory factor—lack of guilt). Given the capitalizing on chance and shrinkage of regression-based scores (e.g., Farrington & Tarling, 1985), Fig. 5.1 may provide a more realistic measure of the degree of discrimination between delinquents and nondelinquents.

CONCLUSION

How do the results compare with other studies? Many explanatory variables for delinquency found in this study were also found in other studies. We briefly

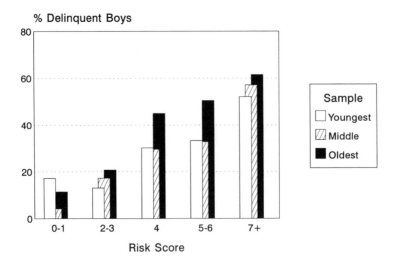

FIG. 5.1. Percentage of delinquent boys as a function of increasing risk score.

discuss explanatory factors for delinquency divided into child, family, and macro (i.e., socioeconomic, demographic, and neighborhood) factors.

Child Variables

Several studies have shown that being a difficult or troublesome child or highly oppositional is related to delinquency (e.g., Sampson & Laub, 1993; West & Farrington, 1973, 1977). We also found that oppositional behavior, nonphysical aggression, and cruelty to people were consistently related to delinquency. However, because we considered these behaviors correlates of delinquency rather than explanatory factors, we did not include them in our explanatory analyses.

Longitudinal (and indeed cross-sectional) surveys have consistently demonstrated that children with low intelligence and academic attainment are disproportionately likely to become delinquents. For example, in the Cambridge Study, low intelligence and attainment predicted both juvenile convictions and self-reported delinquency. This shows that the link between low intelligence/attainment and delinquency was not caused by the less intelligent boys having a greater probability of being caught (West & Farrington, 1973). We also found that low attainment was an important predictor of delinquency.

The most important child factors include HIA problems and low school achievement. Many studies report a link between HIA and delinquency. For example, Satterfield (1987) tracked HIA and matched control boys in Los Angeles between ages 9 and 17 and showed that six times as many of the HIA boys were arrested for serious offenses. Similar results were reported by Gittelman, Mannuzza, Shenker, and Bonagura (1985) in New York. The major problem of interpretation in these types of projects centers on the marked overlap between attention-deficit/hyperactivity and conduct disorder (e.g., Taylor, 1986). Many of the boys in these and other longitudinal studies of attention-deficit/hyperactivity (e.g., Huessy & Howell, 1985; Nylander, 1979; Weiss & Hechtman, 1986) probably displayed both HIA and conduct disorder, making it difficult to know how far the results might have reflected the continuity between childhood antisocial behavior and later offending.

Farrington, Loeber, and Van Kammen (1990) developed a combined measure of HIA at ages 8 to 10 and showed that it significantly predicted juvenile convictions independently of conduct problems at ages 8 to 10. Hence, it might be concluded that HIA is not merely another measure of antisocial personality, but is a possible cause or an earlier stage in a developmental sequence. For example, Richman, Stevenson, and Graham (1982) found that restlessness at age 3 predicted conduct disorder at age 8. Other studies have also concluded that attention-deficit/hyperactivity and conduct disorder are different constructs (e.g., Blouin, Conners, Seidel, & Blouin, 1989; McGee, Williams, & Silva, 1985). We also found that HIA problems and ADHD were important explanatory factors. Finally, we failed to find that low religiosity was related to delinquency, as has been found in several other studies. These studies proposed that the relationship could be explained by means of other mediating factors (Cochran, Wood, & Arneklev, 1994; Evans, Cullen, Dunaway, & Burton, 1995).

Family Variables

Loeber and Dishion (1983) and Loeber and Stouthamer-Loeber (1987) reviewed the predictors of male delinquency. They concluded that poor parental child management techniques, offending by parents and siblings, low intelligence and educational attainment, and separations from parents were all important predictors.

Loeber and Stouthamer-Loeber (1986) also completed a review of family factors as correlates and predictors of juvenile conduct problems and delinquency. They found that poor parental supervision or monitoring, erratic or harsh parental discipline, marital disharmony, parental rejection of the child, and low parental involvement with the child (as well as antisocial parents and large family size) were all important predictors.

In the Cambridge–Somerville study in Boston, McCord (1979) reported that poor parental supervision was the best predictor of both violent and property crimes. Parental aggressiveness (which included harsh discipline, shading into child abuse at the extreme) and parental conflict were significant precursors of violent but not property crimes, whereas the mother's attitude (passive or rejecting) was a significant precursor of property but not violent crimes. In her long-term follow-up studies in St. Louis, Robins (1979) also found that poor supervision and discipline were consistently related to later offending. In the Cambridge Study, West and Farrington (1973) found that harsh or erratic parental discipline; cruel, passive, or neglecting parental attitude; poor supervision; and parental conflict, measured at age 8, all predicted later juvenile convictions. Farrington (1992a) reported that poor parental child rearing behavior (a combination of discipline, attitude, and conflict), poor parental supervision, and low parental interest in education all predicted both convictions and self-reported delinquency.

In addition, researchers and clinicians have emphasized the importance of factors that may interfere with normal family functioning, such as marital discord and stress. For example, Reid and Crisafulli (1990) found that marital discord was consistently related to child behavior problems (but most strongly when the parent was the informant). The authors suggested that the findings were strongest for younger children. This would agree with our study, in which we found that marital problems as evident from the variable unhappy parents were significantly associated with delinquency but only for the youngest sample, even when delinquency was based on the reports of multiple informants.

These results are concordant with the psychological theory (e.g., Patterson, 1982; Trasler, 1962) that antisocial behavior develops when the normal social learning process, based on rewards and punishments from parents, is disrupted by erratic discipline, poor supervision, parental disharmony, and unsuitable (antisocial or criminal) parental models. We also found that poor supervision and harsh discipline (physical punishment) were important explanatory factors for delinquency. In addition, the positive association between parental psychopathology (parent anxiety/depression, parent substance use problems, father behavior problems) and delinquency in the two younger samples is concordant with other studies (see review by Dishion, French, & Patterson, 1995).

Macro Variables

The most important socioeconomic correlates of delinquency are poverty, poor housing, and parental unemployment. Most delinquency theories assume that delinquents disproportionately come from lower class social backgrounds and aim to explain why this is so. For example, Cohen (1955) proposed that lower-class boys found it hard to succeed according to the middle-class standards of the school partly because lower class parents tended not to teach their children to delay immediate gratification in favor of long-term goals. Consequently, lower class boys joined delinquent subcultures by whose standards they could succeed. Cloward and Ohlin (1960) argued that lower class children could not achieve universal goals of status and material wealth by legitimate means and consequently had to resort to illegitimate means.

Beginning with the pioneering self-report research of Nye and Short (1957), it was common in the United States to argue that low social class was related to official offending but not to self-reported offending, and hence that the official processing of offenders was biased against lower class youth. Unfortunately, as Thornberry and Farnworth (1982) pointed out, the voluminous literature on the relationship between SES and offending is characterized by inconsistencies and contradictions. Some reviewers (e.g., Hindelang et al., 1981) have concluded that there is no relationship between SES and either self-reported or official delinquency.

Studies in England have reported more consistent links between low social class and delinquency. In the English national survey, Douglas, Ross, Hammond, and Mulligan (1966) showed that the prevalence of official juvenile delinquency in males varied considerably according to the occupational prestige and educational background of their parents—from 3% in the highest category to 19% in the lowest. Numerous indicators of SES were measured in the Cambridge Study, both for the male's family of origin and for the male as an adult, including occupational prestige, family income, housing, and employment instability. Most of the measures of occupational prestige were not significantly related to delinquency. However, low SES of the family when the boy was ages 8 to 10 significantly predicted his later self-reported, but not official, delinquency. More consistently, low family income and poor housing predicted official and self-reported juvenile and adult offending (Farrington, 1992b). In our Pittsburgh study, low SES and the family on welfare were important explanatory factors.

The most important demographic factors are single-parent families (separation from a biological parent, usually the father), large family size, young mothers, and African American ethnicity. Many projects show that broken families and early separations predict offending. In the Newcastle Thousand Family Study, Kolvin et al. (1990) reported that parental divorce or separation up to age 5 predicted later convictions up to age 33. McCord (1982) carried out an interesting study of the relationship between families broken by loss of the natural father and later serious offending. She found that the prevalence of offending was high for boys reared in broken families without affectionate mothers (62%) and for those reared in united families characterized by parental conflict (52%), irrespective of whether they had affectionate mothers. The prevalence of offending was low for those reared in united families without conflict (26%) or in broken families with affectionate mothers (22%).

These results suggest that it is not so much the broken family (or a single-parent female-headed household) that is criminogenic as the parental conflict that causes it. However, teenage childbearing combined with a single-parent female-headed household is conducive to offending (Morash & Rucker, 1989).

The importance of the cause of the broken family is also shown in the English national longitudinal survey of over 5,000 children born in 1 week in 1946 (Wadsworth, 1979). Boys from families broken by divorce or separation had an increased likelihood of being convicted up to age 21 in comparison with those from families broken by death or from unbroken families. Remarriage (which happened more often after divorce or separation than after death) was also associated with an increased risk of offending. In the Cambridge Study, both permanent and temporary (more than 1 month) separations before age 10 predicted convictions and self-reported delinquency, providing that they were not caused by death or hospitalization (Farrington, 1992b). However, families who split up at an early age (under age 5) were not unusually criminogenic (West & Farrington, 1973). In the Pittsburgh study, a young mother and a broken family were important explanatory factors.

Numerous studies show a link between large family size and delinquency. For example, Wadsworth (1979) reported that offending increased significantly with increasing family size in the English National survey. A similar link between family size and offending was reported by Kolvin et al. (1988) in their follow-up of Newcastle children from birth to age 33, by Rutter et al. (1970) in the Isle of Wight survey, and by Ouston (1984) in the Inner London survey. In the Cambridge Study, large family size predicted official and self-reported juvenile and adult offending (Farrington, 1992b). However, large family size was only weakly associated with delinquency in the Pittsburgh study.

Generally, delinquency rates are highest in inner city, deteriorated neighborhoods. For example, Clark and Wenninger (1962) compared four areas in Illinois and concluded that self-reported offending rates were highest in the inner city, less in a lower class urban area, less still in an upper middle-class urban area, and lowest of all in a rural farm area. In their national self-report survey of American juveniles, Gold and Reimer (1975) also found that self-reported offending was highest for males living in the city centers and lowest for those living in rural areas. Moreover, Shannon (1988) documented how police contact rates over a long period were highest in the inner city (of Racine, Wisconsin) and lowest in the more peripheral areas.

The classic studies by Shaw and McKay (1969) in Chicago and other American cities also showed that juvenile delinquency rates (based on where offenders lived) were highest in inner city areas characterized by physical deterioration, neighborhood disorganization, and high residential mobility. A large proportion of all offenders came from a small proportion of areas, which tended to be the most deprived. Furthermore, these relatively high delinquency rates persisted over time, despite the effect of successive waves of immigration and emigration in changing the demographics of the population in different areas. Shaw and McKay concluded that variations in offending rates reflected variations in the social values and norms to which children were exposed, which in turn reflected the degree of social disorganization of an area.

Later work has tended to cast doubt on the consistency of offending rates over time. Bursik and Webb (1982) tested Shaw and McKay's cultural transmission hypothesis using more recent data in Chicago and more sophisticated quantitative methods. They concluded that the distribution of delinquency was not stable after 1950 but reflected demographic changes. Variations in delinquency rates in different areas were significantly correlated with variations in the percentage on non-Whites, the percentage of foreign-born Whites, and the percentage of overcrowded households. The greatest increase in offending in an area occurred when African Americans moved from the minority to the majority. These results suggest that Shaw and McKay's ideas about community values, which persisted despite successive waves of immigration and emigration, need revising. It was necessary to take account of both the type of area and people living in the area (e.g., Simcha-Fagan & Schwartz, 1986). In the Pittsburgh study, living in a bad neighborhood was an important explanatory factor for delinquency. It should be pointed out that African American ethnicity did not contribute to the explanation of delinquency in the hierarchical multiple regressions for each of the three samples. Instead, it is likely that such factors as single parenthood and bad neighborhood are the important mediators.

A Model of Influences

We have used a model in which the factors most proximal to delinquency are child features. We tested this model in multivariate analyses by first entering child factors, then entering family factors, and last entering macro factors (i.e., socioeconomic, demographic, and neighborhood). In the Methodological Appendix we show that hierarchical multiple regression analyses, in which blocks of variables are entered in the reverse order, produce much the same results in regard to the most important independent predictors of delinquency). In this model, we conceptualize that neighborhoods might affect delinquency through their effects on families and individuals. For example, Rutter et al. (1975a, 1975b) found a much higher incidence of conduct disorder among their Inner London sample of 10-year-olds than in the Isle of Wight (a rural area). They investigated factors that might explain this area difference and found that four sets of variables—family disruption, parental deviance, social disadvantage, and school characteristics—were correlated with conduct disorder in each area. They concluded that the higher rates of disorder in Inner London were at least partly caused by the higher incidence of these four adverse factors.

Clearly, there is an interaction between individuals and the communities in which they live. Some aspect of an inner city neighborhood may be conducive to offending perhaps because the inner city leads to a breakdown of community ties or neighborhood patterns of mutual support, or perhaps because the high population density produces tension, frustration, or anonymity. There may be many interrelated factors. As Reiss (1986) argued, high-crime areas often have a high concentration of single-parent female-headed households with low incomes living in low-cost housing. The weakened parental control in these families—partly caused by the mother having to work and leaving her children unsupervised—meant that the children tended to congregate on the streets. In consequence, they were influenced by a peer subculture that often encouraged and reinforced offending. This interaction of individual, family, peer, and neighborhood factors may be the rule rather than the exception.

6

Explanatory Factors for Substance Use

In chapter 4, we showed that substance use had already started early in the lives of boys in the youngest sample and was quite prevalent in boys in the middle and oldest samples. In this chapter, we address factors that may explain different degrees of substance use involvement and how such factors differ for different age groups. We first examine the relationship among different substances, particularly to investigate the view that substance use develops in a generally orderly fashion and that the strength of relations among the use of different substances varies with age. We then show how substance use is related to the severity of delinquency and petitions to the juvenile court. We then turn to explanatory factors for substance use and correlates of use. We show which combination of explanatory factors in multiple regression analyses best accounts for substance use in each of the three samples, discuss interaction effects, and then show how a risk index of such factors is associated with substance use. The methodological issues discussed in chapter 5 and the Methodological Appendix also apply to this and the following chapters, and are no longer raised here.

MEASUREMENT OF SUBSTANCE USE

In chapter 4, we described our rationale for differentiating among different categories of use and treating them as a substance use scale: first beer or wine, then tobacco, then liquor, then marijuana, and finally other illegal drugs. This categorization and scaling of substance use is based on our earlier findings on the age of onset of different forms of substance use, on the prevalence of use at follow-up (both detailed in chap. 4), and on prior research (e.g., Kandel, 1975; Kandel, Yamaguchi, & Chen, 1992), showing the developmental order of use

131

of different substances. We now follow this categorization. Table 6.1 shows the percentage of boys who reached each level of substance use up to the follow-up interview. As indicated in chapter 4, alcohol consumption with parental consent was excluded.

How strong is the relationship among different types of substance use and does this vary with age? Table 6.2 shows the odds ratios for the various associations for each sample. Remarkably, the associations between beer and wine and between wine and tobacco were strongest for the youngest sample (odds ratios of 9.7 and 10.3, respectively), compared with the middle (4.9 and 3.5, respectively) and oldest samples (3.1 and 4.0, respectively). This indicates that, at a young age, the risk of drinking wine was highly associated with the drinking of beer and tobacco use is strongly associated with the drinking of wine. In comparison, the drinking of beer was less strongly associated with tobacco use (odds ratio 3.3 in the youngest sample), with no major age effects (odds ratios of 3.8 and 4.1 in the middle and oldest samples, respectively).

The use of liquor in the youngest sample was too rare to be compared with the use of other substances. However, Table 6.2 shows that the odds ratios for the associations between beer and liquor and between wine and liquor were high (9.1 and 9.1 in the middle sample and 11.1 and 9.5 the oldest sample, respectively). In the oldest sample, beer use, compared with wine use, was more strongly associated with marijuana use (odds ratio of 8.2 vs. 3.7), but wine use, compared with beer use, was more strongly associated with other illegal drugs (odds ratios of 16.1 and 9.0). In comparison, however, liquor use was most strongly related to use of other drugs (odds ratio of 40.6).

Turning to tobacco use, its association with liquor use was strong in the middle sample (odds ratio of 7.2) but much stronger in the oldest sample (13.8). The association between tobacco use and drug use varied with the seriousness level of drug use: The odds ratio was 8.5 between tobacco use and marijuana use and 20.0 between tobacco use and other drug use.

Table 6.1
Lifetime Substance Use up to the Follow-Up Assessment

	Sample					
	Youngest		Middle		Oldest	
Substance Use	%	(N)	%	(N)	%	(N)
None	83.1	(418)	59.4	(302)	21.9	(111)
Beer/wine	9.3	(47)	25.6	(130)	29.4	(149)
Tobacco	5.8	(29)	9.4	(48)	24.5	(124)
Liquor	1.2	(6)	4.1	(21)	9.9	(50)
Marijuana	0.6	(3)	1.2	(6)	11.1	(56)
Other drugs	—	—	0.2	(1)	3.2	(16)
Total	100	(503)	100	(508)	100	(506)

—, Not assessed in the youngest sample.

TABLE 6.2
Interrelation Among Different Substances (The Odds Ratio of the Second Substance
Given the Presence of the First Substance)

Substances	Odds Ratio
Youngest sample	
Beer–wine	9.7
Beer–tobacco	3.3
Wine–tobacco	10.3
Middle sample	
Beer–wine	4.9
Beer–tobacco	3.8
Beer–liquor	9.1
Wine–tobacco	3.5
Wine–liquor	9.1
Tobacco–liquor	7.2
Oldest sample	
Beer–wine	3.1
Beer–tobacco	4.1
Beer–liquor	11.1
Beer–marijuana	8.2
Beer–other drugs	9.0
Wine–tobacco	4.0
Wine–liquor	9.5
Wine–marijuana	3.7
Wine–other drugs	16.1
Tobacco–liquor	13.8
Tobacco–marijuana	8.5
Tobacco–other drugs	20.0
Liquor–marijuana	6.1
Liquor–other drugs	40.6
Marijuana–other drugs	33.6

Note. $p < .001$ (one-tailed, based on chi-square) in all cases except beer–tobacco in the youngest sample ($p = .003$) and beer–other drugs in the oldest sample ($p = .002$).

In summary, we found an important age trend. The magnitude of the associations between beer and wine use and between wine and tobacco use were greatest in middle childhood compared with late childhood or early adolescence. This may imply that the use of one legal substance at an early age puts boys at risk of using another legal substance as well. At later ages, the deviant early starters are joined by more normal, substance-using boys so the inter-relationships among beer, wine, and tobacco become weaker. Whether this means that these substance-using boys are also at risk of progressing to the use of illegal drugs such as marijuana and cocaine is plausible but could not be demonstrated in these analyses.

Our hypothesis is that the strength of association is greater where the prevalence is lower because a more extreme group of (more deviant) boys is involved. Thus, the relation between beer and wine and between wine and tobacco may be strongest in the youngest sample because the beer, wine, and tobacco users in the youngest sample are more deviant for their age than such users in the older two samples. Similarly, many of the substance users in the oldest sample who have escalated beyond marijuana use are likely to be multiply deviant boys. This may help account for the high odds ratios for the relationships between substances at the higher seriousness levels of use. However, the main finding is the strong overlap between all substances at all ages.

SUBSTANCE USE AND DELINQUENCY

It has long been known that boys who engage in substance use are more prone to engage in delinquent acts (Bukstein, Brent, & Kaminer, 1989; Collins, 1981; Loeber, 1988). It is also known that conduct problems can predict substance use (e.g., Boyle et al., 1992). However, it is less clear whether substance use is associated with the severity of delinquency and whether substance use is related to past and future court petitions for delinquency.

Table 6.3 shows the association between substance use and the lifetime delinquency seriousness scale based on information from the boys, parents, and teachers. Substances distinguished are beer/wine, tobacco, liquor, and marijuana or more serious illegal drugs. However, because of the small number of cases in the youngest sample using the more serious substances, tobacco use was combined with liquor and marijuana use. For the same reason, liquor use in the middle sample was combined with marijuana and other illegal drug use, and marijuana and other illegal drug use were combined in the oldest sample.

Table 6.3 shows that, for all three samples, the different levels of substance use were related to the severity of delinquent acts. In the youngest sample, 28.9% of the tobacco or worse substance use group had engaged in serious forms of delinquency, compared with 6.4% of the boys who had only consumed beer or wine. In the middle sample, only 2.1% of the tobacco users and 3.6% of the liquor or worse substance users had not engaged in any delinquent acts, compared with 14.6% of the boys who had only used beer or wine. About 42% of the tobacco users and liquor or worse drug users had engaged in serious delinquency, compared with 30.8% of the boys who had used beer or wine only and 22.5% of the boys who had used no substance at all.

TABLE 6.3
Substance Use Versus Delinquency

Substance Use	Delinquency								Total
	None		Minor		Moderate		Serious		
	%	(n)	%	(n)	%	(n)	%	(n)	
Youngest sample									
None	43.3	(181)	33.5	(140)	14.4	(60)	8.9	(37)	418
Beer/wine	29.8	(14)	27.2	(13)	36.2	(17)	6.4	(3)	47
Tobacco, etc.	7.9	(3)	31.6	(12)	31.6	(12)	28.9	(11)	38
Total	39.4	(198)	32.8	(165)	17.7	(89)	10.1	(51)	503
Middle sample									
None	26.8	(81)	33.1	(100)	17.5	(53)	22.5	(68)	302
Beer/wine	14.6	(19)	31.5	(41)	23.1	(30)	30.8	(40)	130
Tobacco	2.1	(1)	12.5	(6)	43.8	(21)	41.7	(20)	48
Liquor, etc.	3.6	(1)	21.4	(6)	32.1	(9)	42.9	(12)	28
Total	20.1	(102)	30.1	(153)	22.2	(113)	27.6	(140)	508
Oldest sample									
None	32.4	(36)	21.6	(24)	23.4	(26)	22.5	(25)	111
Beer/wine	24.2	(36)	22.1	(33)	26.8	(40)	26.8	(40)	149
Tobacco	12.1	(15)	23.4	(29)	29.0	(36)	35.5	(44)	124
Liquor	4.0	(2)	22.0	(11)	38.0	(19)	36.0	(18)	50
Marijuana, etc.	0.0	(0)	1.4	(1)	18.1	(13)	80.6	(58)	72
Total	17.6	(89)	19.4	(98)	26.5	(134)	36.6	(185)	506

The results for the oldest sample show similar relationships between substance use and delinquency. In comparison with the middle sample, relatively more of the tobacco and beer/wine users were nondelinquent possibly because beer/wine and tobacco use was more normal at this age. More important, four out of five (80.6%) of the boys who had taken marijuana or other illegal drugs had also engaged in serious forms of delinquency.

Thus, the results indicate that boys' advancement on the substance use pathway is associated with increasingly more serious forms of delinquency, although tobacco and liquor use were similarly related to delinquency. However, it should be understood that these data do not address the extent that progression in substance use predated or followed boys' escalation in the seriousness of their delinquent acts.

How well does the observed relation between substance use and delinquency hold when both variables are dichotomized by identifying the worst quarter of substance users and the worst quarter of delinquents? Such dichotomization allows us to express the strength of the relationship more directly as an odds ratio for each sample. For substance use, the dichotomization for the youngest sample was between no use (418 boys) and beer/wine or tobacco use (85); for the middle sample between no use or beer/wine use (432) and tobacco use, liquor, or illegal drug use (76); and for the oldest sample between no use or wine, beer or tobacco use (384), and liquor or illegal drug use (122). In each case, the aim was to identify the worst quarter of substance users (approximately).

Table 6.4 shows the results of dichotomized substance use against dichotomized delinquency (i.e., in the youngest sample, nondelinquency and minor delinquency vs. moderate to serious delinquency; in the middle and oldest samples, nondelinquency, minor delinquency, and moderate delinquency vs. serious delinquency). The strongest relation between dichotomized substance use and delinquency was for the oldest sample (odds ratio = 9.2), compared with odds ratios of 3.4 and 2.2 for the youngest and middle samples, respectively. The majority of serious substance users in the oldest sample (62.3%) were serious delinquents. Because the cutoffs were different for each sample, conclusions about age trends in the strength of the association should be inferred with caution. However, substance use in the oldest sample (marijuana or other drug use) was more clearly linked to delinquency than substance use in the youngest and middle samples.

Is the relationship between substance use and delinquency also apparent from the juvenile court records? To what extent does substance use predict boys' petitions to the court? The results, presented in Table 6.5, show data for the middle and oldest samples only. As explained in chapter 5, it was rare for boys in the youngest sample to have been petitioned to the juvenile court (up to 1994) and for boys in the middle sample to have been petitioned up to the

TABLE 6.4
Dichotomized Substance Use Versus Dichotomized Delinquency

Dichotomized Values		Delinquency		% Delinquents	Odds Ratio
Youngest sample					3.4
		N	Y		$X^2 = 25.02$ ($p = .0001$)
	N	321	97	23.2	
Substance use	Y	42	43	50.6	
		Delinquency		% Delinquents	
Middle sample					2.2
		N	Y		$X^2 = 8.63$ ($p = .002$)
	N	324	108	25.0	
Substance use	Y	44	32	42.1	
		Delinquency		% Delinquents	
Oldest sample					9.2
		N	Y		$X^2 = 44.45$ ($p = .0001$)
	N	275	109	28.4	
Substance use	Y	46	76	62.3	

Note. N = No; Y = Yes.

TABLE 6.5
Substance Use Versus Juvenile Court Petitions

	Juvenile Court Petitions		
Substance Use	% Delinquency	% Index Offenses	% Drug Offenses
Middle sample after follow-up			
None	26.7	20.4	6.3
Beer/wine	32.0	25.0	7.8
Tobacco	26.7	17.8	4.4
Liquor, etc.	29.6	22.2	0.0
X^2	1.3	1.5	2.6
p	NS	NS	NS
Oldest sample up to follow-up			
None	7.8	5.8	—
Beer/wine	8.5	7.8	—
Tobacco	20.2	16.7	—
Liquor	9.1	4.5	—
Marijuana, etc.	19.7	16.7	—
X^2	13.6	12.5	—
p	.009	.014	—
Oldest sample after follow-up			
None	30.1	23.7	7.5
Beer/wine	32.8	21.6	13.7
Tobacco	37.9	27.6	3.5
Liquor	45.0	40.0	7.5
Marijuana, etc.	47.1	35.3	13.7
X^2	6.2	7.6	7.9
p	NS	NS	.095

Note. p values two-tailed. No boys were petitioned for drug offenses up to follow-up (the first assessment after screening). NS = Not applicable.

follow-up assessment. The prevalence of juvenile court petitions is shown for any delinquency (excluding minor offenses), index offenses, and drug offenses; no boys were petitioned for drug offenses up to the follow-up assessment.

There was no tendency for substance use in the middle sample to predict court petitions. Substance use in the oldest sample was significantly related to court petitions up to the folllow-up assessment; basically, tobacco, marijuana, and other drug use were related to a prior court record, but this was not true of beer, wine, or liquor use. There was a tendency for substance use in the oldest sample to predict court petitions up to age 18 (for delinquency and index offenses), but this tendency did not reach statistical significance. There was little tendency for substance use to predict court petitions for drug offenses, although the marijuana and other drug users at the follow-up assessment had a relatively high prevalence of court petitions for drug offenses. In summary, the worse boys' substance use, the worse their delinquency, especially for the oldest sample. Also, in the oldest sample, the higher the level of substance use, the higher the risk that the boys would be referred to the juvenile court in the next few years for either any offense or for an index offense. However, the data do not indicate the temporal, and possible causal order between substance use and delinquency.

THE EXPLANATION OF SUBSTANCE USE

Which explanatory factors best account for boys' substance use? Table 6.6 shows the results based on dichotomized explanatory variables and substance use. For comparison, the results for key explanatory variables as related to the full three- to five-category substance use scales are shown in the appendix to this chapter (Table A6.1; three, four, and five categories for the youngest, middle, and oldest samples, respectively).

We first discuss replicated findings in Table 6.6. Lack of guilt was a significant explanatory variable in the middle and the two oldest samples only (2.1 and 1.6, respectively) and the same applied to HIA problems (1.9 and 1.8, respectively). In comparison, old for grade, a high ADHD score, and low achievement (according to parent, boy, and teacher) were associated with substance use in all three samples (range: 1.5–2.8), but low achievement as evident from CAT scores was significant only in the youngest sample (1.8). Depressed mood was an explanatory variable in the youngest and middle samples (2.3 and 1.7, respectively). Of the remaining child variables, few friends, high anxiety, and low religiosity showed significant results in a single sample only (all 2.0 or lower).

Among the family variables, poor supervision was a significant explanatory variable in the youngest and oldest samples (1.7 and 2.3, respectively), whereas physical punishment was an explanatory variable in the middle and oldest samples (1.8 and 1.7, respectively). Of the remaining family variables, poor communication, no set time home, boy not involved, unhappy parents, and parent anxiety/depression were significant explanatory variables in one sample only (all 1.9 or lower).

Of the socioeconomic factors, low SES, unemployed mother, and poorly educated mother were explanatory factors for substance use in the youngest and middle samples (all 2.2 or lower), whereas family on welfare was an explanatory factor in the middle sample only (1.7). Ethnicity was of importance only in the youngest sample (1.6), and this also applied to bad neighborhood (1.7).

It might be argued that the results depend on the dichotomization of the data. For that reason, analyses were repeated with the full categorical substance use data, such as no use, beer or wine use, liquor use, and so on (see Table A6.1 in the appendix). The results are largely the same, indicating that most of the

TABLE 6.6
Odds Ratios for Explanatory Variables for Substance Use

	Sample		
Variable	Youngest	Middle	Oldest
Child			
Lack of guilt (PT)	1.5	2.1**	1.6*
Old for grade (P)	1.7*	2.2**	1.5*
HIA problems (PT)	1.3	1.9*	1.8*
High ADHD score (P)	1.6*	2.2**	1.7*
Low achievement (PBT)	1.6*	2.8*	1.8*
Low achievement (CAT)	1.8*	1.2	−1.4
Depressed mood (B)	2.3***	1.7*	1.5
Few friends (PB)	2.0**	1.3	1.3
Anxiety (PT)	1.1	1.8*	−1.1
Low religiosity (B)	1.3	1.6	1.8*
Family			
Poor supervision (PB)	1.7*	1.2	2.3***
Poor communication (PB)	—	2.5***	1.0
No set time home (PB)	1.0	1.2	2.0**
Physical punishment (PB)	1.4	1.8**	1.7*
Boy not involved (PB)	1.2	1.3	1.7*
Disagree on discipline (PB)	—	1.9*	1.2
Unhappy parents (P)	1.9*	1.2	1.0
Parent anxiety/depression (P)	1.2	1.3	1.6*
Macro			
Socioeconomic			
Low SES (P)	1.7*	2.2**	1.2
Family on welfare (P)	1.4	1.7*	1.2
Unemployed mother (P)	1.8*	1.9*	1.2
Poorly educated mother (P)	1.9*	1.7*	1.4
Demographic			
African American (P)	1.6*	−1.5	−1.3
Neighborhood			
Bad neighborhood (P)	1.7*	−1.6	1.2

Note. B = boy; C = census; CAT = California Achievement Test; P = parent; T = teacher.

* $p < .05$. ** $p < .01$. *** $p < .001$. **** $p < .0001$ (one-tailed), based on chi-square with correction for continuity. No significant relationship: low organizational participation, low jobs/chores involvement, shy/withdrawn, low reinforcement, boy not close to mother, high parental stress, parent substance use problems, father behavior problems, parent antisocial attitude, poor housing, unemployed father, large family, young mother, broken family, bad neighborhood (C). —, Variable not measured in this form, because boy was not considered old enough to respond to the relevant questions.

significant explanatory variables identified in the dichotomized analyses were similar to those identified in the categorical analyses.

It also might be argued that if one were to move the cutoff point for serious substance use in the dichotomized analyses, a different set of significant explanatory variables might ensue. To test this, we dichotomized the substance use in the oldest sample so that we could compare the 72 illegal drug users (i.e., mostly marijuana users) against legal substance users and nonusers as a group (434 boys). The results (not shown here) again indicate that most of the significant explanatory variables were identical to those identified with a broader cutoff as shown in Table 6.6.

It should be noted that odds ratios for the explanatory variables for substance use, as shown in Table 6.6, generally were lower than for the explanation of delinquency and never exceeded 2.8. There were no appreciable age effects in the magnitude of the odds ratios.

CORRELATES OF SUBSTANCE USE

The analyses so far excluded correlates of substance use. The association between dichotomized correlates and substance use in the three samples is summarized in Table 6.7. The results show that, as expected, the odds ratios for correlates are much higher than for the explanatory variables. Aside from risk status, several attitudinal variables were associated with substance use in all three samples—particularly a positive attitude to delinquency and a positive attitude to behavior problems. Remarkably, boys' positive attitude to substance use was not related to use in the youngest sample, but it was related to use in the middle and the oldest samples. There were also clear age trends. In three out of the four comparisons for attitudes, the odds ratio increased with age. For instance, the association between a positive attitude to problem behavior and substance use was 5.7 in the oldest sample, compared with 1.9 and 4.1 in the youngest and middle samples, respectively.

Of the behavior problems, running away was a correlate of substance use in all three samples, whereas nonphysical aggression, cruelty to people, and oppositional behavior were associated with substance use in two out of the three samples. Among the problems in school, the following variables were associated with substance use: truancy, low school motivation, and negative attitude to school in the two older samples. School suspension was a significant correlate in all three samples.

In the youngest and middle samples, a poor relationship with a parent was related to substance use, whereas in the middle and oldest samples, a poor relationship with siblings was related to substance use.

The results, shown in Table 6.7, confirm that peer influences are often closely linked to boys' substance use. Both peer delinquency and nonconven-

TABLE 6.7
Odds Ratios for Correlates of Substance Use

Correlate	Sample		
	Youngest	Middle	Oldest
Risk status			
High risk	2.5***	6.5****	6.2****
Attitude			
Positive attitude to delinquency (B)	2.0**	2.6***	2.1***
Positive attitude to problem behavior (B)	1.9**	4.1****	5.7****
Positive attitude to substance use (B)	1.4	2.3**	3.4****
Unlikely to be caught (B)	—	1.1	1.9**
Behavior			
Nonphysical aggression (PT)	1.5	2.8****	2.3****
Cruel to people (PT)	2.0**	1.7	2.8****
Oppositional behavior (P)	1.5	2.5***	2.0***
Runs away (PB)	2.3**	2.3***	2.3****
School			
Suspended (PB)	2.3**	2.4***	2.2***
Truant (PBT)	1.6	2.5***	6.0****
Low school motivation (T)	1.6	2.2**	3.0****
Negative attitude to school (B)	1.5	2.9****	2.4****
Family			
Discipline not persistent (PB)	—	1.1	1.7*
Poor relationship with parent (PB)	2.0**	2.0**	1.5
Poor relationship with siblings (PB)	1.1	2.1**	1.6*
Peers			
Poor relationship with peers (T)	1.8*	1.6	2.6****
Bad friends (PB)	1.1	1.7*	2.4***
Peer delinquency (B)	2.3***	3.0****	3.4****
Nonconventional peers (B)	2.1**	2.0**	2.2***
Peer substance use (B)	—	3.9****	7.4****
Exposed to drugs (B)	—	2.2**	4.3****

Note. B = boy; C = census; CAT = California Achievement Test; P = parent; T = teacher.
*$p < .05$. ** $p < .01$. *** $p < .001$. **** $p < .0001$. p values one-tailed based on chi-square with correction for continuity. No significant relationship: frequent injuries, countercontrol, Don't enjoy boy. —, Variable not measured in this form because boy was not considered old enough to respond to the relevant questions.

tional peers were related to substance use in all three samples, but a poor relationship with peers reached significance in the youngest and oldest samples only. Not surprisingly, peer substance use and exposure to drugs were strongly related to the boys' own substance use in the middle and oldest samples (these were not measured in the youngest sample), with the strongest relationship in the oldest sample.

The odds ratios for correlates of substance use tended to increase with age. In the youngest age group, the odds ratios for the strongest relationship did not exceed 2.5 (e.g., for high-risk status). They were higher for the middle sample (high-risk status 6.5, positive attitude to problem behavior 4.1, and peer substance use 3.9), but highest for the oldest sample (positive attitude to problem behavior 5.7, truant 6.0, and peer substance use 7.4). This suggests that, with age, substance use becomes more closely intertwined with these correlates or, alternatively, that the substance users in the oldest sample are more clearly deviant than those in the youngest sample.

In summary, the analyses of correlates show that many of the factors known from other studies were also associated with substance use in the current samples of boys and that there were major age trends in the correlates. Not surprisingly, the odds ratios for correlates of substance use tended to be higher than the odds ratios for explanatory variables.

REGRESSION ANALYSES

Returning to the explanatory variables, the next question is, which of these variables were independently predictive of substance use in a hierarchical multiple regression? The results of these analyses for the three samples are shown in Table 6.8. Overall, the multiple R's were modest (.253 for the youngest sample, .287 for the middle sample, and .280 for the oldest sample). In all three samples, low achievement featured as highly as ADHD score. Of the family factors, poor supervision contributed in the youngest and oldest samples, whereas poor communication and physical punishment contributed in the middle sample only.

In addition, several explanatory variables were predictive of early forms of substance use (in the youngest and middle samples only), including depressed mood, low SES, unemployed mother, and poorly educated mother. Other predictors of substance use in the middle and oldest samples were: lack of guilt, HIA problems, and physical punishment. It should be noted that the following variables were not predictive of substance use in any of the three samples: low organizational involvement, low jobs/chores involvement, shy/withdrawn, low reinforcement, not close to mother, mother's high stress, parent substance use, father behavior problems, parent antisocial attitude, poor housing, unemployed father, large family, young mother, broken family, and bad neighborhood.

DETECTING INTERACTION EFFECTS

As discussed in chapter 5, we focus on those interaction effects among explanatory variables that survived the multiple regression analyses, showing that the interactions were associated with substance use over and above the main effects of explanatory variables.

TABLE 6.8
Hierarchical Multiple Regression for Substance Use

Variable	Multiple R	F change	p
Youngest sample			
Child			
Depressed mood	.150	10.56	.0006
Few friends	.194	7.16	.004
Low achievement (CAT)	.210	3.01	.042
Old for grade	.221	2.26	.067
High ADHD score	.230	2.03	.077
Family			
Poor supervision	.244	3.08	.040
Macro			
Unemployed mother	.253	1.90	.084
Middle sample			
Child			
Low achievement (PBT)	.183	15.35	.0001
Lack of guilt	.209	4.66	.016
Old for grade	.222	2.62	.053
High ADHD score	.233	2.30	.065
Anxiety	.241	1.67	.098
Family			
Poor communication	.257	3.86	.025
Physical punishment	.265	1.84	.088
Macro			
Low SES	.278	3.07	.040
Unemployed mother	.287	2.02	.078
Oldest sample			
Child			
Low achievement (PBT)	.119	5.47	.010
Low religiosity	.165	5.03	.013
High ADHD score	.186	2.88	.045
Family			
Poor supervision	.231	7.29	.004
No set time home	.254	4.50	.017
Physical punishment	.266	2.42	.060
Parent anxiety/depression	.280	2.88	.045

Note. p values one-tailed. No other variables entered. All weightings positive.

Table 6.9 shows the only four significant interactions that were independently important, which is less than would be expected by chance alone. In
the youngest sample, there was an interaction between a high ADHD score and
an unemployed mother: 38.2% of the boys with both risk factors were substance
users, compared with less than 16% of the boys in the other groups. In the
middle sample, we found an interaction between lack of guilt and low SES,
indicating that only 8.2% of the boys possessing neither of these risk factors
engaged in substance use, compared with 20% or higher of the boys in the other
categories. A similar type of interaction was found between low achievement and
high anxiety. Finally, we also found an interaction between low achievement and old
for grade: The joint occurrence of both risk factors was associated with a much higher
prevalence of substance use (34.3%) than for boys in any of the other groups.

In summary, we found several interaction effects for substance use. However, because the total number of interactions was less than would be expected
by chance alone, the results should be interpreted with caution.

CUMULATIVE EFFECT OF RISK
FACTORS ON SUBSTANCE USE

The last question on substance use concerns how well a risk index, based on
the best explanatory variables (derived from the hierarchical multiple regres-

TABLE 6.9
Interaction Effects for Substance Use

| | | % Substance Use | | | | | | Regression | |
| | | B = No | | B = Yes | | | | | |
Variable A	Variable B	A = No	A = Yes	A = No	A = Yes	LRCS	p	F change	p
Youngest sample (16.9)									
High ADHD score	Unemployed mother	14.2	10.5	15.1	38.2	6.77	.009	10.55	.001
Middle sample (15.0)									
Lack of guilt	Low SES	8.2	23.6	28.8	22.0	7.91	.005	7.35	.007
Low achievement (PBT)	Anxiety	8.2	29.3	19.8	22.0	6.95	.008	4.67	.031
Low achievement (PBT)	Lack of guilt	8.4	28.1	22.0	24.5	5.49	.019	2.83	.093
Low achievement (PBT)	Old for grade	10.8	16.4	12.6	34.3	26.8	.102	4.61	.033
Oldest sample (24.1)									
(no significant interactions)									

Note. LRCS = Likelihood ratio chi-squared. p values two-tailed.

sion), is associated with substance use in the three samples. It should be kept in mind that the contents of each risk index differed for each of the samples, reflecting that partly different explanatory variables contributed to the results of the multiple regression analyses. Also, as before, the dichotomization of substance use, by necessity, varied across the samples.

Figure 6.1 shows that the risk of substance use in the youngest sample more than doubled between the presence of two and three risk factors (from 12.9% to 30.8%). In the middle sample, the percentage of boys engaging in substance use increased especially between two and three risk factors and peaked at 31.8% in the presence of four or more risk factors. Thus, the threshold of highest risk was reached with a lower number of risk factors in the youngest compared with the middle sample.

The risk pattern for the oldest sample differed in a significant manner from that in the two other samples, at least partly because of the higher prevalence of substance use in that sample. Figure 6.1 shows that, already in the presence of two risk factors, almost 30% of the boys engaged in substance use. Also, the percentage of boys using substances peaked at four or more risk factors (44.9%). Thus, almost half of the boys in the oldest sample had advanced to liquor, marijuana use, or hard drug use once they were exposed to four or more risk factors. However, the odds ratio for the comparison of the highest risk group and the remainder was lower in the oldest sample (3.1) than in the other two samples. It should also be noted that these odds ratios for substance use were much lower than for delinquency, showing that the measured variables explained delinquency better than substance use.

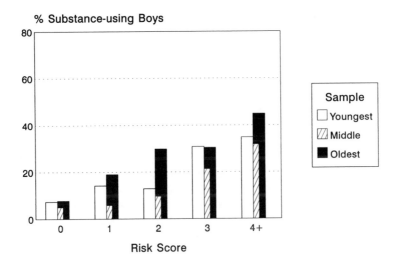

FIG. 6.1. Percentage of substance-using boys as a function of increasing risk score.

CONCLUSION

We briefly summarize and review the results in the context of findings from other studies.

Interrelation Among Different Forms of Substance Use

We found that, for the oldest sample, the magnitude of associations (as expressed by odds ratios) among different forms of substance use increased from tobacco and alcohol to drugs. This trend was contrary to trends in prevalence, which was lowest for the more serious substances and highest for the less serious substances. It is likely that, at the highest level of substance use, the other drug users in the oldest sample are multiply deviant boys who also use other substances. This may account for the high odds ratios for the relationships involving these other drug users. Another interpretation is that, as boys advance through the substance-use progression, the probability of boys' initiating the next step becomes more likely the further they are into the progression. However, only further longitudinal analyses can substantiate this.

For the youngest boys (ages 7–8), few of whom had yet progressed to serious levels of substance use, we found that the associations between beer and wine and between wine and tobacco were stronger than for the middle and oldest samples. This may indicate that, for the youngest boys, legal substance use of one type—even at a low level of seriousness—is strongly associated with legal substance use of another type and may represent a generalized form of deviance, which is less common among the boys in late childhood or early adolescence. We return to this theme when discussing the relationship between substance use and delinquency.

Substance Use and Delinquency

We confirmed that there is a relationship between substance use and delinquency, as found in many other studies (Bukstein et al., 1989; Collins, 1981; Huizinga et al., 1993; Loeber, 1988). In our study, we observed that, for all three samples, the different levels of substance use were related to the severity of delinquent acts. Thus, the results indicate that the further boys advance on the substance use progression the more serious their delinquency. However, the relationship between substance use and court petitions concerning delinquency was weaker than we expected.

Also relevant is whether the strength of association between substance use and delinquency is different with age. Simplistically, there are two lines of reasoning about the association. First, substance use and delinquency early in life are expressions of a strong deviant tendency; as the prevalence of substance use (and delinquency) in adolescence increases, the association between the two becomes weaker because of the emergence of less deviant substance users who are not necessarily involved in serious forms of delinquency (Loeber, 1985). This is indeed what was found by Wechsler and Thum (1973) in their study of junior and senior high school students.

Second, the association between substance use and delinquency increases in magnitude with age because more of the highly deviant youth that emerge over time engage in both behaviors. In the present study, using dichotomized measures, we found a substantially stronger relationship for the oldest sample (odds ratio = 9.2), compared with the youngest and middle samples, respectively (3.4 and 2.2, respectively). A word of caution, however, is in order because the measures of substance use and delinquency for the youngest sample only partly overlapped with those for the two older samples. However, the comparison between the middle and oldest samples was more straightforward and clearly indicates that the strength of relationship between substance use and delinquency in middle adolescence was higher than for late childhood.

This is not to say that we should discount substance use at an early age. First, we showed that, during the elementary school years, the use of one legal substance was associated with the use of other legal substances. Also, we know from other studies that early initiation into any drug use increases the likelihood of subsequent involvement in conduct problems and delinquent acts (Brunswick & Boyle, 1979; O'Donnell & Clayton, 1979).

Explanation of Substance Use

Our results show that child, family, socioeconomic, demographic, and neighborhood variables in univariate analyses all contributed to the explanation of substance use. Overall, however, the strength of relationships with substance use was lower than for delinquency, although the same sets of variables were considered.

Of the child variables that we measured, depressed mood was significantly related to substance use. This agrees with a finding from the Dunedin longitudinal study, showing that depressive symptoms predicted multiple drug use over a 4-year period (Henry et al., 1993). Also, we found that a high ADHD score and low achievement (according to parent, boy, and teacher) were associated with substance use in all three samples—an association that is also known from other studies (e.g., Bukstein et al., 1989; Wilens, Biederman, Spencer, & Frances, 1994). Also, research shows that ADHD or ADD predicts later substance use (Gittelman et al., 1985; Hechtman, Weiss, Perlman, & Amsel, 1984; Klinteberg et al., 1993). The crucial question is whether ADHD predicts substance use once conduct problems are taken into account. For example, in the Christchurch Health and Development Study, Fergusson (1993) found that early attention deficit behaviors did not predict later marijuana use once the association between attention deficit and conduct disorder was partialed out. Likewise, Boyle et al., (1992) found that conduct problems contributed to later marijuana or other hard drug use independently from attention deficit and emotional disorders (Boyle et al., 1992). This agrees with the finding by Alterman and Tarter (1986), who found that conduct disorder rather than hyperactivity places an individual at risk for alcoholism. However, we consider that it is plausible that several processes co-occur in at-risk populations: (a) conduct problems (without ADHD) are associated with increased risk for substance use by juveniles, but (b) the presence of ADHD is associated with an increased comorbidity of disruptive behavior and substance use during childhood or adolescence.

Turning to parental behaviors, we found that parental substance use problems were not related to the juvenile's substance use in any of the three samples. In contrast, Dishion and Loeber (1985) found that the mother's alcohol use (but not the father's alcohol use) was related to the son's marijuana use. Our results are surprising.

However, several of the results in the present study agree with findings reported elsewhere. For example, of the parenting factors, lack of supervision was important in the multivariate analyses, which was a replication of an earlier finding on an Oregon sample of boys (Dishion & Loeber, 1985). We also found that physical punishment was an explanatory variable in the two older samples. Not surprisingly, low SES, unemployed mother and poorly educated mother were all related to substance use in the offspring (in two out of the three samples). However, we did not expect to find that boys' substance use at an early age would be related to bad neighborhood. This may mean that elementary school-age boys living in disadvantaged neighborhoods are especially at risk to start using substances at a young age.

Finally, we found that several factors were not related to substance use in any of the three samples. Contrary to what community activists might think, boys' low involvement in organizations was not related to substance use, or their involvement in jobs or chores. Also, several demographic factors were not related, including poor housing, living in a large family, having a young mother, and a broken family. This indicates that boys' substance use is not necessarily associated with disadvantage at the family level, but that it can occur in families living in any type of housing, in families of any composition, and with mothers of any age group.

Overall, child factors such as depressed mood (in the youngest sample) and low achievement (in all three samples) were the most important explanatory factors for substance use. Poor parental supervision and poor parent–child communication were also important, but macrofactors were relatively unimportant.

APPENDIX

The following table shows the relationship between the key variables and the full three- to five-category substance use scale.

TABLE A6.1
Dichotomized Explanatory Variables Versus Substance Use Scales

Variable	None (N = 418)	Beer/Wine (N = 47)	Tobacco, etc. (N = 38)	Total	p
	Substance Use (%)				
Youngest sample					
Child					
Lack of guilt	20.5	26.7	30.6	21.9	ns
Old for grade	21.3	25.5	39.5	23.1	.035
HIA problems	16.3	17.0	23.7	16.9	ns
High ADHD score	23.9	31.9	36.8	25.6	ns
Low achievement (PBT)	23.0	31.9	34.2	24.7	ns
Depressed mood	20.7	31.9	44.7	23.6	.001
Family					
Poor supervision	22.3	30.4	36.8	24.3	.081
Physical punishment	17.6	14.9	32.4	18.5	.068
Macro					
Socioeconomic					
Low SES	26.1	45.7	28.9	28.1	.020
Family on welfare	49.0	59.1	56.8	50.5	ns
Demographic					
African American	55.7	74.5	57.9	57.7	.048
Parent nonbiological	60.2	73.9	65.7	61.9	ns
Neighborhood					
Bad neighborhood (C)	27.2	39.0	32.4	28.7	ns
Bad neighborhood (P)	24.3	40.4	28.9	26.1	.053

Variable	None (N = 302)	Beer/Wine (N = 130)	Tobacco (N = 48)	Liquor, etc. (N = 28)	Total	p
Middle sample						
Child						
Lack of guilt	25.5	30.4	44.4	41.7	29.5	.035
Old for grade	27.2	30.8	47.9	42.9	30.9	.016
HIA problems	15.6	20.0	22.9	35.7	18.5	.045
High ADHD score	21.9	20.8	37.5	39.3	24.0	.020
Low achievement (PBT)	21.9	20.0	45.8	39.3	24.6	.0005
Depressed mood	17.1	30.8	35.4	25.0	22.8	.002
Family						
Poor supervision	27.6	26.4	27.1	39.3	27.9	ns
Poor communication	19.5	26.9	39.6	42.9	24.6	.001
Physical punishment	32.1	38.5	50.0	46.4	36.3	.053

Middle Sample cont.	None (N = 302)	Beer/Wine (N = 130)	Tobacco (N = 48)	Liquor, etc. (N = 28)	Total	p
Macro						
Socioeconomic						
Low SES	21.7	23.3	41.7	32.1	24.6	.020
Family on welfare	43.2	36.6	56.8	51.9	43.2	.096
Demographic						
African American	59.9	51.5	54.2	35.7	55.9	.053
Parent nonbiological	60.8	57.1	70.8	60.7	60.8	ns
Neighborhood						
Bad neighborhood (C)	28.1	25.6	20.8	11.1	25.8	ns
Bad neighborhood (P)	26.9	21.5	20.8	10.7	24.1	ns

	None N = 101)	Beer/Wine (N = 158)	Tobacco (N = 122)	Liquor (N = 53)	Marijuana, etc. (N = 72)	Total	p
Oldest sample							
Child Variables							
Lack of guilt	23.5	23.5	20.4	35.9	29.0	24.6	ns
Old for grade	42.3	37.6	36.3	32.0	59.7	40.9	.007
HIA problems	13.5	16.1	18.5	26.0	25.0	18.4	ns
High ADHD score	14.4	22.8	23.4	36.0	27.8	23.1	.036
Low achievement (PBT)	20.7	22.8	21.0	26.0	38.9	24.5	.040
Depressed mood	18.0	17.4	28.5	22.0	33.3	23.0	.032
Family							
Poor supervision	14.5	23.6	26.2	30.6	44.9	25.9	.0003
Poor communication	20.9	26.0	27.3	24.0	26.8	25.1	ns
Physical punishment	17.1	15.8	20.5	24.0	29.0	19.9	ns
Macro							
Socioeconomic							
Low SES	31.5	24.3	24.8	24.0	33.3	27.3	ns
Family on welfare	42.9	38.9	31.9	34.7	47.7	38.8	ns
Demographics							
African American	69.4	65.8	41.9	44.0	58.3	57.5	.0001
Parent nonbiological	62.7	68.5	70.6	57.1	74.6	67.4	ns
Neighborhood							
Bad neighborhood (C)	33.3	31.5	24.2	15.6	37.9	29.4	.059
Bad neighborhood (P)	21.8	31.1	19.0	18.4	34.3	25.3	.039

Note. p values two-tailed based on chi-square. PBT = parent, boy, teacher measure; P = parent measure; C = census measure.

7

Explanatory Factors for Sexual Intercourse

Sexual intercourse is of concern in this volume for several reasons. First, sexual intercourse by juveniles can be considered an adult type of behavior, which is age-inappropriate to some extent. Second, boys' sexual intercourse can be viewed as a risk-taking behavior; there is the risk of contracting sexually transmitted diseases and the risk of impregnating female partners. Third, sexual intercourse by adolescents can be viewed as another problem behavior, but without the criminal victimization that is often associated with conduct problems.

This chapter focuses on sexual intercourse in the oldest sample; boys in the other samples were considered too young to be asked questions about their sexual behavior. Chapter 4 reviewed the prevalence of boys' sexual intercourse. For reasons explained later, we examine ethnic differences in the age of first intercourse, frequency of intercourse, and number of sexual partners. We then examine the relationship among sexual intercourse, delinquency and substance use. Next, we show which explanatory variables are related to sexual intercourse and which of these variables are independently related to sexual intercourse in a regression analysis. Finally, we address how far a risk index correctly identifies those boys who have had intercourse.

MEASUREMENT OF SEXUAL INTERCOURSE

For the outcomes discussed in chapters 5 and 6, African-American ethnicity was not a strong explanatory factor, this was not the case for sexual intercourse.

In the oldest sample, 44.2% of the boys had experienced heterosexual intercourse at follow-up, when they were, on average, 13.2 years old. (The prevalence of homosexual intercourse was too low for analyses.) Preliminary
analyses showed that there were large differences between White and African-
American boys; 62.8% of African-American boys had experienced sexual
intercourse, compared with 19.2% of White boys—a highly significant difference (X^2 = 93.2, p < .0001, odds ratio = 7.1).

Table 7.1 shows the relationship among age, sexual intercourse, and ethnicity. It should be noted that, on average, African Americans tended to be older
than Whites, because more of them had been held back to complete a grade and
hence were age-inappropriate in the seventh grade. Table 7.1 shows that 145
(50.3%) of African Americans were age 14 or older, compared with 60 (28%)
of Whites (X^2 = 24.4, p <.001). This raises the issue of how much of the
African-American/White difference in the prevalence of sexual intercourse is
due to the African Americans being older. However, Table 7.1 shows that the
African-American/White difference in the prevalence of sexual intercourse is
seen at all ages, with odds ratios ranging from 5.4 to 8.9. Indeed, this difference
is greater for the younger boys than for the older, age-inappropriate boys.

Prevalence figures only tell part of the story. How frequently did the boys engage
in sexual intercourse and were there also ethnic differences in this respect? Table
7.2 provides information about the number of times boys had intercourse in the last
6 months. Among the sexually experienced boys, there was little difference
between African-American and White boys in the number of times they had sexual
intercourse in the last 6 months (e.g., 24% of active boys in each ethnic group had
sexual intercourse five or more times in that period).

It can be argued from a public health point of view that the critical factor is
the number of sexual partners among the sexually active boys. Table 7.3
addresses this issue and again shows little difference between African-American and White boys in the number of sexual partners in the last 6 months given
that they have had sexual intercourse (e.g., 9.8% of the active White boys had
four or more partners, compared with 12.2% of the active African-American
boys). Of course, the frequency of intercourse in the last 6 months tended to

TABLE 7.1
Sexual Intercourse by Age and Ethnicity (Oldest Sample)

Age	% Had Intercourse (N)		Odds Ratio
	White	African American	
13.00 or less	6.3 (48)	37.2 (43)	8.9
13.01–13.50	15.0 (60)	58.3 (48)	7.9
13.51–13.99	17.4 (46)	55.8 (52)	6.0
14.00 or more	35.0 (60)	74.5 (145)	5.4
Total	19.2 (214)	62.8 (288)	7.1

TABLE 7.2
Frequency of Sexual Intercourse by Ethnicity (Oldest Sample)

Variable	White		African American	
	N	(%)	N	(%)
Never had sexual intercourse	173		107	
Times in last 6 months				
0	13	(31.7)	38	(21.3)
1	9	(22.0)	33	(18.5)
2	3	(7.3)	36	(20.2)
3–4	6	(14.6)	28	(15.7)
5+	10	(24.4)	43	(24.2)
Had sexual intercourse	41		178	

Note. Excludes cases with no data on number of times in last 6 months.

TABLE 7.3
Number of Sexual Partners by Ethnicity (Oldest Sample)

Variable	White		African American	
	N	(%)	N	(%)
Never had sexual intercourse	173		107	
0 13 (31.7) 38 (21.1)				
Number of partners in last 6 months				
1	15	(36.6)	73	(40.6)
2	5	(12.2)	27	(15.0)
3	4	(9.8)	20	(11.1)
4+	4	(98)	22	(122)
Had sexual intercourse	41		180	

Note. Excludes cases with no data on number of sexual partners in last 6 months.

correlate with the number of partners in the last 6 months. In summary, ethnic differences in sexual intercourse concerned prevalence rather than the frequency of intercourse or the number of sexual partners. Subsequent analyses in this chapter focus on prevalence.

SEXUAL INTERCOURSE, DELINQUENCY, AND SUBSTANCE USE

How is sexual intercourse related to delinquency? The answer to this is shown in Fig. 7.1. Fewer than 30% of boys who had remained nondelinquent or

% INTERCOURSE

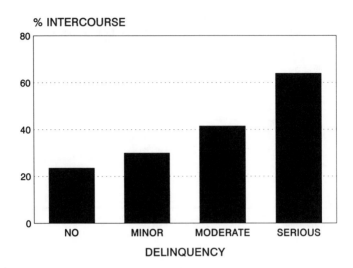

FIG. 7.1. Relationship between sexual intercourse and delinquency (oldest sample).

committed only minor delinquency had experienced sexual intercourse (23.5% and 29.9%, respectively). However, this proportion increased to 41.4% for the moderately delinquent boys and further increased to 63.9% for the seriously delinquent boys. Thus, sexual intercourse was clearly related to the severity of delinquency. The odds ratio linking serious delinquency and sexual intercourse was 3.6 ($X^2 = 44.1, p < .0001$).

Figure 7.2 shows the relationship between sexual intercourse and substance use. The percentage who had had sexual intercourse for boys at several levels of minor substance use, such as beer or wine, smoking, and liquor use, was similar to the percentage in the whole sample. However, 62.5% of the boys who had used marijuana or other drugs also had experienced intercourse. The odds ratio for the comparison of sexual intercourse and marijuana or other drug use was 1.8 ($X^2 = 8.06, p = .003$). When comparing substance use and delinquency in their relation to sexual intercourse, almost two thirds of those at the highest level of either substance use or delinquency also had engaged in sexual intercourse at follow-up.

Sexual intercourse was also related to juvenile court petitions. Table 7.4 shows that only 7.4% of the boys who had not had sexual intercourse had been petitioned to the juvenile court for delinquency up to the follow-up Assessment compared with 18.9% of those who had had sexual intercourse—a highly significant difference ($p < .0002$). Similarly, excluding boys with prior petitions, 26.7% of boys who had not had sexual intercourse were petitioned for delinquency after the follow-up Assessment compared with 50% of boys who had had sexual intercourse ($p < .0001$).

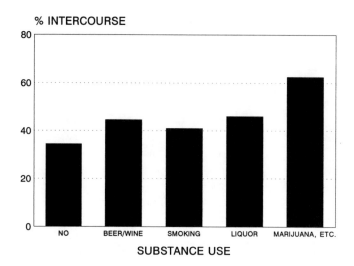

% INTERCOURSE

FIG. 7.2. Relationship between sexual intercourse and substance abuse (oldest sample).

TABLE 7.4
Sexual Intercourse Versus Juvenile Court Petitions (Oldest Sample)

| | Had Sexual Intercourse | | | |
Variable	No	Yes	X^2	p
% Petitions up to follow-up				
Delinquency	7.4	18.9	14.0	.0002
Index offense	4.7	17.0	19.2	.0001
Index violence	1.6	5.3	5.3	.022
Index property	3.1	14.6	20.0	.0001
% Petitions after follow-up				
Delinquency	26.7	50.0	22.4	.0001
Index offense	20.7	35.8	11.1	.0009
Index violence	9.9	18.1	5.5	.018
Index property	16.8	29.6	9.1	.003
Drugs	4.7	16.3	14.7	.0001

Note: p values two-tailed.

In view of the difference between African-American and White boys in the prevalence of sexual intercourse, Table 7.5 shows how far sexual intercourse was related to court referrals after controlling for ethnicity. Generally, the relationships were attenuated but still present. For example, among White boys, 44.4% of those who had had sexual intercourse were petitioned to the court for delinquency in the future, compared with 22.6% of other boys.

TABLE 7.5
Sexual Intercourse Versus Juvenile Court Petitions, Controlling for Ethnicity (Oldest Sample)

	Had Sexual Intercourse			
Variable	No	Yes	x^2	p
% Petitions up to A				
Delinquency (W)	6.2	23.7	10.9	.001
(AA)	9.3	17.9	3.6	.058
Index offenses (W)	4.3	21.1	12.3	.0005
(AA)	5.2	16.1	6.9	.009
% Petitions after A				
Delinquency (W)	22.6	44.4	5.6	.017
(AA)	33.7	51.1	6.4	.011
Index Offenses (W)	15.8	33.3	4.7	.031
(AA)	29.1	36.3	1.2	NS

Note. W = White, AA = African American. *p* values two-tailed. NS = Nonsignificant.

Among African-American boys, 51.1% of those who had had sexual intercourse were petitioned to the court for delinquency in the future, compared with 33.7% of other boys.

In summary, sexual intercourse was common among boys who engaged in serious delinquency or illegal drug use. Sexual intercourse was related to petitions to the juvenile court in the past and was predictive of court petitions in the next 4 years.

THE EXPLANATION OF SEXUAL INTERCOURSE

Which explanatory variables were especially related to sexual intercourse? Table 7.6 shows that those boys in the oldest sample who had had sexual intercourse displayed lack of guilt (odds ratio = 2.1), tended to be old for their grade (3.7), had HIA problems (1.8), had low academic achievement (about 2), and experienced depressed mood (1.5). In terms of family interactions, poor supervision and the boy not being involved with the family increased the risk of sexual intercourse by a factor of about 2. Of the remaining risk factors, the following were the strongest: family on welfare (3.3), African-American ethnicity (7.1), broken family (3.9), and bad neighborhood (4.0).

In summary, leaving aside ethnicity, the strongest explanatory factors were family on welfare, broken family, and bad neighborhood. However, it is clear that child and family variables (such as lack of supervision) were also associated with boys' sexual intercourse.

THE CORRELATES OF SEXUAL INTERCOURSE

Table 7.7 summarizes the correlates of sexual intercourse. As might be expected, risk status increased the chance of sexual intercourse by a factor of about 2. Several attitudinal variables, including a positive attitude to problem behavior and substance use, increased the chance of boys' intercourse. Of all the problem behaviors, only cruel to people was associated with an increased risk of intercourse. However, several school-related problems, such as being

TABLE 7.6
Odds Ratios for Explanatory Variables for Sexual Intercourse (Oldest Sample)

Variable	Sexual Intercourse
Child	
Lack of guilt (PT)	2.1***
Old for grade (P)	3.7****
HIA problems (PT)	1.8**
Low achievement (PBT)	1.8**
Low achievement (CAT)	2.1***
Depressed mood (B)	1.5*
Family	
Poor supervision (PB)	2.3****
Boy not involved (PB)	1.8**
Macro	
Socioeconomic	
Low SES (P)	1.8**
Family on welfare (P)	3.3***
Small house (P)	1.8**
Unemployed father (P)	1.9*
Poorly educated mother (P)	2.1***
Demographic	
African American (P)	7.1****
Young mother (P)	1.7**
Broken family	3.9****
Neighborhood	
Bad neighborhood (C)	4.0****
Bad neighborhood (P)	1.9**

Note. B = boy; C = census; CAT = California Achievement Test; P = parent; T = teacher. * $p < .05$. ** $p < .01$. *** $p < .001$. **** $p < .0001$. p values one-tailed based on chi-square with correction for continuity. No significant relationship: ADHD score, anxiety, shy/withdrawn, few friends, low organizational participation, low jobs/chores involvement, low religiosity, poor communication, no set time home, low reinforcement, physical punishment, disagree on discipline, unhappy parents, boy not close to mother, high parental stress, parent antisocial attitude, parent substance use problems, parent anxiety/depression, father behavior problems, poor housing, unemployed mother, and large family.

TABLE 7.7
Odds Ratios for Correlates of Sexual Intercourse (Oldest Sample)

Correlate	Sexual Intercourse
Risk status	
High risk	1.9***
Attitude	
Positive attitude delinquency (B)	2.8****
Positive attitude problem behavior (B)	2.3****
Positive attitude substance use (B)	1.9**
Unlikely to be caught (B)	2.7****
Behavior	
Cruel to people (PT)	2.1***
School	
Suspended (PB)	3.8****
Truant (PBT)	3.1****
Low school motivation (T)	2.4****
Peers	
Bad friends (PB)	1.6*
Peer delinquency (B)	4.4****
Peer substance use (B)	3.2****
Exposed to drugs (B)	2.9****

Note. B = boy; C = census; P = parent; T = teacher. * $p < .05$. ** $p < .01$. *** $p < .001$. **** $p < .0001$. p values one-tailed based on chi-square with correction for continuity.

suspended, truant, and low school motivation, increased the risk of intercourse, with suspended being associated with the highest risk (3.8). Finally, Table 7.7 shows that several peer factors were related to boys' sexual intercourse, including bad friends (1.6), peer delinquency (4.4), peer substance use (3.2), and exposure to drugs (2.9).

Many variables were not related to boys' sexual intercourse in any of the three samples: high ADHD score, anxiety, shy/withdrawn, few friends, low organizational participation, low jobs/chores involvement, low religiosity, poor communication, no set time home, low reinforcement, physical punishment, disagree on discipline, unhappy parents, boy not close to mother, high parental stress, parent antisocial attitude, parent substance use problems, parent anxiety/depression, father behavior problems, poor housing, unemployed mother, and large family. Thus, most of the family factors were not related to sexual intercourse and neither were forms of parental pathology.

In summary, sexual intercourse is associated with boys' positive attitudes to problem behavior, delinquency, and substance use, and with boys' association with peers engaging in such behaviors. Cruelty to people was the only correlate among the behavior problems outside of school associated with intercourse at this age.

REGRESSION ANALYSES

To return to the explanatory variables, which of these were independently related to sexual intercourse in a hierarchical multivariate analysis? The top portion of Table 7.8 shows that the multiple R was .515 for explaining sexual intercourse in the oldest sample. Of the child variables, old for grade and lack of guilt were the only variables that predicted sexual intercourse; these were followed by poor supervision and several other variables, including African American, family on welfare, and broken family.

Because ethnicity came into the analyses, we repeated the multivariate analyses with ethnicity entered last so that we could examine whether ethnicity predicted sexual intercourse after controlling for all other important variables. The results of these analyses are shown in the bottom portion of Table 7.8. The same child and parent variables entered into the equation, of course, but the pattern of the remaining variables changed: Bad neighborhood now entered first, followed by broken family and family on welfare. However,

TABLE 7.8
Hierarchical Multiple Regression for Sexual Intercourse (Oldest Sample)

Variable	Multiple R	F change	p
Child			
Old for grade	.313	47.96	.0001
Lack of guilt	.330	5.59	.009
Family			
Poor supervision	.345	4.99	.013
Macro			
African American	.500	72.33	.0001
Family on welfare	.510	5.09	.012
Broken family	.515	3.24	.036
Alternative analyses with ethnicity entered last			
Child			
Old for grade	.313	47.96	.0001
Lack of guilt	.330	5.59	.009
Family			
Poor supervision	.345	4.99	.013
Macro			
Bad neighborhood (C)	.427	31.95	.0001
Broken family	.457	13.59	.0002
Family on welfare	.465	4.05	.022
African American	.520	30.18	.0001

Note: p values one-tailed. No other variables entered. All weightings positive.

African-American ethnic status was still predictive of sexual intercourse independently of all other variables.

In summary, African-American ethnicity was a significant predictor in the multivariate analyses even when it was entered last. Hence we have not been able to identify the variables that mediated the link between ethnicity and sexual intercourse. Possibly, more is known about the risk factors for delinquency than about risk factors for sexual intercourse. Of the remaining significant explanatory child variables, the most important ones were older age (reflecting low attainment) and lack of guilt. Other significant predictors included poor supervision, which probably facilitated boys' freedom to have intercourse, and disadvantaged family circumstances, such as a bad neighborhood, the family being on welfare, and a broken family.

INTERACTION EFFECTS

We found only one significant interaction effect—between lack of guilt and ethnicity (LRCS = 11.07, p = .0009). Among the White boys, 10.9% who felt guilt had sexual intercourse, compared with 42.1% of the boys who lacked guilt. Among the African-American boys, similar percentages of boys had sexual intercourse irrespective of the presence or absence of guilt (61.5% and 63.4%, respectively). The interaction effect was still significant in the multiple regression analysis (F change = 9.42, p = .0002), indicating that this interaction was associated with sexual intercourse over and above the main effects. Thus, guilt feelings were associated with a lower prevalence of intercourse among White boys but not among African-American boys. Guilt seemed to have an internal inhibition effect for White boys but not for African-American boys.

CUMULATIVE EFFECT OF RISK
FACTORS ON SEXUAL
INTERCOURSE

If one were to make a risk score based on the most powerful explanatory variables, what percentage of the sample would be correctly identified as having had sexual intercourse? Figure 7.3 shows that the percentage of boys who had engaged in sexual intercourse increased with the number of risk factors, but increments were greater at the low compared with the high end of the risk scale. Four-fifths (78.1%) of those boys with five or more risk factors experienced

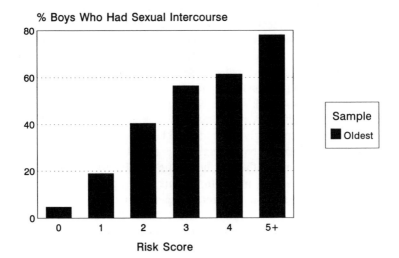

FIG. 7.3. Percent boys who had intercourse as a function of increasing risk score (oldest sample).

intercourse, compared with 4.7% of the boys with none of the risk factors. However, the odds ratio for sexual intercourse, comparing the high-risk boys with the remainder, was only 5.7—less than the odds ratio for the single variable of ethnicity (7.1).

CONCLUSION

As in other studies (e.g., Costa, Jessor, Donovan, & Fortenberry, 1995; Zelnik & Shah, 1983), we found that African-American boys were more sexually active than White boys. In our study, the prevalence of sexual intercourse by age 13 was 15% to 17% for White boys and 56% to 58% for African-American boys. For each ethnic group, these findings are substantially higher than the respective prevalence rates of 6.8% and 30.4% reported by Mott and Haurin (1988) for 1983–1984, but lower than the inner city African Americans studied by Clark, Zabin, and Hardy (1984), 81.3% of whom had experienced intercourse by age 14.

We found no significant ethnic differences in the frequency of sexual intercourse or the number of sexual partners. Thus, the only major difference found was that more African-American boys had experienced sexual intercourse more than White boys.

We also saw that sexual intercourse in the age range studied was related to both delinquency and substance use. Although this was known from other studies (e.g., Donovan, Jessor, & Costa, 1988; Jessor & Jessor, 1977), we demonstrated that the more serious the delinquency or substance use, the higher the likelihood that boys had engaged in sexual intercourse. Sexual intercourse was also predictive of petitions to the juvenile court for a delinquent act.

We found that several risk factors were associated with sexual intercourse, especially lack of guilt, HIA problems, low academic achievement, and depressed mood. Not surprisingly, the older the boy was for his grade, the higher was his likelihood of having had sexual intercourse. In terms of family interactions, poor supervision and the boy not being involved with the family also increased the risk of sexual intercourse. This is in agreement with findings reported in other studies that poor parental supervision is related to early sexual behavior (Biglan et al., 1990; Miller, McCoy, Olson, & Wallace, 1986).

In the present study, we also found that additional risk factors were: family on welfare, African-American ethnicity, broken family, and bad neighborhood. Multivariate analyses showed that, of these risk factors, the following were independently important: old for grade, lack of guilt, poor supervision, African-American ethnicity, family on welfare, and broken family. Even when African-American ethnicity was entered last, this variable was important in the multivariate analyses. In fact, for all outcomes considered in this book (delinquency, substance use, sexual intercourse, ADHD score, conduct problems, physical aggression, depressed mood, and shy/withdrawn behavior), ethnicity was a significant contributor only to the multivariate explanation of sexual intercourse.

Several of the risk factors identified in this study are also known from other studies, including a broken family and bad neighborhood (see the review by Miller & Dyk, 1993). In contrast to other studies, we did not find that low religiosity, a young mother, or poor family communication (although not necessarily referring to talk about sexual matters) were related to boys' sexual intercourse. Also, we did not find that any of the measures of parental pathology—as expressed in parent substance use problems, father behavior problems, parent antisocial attitude, or parent anxiety/depression—were related to boys' sexual intercourse. Our results stress the role of parents' poor supervision and the lack of involvement of the boy in family activities as risk factors for boys' sexual intercourse.

It should be noted that hormonal factors, although not measured in this study, play a role in the emergence of sexual behaviors. However, as Udry (1988) has shown, hormonal factors do not sufficiently explain sexual intercourse: It is the interaction between hormonal and social factors that appears to be important.

Finally, we demonstrated the cumulative effect of risk factors on the likelihood of the boys' having sexual intercourse. The results show that, even with as few as two or three risk factors present, the risk of sexual intercourse increased substantially.

Elsewhere we have shown (Stouthamer-Loeber & Wei, in press) the potentially hazardous nature of sexual intercourse in the oldest sample at the eighth follow-up assessment in terms of the relatively low rate of condom use in this population of boys about 40% did not protect themselves from impregnating a female. By ages 18 to 19, 18.5% of these boys had impregnated a girl and 12.3% were fathers. Thus, by their sexual activity, the boys not only influenced their own future, but that of their sexual partners and offspring as well.

8

Explanatory Factors for
Attention Deficit/Hyperactivity
and Conduct Problems

Of all the psychiatric syndromes, attention deficit hyperactivity disorder (ADHD) and conduct disorder (CD) are the most closely related to delinquency. We discuss these two syndromes in this chapter (followed by physical aggression and covert behaviors in chap. 9 and depressed mood and shy/withdrawn behavior in chap. 10). Therefore, the later chapters in this volume concern the mental health aspects of disruptive child behaviors. ADHD score, depressed mood, and shy/withdrawn behavior were considered earlier as explanatory variables, but they are treated as outcome variables in these chapters.

Typically, the symptoms of CD "result in the violation of the basic rights of others and major age-appropriate societal norms or rules" (American Psychiatric Association, 1994). CD has much in common with delinquency, but it includes behaviors harmful to others, irrespective of whether they are illegal. Conduct problems as defined in this chapter conform with the *DSM–III–R* definition of the symptoms of CD. In contrast, delinquency, as defined in chapter 3, is a subset of conduct problems.

The second set of problems considered in this chapter are the symptoms of ADHD, consisting of a constellation of symptoms of hyperactivity, impulsive behaviors, and attention deficit. An example of hyperactive behavior is when youth have difficulty sitting still or fidget excessively. An example of impulsive behavior is when youth shift excessively from one activity to another. Further, an example of attention deficit is when youth are easily distracted.

Thus, attention deficit, impulsiveness and hyperactive behavior are conceptually independent from delinquent acts.

The Gluecks (Glueck & Glueck, 1943) were probably the earliest researchers who pointed out that hyperactivity might play a role in the development of delinquency. This may be because hyperactive children do not give sufficient consideration to the possible consequences of their behavior. Much of our knowledge about hyperactivity and associated attention deficit comes from psychiatric rather than criminological studies. Several studies have suggested that CD is more severe and persistent when children also score high on an index of attention-deficit and hyperactivity (Abikoff & Klein, 1992; August & Stewart, 1982; Cantwell & Baker, 1992; Hechtman et al., 1984; Magnusson, 1988; Offord, Sullivan, Allen, & Abrams, 1979; Schachar, Rutter, & Smith, 1981; but for an exception, see Forehand, Wierson, Frame, Kempton, & Armistead, 1991). In reviewing the literature, Hinshaw, Lahey, and Hart (1993) concluded that children with CD and comorbid ADHD (a) have an earlier age of onset of CD, (b) exhibit more physical aggression, and (c) exhibit more persistent CD than other children with CD.

However, as indicated in our review in chapter 4, attention-deficit/hyperactivity and conduct problems are believed to be distinct disorders. For example, Farrington, Loeber, and Van Kammen (1990) reported that ratings of hyperactivity/impulsivity/attention deficit (HIA) and conduct problems in childhood both independently predicted chronic adult offending, with HIA being the better predictor of an early onset of convictions. More recently, Loeber, Green, Keenan, and Lahey (1995) confirmed that ADHD is predictive of an early onset of CD. Mannuzza, Klein, Konig, and Giampino (1989) and Mannuzza, Klein, Bessler, Malloy, and LaPadula (1993) reported that clinic-referred children with hyperactivity who do not exhibit CD at the time of referral are, nevertheless, at increased risk for the development of either CD during late adolescence or antisocial personality disorder (APD) in early adulthood. These findings suggest that ADHD *alone* may be a precursor to APD, again indicating the distinctiveness of ADHD and conduct disorder.

In addition, Loeber (Loeber, 1988; Loeber, Stouthamer-Loeber, & Green, 1991) and Moffitt (1993) have drawn attention to the fact that many of the inattentive, hyperactive youth who are also criminal experienced an early onset of problem behaviors—often as early as the preschool years. An important issue is whether explanatory variables for attention-deficit/hyperactivity are the same as those for conduct problems. This is not always easy to determine because attention deficit, hyperactivity and conduct problems often co-occur in the same boys and, as a consequence, are fairly highly correlated.

This chapter first reports the relationship between ADHD and conduct problems symptom scores and diagnoses. Then it shows the interrelation among attention-deficit/hyperactivity, conduct problems, and other problem behaviors. It then examines explanatory variables and correlates of a high ADHD score and conduct problems. Then it shows which explanatory variables were independently associated with each outcome while controlling for other explanatory variables. It also examines the interaction effects among the significant explanatory variables. Next, it attempts to disentangle the explanatory variables for ADHD score as distinct from those associated with conduct problems. Finally, on the basis of the multiple regression results, it makes a risk index and illustrates how well this identifies youth with the worst ADHD score and the worst conduct problems.

SYMPTOM SCORES AND DIAGNOSES

As explained in chapter 3, disruptive behavior symptom scores were derived from the Diagnostic Interview Schedule for Children (DISC-P). The ADHD score was based on 28 questions, whereas the conduct problems score was based on 25 questions and the oppositional behavior score was based on 13 questions. All these scores were dichotomized into the highest 25% (approximately) versus the remainder. However, the dichotomized oppositional behavior score was highly related to the ADHD score. In the youngest sample, 66.9% of oppositional boys also had a high ADHD score (odds ratio = 14.1). In the middle sample, 65% of oppositional boys also a high ADHD score (odds ratio = 14.5), and this was true of 61.7% of oppositional boys in the oldest sample (odds ratio = 12.8). Because oppositional behavior was so closely related to the ADHD score, oppositional behavior is not analyzed further in this book.

The overlap between a high ADHD score and the conduct problems symptom score was less. In the youngest sample, 55.4% of conduct problem boys also had a high ADHD score (odds ratio = 6.0). In the middle sample, 54.8% of conduct problem boys had a high ADHD score (odds ratio = 7.5), whereas this was true of 46.7% of conduct problem boys in the oldest sample (odds ratio = 5.2). Although they were interrelated, we considered that the overlap of the ADHD score and conduct problems was not so great as to prevent us from studying them both separately. Later in this chapter, we disentangle boys with a high ADHD score and those with a high conduct problem score.

DSM-III-R diagnoses were also derived from the DISC (*DSM-IV* had not been developed at the time). The conduct disorder diagnosis required 3 out of

13 specified symptoms, whereas the ADHD diagnosis required 8 out of 14 specified symptoms (and, in both cases, also a disturbance lasting at least 6 months). Almost all the boys who received a diagnosis of ADHD were among the highest quarter in their ADHD score: 84 out of 86 in the youngest sample, 60 out of 62 in the middle sample, and 44 out of 46 in the oldest sample. The percentages of boys who received a diagnosis of conduct disorder who were among the highest quarter in their conduct problems symptom scores were somewhat less but still high: 78.8% in the youngest sample, 69.4% in the middle sample, and 75.4% in the oldest sample. Although this chapter focuses on ADHD score and conduct problems symptom scores, it is clear that the results would also apply, in large part, to the corresponding diagnoses.

ATTENTION DEFICIT HYPERACTIVITY, CONDUCT PROBLEMS, AND OTHER PROBLEM BEHAVIORS

We know that attention deficit overlaps with conduct problems and other manifestations of disruptive behavior such as delinquency and possibly substance use, but is less associated with nondisruptive behaviors such as sexual intercourse. Table 8.1 shows the relationship among ADHD score, conduct problems, and delinquency, substance use, and sexual intercourse. Across the three samples, the odds ratio for the relationship between a high ADHD score and delinquency ranged from about 2 to 3, indicating that a high ADHD score increased the risk of delinquency by a factor of 2 to 3. The odds ratio for conduct problems and delinquency ranged from 3 to 4, with the highest odds ratio for the youngest sample (4.3). It is not surprising that conduct problems, compared

TABLE 8.1
Relationship Among ADHD Score, Conduct Problems,
Delinquency, Substance Use, and Sexual Intercourse (Odds Ratio)

	Sample		
Variable	Youngest	Middle	Oldest
High ADHD score–delinquency	2.2***	2.8****	1.8**
Conduct problems–delinquency	4.3***	3.1****	2.8****
High ADHD score–substance use	1.6*	2.2**	1.7*
Conduct problems–substance use	1.5	2.1**	1.6*
High ADHD score–sexual intercourse	—	—	1.1
Conduct problems–sexual intercourse	—	—	1.3
High ADHD score–conduct problems	6.0****	7.5****	5.2****

Note. * $p < .05$. ** $p < .01$. *** $p < .001$. **** $p < .0001$. p values one-tailed based on chi-square with correction for continuity. —, sexual intercourse not measured.

with ADHD score, were more strongly related to delinquency because some symptoms of conduct problems describe delinquent acts. However, one important difference was that the measure of conduct problems was based on parent report only, whereas the delinquency seriousness scale was based on child, teacher, and parent reports.

Table 8.1 also shows that a high ADHD score raised the risk of substance use across all samples, even for the youngest boys, by a factor of 1.6 to 2.2. The presence of conduct problems was also related to substance use, but this reached statistical significance in the middle and oldest samples only (odds ratios 2.1 and 1.6, respectively). Neither a high ADHD score nor conduct problems was related to sexual intercourse. In summary, a high ADHD score and conduct problems were related to delinquency and substance use, but not to sexual intercourse.

THE EXPLANATION OF ATTENTION-DEFICIT/ HYPERACTIVITY AND CONDUCT PROBLEMS

Attention-Deficit/Hyperactivity

We first examine which explanatory variables are related to a high ADHD score. Table 8.2 shows that most of the results were replicated over the three samples. Lack of guilt substantially increased the odds of a high ADHD score (4.0 – 5.5). Less but still considerable effects were observed for low achievement, either measured by ratings or CAT scores (1.7– 3.2). We also found that internalizing problems were associated with a high ADHD score— notably depressed mood (1.8–2.3), anxiety (1.9–2.2), and shy/withdrawn behavior (2.3–2.5). Having few friends was related to a high ADHD score, but not strongly and in the middle sample only (1.6).

Which family variables are related to the boys' high ADHD score? Table 8.2 indicates that only two variables were related across the three samples: poor supervision (1.6–2.2) and parent anxiety/depression (1.9–2.0). Several of the remaining family variables were related to a high ADHD score, but for the middle and the oldest samples only: poor communication (3.4, 3.6; not measured in the youngest sample), low parental reinforcement (2.1, 1.8), physical punishment (2.5, 1.6), disagree on discipline (2.4, 1.8; not measured in the youngest sample), and unhappy parents (2.3, 1.8). Parent substance use problems was also related, but for the youngest and middle samples only (2.5, 2.3). Father behavior problems was strongly related to a high ADHD score, but in the youngest sample only (3.3).

TABLE 8.2
Odds Ratios for Explanatory Variables for ADHD Score

Variable	Sample		
	Youngest	Middle	Oldest
Child			
Lack of guilt (PT)	5.5****	4.0****	5.0****
Old for grade (P)	1.2	2.1***	1.2
Low achievement (PBT)	2.8****	3.2****	2.6****
Low achievement (CAT)	1.7*	2.0**	1.7*
Depressed mood (B)	1.8**	2.3***	2.3***
Anxiety (PT)	1.9**	2.2***	2.2***
Shy/withdrawn (PT)	2.3***	2.5****	2.3****
Few friends (PB)	−1.2	1.6*	1.1
Family			
Poor supervision (PB)	2.2***	1.8**	1.6*
Poor communication (PB)	—	3.6****	3.4****
Low reinforcement	1.1	2.1***	1.8**
Physical punishment (PB)	1.3	2.5****	1.6*
Boy not close to mother (B)	—	1.7*	1.7*
Boy not involved (PB)	1.2	1.6*	1.3
Disagree on discipline (PB)	—	2.4**	1.8*
Unhappy parents (P)	1.6	2.3**	1.8*
High parental stress (P)	1.5	2.8****	2.8****
Parent antisocial attitude (P)	1.5*	1.1	1.0
Parent substance use problems (P)	2.5****	2.3****	1.2
Parent anxiety/depression (P)	2.0***	2.0***	1.9**
Father behavior problems (P)	3.3****	1.5	1.3
Macro			
Socioeconomic			
Low SES (P)	1.4	1.6*	1.2
Family on welfare (P)	1.7**	1.3	1.3
Poor housing (P)	−1.2	1.3	1.8**
Demographic			
Broken family (P)	3.1****	2.2***	1.3
Neighborhood			
Bad neighborhood (P)	1.4	1.1	1.6*

Note. * $p < .05.$ ** $p < .01.$ *** $p < .001.$ **** $p < .0001.$ p values one-tailed based on chi-square with correction for continuity. —, Variable not measured for this sample because boy was not considered old enough to respond to the relevant questions. Variable not included: HIA problems. No significant relationship: low organizational participation, low jobs/chores involvement, low religiosity, no set time home, large family, small house, young mother, unemployed mother, unemployed father, poorly educated mother, African American, and bad neighborhood (C). Variables not included: HIA problems and conduct problems. B = boy; C = census; CAT = California Achievement Test; P = parent, T = teacher

The bottom part of Table 8.2 shows that indicators of socioeconomic status (SES) were not consistently or strongly associated with a high ADHD score. The same was true for bad neighborhood as reported by the parent. However, a broken family was associated with boys' high ADHD score in the youngest and middle samples (3.1, 2.2).

Several factors were not related to a high ADHD score, including low organizational participation, low jobs/chores involvement, low religiosity, no set time home, large family, small house, young mother, mother unemployed, father unemployed, poor education of mother, African American ethnic status, and bad neighborhood (as measured by the census data). HIA problems were not considered as a possible explanatory variable for the ADHD score and conduct problems, nor was the ADHD score considered as a possible explanatory variable for conduct problems.

Conduct Problems

We briefly review the results of bivariate analyses to investigate which explanatory variables are related to conduct problems (Table 8.3). Several other child behaviors increased the odds of conduct problems across the three samples: lack of guilt (2.8–5.5; strongest in the two youngest samples), low achievement (rated; 2.4–3.2), and depressed mood (1.5–2.1). A few variables were related in the middle and oldest samples only, including old for grade (1.9, 1.7), low achievement as measured by CAT scores (1.8, 1.9), and anxiety (1.6, 1.5). Shy/withdrawn behavior was also associated with conduct problems, but for the youngest and middle samples only (2.9, 2.4).

Turning to family variables, both parenting practices and parent characteristics increased the odds of boys' conduct problems. Of the parenting practices, only poor supervision was related across all three samples (2.1–2.9). However, several other practices were related in the middle and oldest samples, including poor communication (3.4, 3.2), low parental reinforcement (1.9, 2.0), physical punishment (2.1, 1.7), and disagree on discipline (2.2, 2.5). Parental psychopathology was consistently associated with boys' conduct problems in all three samples. This was evident for parent substance use problems (2.0–3.4), parent anxiety/depression (1.6–2.5), and father behavior problems (2.1–2.8).

Table 8.3 also shows that various socioeconomic indicators were associated with an increased risk of conduct problems, but most of the findings were not consistent across samples. An exception was family on welfare (1.7–2.3). A broken family also increased the risk of conduct problems in each of the samples (2.1–2.7). Finally, the effects of bad neighborhood were less consistent, but appeared particularly relevant for the youngest sample on both indicators (1.8–2.1).

TABLE 8.3
Odds Ratios for Explanatory Variables for Conduct Problems

	Sample		
Variable	Youngest	Middle	Oldest
Child			
Lack of guilt (PT)	5.5****	5.1****	2.8****
Old for grade (P)	1.2	1.9**	1.7**
Low achievement (PBT)	2.4****	2.4****	3.2****
Low achievement (CAT)	1.4	1.8**	1.9**
Low organizational participation (PB)	1.5*	1.4	1.3
Depressed mood (B)	2.1**	1.5*	1.8**
Anxiety (PT)	−1.1	1.6*	1.5*
Shy/withdrawn (PT)	2.9****	2.4****	1.4
Few friends (PB)	1.4	1.7*	−1.2
Family			
Poor supervision (PB)	2.9****	2.2***	2.1***
Poor communication (PB)	—	3.4****	3.2****
Low reinforcement (PB)	1.2	1.9**	2.0***
Physical punishment (PB)	1.3	2.1***	1.7*
Boy not close to mother (B)	—	1.4	1.9**
Boy not involved (PB)	1.5	1.5*	1.6*
Disagree on discipline (PB)	—	2.2**	2.5**
Unhappy parents (P)	2.3**	1.8*	1.6
High parental stress (P)	1.8**	2.7****	3.2****
Parent antisocial attitude (P)	2.1***	1.5*	−1.1
Parent substance use problems (P)	2.0**	3.4****	2.0***
Parent anxiety/depression (P)	2.3***	1.6*	2.5****
Father behavior problems (P)	2.6***	2.8****	2.1**
Macro			
Socioeconomic			
Low SES (P)	1.5	2.0**	1.5*
Family on welfare (P)	2.2***	1.7*	2.3***
Poor housing (P)	1.1	1.7*	1.6*
Unemployed father (P)	1.3	2.2**	−1.1
Unemployed mother (P)	1.5*	1.2	1.0
Poorly educated mother (P)	1.5*	1.4	2.2***
Demographic			
Large family (P)	1.8**	1.2	1.1
Broken family (P)	2.7****	2.2***	2.1**
Neighborhood			
Bad neighborhood (C)	1.8*	−1.1	1.0
Bad neighborhood (P)	2.1***	1.3	2.0*

Note. $^* p < .05.$ $^{**} p < .01.$ $^{***} p < .001.$ $^{****} p < .0001.$ *p* values one-tailed, based on chi-square with correction for continuity. —, Variable not measured for this sample because boy was not considered old enough to respond to the relevant questions. No statistical relationship: low jobs/chores involvement, low religiosity, no set time home, young mother, small house, and African American. Variables not included: HIA problems and high ADHD score. B = boy; C = census; CAT = California Achievement Test; P = parent, T = teacher.

The following variables were not related to conduct problems: low jobs/chores involvement, low religiosity, no set time home, young mother, small house, and African American ethnicity.

REGRESSION ANALYSES

Table 8.4 summarizes the results of the hierarchical multiple regression with the ADHD score as the dependent variable. The multiple R's were moderately high and of the same magnitude across the samples: .435 for the youngest sample, .432 for the middle sample, and .431 for the oldest sample. For all three samples, lack of guilt entered first. Low academic achievement also entered the equation for all three samples. In addition, two internalizing behaviors recurred in the three samples: depressed mood and anxiety. Moreover, a third internalizing behavior—namely, shy/withdrawn behavior—contributed to the equation in the youngest sample. In all, there was a remarkable agreement across the three samples in the child variables that independently predicted a high ADHD score.

Table 8.4 also shows which other variables entered into the equation. As can be seen, no demographic, socioeconomic, or neighborhood variables contributed. Instead, the remaining variables were limited to family characteristics, but these varied from sample to sample. For instance, in the youngest sample, the father's behavior problems, poor supervision by parents, and parent substance use problems were of importance. In the middle sample, physical punishment was of most importance. In the oldest sample, high parental stress and parent anxiety/depression predicted a high ADHD score. Only poor parent–child communication recurred in the analyses for the middle and the oldest samples.

We now turn to the hierarchical multiple regression for conduct problems (Table 8.5). The multiple R was moderately high and about equal for the three samples: .456 in the youngest sample, .468 in the middle sample, and .436 in the oldest sample. Across the three samples, lack of guilt was one of the first variables to enter the equation, followed by shy/withdrawn behavior (youngest and middle samples), depressed mood (youngest and oldest samples), and low achievement (middle and oldest samples).

Turning to family variables, Table 8.5 shows that high parental stress and poor communication contributed in both the middle and oldest samples, whereas parent substance use problems contributed to the equation in the middle sample. Poor supervision and unhappy parents were variables that were independently predictive of conduct problems in the youngest sample only. Finally, parent anxiety/depression predicted conduct problems in the

TABLE 8.4
Hierarchical Multiple Regression for ADHD Score

Variable	Multiple R	F Change	p
Youngest sample			
Child			
Lack of guilt	.345	62.20	.0001
Low achievement (PBT)	.365	7.52	.003
Shy/withdrawn	.377	4.67	.016
Depressed mood	.385	3.02	.042
Anxiety	.391	2.61	.053
Family			
Father behavior problems	.425	14.12	.0001
Poor supervision	.430	2.33	.064
Parent substance use problems	.435	2.43	.060
Middle sample			
Child			
Lack of guilt	.291	40.73	.0001
Low achievement (PBT)	.345	17.38	.0001
Shy/withdrawn	.376	11.16	.0005
Depressed mood	.387	4.26	.020
Anxiety	.393	2.58	.054
Family			
Poor communication	.417	10.09	.0008
Physical punishment	.432	6.98	.004
Oldest sample			
Child			
Lack of guilt	.325	52.45	.0001
Depressed mood	.357	11.30	.0004
Anxiety	.374	6.44	.006
Low achievement (PBT)	.379	1.88	.085
Family			
Poor communication	.413	14.08	.0001
High parental stress	.423	4.68	.016
Parent anxiety/depression	.431	3.51	.031

Note. p values one-tailed. No other variables entered. All weightings positive.

youngest and oldest samples. Remarkably, of the demographic, socioeconomic, and neighborhood variables, only family on welfare in the youngest sample and poorly educated mother in the oldest sample predicted conduct problems and then only at a marginally significant level.

TABLE 8.5
Hierarchical Multiple Regression for Conduct Problems

Variable	Multiple R	F Change	p
Youngest sample			
Child			
Lack of guilt	.337	58.70	.0001
Shy/withdrawn	.369	11.92	.0003
Depressed mood	.386	7.03	.004
Family			
Unhappy parents	.408	5.10	.012
Poor supervision	.426	4.54	.017
Parent anxiety/depression	.441	4.16	.021
Parent antisocial attitude	.449	2.04	.077
Macro			
Family on welfare	.456	2.09	.075
Middle sample			
Child			
Lack of guilt	.342	57.24	.0001
Shy/withdrawn	.374	11.33	.0004
Low achievement (PBT)	.388	5.43	.010
Few friends	.394	2.24	.068
Family			
Parent substance use problems	.445	22.79	.0001
Poor communication	.460	7.31	.004
High parental stress	.468	4.32	.019
Oldest sample			
Child			
Low achievement (PBT)	.242	27.74	.0001
Lack of guilt	.277	8.75	.002
Depressed mood	.295	4.89	.014
Family			
High parental stress	.423	4.68	.016
Parent anxiety/depression	.431	3.51	.031
Poor communication	.413	14.08	.0001
Disagree on discipline	.428	2.33	.064
Macro			
Poorly educated mother	.436	1.74	.094

Note: p values one-tailed. No other variables entered. All weightings positive.

A comparison of the regression results for the high ADHD score and conduct problems shows some similarities and differences. Because the two variables are correlated, there is a need to disentangle those explanatory variables applicable to one while controlling for the other. For a discussion of these and other interaction effects, see chapter 11.

DETECTING INTERACTION EFFECTS

A search was made for significant interaction effects among the independent explanatory factors for a high ADHD score and conduct problems. Table 8.6 shows interaction effects that were not only statistically significant, but also related to a high ADHD score or conduct problems, respectively, independently of all other variables.

In the youngest sample, lack of guilt was associated with a high ADHD score especially if the boy was not shy/withdrawn or alternatively shy/withdrawn behavior was associated with a high ADHD score only if the boy did not lack guilt. Shy/withdrawn behavior was associated with a high ADHD score only if the boy was not anxious or, conversely, the boy's anxiety was associated with a high ADHD score only if he was not shy/withdrawn. In the middle sample, low achievement was associated with a high ADHD score especially in the absence of physical punishment or, alternatively, physical punishment was associated with a high ADHD score only in the absence of low achievement. Also, lack of guilt was associated with a high ADHD score especially in the presence of physical punishment or, alternatively, physical punishment was associated with attention-deficit only in the presence of lack of guilt. Therefore, guilt acted as a protective factor against the effects of physical punishment. In the oldest sample, low achievement was associated with a high ADHD score especially in the absence of parental stress or, alternatively, high parental stress was associated with a high ADHD score especially in the absence of low achievement.

In the youngest sample, parent anxiety/depression was associated with conduct problems only if the boy was depressed or, conversely, depressed mood was associated with conduct problems only if the parents had anxiety/depression. The combination of a depressed boy and an anxious/depressed parent was especially linked to conduct problems. Therefore, parents without anxiety/depression acted as a protective factor against depressed mood or a nondepressed boy acted as a protective factor against parent anxiety/depression. In the middle sample, shy/withdrawn behavior

TABLE 8.6
Independent Interaction Effects for ADHD Score and Conduct Problems

Variable A	Variable B	B = No		B = Yes		LRCS	p	Regression	
		A = No	A = Yes	A = No	A = Yes			F change	p
ADHD score									
Youngest sample (25.6)									
Lack of guilt	Shy/ withdrawn	14.1	58.1	30.4	46.2	7.96	.005	6.54	.011
Shy/withdrawn	Anxiety	19.3	39.7	35.2	38.0	3.18	.075	4.74	.030
Middle sample (24.0)									
Low achievement (PBT)	Physical punishment	11.2	41.4	31.8	43.4	7.12	.008	7.50	.006
Oldest sample (23.1)	(No significant interactions)								
Conduct problems									
Youngest sample (22.3)									
Depressed mood	Parent anxiety/ depression	18.0	20.5	22.9	57.5	7.02	.008	7.57	.006
Middle sample (24.8)									
Shy/withdrawn	Low achievement (PBT)	14.6	36.3	39.2	37.3	7.84	.005	8.48	.004
Low achievement (PBT)	Poor communication	17.4	23.7	31.2	63.8	3.94	.047	9.24	.003
Oldest sample (27.1)									
Lack of guilt	Poorly educated mother	14.9	41.2	35.1	40.5	5.10	.024	3.03	.083

Note: LRCS = Likelihood ratio chi-squared; *p* values two-tailed.

was associated with conduct problems only if the boy was not a low achiever or, alternatively, low achievement was associated with conduct problems only if the boy was not shy/withdrawn. Low achievement was associated with conduct problems especially if there was poor parent–child communication or, alternatively, poor communication was associated with conduct problems especially if there was low achievement. Good parent-child communication acted as a protective factor against the effects of low achievement. In the oldest sample, a poorly educated mother was associated with conduct problems only in the absence of lack of guilt or, alternatively, lack of guilt was associated with conduct problems especially where the mother was not poorly educated.

DISENTANGLING EXPLANATORY FACTORS FOR ATTENTION-DEFICIT/HYPERACTIVITY AND CONDUCT PROBLEMS

As described earlier, there was some overlap between attention-deficit/hyperactivity and conduct problems. In the community and in child clinics, it is quite common to see that boys scoring high on attention-deficit/hyperactivity also score high on conduct problems. Therefore, it is crucial to determine which explanatory variables contribute to the explanation of one outcome while controlling for the other outcome. Table 8.7 displays results of analyses in which first explanatory variables are related to the ADHD score while controlling for the presence or absence of conduct problems; then explanatory variables are related to conduct problems while controlling for presence or absence of a high ADHD score.

The results show that low academic achievement, anxiety, and depressed mood were associated with a high ADHD score in all three samples even in the absence of conduct problems. Less consistent results across the samples were found for few friends and father behavior problems.

In regard to explanatory variables that were mainly associated with conduct problems rather than the ADHD score, these included socialization factors such as poor supervision, unhappy parents, and parental disagreement about discipline, but the results did not replicate across samples. Several parent characteristics were also mainly related to conduct problems, including parent anxiety/depression (youngest and oldest samples), family on welfare, parent substance use problems, and poorly educated mother.

Finally, several explanatory variables were related to both the ADHD score and conduct problems even in the absence of the other, including lack of guilt (all three samples), poor communication, and high parental stress (middle and oldest samples). Also, the boys' shy/withdrawn behavior and parent substance use problems fell in this category, but these results were not replicated across samples.

Poor academic performance was associated with the ADHD score, but poor academic performance may be primarily a result of attention-deficit and hyperactivity. This conclusion is reinforced by a meta-analysis of studies on the relationship between academic achievement and delinquency, showing that attention deficit can explain both and, when statistically controlled, reduces the relationship between academic achievement and delinquency to nonsignificance (Maguin & Loeber, 1996). However, it is less clear why internalizing problems such as depressed mood and anxiety are related to attention-deficit and hyperactivity. In contrast, conduct problems were mostly related to socialization factors and parental characteristics.

CUMULATIVE EFFECT OF RISK FACTORS ON ATTENTION-DEFICIT/HYPERACTIVITY AND CONDUCT PROBLEMS

Figures 8.1 and 8.2 show the cumulative effect of risk factors on ADHD score and conduct problems. The risk of a high ADHD score increased disproportionally in the highest risk group (with four or more risk factors) for the

TABLE 8.7
Disentangling ADHD Score and Conduct Problems

Variables	ADHD Score		Conduct Problems	
	CP = No	CP = Yes	AD = No	AD = Yes
Effect mainly for ADHD score				
Child				
Low achievement # (Y)	2.0*	3.2*	1.4	2.2*
Low achievement # (M)	3.5****	1.7	2.3**	1.1
Low achievement # (O)	2.8**	1.2	3.6****	1.5
Anxiety (Y)	2.2**	2.6	−1.7	−1.4
Anxiety(M)	2.8***	1.2	1.7	−1.4
Anxiety(O)	2.7***	1.4	1.6	−1.3
Depressed mood (Y)	1.4	1.5	1.8	1.9
Depressed mood (M)	2.0*	2.4*	1.0	1.2
Depressed mood (O)	2.0*	2.0*	1.5	1.5
Few friends (M)	1.9*	−1.3	—	—
Physical punishment (M)	2.2**	2.0*	1.6	1.5
Family				
Father behavior problems (Y)	2.3*	3.4*	1.4	2.1
Effect mainly for conduct problems				
Child				
Shy/withdrawn (Y)	1.8*	1.6	2.5**	2.2*

TABLE 8.7 (continued)

Variables	ADHD Score		Conduct Problems	
	CP = No	CP = Yes	AD = No	AD = Yes
Family				
Poor supervision (Y)	1.3	2.2*	1.9*	3.2**
Unhappy parents (Y)	1.5	−1.1	2.6*	1.6
Parent anxiety/depression (Y)	1.7	1.5	2.0*	1.8
Parent anxiety/depression (O)	1.9*	1.1	2.7***	1.5
Parent antisocial attitude (Y)	1.4	−1.1	2.3**	1.5
Family on welfare (Y)	1.1	2.4*	1.4	3.1**
Parent substance use problems (M)	2.0*	1.0	3.8****	1.9
Disagree on discipline (O)	1.6	1.0	2.7*	1.7
Poorly-educated mother (O)	1.3	−1.4	2.7***	1.4
Effect about equal				
Child				
Lack of guilt (Y)	4.5****	2.9**	4.4****	2.9**
Lack of guilt (M)	4.4****	1.1	6.2****	1.6
Lack of guilt (O)	4.8****	3.2**	2.2*	1.4
Shy/withdrawn (M)	2.4**	1.5	2.1**	1.4
Family				
Parent substance use problems (Y)	3.2****	1.0	2.5**	−1.2
Poor communication (M)	3.0***	2.1*	2.7**	1.9
Poor communication (O)	2.7**	2.3*	2.6***	2.2*
High parental stress (M)	2.2*	2.1*	2.0*	1.9
High parental stress (O)	2.7**	1.4	3.2****	1.8

Note. Odds ratios shown. * $p < .05$. ** $p < .01$. *** $p < .001$. **** $p < .0001$. CP = conduct problems; AD = high ADHD score; # PBT = construct based on parent, boy, and teacher ratings.

youngest and middle samples. For the oldest sample, the highest risk group was only slightly worse than the next group (with three risk factors). The odds ratio for the comparison of high risk and ADHD score was highest in the youngest (6.1) and middle (5.5) samples and lowest in the oldest (4.2) sample. These odds ratios were not markedly greater than those for the single variable of lack of guilt (5.5 youngest, 4.0 middle, 5.0 oldest).

Similarly, the risk of conduct problems increased disproportionally in the highest risk group (with four or more risk factors) for the youngest and middle samples, but less for the oldest sample. The odds ratio for the comparison of high risk and conduct problems was highest in the middle (7.9) and youngest (6.3) samples and again lowest in the oldest sample (5.0). These odds ratios were higher than the single variable of lack of guilt (5.5 youngest, 5.1 middle, 2.8 oldest), showing that there is some increase in predictive efficiency by developing a risk score.

CONCLUSION

Unique Explanatory Factors for Attention-Deficit/Hyperactivity and Conduct Problems

We first carried out separate analyses on the explanatory variables for ADHD score and conduct problems, which showed that several of the explanatory variables for one applied to the other as well. This was reinforced by the hierarchical multiple regressions, which showed that the following variables predicted a high ADHD score and conduct problems (while controlling for other explanatory variables). These common variables were: lack of guilt, depressed mood (youngest, middle, and oldest samples), shy/withdrawn behavior (youngest and middle samples), and poor communication (middle and oldest samples).

Because many boys with attention-deficit/hyperactivity also have conduct problems, we undertook separate analyses to examine which explanatory factors were related to one while controlling for the other. Briefly, we found that low achievement, anxiety, and depressed mood were associated with a high ADHD score in all three samples even when conduct problems were controlled. In contrast, socialization factors such as poor supervision,

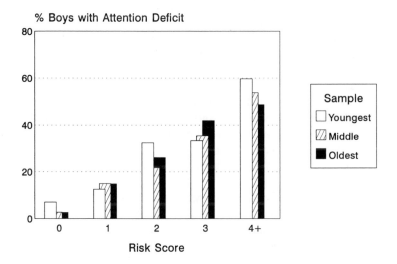

FIG. 8.1. Percentage of boys with attention deficit as a function of increasing risk score.

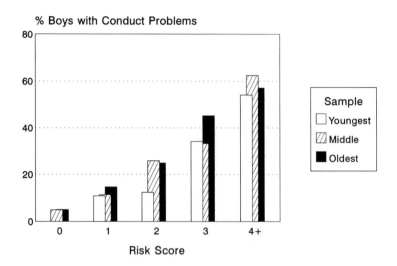

FIG. 8.2. Percentage of boys with conduct problems as a function of increasing risk score.

unhappy parents, physical punishment, and parental disagreement about discipline were related to conduct problems even when the ADHD score was controlled, but the results did not replicate across samples. The same applied to several parent characteristics, including parent anxiety/depression (youngest and oldest samples), family on welfare, parent substance use problems, and poorly educated mother. Hence, child factors are more related to ADHD, whereas family factors are more related to conduct problems.

How do these results compare with other studies? Loeber, Brinthaupt, and Green (1990) addressed the same question in another sample of 4th-, 7th-, and 10th-grade boys. They found that some sets of factors were more related to HIA than to conduct problems when controlling for each. The results show that HIA was uniquely related to academic problems in the older age boys and to family mental health factors (such as parent substance abuse). In contrast, social interactional factors (such as childrearing practices) were mostly related to conduct problems.

Loeber et al. (1990) also reviewed many other studies of factors related to attention deficit and conduct problems. They concluded that poor parent–child interactions were more related to conduct problems than to HIA. In contrast, it was more difficult to identify unique etiological factors for HIA over numerous studies. Such factors may need to be sought more in constitutional, genetic, and psychophysiological domains (see Biederman, Munir, & Knee, 1987; Faraone, Biederman, Keenan, & Tsuang, 1991).

The Role of Internalizing Problems

One of the findings of the present study is that internalizing problems such as depressed mood and anxiety were uniquely associated with the ADHD score. Furthermore, in a separate set of analyses (Loeber, Russo, Stouthamer-Loeber, & Lahey, 1994), we found that internalizing problems in the middle and oldest samples were more associated with a diagnosis of ADHD than with conduct disorder. These findings agree with the results from other studies showing that ADHD children have an above average comorbidity with the internalizing spectrum of anxiety disorders (Biederman, Newcorn, & Sprich, 1991; Lahey et al., 1989; Lahey et al., 1987; Pliszka, 1992). It also has become clear, as we found in our study, that this comorbidity extends to depression as well (Biederman et al., 1991; Jensen, Shervette, Xenakis, & Richters, 1993; Kolko, 1993). Likewise, in an Australian sample, Rey (1994) found that depression was related to ADHD but not to CD.

Other studies have noted (Biederman et al., 1991; Rey, 1994; Pliszka, 1992) that anxiety and depressed mood are more associated with attention-deficit/hyperactivity than with conduct problems. In contrast, socialization variables and parental problem behaviors and disadvantaged circumstances were more related to conduct problems rather than to attention deficit in boys. This confirms the earlier cited findings by Loeber, Brinthaupt, and Green (1990). Finally, boys' lack of guilt and poor communication in families were related to both ADHD score and conduct problems. Only further follow-up data can determine the causal links among these variables. It is even possible that attention-deficit/hyperactivity causes lack of guilt and poor parent–child communication rather than the reverse, as assumed in the analyses in this chapter. The rearing of children with attention-deficit and hyperactivity is a great challenge to parents. Our finding that high parental stress is associated with boys' high ADHD score is also replicated in other studies (Anastopoulos, Guevremont, Shelton, & DuPaul, 1992; Barkley, 1990). However, although some of the stress appears to be the result of children's problem behavior (Anastopoulos et al., 1992), it is less clear to what extent parents of ADHD children are more vulnerable to stressors in general. The association between parental anxiety/depression and boys' ADHD score makes this a plausible hypothesis.

9

Explanatory Factors for Physical Aggression and Covert Behaviors

Because we considered psychiatric dimensions of disruptive behavior in the last chapter, we now shift to more psychological constructs. There is mounting evidence that there are two important constructs in disruptive behaviors in children and juveniles: overt or confrontational acts and covert or nonconfrontational acts. These may also be conceptualized as consisting of a single dimension with two poles, as indicated by a meta-analysis of rating scales filled out by parents and teachers on 28,401 youth (Frick et al., 1993; see also Loeber & Schmaling, 1985a).

Although covert acts include theft and vandalism, for this chapter we are particularly concerned with those covert acts that are usually considered not criminal and that rarely lead to criminal prosecution in the juvenile court. Non-criminal covert behaviors of special concern are concealing behaviors (i.e., the boy concealing his activities from his parents), the boy being untrustworthy, and his tendency to manipulate others against their best interests. We consider these behaviors important because they often emerge early in children's lives and probably are stepping stones to delinquent acts, which often require these covert activities for success. Thus, it should be understood that the covert behavior construct used in the following analyses is based on an index of boys' unaccountability (concealing his activities), untrustworthiness, and manipulativeness as reported by parents and teachers. None of these elements was involved in our delinquency construct of course. Thus, the construct is more restricted than that used by Loeber and Schmaling (1985a), which included more serious delinquent acts such as firesetting and theft.

Of all possible overt problem behaviors, we decided to focus on physical fighting. First, physical aggression causes direct harm to others. Second, aggression in general has a high stability over time (Olweus, 1979), whereas early aggression predicts later violence and chronic offending (Farrington, 1991; Justice, Justice, & Kraft, 1974; Loeber & Stouthamer-Loeber, 1987). Third, physical aggression predicts a wide variety of other deviant outcomes, including covert delinquent acts (Loeber et al., 1993; Loeber, Tremblay, Gagnon, & Charlebois, 1989) and poly-drug use (Robins, Darvish, & Murphy, 1970; Simcha-Fagan, Gersten, & Langner, 1986). Our construct of physical aggression refers specifically to physical fighting, including such behaviors as starts physical fights and hits teacher. Because the construct does not refer to serious violence such as aggravated assault, rape, or robbery, it is reasonably independent of our construct of delinquency.

PHYSICAL AGGRESSION, COVERT BEHAVIORS, AND OTHER PROBLEMS

To what extent are physical aggression and covert behavior associated with any of the problem behaviors reviewed thus far? Table 9.1 shows the interrelationship between physical aggression and covert behavior. This relationship is strongest for the youngest sample (odds ratio = 8.4), slightly less strong for the middle sample (7.2), and least strong for the oldest sample (4.9). It should be noted that the relatively strong magnitude of the odds ratio between physical

TABLE 9.1
Relationships Among Physical Aggression and Covert Behavior, Delinquency, Substance Use, Sexual Intercourse, ADHD Score, and Conduct Problems

	Sample		
Variable	Youngest	Middle	Oldest
Physical aggression–covert behavior	8.4****	7.2****	4.9****
Physical aggression–delinquency	4.6****	5.8****	3.6****
Covert behavior–delinquency	3.8****	4.6****	4.2****
Physical aggression–substance use	1.6*	1.8*	2.0**
Covert behavior–substance use	1.2	2.5***	2.2***
Physical aggression–sexual intercourse	—	—	1.8**
Covert behavior–sexual intercourse	—	—	2.3***
Physical aggression–high ADHD score	4.3****	3.9****	4.1****
Covert behavior–high ADHD score	5.1****	4.1****	5.3****
Physical aggression–conduct problems	4.8****	4.2****	3.1****
Covert behavior–conduct problems	6.8****	7.4****	6.0****

Note. $* p < .05.$ $** p < .01.$ $*** p < .001.$ $**** p < .0001;$ — = sexual intercourse not measured.

aggression and covert behavior (manipulativeness, untrustworthiness, and concealing behavior) does not imply that all overt forms of conduct problems are as highly associated with all covert forms of conduct problems.

Physical aggression and covert behavior were both associated with delinquency. There was a trend for the association between physical aggression and delinquency to be slightly weaker for the oldest sample (3.6), compared with the two younger samples (4.6 and 5.8). In comparison, the relationship between covert behavior and delinquency was more stable with age (3.8, 4.6, and 4.2, for the youngest, middle, and oldest samples, respectively).

Physical aggression and covert behavior were somewhat related to substance use (aggression 1.6–2.0; covert behavior 1.2–2.5), but not as strongly as to delinquency. The relationship between aggression and substance use was rather constant with age, but covert behavior was nonsignificantly related to substance use in the youngest sample. In the oldest sample, physical aggression and covert behavior were about equally strongly related to sexual intercourse (1.8 and 2.3, respectively). Both physical aggression and covert behaviors were related to ADHD score, but covert behavior was slightly more strongly related (aggression 3.9–4.3; covert behavior 4.1–5.3). The same applied to conduct problems (aggression 3.1–4.8; covert behavior 6.0–7.4). The relationships between covert behavior and conduct problems was rather stable with age, whereas the relationship between physical aggression and conduct problems decreased in magnitude with age (4.8 for the youngest sample, 4.2 for the middle sample, and 3.1 for the oldest sample).

In summary, the relationship between physical aggression and covert behavior was strong, but declined with age. Over the three samples, physical aggression and covert behavior were about equally strongly related to delinquency and the ADHD score. An exception was conduct problems, to which covert behavior was more strongly related than was aggression. In contrast, physical aggression and covert behavior were about equally strongly related to substance use and sexual intercourse. However, the magnitude of the associations, compared with the relationships among substance use or sexual intercourse and delinquency, ADHD score, and conduct problems, was much weaker.

THE EXPLANATION OF PHYSICAL AGGRESSION AND COVERT BEHAVIOR

We now turn to explanatory variables for physical aggression and covert behavior.

Physical Aggression

Table 9.2 shows that, of the child behaviors, the following variables were consistently and strongly associated with physical aggression in all three samples: lack of guilt (5.0–6.5), HIA problems (4.2–6.1), and high ADHD score (3.9–4.3). Physical aggression was less strongly related to old for grade (1.5–2.4) and less clearly associated with a high ADHD score than with HIA problems, possibly because HIA problems, as measured, reflect more the cross-situational consistency of the hyperactivity, impulsivity, and attention problems. Weaker relationships were found with low achievement (measured by ratings or the CAT test) and shy/withdrawn behavior in each of the three samples. Depressed mood was associated with physical aggression but weakly and only significantly in the middle sample (1.6).

Turning to family factors, Table 9.2 shows that, across the three samples, poor supervision (1.5–2.2) and physical punishment (1.9–4.6) were related to physical aggression. Only physical punishment showed a clear age trend, with the risk of physical aggression doubling between the youngest and oldest samples. Poor communication was related to physical aggression in the middle and oldest samples (2.5 and 2.8; it was not measured in the youngest sample). In addition, low parental reinforcement was related to physical aggression in the middle and oldest samples only (1.6 and 2.0), whereas unhappy parents (2.8 and 1.8), parent anxiety/depression (2.1 and 1.8), and father behavior problems (1.8 and 1.8) were related to physical aggression in the youngest and middle samples only.

Turning to contextual factors, whereas low SES was associated with physical aggression in the youngest and middle samples only, poor housing, unemployed mother, and African American ethnicity were only of importance for the oldest sample. In contrast, large family was related to physical aggression in the youngest sample only, but a broken family was related to physical aggression in all three samples. Finally, a bad neighborhood, as rated by the parent, was related to physical aggression in two out of the three samples (but bad neighborhood according to the census was not related to physical aggression in any of the samples). Contrary to the generally accepted view that aggressive boys tend to be rejected by their peers (Parker & Asher, 1987), physical aggression was not associated with having few friends. Nor was it associated with boys' low participation in organizations or jobs and chores. Also, physical fighting was not associated with low religiosity, no set time home, living in a small house, an unemployed father, a poorly educated mother, or a young mother.

In summary, the strongest explanatory variables for physical aggression were child factors such as lack of guilt, HIA problems, and ADHD score. Of the childrearing practices, poor supervision and physical punishment were

TABLE 9.2
Explanatory Variables for Physical Aggression

Variable	Sample		
	Youngest	Middle	Oldest
Child			
Lack of guilt (PT)	6.5****	5.0****	5.9****
Old for grade (P)	2.4***	1.5*	1.7**
HIA problems (PT)	5.2****	4.2****	6.1****
High ADHD score (DISC)	4.3****	3.9****	4.1****
Low achievement (PBT)	1.9**	2.0***	2.0**
Low achievement (CAT)	2.0**	1.6*	2.0**
Depressed mood (B)	1.5	1.6*	−1.1
Anxiety (PT)	2.0**	1.5*	1.6*
Shy/withdrawn (PT)	2.5****	2.4****	1.8**
Family			
Poor supervision (PB)	2.2***	1.5*	1.7*
Poor communication (PB)	—	2.5****	2.8****
Low reinforcement (PB)	1.2	1.6*	2.0**
Physical punishment (PB)	1.9**	2.0***	4.6****
Boy not involved (PB)	1.5*	1.2	1.2
Disagree on discipline (PB)	—	1.7*	−2.0
Unhappy parents (P)	2.8**	1.8*	1.8
Boy not close to mother (B)	—	1.0	1.6*
High parental stress (P)	1.8**	2.6****	1.9**
Parent substance use problems (P)	2.0**	1.4	1.4
Parent anxiety/depression (P)	2.1**	1.8**	1.3
Father behavior problems (P)	1.8*	1.8*	1.6
Macro			
Socioeconomic			
Low SES (P)	1.9**	1.7**	1.5
Family on welfare (P)	1.5*	1.2	2.1***
Poor housing (P)	1.1	1.1	2.0**
Unemployed mother (P)	1.1	1.0	1.6*
Demographic			
African American (P)	1.2	1.2	1.5*
Large family (P)	1.6*	1.4	−1.2
Broken family (P)	2.0**	1.7**	2.2**
Neighborhood			
Bad neighborhood (P)	1.9**	1.2	2.2***

Note. * *p* < .05. ** *p* < .01. *** *p* < .001. **** *p* <.0001. No significant relationship: few friends, low organizational participation, low jobs/chores involvement, low religiosity, no set time home, small house, unemployed father, parent antisocial attitude, poorly educated mother, young mother, and bad neighborhood (C) Parent antisocial attitude was not significant; — = not measured in youngest sample.

especially related to physical aggression; the relationship with physical punishment increased in strength with age. Physical fighting was also related to the boy living in a broken family.

Covert Behavior

Table 9.3 shows the explanatory variables related to covert behavior. This was most strongly related to lack of guilt (4.7–6.2), HIA problems (3.7–5.5), and high ADHD score (4.1–5.3). Covert behavior was less strongly related to old for grade in the three samples (1.6–2.7), low achievement (2.1–2.9, for ratings and 1.6–2.1 for CAT scores), high anxiety (1.6–2.0), and shy/withdrawn (2.0–3.4). Less consistently related (i.e., in two of the three samples) was depressed mood (1.7 and 1.9).

Of the family factors, only one (boy not involved in family activities) was related to covert behavior across the three samples. A few variables were related to covert behavior in the youngest and middle samples: physical punishment (1.6 and 1.8), parent substance use problems (1.6 and 2.1), and father behavior problems (2.3 and 1.8). In contrast, several variables were associated with covert behavior in the middle and oldest samples only, including poor supervision (2.0 and 3.3), poor communication (3.8 and 4.1, not measured in the youngest sample), and low reinforcement (2.2 and 2.4). Less consistent relationships were found for unhappy parents, not close to mother, and parent anxiety/depression. An age trend was observed for poor supervision, which was most strongly related to covert behavior in the oldest sample.

Socioeconomic factors, with the exception of the family on welfare (1.6–1.8), were not consistently related to covert behavior. For the younger two samples, only small house was weakly associated (1.5); for the middle and oldest samples, low SES (1.5–1.8), poor housing (1.5–1.8), and a poorly educated mother (1.6–2.2). Ethnicity was not consistently related (only significant for the middle sample), but a broken family was associated with covert behavior in all three samples (1.9–2.6). Also, a bad neighborhood was related to covert behavior in the middle and oldest samples only, but rather weakly (1.9 and 1.7).

A few variables were not related to covert behavior across the three samples: few friends, low religiosity, no set time home, parents disagree on discipline, unemployed father, large family, young mother, and bad neighborhood according to the census.

In summary, boys' covert behavior was most strongly related to lack of guilt, ADHD score, and HIA problems. Less strong but very consistent explanatory factors were poor academic achievement and internalizing behaviors (especially anxiety, shy/withdrawn behavior, and, to a slightly lesser extent, de-

TABLE 9.3
Explanatory Variables for Covert Behavior

Variable	Sample		
	Youngest	Middle	Oldest
Child			
Lack of guilt (PT)	4.7****	6.0****	6.2****
Old for grade (P)	1.6*	2.7****	1.9***
HIA problems (PT)	5.4****	3.7****	5.5****
High ADHD score (DISC)	5.1****	4.1****	5.3****
Low achievement (PBT)	2.1***	2.9****	2.9****
Low achievement (CAT)	1.6*	2.1***	1.7*
Low organizational participation (PB)	−1.1	1.3	1.7*
Low jobs/chores involvement (PB)	−1.1	1.6*	1.5*
Depressed mood (B)	1.7*	1.4	1.9**
Anxiety (PT)	1.6*	1.9**	2.0**
Shy/withdrawn (PT)	3.4****	2.5****	2.0***
Family			
Poor supervision (PB)	1.4	2.0***	3.3****
Poor communication (PB)	—	3.8****	4.1****
Low reinforcement (PB)	1.5	2.2***	2.4****
Physical punishment (PB)	1.6*	1.8**	1.5
Boy not involved (PB)	2.1***	1.9**	1.9**
Unhappy parents (P)	1.7	2.1**	1.6
Boy not close to mother (B)	—	1.2	2.5***
High parental stress (P)	2.2****	2.5****	3.5****
Parent antisocial attitude (P)	2.3****	1.3	1.4
Parent substance use problems (P)	1.6*	2.1***	1.4
Parent anxiety/depression (P)	2.1***	1.4	2.7****
Father behavior problems (P)	2.3**	1.8*	1.3
Macro			
Socioeconomic			
Low SES (P)	1.4	1.5*	1.8**
Family on welfare (P)	1.6*	1.7**	1.8**
Poor housing (P)	1.2	1.5*	1.8*
Small house (P)	1.5*	1.5*	−1.1
Unemployed mother (P)	1.9**	1.5	1.4
Poorly educated mother (P)	1.4	1.6*	2.2***
Demographic			
African American (P)	1.0	1.8**	1.1
Broken family (P)	1.9**	2.6****	1.9**
Neighborhood			
Bad neighborhood (P)	1.3	1.9**	1.7*

Note. * $p < .05$. ** $p < .01$. *** $p < .001$. **** $p < .0001$. No significant relationship: few friends, low religiosity, no set time home, disagree on discipline, unemployed father, large family, young mother, and bad neighborhood (C).

pressed mood). With the exception of the boy not involved in family activities, family variables were less consistently associated with covert behavior across the three samples. However, physical punishment, poor supervision, and poor communication were associated with covert behavior in two out of the three samples. It is noteworthy that parent substance use problems and father behavior problems were associated with the early emergence of covert behavior. In general, covert behavior was weakly associated with socioeconomic and neighborhood factors. Of all demographic factors, only a broken family was consistently related to covert behavior.

REGRESSION ANALYSES

Hierarchical multiple regressions were carried out to examine which variables were independently related to physical aggression and, in a separate analysis, which variables were independently related to covert behavior.

Physical Aggression

Table 9.4 shows the results for physical aggression for each of the three samples. The amount of explained variance was about the same for each sample ($R =$ .518, .459, and .473 for the youngest, middle, and oldest samples, respectively). Lack of guilt entered each equation first, HIA problems second, and ADHD score third in all three samples. Less consistent results were found for the family variables. With the exception of poor communication in the oldest sample, none of the childrearing variables entered the equation. Of the background variables, low SES independently predicted physical aggression in the youngest and middle samples, and bad neighborhood and family on welfare independently predicted physical aggression in the oldest sample.

Covert Behavior

Table 9.5 summarizes the results of the hierarchical multiple regression analyses for covert behavior. Again, the amount of variance explained was similar across the three samples ($R =$ .510, .501, and .553 for the youngest, middle, and oldest samples, respectively). Results were highly consistent across the three samples. Of the child variables, ADHD score, HIA problems, and lack of guilt were predictors of covert behavior in the three samples. In addition, shy/withdrawn contributed in the youngest and middle samples, old for grade contrib-

TABLE 9.4
Hierarchical Multiple Regression for Physical Aggression

Variable	Multiple R	F Change	p
Youngest sample			
Child			
Lack of guilt	.375	75.15	.0001
HIA problems	.428	23.99	.0001
High ADHD score	.453	12.32	.0003
Old for grade	.472	10.40	.0007
Anxious	.478	3.40	.033
Family			
Unhappy parents	.504	8.32	.002
Parent anxiety/depression	.512	2.74	.050
Macro			
Low SES	.518	2.11	.074
Middle sample			
Child			
Lack of guilt	.350	61.82	.0001
HIA problems	.399	19.24	.0001
High ADHD score	.428	12.99	.0002
Shy/withdrawn	.442	6.40	.006
Family			
High parental stress	.454	5.90	.008
Macro			
Low SES	.459	2.80	.048
Oldest sample			
Child			
Lack of guilt	.355	64.24	.0001
HIA problems	.422	27.96	.0001
High ADHD score	.447	12.30	.0003
Family			
Poor communication	.458	5.12	.012
Macro			
Bad neighborhood (P)	.468	4.95	.013
Family on welfare	.473	2.65	.052

Note. p values one-tailed. No other variables entered. All weightings positive.

uted in the middle and oldest samples, and depressed mood independently predicted covert behavior in the oldest sample only.

Of the family interaction variables, only poor communication predicted covert behavior in the middle and oldest samples. Other family variables predicted less consistently (boy not involved in the youngest sample, poor

TABLE 9.5
Hierarchical Multiple Regression for Covert Behavior

Variable	Multiple R	F Change	p
Youngest sample			
Child			
High ADHD score	.337	58.62	.0001
HIA problems	.413	31.55	.0001
Shy/withdrawn	.444	15.17	.0001
Lack of guilt	.465	11.34	.0004
Family			
Boy not involved	.481	8.86	.002
Parent antisocial attitude	.494	7.28	.004
Parent anxiety/depression	.501	4.38	.019
Macro			
Unemployed mother	.510	4.74	.015
Middle sample			
Child			
Lack of guilt	.379	74.24	.0001
High ADHD score	.422	18.81	.0001
Old for grade	.444	10.01	.0009
Shy/withdrawn	.462	8.92	.002
Low jobs/chores involvement	.471	4.76	.015
HIA problems	.478	4.14	.021
Family			
Poor communication	.494	8.54	.002
Macro			
Bad neighborhood (P)	.501	4.07	.022
Oldest sample			
Child			
Lack of guilt	.374	72.27	.0001
High ADHD score	.438	28.67	.0001
HIA problems	.472	17.78	.0001
Depressed mood	.477	2.45	.059
Old for grade	.481	2.10	.074
Family			
Poor communication	.510	16.98	.0001
Parent anxiety/depression	.530	12.45	.0003
High parental stress	.543	9.06	.001
Poor supervision	.549	4.12	.021
Macro			
Poorly educated mother	.553	2.64	.053

Note. p values one-tailed. No other variables entered. All weightings positive.

supervision in the oldest sample). In addition, several parent characteristics independently predicted covert behavior—notably parent anxiety/depression (youngest and oldest samples) and parent antisocial attitude (youngest sample). High parental stress only predicted in the oldest sample. Finally, none of the macrofactors was consistently predictive across the samples: unemployed mother (youngest sample only), bad neighborhood (middle sample only), and poorly educated mother (oldest sample only).

DETECTING INTERACTION EFFECTS

A systematic search was made for significant interaction effects between the independent explanatory factors for physical aggression and covert behavior. Table 9.6 shows interaction effects that were not only statistically significant but were also associated with physical aggression or covert behavior independently of all main effects.

In the youngest sample, lack of guilt was associated with physical aggression especially if the parents had low anxiety/depression. Alternatively, parent anxiety/depression was associated with physical aggression only if the boy felt guilt. Unhappy parents were associated with physical aggression especially if the parents also had anxiety/depression or, alternatively, parent anxiety/depression was associated with physical aggression only if the parents were unhappy. In the middle sample, shy/withdrawn behavior was associated with physical aggression only if the boy felt guilt or alternatively, lack of guilt was associated with physical aggression especially if the boy was not shy/withdrawn. Low SES was associated with physical aggression only if the boy did not have HIA problems or, alternatively, HIA problems were associated with physical aggression especially in the absence of low SES. In other words, HIA problems and low SES may be alternative routes to physical aggression.

In the youngest sample, HIA problems were associated with covert behavior especially if the boy felt guilt or, alternatively, lack of guilt was associated with covert behavior only in the absence of HIA problems. In the middle sample, HIA problems and poor parent–child communication were associated with covert behavior only in the absence of a bad neighborhood or, alternatively, a bad neighborhood was associated with covert behavior only in the absence of HIA problems or poor communication. In the oldest sample, a high ADHD score was associated with covert behavior especially in the absence of HIA problems or, alternatively, HIA problems were associated with covert behavior especially in the absence of a high ADHD score. Parent anxiety/de-

TABLE 9.6
Interaction Effects (%) for Physical Aggression and Covert Behavior

| | | B = No | | B = Yes | | | | Regression | |
| | | A = No | A = Yes | A = No | A = Yes | | | F | |
Variable A	Variable B	No	Yes	No	Yes	LRCS	p	change	p
Physical aggression									
Youngest sample (22.9)									
Lack of guilt	Parent anxiety/ depression	10.8	54.1	26.5	48.1	5.76	.016	4.41	.037
Unhappy parents	Parent anxiety/ depression	16.3	26.8	10.0	61.5	5.56	.018	8.83	.003
Middle sample (28.7)									
Lack of guilt	Shy/withdrawn	11.8	54.3	37.0	54.0	10.09	.001	8.83	.003
HIA problems	Low SES	18.5	55.4	34.6	52.6	2.74	.098	3.40	.066
Oldest sample									
No significant interactions									
Covert Behavior									
Youngest sample (24.9)									
HIA problems	Lack of guilt	13.7	52.6	46.0	57.9	7.02	.008	2.95	.087
Middle sample (25.2)									
HIA problems	Bad neighborhood (P)	15.4	51.4	35.4	31.8	11.59	.0007	13.00	.0003
Poor communication	Bad neighborhood (P)	14.2	48.2	32.5	39.5	8.53	.003	5.64	.018
Oldest sample (24.1)									
High ADHD score	HIA problems	11.3	44.2	47.2	62.5	5.32	.021	3.35	.068
Parent anxiety/ depression	Poorly educated mother	15.8	28.4	22.4	57.8	2.82	.093	3.52	.061

Note. LRCS = likelihood ratio chi-squared; *p* values two-tailed.

pression was associated with covert behavior especially if the mother was poorly educated or, alternatively, a poorly educated mother was associated with covert behavior especially if the parents had anxiety/depression. Conversely, a well-educated mother acted as a protective factor against the effects of parent anxiety/depression or parents without affective problems acted as a protective factor against a poorly educated mother.

In summary, most of the interaction effects involved the predictive impact of one variable only in the absence of another variable. This type of interaction is of practical and theoretical importance because it hints at different etiological pathways to the same outcomes. For instance, HIA problems were associated with covert behavior only in better neighborhoods, whereas a bad neighborhood was associated with covert behavior only in the absence of HIA problems. Likewise, HIA problems were associated with physical aggression only in families with a higher SES, whereas a low SES also was associated with physical aggression only in the absence of HIA problems. These and other similar interaction effects can help explain the presence of problem behaviors in better neighborhoods, in families who are reasonably well off, and in boys who have normal prosocial skills.

CUMULATIVE EFFECT OF RISK FACTORS ON COVERT BEHAVIOR AND PHYSICAL AGGRESSION

Figures 9.1 and 9.2 show how far risk indexes, based on variables identified in the hierarchical multiple regression, were associated with covert behavior and physical aggression.

As to covert behavior, Fig. 9.1 shows that the risk for covert acts in the youngest sample increased nonlinearly. Specifically, the risk was less than

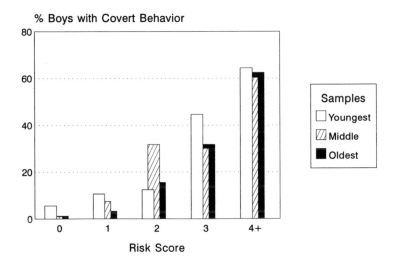

FIG. 9.1. Percentage of boys with covert behavior as a function of increasing risk score.

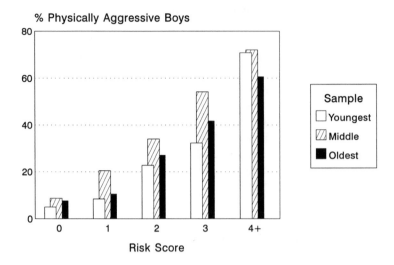

FIG. 9.2. Percentage of physically aggressive boys as a function of increasing risk score.

13% in the presence of either no, one, or two risk factors, but jumped to 44.7% in the presence of three risk factors and to over 60% for four or more risk factors. Nonlinear increases were also seen for the middle and oldest samples. In the middle sample, the percentage of boys engaging in covert acts increased especially between one and two risk factors (from 7.4% at one risk factor to 31.8% at two risk factors). Remarkably, at four or more risk factors, about 60% of the boys in each of the samples engaged in covert acts and the odds ratios were high (7.5–9.4).

Figure 9.2 shows that the risk of a boy engaging in physical aggression steadily increased with the number of risk factors, peaking at over 70% for boys in the youngest and middle samples. The odds ratio were high (7.7–13.9), showing quite effective prediction.

CONCLUSION

Relationships Among Problem Behaviors

We found that the relationship between physical aggression and covert behavior was strongest in middle childhood and weakest in early adolescence. One possible interpretation is that the two behaviors jointly occur especially when deviance emerges early in life and are representative of a strong antisocial tendency at that phase of life. However, it should be noted that many nonaggressive forms of delinquent behavior patterns emerge in late childhood and adolescence (Loeber, 1985), but these probably occur mostly in nonaggressive individuals, which would explain a weaker association between physical fighting and covert behavior during adolescence.

We found that physical aggression and covert behavior were about equally strongly related to delinquency. Similarly, they were about equally related to substance use and sexual intercourse, but the magnitude of these associations was smaller than for delinquency. The implication is that physical aggression and covert behavior probably function developmentally as stepping stones toward more serious deviance, although more strongly for delinquency than for substance use or sexual intercourse.

There was a trend for the association between physical aggression and delinquency to be slightly weaker for the oldest sample (3.6), compared with the two younger samples (4.6 and 5.8). This is in contrast to the finding reported by Roff and Wirt (1984) showing a lower correlation between aggression and delinquency in young (third- and fourth-grade) boys compared with older (fifth- and sixth-grade) boys.

Comparison of Explanatory Factors for Physical Aggression and Covert Behavior

Were there explanatory variables that were mostly linked to either physical aggression or covert behavior? The univariate results in Tables 9.2 and 9.3 show that the child factors were most strongly related to both problem behaviors.

For example, attention-deficit/hyperactivity was related to both physical aggression and covert behavior—a finding that was replicated across the three samples. This is an important point because several authors have emphasized a link between attention-deficit/hyperactivity and aggression or violence (e.g., Hinshaw et al., 1993; Klinteberg et al., 1993). However, in the light of the present findings, it is more likely that attention-deficit/hyperactivity has a less specific relationship with aggressive and covert disruptive behaviors, at least in males.

As to explanatory factors, we found some specificity in their association with physical aggression compared with covert behavior. Our findings show that the link between physical aggression and physical punishment administered by the parents increased with age. Also, boys' low involvement in family activities was more consistently associated with covert behavior than with physical aggression, and the same applied to parent substance use problems. In contrast, unhappy parents were more associated with physical aggression than with covert behavior.

However, these conclusions had to be modified when we compared the results of the multivariate analyses for physical aggression with those for covert behavior. Tables 9.4 and 9.5 show that several child factors were relevant for the explanation of both (notably lack of guilt, high ADHD score, and HIA problems). However, shy/withdrawn and depressed mood were associated more with covert behavior than with physical aggression. Of the childrearing practices, poor communication and poor supervision were more related to covert behavior than to physical aggression. In contrast, low SES and family on welfare were independently related to physical aggression but were not related to covert behavior.

It should be kept in mind that there was considerable comorbidity between covert behavior and physical aggression, although this comorbidity was higher in middle and late childhood than in early adolescence. This may suggest that boys who physically fight in childhood are already covertly deviant as well. It is likely that these constitute the early onset youths, who are likely to become worse in their antisocial behavior over time (Loeber, 1988; Moffitt, 1993). In contrast, the lower odds ratio linking covert behavior and physical aggression during early adolescence may indicate more specialization in each area in that phase of children's lives. Differences in the degree of comorbidity inherently influence our knowledge about etiological factors for different forms of problem behavior. Therefore, it comes as no surprise that we found some explanatory factors that were shared and some that appear unique to either covert acts or physical aggression.

The covert acts and physical aggression were measured in such a way that they did not qualify for inclusion in the delinquency construct. However, they were related to delinquency, as evident from the odds ratios that ranged from 3.6 to 5.8 (see Table 9.1). We argue that the importance of covert behavior and physical aggression does not rest just on their concurrent association with delinquency, but on their being developmental precursors of delinquency (for some longitudinal evidence, see Loeber et al., 1993, 1997).

10

Explanatory Factors for Depressed Mood and Shy/Withdrawn Behavior

The preceding chapters concentrated on externalizing behaviors. We now switch to internalizing problems—particularly depressed mood and shy/withdrawn behavior—to examine how such problems relate to externalizing problems and what the explanatory factors are for depressed mood and shy/withdrawn behaviors.

In chap.8 we saw that Attention Deficit/Hyperactivity was related to internalizing problems. Factor analytic work on child problem behavior has often identified two major dimensions of externalizing and internalizing problems (Achenbach et al., 1989). Although this is a valuable distinction, researchers have started to challenge the independence of the dimensions (Biederman, Newcorn, & Sprich, 1991; Coie, Lochman, Terry, & Hyman, 1992; Russo & Beidel, 1994). Clinical and population studies show that there often is a considerable degree of comorbidity between disruptive behavior disorders such as conduct disorder and oppositional defiant disorder and internalizing disorders such as depressive and anxiety disorders (Anderson, Williams, McGee, & Silva, 1987; Caron & Rutter, 1991; Loeber & Keenan, 1994; Puig-Antich, 1982; Russo & Beidel, 1994).

For example, investigations of the relationship between conduct disorder and depressed symptomatology show that the two often co-occur. However, studies of their temporal relationship have produced more controversial results (Capaldi, 1992; Holmes & Robins, 1987; Kovacs et al., 1988; Masten, 1988; Puig-Antich et al., 1989). Other researchers have stressed the importance of shy/withdrawn behaviors in the etiology of disruptive behaviors (Kellam, Brown, Rubin, & Ensminger, 1983; Kellam et al., 1991; Serbin, Moskowitz, Schwartzman, & Ledingham, 1991). It is unclear, however, whether shy/withdrawn behavior and depressed mood are equally strongly related to externalizing problems. For example, it seems likely that, because physical aggression is often accompanied by social skills deficits, shy/withdrawn behavior may be more related to physical aggression than is depressed mood. On the other hand, depression may cause aggression. However, there is a scarcity of studies that have measured both forms of internalizing problems in relation to disruptive behaviors in general.

Another area in need of investigation is the risk factors associated with internalizing problems. Are the risk factors for shy/withdrawn behavior the same as those for depressed mood? What are some of the most important risk factors? For instance, Kellam et al. (1991) found that poor academic achievement and concentration problems best predicted depression in elementary school-age children. Also, it is plausible that depressed mood and shy/withdrawn behavior are more common in families with inadequate communication patterns between adults and children and in families in which the parents show anxiety or depressive symptoms (Beardslee, Bemporad, Keller, & Klerman, 1983). Moreover, there are indications that depressed parents' childrearing practices often are disrupted (Patterson & Forgatch, 1990). In contrast to explanatory factors for disruptive behaviors, it is not known what explanatory factors in juveniles' macroenvironment (such as the neighborhood in which they live) are associated with internalizing problems.

To investigate these issues, this chapter first examines the relationship between these internalizing behaviors and other forms of problem behavior. It then shows which explanatory variables were related to depressed mood and shy/withdrawn behavior, respectively, which of these variables made independent contributions in multiple regression analyses, and which interacted with each other. To enhance the comparability among explanatory factors across different outcomes, for depressed mood and shy/withdrawn behavior we kept to the explanatory variables listed in the preceding chapters, although a case could be made that some of the correlates mentioned in those chapters could serve as well as explanatory factors for depressed mood and shy/withdrawn behavior. Finally, this chapter shows how well a risk index based on the best explanatory factors accounts for each outcome for each of the three samples of boys.

INTERRELATION AMONG DEPRESSED MOOD, SHY/WITHDRAWN BEHAVIOR, AND OTHER PROBLEM BEHAVIORS

Table 10.1 shows the extent that depressed mood and shy/withdrawn behavior are interrelated as well as related to other problem behaviors. Depressed mood

TABLE 10.1
Relationship Among Depressed Mood, Shy/Withdrawn Behavior, and ADHD Score,
Conduct Problems, Delinquency, Substance Use, and Sexual Intercourse

Variable	Sample		
	Youngest	Middle	Oldest
Depressed mood–shy/withdrawn	1.3	1.9**	2.1***
Depressed mood–delinquency	2.6***	1.8**	1.7**
Shy/withdrawn–delinquency	1.5*	1.6*	−1.2
Depressed mood–substance use	2.3***	1.7*	1.5
Shy/withdrawn–substance use	1.3	1.3	−1.5
Depressed mood–sexual intercourse	—	—	1.5*
Shy/withdrawn–sexual intercourse	—	—	−1.3
Depressed mood–high ADHD score	1.8**	2.3***	2.3***
Shy/withdrawn–high ADHD score	2.3***	2.5****	2.3***
Depressed mood–conduct problems	2.1**	1.5*	1.8**
Shy/withdrawn–conduct problems	2.9****	2.4****	1.4
Depressed mood–physical aggression	1.5	1.6*	−1.1
Shy/withdrawn–physical aggression	2.5****	2.4****	1.8**
Depression–covert behavior	1.7*	1.4	1.9**
Shy/withdrawn–covert behavior	3.4****	2.5****	2.0***

Note. * $p < .05$. ** $p < .01$. *** $p < .001$. **** $p < .0001$. — = not applicable.

was related to shy/withdrawn behavior, but not strongly and only in the middle
and oldest samples (odds ratios = 1.9 and 2.1). Because of this relatively weak
overlap, we did not think it was necessary to disentangle depressed mood and
shy/withdrawn behavior as we had previously disentangled attention-defi-
cit/hyperactivity and conduct problems.

How are depressed mood and shy/withdrawn behavior related to other
problem behaviors? Depressed mood was significantly related to delinquency,
but there was a slight trend for the relation to decrease in magnitude with age
(2.6, 1.8, and 1.7 for the youngest, middle, and oldest samples, respectively).
Likewise, shy/withdrawn behavior was weakly related to delinquency in the
youngest and middle samples, but not in the oldest sample. Depressed mood,
but not shy/withdrawn behavior, was related to substance use, but significantly
only in the youngest and middle samples (2.3 and 1.7). Also, depressed mood,
but not shy/withdrawn behavior, was related to sexual intercourse and then only
weakly (1.5). Both shy/withdrawn and depressed mood were related to a high
ADHD score (odds ratios = 2) and to conduct problems, but the magnitude for
shy/withdrawn was slightly larger (with the exception of the oldest sample,
which was nonsignificant). Finally, shy/withdrawn was more consistently and
strongly related to physical aggression (2.5, 2.4, and 1.8) and covert behavior
(3.4, 2.5, and 2.0) than was depressed mood (1.5, 1.6, -1.1, and 1.7, 1.4, 1.9,
respectively).

In summary, the results support our distinction between shy/withdrawn and depression, in that each has some distinct relations with other problem behaviors. Across the three samples, depressed mood, compared with shy/withdrawn behavior, was more related to delinquency and substance use. They were about equally related to a high ADHD score. However, shy/withdrawn behavior was more strongly related to physical aggression and covert behavior. It should be noted that, for both depressed mood and shy/withdrawn behavior, the magnitudes of the relationships with other problem behaviors were relatively weaker in comparison with some of the associations discussed in earlier chapters, and much weaker than, for example, the relationship between physical aggression and covert behavior.

THE EXPLANATION OF DEPRESSED MOOD AND SHY/WITHDRAWN BEHAVIOR

Which of our list of explanatory variables best predicts depressed mood and which predicts shy/withdrawn behavior? Because we were unsure about causal linkages, we did not include depressed mood and shy/withdrawn behavior as explanatory variables for each other and neither did we include boys' anxiety or their having few friends as explanatory factors because of the possible conceptual overlapping. However, we did include the ADHD score as a possible explanatory factor for shy/withdrawn behavior and depressed mood, just as we included shy/withdrawn behavior and depressed mood as potential explanatory factors for the ADHD score.

Depressed Mood

Table 10.2 shows the explanatory variables for depressed mood. A high ADHD score and ratings of low achievement were consistently related to depressed mood over all three samples (odds ratios = 1.7–2.3). Old for grade and low achievement as measured by CAT scores were related to depressed mood in the youngest and middle samples only (1.9 and 1.6, and 1.5 and 2.4, respectively). HIA problems were slightly related to depressed mood in the middle and oldest samples only (1.8 and 1.6). Remarkably, religiosity was related to depressed mood, but in the opposite direction to that expected; high religiosity was associated with depressed mood in the oldest sample (−1.8).

Turning to the family interaction factors, Table 10.2 shows that physical punishment was consistently related to depressed mood across the three samples (2.0, 2.1, 1.9). Poor communication, poor supervision, and not close to

TABLE 10.2
Explanatory Variables for Depressed Mood

Variable	Sample		
	Youngest	Middle	Oldest
Child			
Lack of guilt (PT)	1.5	1.6*	1.2
Old for grade (P)	1.9**	1.6*	1.4
HIA problems (PT)	1.6	1.8*	1.6*
High ADHD score (DISC)	1.8**	2.3***	2.3***
Low achievement (PBT)	2.0**	2.2***	1.7*
Low achievement (CAT)	1.5*	2.4****	1.5
Low religiosity (B)	1.3	1.3	−1.8*
Family			
Poor supervision (PB)	1.4	1.7**	1.6*
Poor communication (PB)	—	3.3****	1.9**
Low reinforcement (PB)	1.1	1.6*	1.0
Physical punishment (PB)	2.0**	2.1***	1.9**
Disagree on discipline (PB)	—	1.8*	1.6
Unhappy parents (P)	−2.4*	1.5	2.0*
Boy not close to mother (B)	—	2.5***	1.7*
High parental stress (P)	1.3	1.6*	1.3
Parent antisocial attitude (P)	1.5*	−1.1	−1.1
Parent substance use problems (P)	1.5	1.5*	1.1
Parent anxiety/depression (P)	1.9**	−1.1	1.5*
Father behavior problems (P)	2.0**	1.5	1.4
Macro			
Socioeconomic			
Low SES (P)	1.6*	1.5	1.1
Family on welfare (P)	1.9**	1.7*	1.3
Unemployed father (P)	1.9**	1.2	1.0
Unemployed mother (P)	−1.1	2.7***	−1.1
Poorly educated mother (P)	1.5*	1.3	1.3
Demographic			
African American (P)	2.4****	1.0	1.1
Broken family (P)	2.7****	1.5	1.5
Neighborhood			
Bad neighborhood (C)	1.7*	1.4	1.0
Bad neighborhood (P)	2.1***	1.1	1.0

Note. * $p < .05$. ** $p < .01$. *** $p < .001$. **** $p < .0001$. No significant relationship: low organizational participation, low jobs/chores involvement, no set time home, boy not involved, poor housing, small house, poorly educated mother, large family, and young mother. Variables not included: anxiety, shy/withdrawn behavior, and few friends. — = not applicable.

mother were also related to depressed mood (in the middle and oldest samples; not measured in the youngest sample). Relationships between other family interaction variables and depressed mood were less consistent.

The same was true for the background factors. Aside from family on welfare, none of the significant relationships was seen in more than one sample. It should be noted that several factors were related to depressed mood for the youngest sample only: low SES (1.6), family on welfare (1.9), unemployed father (1.9), poorly educated mother (1.5), African American ethnicity (2.4), broken family (2.7), and bad neighborhood (measured either by census or parental ratings; 1.7 and 2.1). That explanatory factors for depressed mood were common in the youngest sample compared with the older samples may be due to the fact that the prevalence of depressed mood was much higher among the younger than the older boys (see Angold et al., 1996).

Shy/Withdrawn Behavior

The results for shy/withdrawn behavior are shown in Table 10.3. Remarkably, religiosity was related to shy/withdrawn behavior in the youngest sample, but in the opposite direction to that anticipated (-2.0), with a high score on religiosity being associated with shy/withdrawn behavior. Old for grade was slightly related to shy/withdrawn behavior, but not consistently across samples. Table 10.3 also shows that most of the family interaction variables were related to shy/withdrawn behavior in the middle and oldest samples, compared with the youngest sample. Examples were: poor supervision (1.9 and 1.8), poor communication (2.3 in each sample, but not measured in the youngest sample), and low parental reinforcement (1.6 and 1.8). High parental stress was significantly related to shy/withdrawn behavior in all three samples. Other variables were less consistently related to shy/withdrawn behavior. Of the macrofactors, poor housing was weakly associated with shy/withdrawn behavior in the middle and oldest samples (1.7 and 1.9). The other factors listed in Table 10.3 (African American ethnicity, large family, bad neighborhood) were related in the youngest sample only.

In summary, relationships between explanatory factors and depressed mood were more significant in the youngest sample than for the two older samples. However, such an age effect was not in evidence for shy/withdrawn behavior, for which explanatory factors were about equally distributed across the three age groups. For all three samples, although there were some minor variations in the patterns of odds ratios, attention deficit/hyperactivity and low achievement were related to depressed mood and shy/withdrawn behavior. Physical punishment was among the most consistent factors associated with depressed mood, but not with shy/withdrawn behavior. In contrast, high parental stress

TABLE 10.3
Explanatory Variables for Shy/Withdrawn Behavior

Variable	Youngest	Middle	Oldest
		Sample	
Child			
Lack of guilt (PT)	2.7****	1.5*	2.3**
Old for grade (P)	1.7*	1.3	1.4*
HIA problems (PT)	2.5***	2.6****	2.3****
High ADHD score (DISC)	2.3***	2.5****	2.6****
Low achievement (PBT)	2.2***	1.9**	2.8****
Low achievement (CAT)	1.4	1.4	1.9**
Low organizational participation (PB)	1.4	1.3	1.8**
Low religiosity (B)	−2.0*	1.1	1.0
Family			
Poor supervision (PB)	1.3	1.9**	1.8**
No set time home (PB)	1.2	1.7*	1.1
Poor communication (PB)	—	2.3****	2.3****
Low reinforcement (PB)	1.5	1.6*	1.8**
Unhappy parents (P)	1.4	2.1**	1.2
Boy not close to mother (B)	—	1.4	2.2***
High parental stress (P)	1.9**	1.7**	1.8**
Parent antisocial attitude (P)	1.4	1.7**	1.1
Parent substance use problems (P)	1.8**	−1.1	1.2
Parent anxiety/depression (P)	1.7*	1.2	1.4
Macro			
Socioeconomic			
Poor housing (P)	1.0	1.7*	1.9**
Demographic			
African American (P)	1.7*	1.0	1.0
Large family (P)	2.0**	−1.4	−1.3
Neighborhood			
Bad neighborhood (C)	1.5*	1.0	−1.3

Note. * $p < .05$. ** $p < .01$. *** $p < .001$. **** $p < .0001$. No significant relationship: low jobs/chores involvement, physical punishment, boy not involved, disagree on discipline, father behavior problems, low SES, family on welfare, small house, unemployed mother, unemployed father, poorly educated mother, broken family, young mother, and bad neighborhood (P). Variables not included: anxiety, depressed mood, and few friends.

was slightly more related to boys' shy/withdrawn behavior than to the boys' depressed mood. As to macrovariables, few were related to shy/withdrawn behavior and more to depressed mood, but almost exclusively for the youngest boys.

REGRESSION ANALYSES

This section establishes which explanatory variables were independently associated with depressed mood and shy/withdrawn behavior.

Depressed Mood

Table 10.4 summarizes the results of the hierarchical multiple regression analyses with depressed mood as the dependent variable. The amount of explained variance was relatively low ($R = .282, .311$, and $.233$ for the youngest, middle, and oldest samples, respectively). Which explanatory factors best

TABLE 10.4
Hierarchical Multiple Regression for Depressed Mood

Variable	Multiple R	F Change	p
Youngest sample			
Child			
Low achievement (PBT)	.131	8.78	.002
Old for grade	.165	5.08	.012
High ADHD score	.187	3.99	.023
Family			
Physical punishment	.221	6.63	.005
Father behavior problems	.241	4.61	.016
Macro			
African American	.271	6.43	.006
Unemployed mother	.282	2.81	.047
Middle sample			
Child			
Low achievement (CAT)	.171	14.50	.0001
High ADHD score	.219	9.60	.001
Family			
Poor communication	.288	17.96	.0001
Not close to mother	.302	4.42	.018
Physical punishment	.311	2.90	.045
Oldest sample			
Child			
High ADHD score	.158	12.81	.0002
Low achievement (PBT)	.171	2.35	.063
Family			
Unhappy parents	.206	3.51	.031
Physical punishment	.233	3.26	.036

Note. p values one-tailed. No other variables entered. All weightings positive.

predicted depressed mood when controlling for the other factors? A high ADHD score and low achievement (ratings), but not HIA problems, predicted depressed mood. Of the family variables, only physical punishment was significant across the three samples. Other family variables contributed less consistently: father behavior problems (youngest sample), poor communication and boy not close to mother (middle sample), and unhappy parents (oldest sample). Perhaps important, in the middle and oldest samples, macrofactors did not independently predict depressed mood; only African American ethnicity and unemployed mother were predictive in the youngest sample. Thus, such factors as low SES, family on welfare, poor housing, and bad neighborhood did not predict depressed mood in any of the samples.

Shy/Withdrawn Behavior

Table 10.5 shows the results of the hierarchical multiple regression analyses for shy/withdrawn behavior. The total variance explained was similar for the three samples (R = .299, .322, and .318, for the youngest, middle, and oldest samples, respectively). Note that the amount of variance explained was lower than in the case of physical aggression or covert behavior (see chap. 9). In contrast to those outcomes, lack of guilt only contributed to shy/withdrawn behavior in the youngest sample. However, HIA problems and a high ADHD score independently predicted shy/withdrawn behavior in all three samples and low achievement (ratings) in two out of the three samples. None of the family variables replicated well in these analyses across the samples, with the exception of poor communication (middle and oldest samples; not measured in the youngest sample). Macrofactors rarely made any contribution.

In summary, there are some risk factors shared by depressed mood and shy/withdrawn behavior, including low achievement and attention-deficit/hyperactivity. In contrast, the multivariate analyses showed that shy/withdrawn behavior but not depressed mood was predicted by HIA problems (in all three samples). Also, physical punishment was related to depressed mood but not to shy/withdrawn behavior in all three samples. Thus, although there were several explanatory factors germane to both depressed mood and shy/withdrawn behavior, there were some distinctive risk factors as well.

DETECTING INTERACTION EFFECTS

Table 10.6 shows those interaction effects that were significantly associated with depressed mood and shy/withdrawn behavior over and above the main effects. For depressed mood, we found only a single interaction effect—between low achievement and a high ADHD score. For boys without low achievement the presence of a high ADHD score was associated with depressed mood or, alternatively for boys without a high ADHD score the presence of low achievement was associated with depressed mood.

TABLE 10.5
Hierarchical Multiple Regression for Shy/Withdrawn Behavior

Variable	Multiple R	F Change	p
Youngest sample			
Child			
Lack of guilt	.190	17.18	.0001
HIA problems	.220	5.97	.007
High ADHD score	.239	4.15	.021
Old for grade	.251	2.91	.044
Low achievement (PBT)	.260	2.16	.071
Family			
High parental stress	.274	3.84	.025
Parent substance use problems	.283	2.32	.064
Macro			
Large family	.299	4.69	.015
Middle sample			
Child			
High ADHD score	.193	19.67	.0001
HIA problems	.238	10.18	.0008
Low achievement (PBT)	.244	1.70	.096
Family			
Unhappy parents	.271	4.20	.021
No set time home	.296	4.43	.018
Parent antisocial attitude	.313	3.21	.037
Poor communication	.322	1.78	.092
Oldest sample			
Child			
Low achievement (PBT)	.217	24.81	.0001
HIA problems	.257	10.27	.0007
High ADHD score	.279	6.31	.006
Low organizational participation	.287	2.49	.058
Family			
Poor communication	.308	6.95	.004
Macro			
Poor housing	.318	3.26	.036

Note. p values one-tailed. No other variables entered. All weightings positive.

TABLE 10.6
Interaction Effects % for Depressed Mood and Shy/Withdrawn Behavior

		B = No		B = Yes				Regression	
Variable A	Variable B	A = No	A = Yes	A = No	A = Yes	LRCS	p	F change	p
Depressed mood									
Youngest sample									
No significant interactions									
Middle sample (22.8)									
Low achievement (CAT)	High ADHD score	15.0	36.3	35.6	35.0	5.75	.016	4.66	.031
Oldest sample									
No significant interactions									
Shy/Withdrawn Behavior									
Youngest sample (23.5)									
Lack of guilt	HIA problems	16.8	39.7	39.5	36.8	5.34	.021	4.60	.033
Old for grade	High parental stress	20.0	21.1	25.5	46.7	3.05	.081	4.71	.031
Middle sample									
No significant interactions									
Oldest sample (29.4)									
High ADHD score	Low organizational participation	21.1	45.2	39.5	39.4	5.32	.021	6.87	.009

Note: LRCS = Likelihood ratio chi-squared. p values two-tailed.

The interaction effects for shy/withdrawn behavior are also shown in Table 10.6. For the youngest sample, lack of guilt significantly interacted with HIA problems. For boys who did not lack guilt HIA problems were associated with shy/withdrawn behavior or, alternatively, for boys without HIA problems lack of guilt was associated with shy/withdrawn behavior. A second interaction in the youngest sample concerned old for grade and high parental stress. Old for grade was associated with shy/withdrawn behavior only among boys with high parental stress or, alternatively, high parental stress was associated with shy/withdrawn behavior especially among those who were old for their grade. The absence of parental stress acted as a protective factor against the effect of old for grade. Finally, in the oldest sample, we found an interaction between ADHD score and low participation in organizations. A high ADHD score was associated with shy/withdrawn behavior only among boys who participated in organizations or, alternatively, low organizational participation was associated with shy/withdrawn behavior only among boys without a high ADHD score.

In summary, we found several interaction effects. However, none of these interactions was replicated across the three samples, which diminishes their utility.

CUMULATIVE EFFECT OF RISK FACTORS ON DEPRESSED MOOD AND SHY/WITHDRAWN BEHAVIOR

To what extent does a risk score based on the variables identified through the hierarchical multiple regression identify boys with depressed mood or shy/withdrawn behavior? Figure 10.1 shows the results for depressed mood. For all three samples, there was a linear increase in the percentage of depressed boys as a function of increasing risk. At three or more risk factors, 38.3% of the boys in the youngest sample manifested depressed mood and slightly higher percentages in the middle and oldest samples. The odds ratios obtained by comparing the high-risk category with depressed mood was highest in the oldest sample (5.6), compared with the youngest and middle samples (3.1 and 3.6).

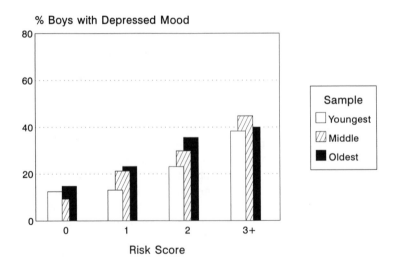

FIG. 10.1. Percentage of depressed boys as a function of increasing risk score.

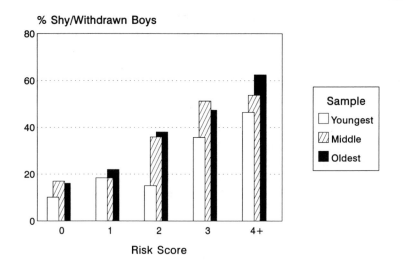

FIG. 10.2. Percentage of shy/withdrawn boys as a function of increasing risk score.

Turning to shy/withdrawn behavior, Fig. 10.2 shows that the risk for such behavior increased linearly in the oldest sample. Boys with four or more risk factors included 62.5% who were shy/withdrawn in the oldest sample and smaller percentages in the youngest and middle samples (46.4% and 53.8%). As with depressed mood, the odds ratios were strongest in the oldest sample (4.6), compared with the youngest (3.7) and middle samples (3.4).

In summary, a risk score of three or more was associated with about 4 out of 10 boys who were depressed, whereas a risk score of four or more was associated with 5 to 6 out of each 10 boys who were shy/withdrawn. For each outcome, predictions at adolescence were better than predictions in childhood.

CONCLUSION

We found some distinct patterns but also some shared patterns of relationships among the two internalizing and various externalizing problems. Depressed mood and shy/withdrawn behavior were both about equally strongly related to a high ADHD score. In this respect, Fergusson (1993), in his New Zealand study showed that the odds ratios for the co-occurrence of mood disorder and ADHD (both measured over a half-year period) was 3.6. Although this association is about twice as high as we found, it may result from different measurement techniques used in the two studies (we used measures of depressed mood over the last 2 weeks and shy/withdrawn behavior over the last year).

In terms of other associations between internalizing and externalizing problems, we found that depressed mood, compared with shy/withdrawn behavior, was more strongly related to delinquency and substance use, whereas shy/withdrawn behavior was more strongly related to physical aggression and covert behavior. Covert behavior and delinquency can be considered as, respectively, lower and higher steps on a continuum of disruptive behaviors (Loeber et al., 1993). Accordingly, in separate analyses, we found that shy/withdrawn behavior was especially associated with the less serious disruptive behaviors, whereas depressed mood was more associated with the serious delinquent acts. This finding particularly applied to boys in the youngest sample. This suggests that boys' internalizing problems may worsen (considering that depressed mood is worse than shy/withdrawn behavior) as they engage in more serious delinquent acts.

Along that line, in the present book, we found that shy/withdrawn behavior also was associated with physical aggression. This may reflect the lack of social skills and social competence that often is germane to both (Patterson, 1982; Feehan, 1993). Finally, that depressed mood is associated with substance use has also been found by other researchers (e.g., Paykel, 1971). This relationship was strongest for the youngest compared with the middle and oldest samples.

Explanatory Factors

Several explanatory factors were related to both depressed mood and shy/withdrawn behavior, including low academic achievement and HIA problems (the latter measuring parent and teacher ratings of hyperactivity, impulsivity, and attention deficit). Kellam, Rebok, Mayer, Ialongo, and Kalodner (1994) and Reinherz et al. (1993) also found a strong relationship between depressed mood and poor educational performance.

In our study, high religiosity was associated with each category of internalizing problems, but in the opposite direction than we expected, with high religiosity co-occurring with both depressed mood and shy/withdrawn behavior. Several other factors were associated with either form of internalizing behavior, but in the predicted direction. For example, physical punishment was more related to depressed mood than to shy/withdrawn behavior. In contrast, low parental reinforcement was more related to shy/withdrawn behavior than to depressed mood. However, poor communication and poor supervision in the middle and oldest samples were related to both depressed mood and shy/withdrawn behavior. Surprisingly, most of these aspects of family functioning have not been measured in other studies, but Lewinsohn and his colleagues found that adolescents' conflict with parents was predictive of depression (Lewinsohn et al., 1994). Also, Capaldi (1991) found that poor discipline was related to conduct problems rather than depressive symptoms, but poor monitoring (what we call *poor supervision*) was related to both.

In another category of family factors, the results show that high parental stress was consistently related to the boys' shy/withdrawn behavior, but not to their depressed mood. This finding suggests that the stress that parents experience from hassles and difficulties in life also affects their children's behavior rather than their mood. In contrast, child internalizing problems and parent anxiety/depression were less consistently related (three out of six significant odds ratios).

It is remarkable that, of the macrovariables, few were associated with either depressed mood or shy/withdrawn behavior (see also Lewinsohn et al., 1994). This suggests that the explanatory factors for these forms of internalizing problems, unlike externalizing problems, are mostly located within the boys themselves and in their family environment, rather than in the larger community context. This finding is also supported by the hierarchical multiple regression analyses.

Age Effects

Finally, we found several distinct age effects. Elementary school-age boys were particularly prone to display both depressed mood and delinquency or depressed mood and substance use. This suggests that the early onset of delinquency and substance use is particularly associated with internalizing problems as expressed through shy/withdrawn behavior and depressed mood. The second age effect concerned the explanatory factors. We found that factors associated with depressed mood were particularly salient for the youngest elementary school-age boys, compared with boys of an older age. This age effect was not seen for the explanatory factors associated with shy/withdrawn behavior, which were more equally spread across the age groups. However, it should be noted that, when we used a cumulative index of risk factors, the strength of association was generally highest for the oldest compared with the two younger samples. Thus, multiple risk factors were most strongly associated with depressed mood and shy/withdrawn behavior in older compared with younger youth. However, depressed mood was more common among boys in the youngest compared with the older samples (Angold et al., 1996).

In summary, the results reinforce themes emphasized in the introduction to this chapter. There are close links between internalizing problems and externalizing problems, but these links varied depending on whether shy/withdrawn behavior or depressed mood were considered. Also, the findings support the notion developed in prior research that these internalizing prob-

lems are associated with attention deficit and hyperactivity. As to the explanatory factors for shy/withdrawn behavior and depressed mood, many of these,
with the exception of macrofactors, were associated with other outcomes
reviewed in preceding chapters, such as delinquency, substance use, and sexual
intercourse. The findings make it clear that there are several nonspecific risk
factors that are associated with a variety of child outcomes. We further explore
this important point in the next chapter.

11

Explanatory Factors for Multiple Risk and Multiple Problem Boys

So far, we have reviewed different outcomes in separate chapters. We now bring together information about the interrelationships among different types of problem behavior and examine the extent that some types of problem behavior are more related to other types of problem behaviors, and whether there are age-related shifts in the patterns of interrelationships among problem behaviors. Second, we examine the degree to which each explanatory factor is associated with a diversity of outcomes. This issue is of great importance for the evaluation of a general problem theory (discussed in chap. 1 and more in detail in chap. 12). Information about general explanatory factors that apply across several different child problem behaviors is of potential importance for interventions, because targeting such factors could have a broad impact on a diversity of outcomes.

The interrelationship among explanatory variables and diverse outcomes, however, does not tell us about characteristics of individual boys. Therefore, the third theme of this chapter is to examine multiproblem boys—that is, those who show several types of problem behavior. A focus on such boys is important because multiproblem boys constitute a large proportion of the individuals who inflict the most damage on society and consume the most time of treatment professionals, particularly by receiving mental health services, remedial or special education, and referral to the juvenile court. We identify the multiproblem boys and summarize which outcomes are most characteristic of them. One related question that is addressed is the extent that explanatory factors associated with multiproblem boys are the same as those for less problematic boys or whether there are qualitative differences. Magnusson and Bergman (1988), noting the clustering of both risk factors and outcomes, argued that many of the significant relationships between single risk factors and single outcomes might reflect the characteristics of multiproblem boys. When these authors excluded the 13% of boys with multiple risk factors from their analyses, many of the significant relationships disappeared. We also investigate the effect of excluding multiproblem boys from our analyses and compare the explanatory factors for the multiproblem boys with those for less problematic boys.

INTERRELATIONSHIPS AMONG OUTCOME VARIABLES

Chapters 5 through 10 examined the interrelationships among different problem behaviors in a piece-meal fashion. For that reason, we return to this topic and present a summary of the interrelationships among all outcomes (Table 11.1).

Generally, there was little evidence of two separate clusters of externalizing and internalizing problems. Also, we found little tendency for the strength of associations to vary with age, which indicates that results were replicated across the three samples. Excluding sexual intercourse (which was only measured in the oldest sample), the number of odds ratios of 2.0 or greater was 18 in the oldest sample, 19 in the middle sample, and 18 in the youngest sample (out of 28 in each case).

The majority of all outcomes tended to be significantly related to all other outcomes, but the strength of associations varied greatly among sets of outcomes. For instance, across the three samples, the most interlinked behaviors were a high ADHD score (20 significant odds ratios out of a possible 21), covert behavior (20), physical aggression (19), conduct problems (19), and delinquency (19). In contrast, the least interconnected behaviors were depressed mood (16), shy/withdrawn behavior (15), and substance use (15), but even these were significantly interrelated in the majority of comparisons. In general, the strength of the associations between internalizing and externalizing behaviors was weaker than among externalizing behaviors.

Overall, behaviors that were developmentally more proximal to each other (see Fig. 1.1 in chap. 1) showed stronger associations than behaviors that were developmentally more distal. Thus, across the three samples, a high ADHD score was more strongly related to physical aggression and covert behavior than to delinquency or substance use. As another example, physical aggression and covert behavior were more strongly related to delinquency than to substance use. Also, delinquency was more strongly related to the more proximal substance use than to the more distal high ADHD score.

TABLE 11.1
Interrelationships Among Outcome Variables (Odds Ratios)

Variable	Substance Use	High ADHD Score	Conduct Problems	Physical Aggression	Covert Behavior	Depressed Mood	Shy/ Withdrawn	Sexual Intercourse
Youngest sample								
Delinquency	3.4	2.2	4.3	4.6	3.8	2.6	1.5	
Substance use		1.6	1.5*	1.6	1.2*	2.3	1.3*	
High ADHD score			6.0	4.3	5.1	1.8	2.3	
Conduct problems				4.8	6.8	2.1	2.9	
Physical aggression					8.4	1.5*	2.5	
Covert behavior						1.7	3.4	
Depressed mood							1.3*	
Middle sample								
Delinquency	2.2	2.8	3.1	5.8	4.6	1.8	1.6	
Substance use		2.2	2.1	1.8	2.5	1.7	1.3*	
High ADHD score			7.5	3.9	4.1.	2.3	2.5	
Conduct problems				4.2	7.4	1.5	2.4	
Physical aggression					7.2	1.6	2.4	
Covert behavior						1.4*	2.5	
Depressed mood							1.9	
Oldest sample								
Delinquency	4.2	1.8	2.8	3.6	4.2	1.7	-1.2*	3.6
Substance use		1.7	1.6	2.0	2.2	1.5*	-1.5*	1.8
High ADHD score			5.2	4.1	5.3	2.3	2.3	1.1*
Conduct problems				3.1	6.0	1.8	1.4*	1.3*
Physical aggression					4.9	-1.1*	1.8	1.8
Covert behavior						1.9	2.0	2.3
Depressed mood							2.1	1.5
Shy/withdrawn								-1.3*

* Not significant.

Specifically, in the youngest sample, the strongest associations were between early externalizing problems, including a high ADHD score, physical aggression, covert behavior, and conduct problems (odds ratios ranged from 4.3 to 6.8). Note that shy/withdrawn behavior was also related to these behaviors but at a lower magnitude of strength (ranging from 2.3 to 2.9) and only marginally to delinquency (1.5). Physical aggression, covert behavior, and conduct problems were about equally related to delinquency (ranging from 3.8 to 4.6), whereas a high ADHD score and shy/withdrawn behavior were also related to delinquency but at a lower magnitude (2.2).

Delinquency at this young age was weakly related to physical aggression (1.6) and, as mentioned, to a high ADHD score, but strongly to substance use (3.4). Alongside these relationships, depressed mood was related to some forms of early externalizing problems (a high ADHD score, 1.8, and covert behavior, 1.7), but not to physical aggression. In addition, depressed mood was related to conduct problems, delinquency, and substance use (2.1, 2.6, and 2.3).

Thus, for the youngest sample, the results show a network of interrelationships between externalizing and internalizing behaviors. Although the two internalizing problems— shy/withdrawn behavior and depressed mood—were not interrelated, each was associated with several externalizing problems. Some differences should be pointed out: At this early age, depressed mood but not shy/withdrawn behavior was related to substance use. Also, shy/withdrawn behavior but not depressed mood was related to physical aggression.

The pattern of associations among externalizing problems observed for the youngest sample was largely replicated for the middle sample, but the number of significant associations increased. Covert behavior and conduct problems (but not physical aggression) became associated with substance use (2.5, 2.1). As to internalizing problems, shy/withdrawn behavior became associated with depressed mood (1.9).

Finally, the results for the oldest sample largely replicated the results for externalizing problems in the youngest and middle samples. Also, whereas covert behavior remained associated with substance use (2.2), substance use was also associated with physical aggression (2.0). Turning to internalizing problems, shy/withdrawn behavior remained embedded in most of the early manifestations of externalizing problems. Depressed mood, as in the youngest and middle samples, remained associated with a high ADHD score. Shy/withdrawn behavior was associated with depressed mood (2.1). Sexual intercourse, measured for the first time in the oldest sample, was related to both covert behavior and delinquency, but not to substance use.

In summary, across the three samples, the strongest associations were found among externalizing problems, particularly a high ADHD score, covert behavior, physical aggression, and conduct problems, and slightly less strongly for delinquency and substance use. Behaviors that tended to be developmentally proximal were most closely interrelated and behaviors that were developmentally more distal were less strongly interrelated. Externalizing problems were consistently related to internalizing problems, but the strength of association was lower than among externalizing problems. It should be noted that, across the three samples, depressed mood but not shy/withdrawn behavior was related to substance use.

Already at age 7, depressed mood was particularly associated with several externalizing problems, including a high ADHD score and substance use. Thus, at an early age, negative mood was implicated in externalizing problems. With age, the relationship between a high ADHD score and depressed mood became more distinct (particularly in the middle and oldest samples). This corresponds with findings reported by Rey (1994) on 12- to 16 year-olds in a referred sample, showing that a diagnosis of depression was significantly related to a diagnosis of ADHD, but not to a diagnosis of conduct disorder. Also, other studies confirm the comorbidity between ADHD and depression (Biederman et al., 1991; Rey, 1994). However, the crucial test is to investigate whether comorbidity between ADHD and conduct problems holds up when controlling for other outcomes. As indicated in chapter 8, depressed mood was particularly related to a high ADHD score rather than conduct problems.

As to shy/withdrawn behavior, we see this not necessarily as an inherent feature of the child, but more as a result of boys' interactions with other children and whether they are accepted or rejected, resulting in socially distancing behaviors. This would agree with observations by Erhardt and Hinshaw (1994), showing that boys with ADHD were rejected by their peers more often than were nondisordered boys. Here again the association with externalizing problems should be taken into account as well because a proportion of aggressive boys also tend to be rejected by their peers (Dodge et al., 1982).

OVERLAP AMONG EXPLANATORY VARIABLES PREDICTING DIFFERENT OUTCOMES

We now review the number of associations among explanatory factors and various outcomes (excluding sexual intercourse). This is important information because it can show the extent that diverse outcomes, such as delinquency and depressed mood, are associated with similar explanatory factors. Comparisons of explanatory factors for different outcomes can also shed light on the extent that explanatory factors are unique to some outcomes or are shared between pairs of outcomes.

Unique explanatory factors are shown when the proportion of explanatory factors for Outcome A that are also associated with Outcome B is substantially larger than the proportion of explanatory factors for Outcome B that are also associated with Outcome A. Thus, asymmetry in the relative proportions of explanatory factors among pairs of outcomes can indicate unique explanatory factors that are not shared by the two outcomes.

Overall, Table 11.2 shows that there was a high degree of symmetrical overlap in the proportions of explanatory factors shared among most pairs of outcomes. (The table shows the percentage of significant explanatory variables shared by pairs of outcomes based on the number of significant odds ratios as a proportion of the total number of possible odds ratios.) This applied not only for outcomes that had some similarities, such as delinquency and conduct problems, physical aggression, and covert behavior, but also for outcomes associated with a high ADHD score.

We now focus on asymmetrical relationships. The first column in Table 11.2 shows the percentage of explanatory factors associated with each single outcome in each of the three samples. For example, in the oldest sample, 22 of the 40 explanatory variables (55%) were significant predictors of delinquency (see Table 5.6). The third column in Table 11.2 shows that, of these 22 explanatory factors, 9 (41%) were also significant predictors of substance use. How does this compare when we take substance use as a starting point? The first column in Table 11.2 shows that 11 of the 40 explanatory variables (28%) were significant predictors of substance use. Of these 11, 9 (82%) were also significant predictors of delinquency. Thus, most explanatory factors associated with substance use are nested within the explanatory factors associated with delinquency, but over half of the explanatory factors associated with delinquency were not predictive of substance use. The results were replicated across the three samples.

As shown in Table 11.2, similar asymmetries of this kind applied to the youngest and middle samples. However, this does not imply that exactly the same explanatory factors are shared or not shared across the samples. In judging other results in Table 11.2, one should keep in mind that the percentages of explanatory factors that are shared are generally higher for outcomes with fewer significant predictors.

Inspection of Table 11.2 shows several other pairs of problem behaviors with asymmetries in the proportion of explanatory factors. For example, only 29% of the predictors of conduct problems in the youngest sample were also among the predictors of depressed mood. However, the converse percentage was high: 86% of the predictors of depressed mood were among the predictors of conduct

TABLE 11.2
Percentage of Significant Explanatory Variables Shared by Different Outcomes (Based on Significant Odds Ratios)

Outcome A		% Sig.	Delinquency	Substance Use	High ADHD Score	Conduct Problems	Physical Aggression	Covert Behavior	Depressed Mood	Shy/ Withdrawn
						Outcome B				
Delinquency	Y	55	—	41	45	75	64	73	29	43
	M	65	—	46	63	75	65	69	50	38
	O	68	—	40	39	70	68	60	39	70
Substance use	Y	28	82	—	44	78	64	73	55	55
	M	35	86	—	75	83	79	79	67	58
	O	35	77	—	17	29	62	46	26	30
High ADHD score	Y	45	53	24	—	88	76	82	50	57
	M	55	71	43	—	95	81	76	71	41
	O	37	69	31	—	85	77	92	23	27
Conduct problems	Y	61	65	30	65	—	65	83	29	48
	M	66	72	40	80	—	72	68	57	43
	O	54	84	37	58	—	63	63	30	43
Physical aggression	Y	50	70	35	72	83	—	85	39	67
	M	50	85	55	94	100	—	85	71	53
	O	54	85	40	43	52	—	75	29	48
Covert behavior	Y	60	67	33	64	86	71	—	33	62
	M	65	69	42	67	71	65	—	54	42
	O	54	75	30	52	52	75	—	36	41
Depressed mood	Y	25	67	67	100	86	78	78	—	67
	M	42	80	53	92	92	80	87	—	53
	O	36	75	50	21	29	75	67	—	50
Shy/withdrawn	Y	36	69	46	82	91	92	100	46	—
	M	36	69	54	64	82	69	77	62	—
	O	52	94	41	26	43	65	53	35	—

Note. % Sig. is % of explanatory variables significantly predicting the outcome. Values above diagonal are percent explanatory variables for A that are also significant for B. Values below diagonal is percent explanatory variables for B that also apply to A. Y = youngest; M = middle, O = oldest. — = non-applicable.

223

problems. These asymmetrical results were replicated in the two other samples. Thus, although most explanatory factors applicable to depressed mood were also explanatory factors for conduct problems, a substantial proportion of explanatory factors were unique to conduct problems. Similar asymmetries were identified between depressed mood and several other outcomes: delinquency, covert behavior, and, in two out of the three samples, high ADHD score and physical aggression. The results were virtually the same for shy/withdrawn behavior, with most explanatory factors for that behavior being nested within the explanatory factors associated with the other mentioned outcomes.

In contrast, however, the proportion of explanatory factors for substance use not shared with conduct problems, physical aggression, or covert behavior was relatively high, whereas most explanatory factors associated with these outcomes tended to be nested within the explanatory factors predictive of substance use.

There was only one case where both percentages were less than 50% in more than one of the samples. In the youngest sample, only 24% of the predictors of a high ADHD score were also among the predictors of substance use and only 44% of the predictors of substance use were among the predictors of a high ADHD score. In the oldest sample, only 31% of the predictors of a high ADHD score were also among the predictors of substance use and only 17% of the predictors of substance use were among the predictors of a high ADHD score. Hence, there was least overlap between the explanatory factors for a high ADHD score and substance use. This was not obvious from Table 11.1 (the association among different problem behaviors), which shows a significant overlap between a high ADHD score and substance use and nonsignificant overlaps in the case of five other outcomes.

EXPLANATORY VARIABLES PREDICTING DIVERSE OR SPECIFIC OUTCOMES

If a general problem theory applies to our data, we would expect that explanatory factors would affect different outcomes to the same degree. Thus, the question raised here is whether specific explanatory factors are equally strongly related to diverse outcomes.

Generalized Associations

Table 11.3 summarizes all the relationships (using odds ratios) between the explanatory variables and all outcomes. We first focus on explanatory factors

TABLE 11.3
Explanatory Variables Versus All Outcomes (Odds Ratios)

Variable		Delinquency	Substance Use	High ADHD Score	Conduct Problems	Physical Aggression	Covert Behavior	Depressed Mood	Shy/Withdrawn
Child									
High ADHD score	Y	2.2	1.6	NA	6.0	4.3	5.1	1.8	2.3
	M	2.8	2.2	NA	7.5	3.9	4.1	2.3	2.5
	O	1.8	1.7	NA	5.2	4.1	5.3	2.3	2.6
Low achievement (PBT)	Y	1.7	1.6	2.8	2.4	1.9	2.1	2.0	2.2
	M	2.6	2.8	3.2	2.4	2.0	2.9	2.2	1.9
	O	2.6	1.8	2.6	3.2	2.0	2.9	1.7	2.8
Lack of guilt	Y	3.4	—	5.5	5.5	6.5	4.7	—	2.7
	M	4.7	2.1	4.0	5.1	5.0	6.0	1.6	1.5
	O	3.5	1.6	5.0	2.8	5.9	6.2	—	2.3
HIA problems	Y	2.1	—	4.0	4.0	5.2	5.4	—	2.5
	M	1.9	1.9	4.0	2.5	4.2	3.7	1.8	2.6
	O	2.7	1.8	3.3	2.5	6.1	5.5	1.6	2.3
Shy/withdrawn	Y	1.5	—	2.3	2.9	2.5	3.4	NA	NA
	M	1.6	—	2.5	2.4	2.4	2.5	NA	NA
	O	—	—	2.3	—	1.8	2.0	NA	NA
Depressed mood	Y	2.0	2.3	1.8	2.1	—	1.7	NA	—
	M	1.8	1.7	2.3	1.5	1.6	—	NA	1.9
	O	1.7	—	2.3	1.8	—	1.9	NA	—
Old for grade	Y	1.9	1.7	—	—	2.4	1.6	1.9	1.7
	M	2.7	2.2	2.1	1.9	1.5	2.7	1.6	—
	O	2.3	1.5	—	1.7	1.7	1.9	—	1.4

Table 11.3 (continued)

Variable		Delinquency	Substance Abuse	High ADHD Score	Conduct Problems	Physical Aggression	Covert Behavior	Depressed Mood	Shy/Withdrawn
Low achievement (CAT)	Y	—	1.8	1.7	—	1.6	—	1.5	—
	M	3.0	—	2.0	1.8	2.1	—	2.4	—
	O	1.6	—	1.7	1.9	1.7	—	—	1.9
Anxiety	Y	—	—	1.9	—	2.0	1.6	NA	NA
	M	—	1.8	2.2	1.6	1.5	1.9	NA	NA
	O	—	—	2.2	1.5	1.6	2.0	NA	NA
Few friends	Y	—	2.0	—	—	—	—	NA	NA
	M	—	—	1.6	1.7	—	—	NA	NA
	O	—	—	—	—	—	—	NA	NA
Low organizational participation	Y	1.5	—	—	1.5	—	—	—	—
	M	1.6	—	—	—	—	—	—	—
	O	—	—	—	—	1.7	—	—	1.8
Low jobs/chores involvement	Y	—	—	—	—	—	—	—	—
	M	—	—	—	—	—	1.6	—	—
	O	—	1.8	—	—	—	-1.8	—	-2.0
Low religiosity	Y	—	—	—	—	—	—	—	—
	M	—	—	—	—	—	—	—	—
	O	—	1.8	—	—	—	1.8	—	2.0
Family									
Poor communication	Y	—	—	3.6	3.4	2.5	3.8	3.3	—
	M	2.4	2.5	3.4	3.2	2.8	4.1	1.9	2.3
	O	1.5	—	2.2	2.9	2.2	—	—	2.3
Poor supervision	Y	1.9	1.7	1.8	2.2	1.5	2.0	1.7	—
	M	1.5	—	1.8	2.2	1.5	3.3	1.6	1.9
	O	2.6	2.3	1.6	2.1	1.7	—	—	1.8

Table 11.3 (continued)

Variable		Delinquency	Substance Use	High ADHD Score	Conduct Problems	Physical Aggression	Covert Behavior	Depressed Mood	Shy/Withdrawn
Parental stress	Y	1.7	—	—	1.8	1.8	2.2	—	1.9
	M	1.9	—	2.8	2.7	2.6	2.5	1.6	1.7
	O	—	—	2.8	3.2	1.9	3.5	—	1.8
Physical punishment	Y	1.7	—	—	—	1.5	1.6	2.0	—
	M	2.0	1.8	2.5	2.1	2.0	1.8	2.1	—
	O	1.9	1.7	1.6	1.7	4.6	—	1.9	—
Parent substance use problem	Y	1.9	—	2.5	2.0	2.0	1.6	—	1.8
	M	1.6	—	2.3	3.4	—	2.1	1.5	—
	O	—	—	—	2.0	—	—	—	—
Unhappy parents	Y	2.0	1.9	—	2.3	2.8	—	-2.4	2.1
	M	—	—	2.3	1.8	1.8	2.1	—	—
	O	—	—	1.8	—	—	—	—	—
Parent anxiety/depression	Y	1.5	—	2.0	2.3	2.1	2.1	1.9	1.7
	M	1.8	—	2.0	1.6	1.8	—	—	—
	O	—	1.6	1.9	2.5	—	2.7	1.5	—
Disagree on discipline	Y	2.1	1.9	2.4	2.2	1.7	1.8	—	—
	M	—	—	1.8	2.5	—	—	—	—
	O	—	—	—	—	—	—	—	—
Father behavior problems	Y	—	—	2.3	2.6	1.8	2.3	2.0	—
	M	1.7	—	—	2.8	1.8	1.8	—	—
	O	—	—	—	2.1	—	—	—	—
Low reinforcement	Y	—	—	—	—	—	—	—	—
	M	—	—	2.1	1.9	1.6	2.2	1.6	1.6
	O	—	—	1.8	2.0	2.0	2.4	—	1.8
Boy not close to mother	M	—	—	1.7	—	1.6	—	2.5	—
	O	—	—	1.7	1.9	1.6	2.5	1.7	2.2

Table 11.3 (continued)

Variable		Delinquency	Substance Use	High ADHD Score	Conduct Problems	Physical Aggression	Covert Behavior	Depressed Mood	Shy/Withdrawn
Parent antisocial attitude	Y	—	—	1.5	2.1	—	2.3	1.5	—
	M	—	—	—	1.5	—	—	—	1.7
	O	—	—	—	—	—	—	—	—
No set time home	Y	—	—	—	—	—	—	—	—
	M	—	—	—	—	—	—	—	1.7
	O	1.5	2.0	—	—	—	—	—	—
Boy not involved	Y	1.6	—	1.6	—	1.5	2.1	—	—
	M	—	—	—	1.5	—	1.9	—	—
	O	1.8	1.7	—	1.6	—	1.9	—	—
Macro									
Broken family	Y	2.0	—	3.1	2.7	2.0	1.9	2.7	—
	M	2.9	—	2.2	2.2	1.7	2.6	—	—
	O	2.8	—	—	2.1	2.2	1.9	—	—
Family on welfare	Y	2.1	—	1.7	2.2	1.5	1.6	1.9	—
	M	2.5	1.7	—	1.7	—	1.7	1.7	—
	O	2.4	—	—	1.6	2.1	1.8	—	—
Bad neighborhood (P)	Y	2.2	—	—	2.1	1.9	—	2.1	—
	M	1.8	—	—	—	—	1.9	—	—
	O	2.0	1.7	1.6	2.0	2.2	1.7	—	—
Bad neighborhood (C)	Y	2.0	—	—	1.8	—	—	1.7	1.5
	M	1.8	—	—	—	—	—	—	—
	O	2.1	—	—	—	—	—	—	—
African American	Y	1.9	1.6	—	—	—	—	2.4	1.7
	M	2.5	—	—	—	—	1.8	—	—
	O	2.3	—	—	—	1.5	—	—	—

Table 11.3 (continued)

Variable		Delinquency	Substance Use	High ADHD Score	Conduct Problems	Physical Aggression	Covert Behavior	Depressed Mood	Shy/Withdrawn
Low SES	Y	1.5	1.7	—	—	1.9	—	1.6	—
	M	2.2	2.2	1.6	2.0	1.7	1.5	—	—
	O	1.5	—	—	1.5	—	1.8	—	—
Poorly educated mother	Y	2.1	1.9	—	1.5	—	1.6	1.5	—
	M	—	1.7	—	—	—	—	—	—
	O	1.9	—	—	2.2	—	2.2	—	—
Unemployed mother	Y	—	1.8	—	1.5	—	1.9	—	—
	M	1.5	1.9	—	—	—	—	2.7	—
	O	—	—	—	—	1.6	—	—	—
Poor housing	Y	—	—	—	—	—	—	—	—
	M	—	—	—	1.7	—	1.5	—	1.7
	O	1.7	—	1.8	1.6	2.0	1.8	—	1.9
Unemployed father	Y	2.2	—	—	—	—	—	1.9	—
	M	2.6	—	—	2.2	—	—	—	—
	O	—	—	—	—	—	—	—	—
Large family	Y	1.7	—	—	1.8	1.6	—	—	2.0
	M	—	—	—	—	—	—	—	—
	O	—	—	—	—	—	—	—	—
Young mother	Y	—	—	—	—	—	—	—	—
	M	1.9	—	—	—	—	—	—	—
	O	2.1	—	—	—	—	—	—	—
Small house	Y	1.7	—	—	—	—	1.5	—	—
	M	—	—	—	—	—	1.5	—	—
	O	1.7	—	—	—	—	—	—	—

Note. Y = youngest sample; M = middle sample; O = oldest sample; — = nonsignificant odds ratio; NA = not applicable to avoid confounds; P = parent; B = boy; T = teacher; C = census.

229

that apply to most outcomes. Table 11.3 shows that low achievement (based on parent, boy, teacher ratings) was the only explanatory factor that was related to all outcomes in all three samples (1.6–2.8 for the youngest sample, 1.9–3.2 for the middle sample, and 1.7–3.2 for the oldest sample). Two other factors—a high ADHD score and HIA problems—that are often associated with poor academic achievement were also related to most outcomes, but more strongly to most externalizing problems (conduct problems, physical aggression, and covert behavior) than to internalizing problems (depressed mood, shy/with-drawn behavior) or delinquency. Along this line, Table 11.3 shows that being old for the grade, which is a result of poor academic performance, was associated with almost all outcomes.

Of the family factors, poor supervision was related to all externalizing and internalizing problems in two or three of the samples. Likewise, poor commu-nication (only measured in the middle and oldest samples) was related to all externalizing outcomes (most strongly to covert behavior) and internalizing outcomes. None of the macrofactors was consistently related across all out-comes.

Specific Associations

Which outcomes were mostly related to externalizing problems? In each of the three samples, lack of guilt was most strongly related to conduct problems, physical aggression, delinquency, and a high ADHD score; less strongly to shy/withdrawn behavior; and weakly to depressed mood and substance use. Several other factors were mostly related to externalizing problems and far less consistently to internalizing problems: broken family, low SES, parent sub-stance use problems, father behavior problems, African-American ethnicity, and bad neighborhood (parent rating).

A few factors were practically only related to delinquency, including boys' low participation in organizations, African American ethnicity, young mother, and a bad neighborhood (according to census). For example, African American ethnicity was significantly related to delinquency in all three samples (odds ratio = 1.9, 2.5, and 2.3 in youngest, middle, and oldest samples, respectively). It was not significantly related to any other outcome in more than one sample and had only one other strong relationship (with depressed mood in the youngest sample, odds ratio = 2.4). Similarly, a bad neighborhood (according to census measures) was significantly related to delinquency in all three samples (odds ratio = 2.0, 1.8, and 2.1, respectively), but was not significantly related to any other outcome (including internalizing problems) in more than one sample and had no other strong relationships. Bad neighborhood (parent rating) was most consistently related (i.e., across the three samples) to delinquency and physical aggression, but much less to substance use, a high ADHD score, covert behavior, and depressed mood and not related to shy/withdrawn behavior. Moreover, the 13 macrovariables had 17 strong relationships with delinquency, 10 with conduct problems, and 15 with the other 6 outcomes, suggesting a possible specific link between macrovariables and delinquent behavior.

Turning to other specific relationships, three factors were primarily related to covert behavior: low involvement in jobs and chores, boy not involved in family activities, and living in a small house. These findings shed a new light on familial interactions by covert boys, which heretofore had been seen as resulting mostly from neglectful parenting (Loeber & Stouthamer-Loeber, 1986). The present findings may indicate that covert boys distance themselves from involvement in family matters.

Turning to physical aggression, we did not find factors that were related to physical aggression only. In fact, variables related to physical aggression also tended to be related to delinquency (e.g., shy/withdrawn behavior, low SES, and bad neighborhood, according to parent).

Among the family factors, high parental stress was particularly associated with externalizing problems, such as conduct problems, physical aggression, covert behavior, and a high ADHD score, but for the two older age groups only. High parental stress was less strongly related to shy/withdrawn behavior and not related to depressed mood.

As pointed out in chapter 8, several explanatory factors discriminated between high ADHD score and conduct problems. Low achievement, anxiety, and depressed mood were associated with a high ADHD score in all three samples even in the absence of conduct problems. In contrast, parental childrearing practices, such as poor supervision, physical punishment, and parental disagreement about discipline, were mostly related to conduct problems (but not in all samples). Moreover, as shown in the multiple regressions in chapter 10, shy/withdrawn behavior in contrast to depressed mood was particularly related to HIA problems. In addition, several parent characteristics were also mainly related to conduct problems (rather than a high ADHD score), including parent anxiety/depression, unhappy parent, family on welfare, parental substance use problems, and a poorly educated mother. In turn, physical punishment and family on welfare were more consistently related to depressed mood but not to shy/withdrawn behavior.

Age Effects

Earlier we examined the extent to which an explanatory factor had an increasing or decreasing impact across the three grade samples. Table 11.3 allows us to examine the extent that the strength of association between an explanatory factor and an outcome stays the same or changes across the three grade samples. In most instances, the strength of association between explanatory variables and outcomes was quite similar across the three age groups. However, a few exceptions should be noted. For example, physical punishment became increasingly related to physical aggression, particularly between late childhood and adolescence (odds ratio = 1.9, 2.0, and 4.6, for the youngest, middle, and oldest samples, respectively). Also, poor supervision became increasingly related to covert behavior (1.4, 2.0, and 3.3 for the respective samples). However, these increases in strength of association were specific and did not apply to other outcomes.

In summary, the results show only a few instances in which the strength of association between an explanatory factor and an outcome changed with age. In most instances, the magnitudes of the relationships were similar across the three grade samples.

EXPLANATORY VARIABLES PREDICTING SEVERAL OUTCOMES

We now investigate to what extent explanatory factors for each of the outcomes were the same. In this and subsequent presentations of results, sexual intercourse is excluded because it was only measured in the oldest sample. Therefore, most analyses are based on eight outcomes: delinquency, substance use, high ADHD score, conduct problems, physical aggression, covert behavior, depressed mood, and shy/withdrawn behavior. A few precautions against confounds should be noted. A high ADHD score and HIA problems were not studied as predictors of a high ADHD score or conduct problems (which were both derived from the DISC), and depressed mood, shy/withdrawn, anxiety, and few friends were not studied as predictors of depressed mood or shy/withdrawn. Hence, for these explanatory variables, percentages are based on six outcomes.

Table 11.4 shows the percentage of outcomes significantly predicted by each explanatory variable and the percentage of relatively strong relationships (with odds ratios = 2.0 or greater). (The ordering of variables in Table 11.4 is based on the percentage of outcomes with odds ratios = 2.0 or greater.) Several explanatory factors were significantly related to all or nearly all outcomes—a finding that was replicated in all three samples. This was true for several child behaviors, including high ADHD score, low achievement (based on parent, boy, and teacher ratings), and lack of guilt. Similarly, several family factors had a generalized impact, including poor parent–boy communication and, to a slightly lesser extent, poor parental supervision.

Overall, the child variables were stronger predictors than the family variables, which in turn were stronger predictors than the macrovariables. No

TABLE 11.4

Percentage of Significant Outcomes for Each Explanatory Variable (Delinquency, Substance Use, Conduct Problems, High ADHD Score, Physical Aggression, Covert Behavior, Depressed Mood, Shy/Withdrawn Behavior)

| | Sample | | | | | |
| | Youngest | | Middle | | Oldest | |
Variable	% Sig.	OR = 2+	% Sig.	OR = 2+	% Sig.	OR = 2+
Child						
High ADHD score	100	67	100	100	100	67
Low achievement (PBT)	100	63	100	88	100	75
Lack of guilt	75	75	100	75	88	75
HIA problems	67	67	100	50	100	67
Shy/withdrawn	83	67	83	67	50	33
Depressed mood	83	50	83	17	67	17
Old for grade	75	13	87	50	75	13
Low achievement (CAT)	63	13	75	50	75	13
Anxiety	50	17	67	17	67	33
Few friends	17	17	33	0	0	0
Low organizational participation	25	0	13	0	25	0
Low jobs/chores involvement	0	0	13	0	13	0
Low religiosity	0	0	0	0	13	0
Family						
Poor communication	—	—	100	100	100	63
Poor supervision	63	38	88	25	100	50
High parental stress	63	13	88	50	63	38
Physical punishment	50	13	88	63	75	13
Parent substance use problems	75	38	63	38	13	13

Table 11.4 (continued)

| | Sample | | | | | |
| | Youngest | | Middle | | Oldest | |
Variable	% Sig.	OR = 2+	% Sig.	OR = 2+	% Sig.	OR = 2+
Unhappy parents	50	38	63	38	25	13
Parent anxiety/depression	88	50	50	13	63	25
Disagree on discipline	—	—	75	38	25	13
Father behavior problems	63	50	50	13	13	13
Low reinforcement	0	0	75	25	63	38
Not close to mother	—	—	25	13	75	25
Parent antisocial attitude	50	25	25	0	0	0
Boy not involved	38	13	38	0	50	0
No set time home	0	0	13	0	25	13
Macro						
Broken family	75	63	63	50	50	38
Family on welfare	75	25	63	13	50	38
Bad neighborhood (P)	50	38	25	0	63	38
African American	50	13	25	13	25	13
Low SES	50	0	75	38	38	0
Poorly educated mother	50	13	25	0	38	25
Unemployed father	25	13	25	25	0	0
Bad neighborhood (C)	50	13	13	0	13	13
Poor housing	0	0	38	0	75	13
Unemployed mother	38	0	38	13	13	0
Large family	50	13	0	0	0	0
Young mother	0	0	13	0	13	13
Small house	25	0	13	0	13	0

Notes. OR = odds ratio; Sig = % of significant outcomes usually calculated on basis of eight outcomes (see text); 2+ = % of outcomes with odds ratios = 2.0 or greater; —, not measured at this age.

macrovariable was strongly (odds ratio = 2.0 or greater) related to the majority of outcomes, compared with five child variables and one family variable (poor parent–boy communication). A broken family was strongly related to half of all outcomes. Generally, the explanatory variables that were only related to a few outcomes tended to be rather weakly related to them and were not significantly related to the same outcomes in all samples.

Age Effects

In some instances, the impact of an explanatory factor on several outcomes narrowed with age, as shown by a larger number of associations at a young age compared with the number of associations at an older age. For the child factors, shy/withdrawn behavior was more related to a variety of outcomes in the youngest and middle samples than in the oldest sample. Also, parent deviant behavior and attitudes (parent substance use, father behavior problems, parent antisocial attitude, and, to a lesser extent, parent anxiety/depression) were more related to diverse outcomes for the youngest sample, slightly less related for the middle sample, and even less related for the oldest sample. Likewise, the percentage of significant associations for unhappy parents was higher for the youngest and middle samples compared with the oldest sample.

Similar age trends were found for several of the macrofactors, such as African American ethnicity, bad neighborhood (census, but not according to parent report), unemployed mother, and large family. These results strongly indicate the pervasive effect that family psychopathology, ethnicity, and some social handicaps have on diverse juvenile problem outcomes at a young age but less at a later age. In contrast, such age effects were not noted for child explanatory factors (see Table 11.4).

In a few instances, the impact of an explanatory factor across several outcomes increased with age. For example, the percent of significant outcomes associated with HIA increased from 67% in the youngest sample to 100% in the middle and oldest samples. Similarly, some childrearing practices, particularly poor supervision and physical punishment, became associated with a higher number of problem behaviors for the middle, and oldest sample compared with the youngest sample (poor supervision: 63%, 88%, 100%, in the youngest, middle and oldest samples, respectively; physical punishment: 50%, 88%, 75%).

The results show age shifts in the pattern of explanatory factors, with some explanatory factors becoming associated with a higher diversity of problem behaviors over time and other explanatory factors showing a narrowing down of associated outcomes with age. It should be kept in mind that several of the associations between explanatory factors, (e.g., African American ethnicity) and outcomes did not survive in multivariate analyses. We review this in the next section.

INDEPENDENTLY IMPORTANT EXPLANATORY VARIABLES

So far the results consider bivariate relations between explanatory factors and outcomes. The next question is to what extent the results hold in hierarchical multivariate analyses. Also, multivariate analyses can help address the extent that explanatory factors associated with different outcomes agree with the model that we formulated earlier, with child factors being related most strongly to an outcome, followed by family factors, followed by macrofactors. For that purpose, Table 11.5 narrows down the explanatory factors listed in Table 11.4 to those that independently contribute to one or more outcomes in hierarchical regression analyses.

The following were the most important predictors, each predicting at least half of the possible outcomes: a high ADHD score, lack of guilt, HIA problems (all replicated across the three samples), and, for two out of the three samples, low achievement (based on the parent, boy, and teacher ratings), shy/withdrawn behavior, and poor parent–boy communication.

In agreement with our sequential model (Fig. 1.2), there was little tendency for macrovariables to predict outcomes after controlling for child and family variables. The most important macrovariable—bad neighborhood (based on the parent rating)—was an independent predictor of only one outcome (delinquency) in the youngest sample, one outcome (covert behavior) in the middle sample, and two outcomes (delinquency and physical aggression) in the oldest sample. However, poor parent–boy communication (middle and oldest samples) was important independently of child variables for slightly more than half of the outcomes (63%). This suggests that some revision of our sequential model is needed, allowing for a direct effect of at least one family variable rather than indirect effects via child variables.

Age Effects

A few age effects, noted in the preceding section, reemerged in the hierarchical analyses: The number of associations between HIA problems and the number of outcomes increased somewhat (from 50% in the youngest sample to 67% in the middle and oldest samples). Similarly, an increase was observed for

TABLE 11.5

Percentage of Eight Outcomes Where Explanatory Variables Were Independently Important in Hierarchical Regressions

		Sample	
Variable	Youngest	Middle	Oldest
Child			
High ADHD score	100	100	83
Lack of guilt	75	75	63
HIA problems	50	67	67
Low achievement (PBT)	25	50	75
Shy/withdrawn	50	83	17
Depressed mood	50	17	67
Old for grade	63	38	25
Anxiety	33	33	17
Low achievement (CAT)	25	25	0
Few friends	33	17	0
Low organization participation	0	13	13
Low jobs/chores involvement	0	13	0
Low religiosity	0	0	13
Family			
Poor communication	—	63	63
Parent anxiety/depression	50	13	38
Physical punishment	13	38	25
High parental stress	13	25	38
Poor supervision	38	0	25
Unhappy parents	38	13	13
Parent substance use problems	25	13	0

237

Table 11.5 (continued)

Variable	Sample		
	Youngest	Middle	Oldest
Parent antisocial attitude	25	13	0
Father behavior problems	25	0	0
Not close to mother	—	13	0
Boy not involved	13	0	0
No set time home	0	13	0
Disagree on discipline	—	0	0
Low reinforcement	0	0	0
Macro			
Bad neighborhood (P)	13	13	25
Unemployed mother	38	13	0
Low SES	13	25	0
Family on welfare	13	0	13
African American	13	13	0
Unemployed father	13	13	0
Young mother	0	13	13
Poorly educated mother	0	0	25
Broken family	0	0	13
Bad neighborhood (C)	0	0	13
Poor housing	0	0	13
Large family	13	0	0
Small house	0	0	0

Note. —, Not measured at this age.

physical punishment (13% in the youngest sample, 38% in the middle sample, and 25% in the oldest sample), high parental stress (from 13% in the youngest sample to 25% and 38% in the middle and oldest samples, respectively), and bad neighborhood (according to parent rating: 13% in the youngest and middle samples, and 25% in the oldest sample).

In contrast, for several other explanatory factors, the hierarchical multiple regression results suggest that their impact across different outcomes narrowed with age. This was the case for shy/withdrawn behavior, old for grade, low achievement according to CAT scores, and having few friends. For example, old for grade was associated with 63% of the outcomes for the youngest sample, 38% for the middle sample, and 25% in the oldest sample. The decrease may be linked to the fact that being old for the grade was most deviant for first grade boys. The decreasing impact across different outcomes also applied to several explanatory factors in the family, including unhappy parents, parent substance use problems, parent antisocial attitude, father problem behavior, and unemployed mother.

The multivariate findings are hard to compare with other studies. First, there are few studies that have compared explanatory factors across externalizing behaviors, internalizing behaviors, ADHD, and substance use. The only study that did this consisted of a select sample of hyperactive children and controls between the ages of 4 and 12 (Fischer, Barkley, Fletcher, & Smallish, 1993). That study, using multiple regression methods, found more indication of different explanatory factors for different outcomes than shared factors. In contrast, we found more evidence of shared explanatory factors than of separate explanatory factors across different outcomes.

REPLICATED INTERACTION
EFFECTS

Which explanatory factors showed interactions in the hierarchical multiple regression analyses across the different outcomes? Unfortunately, there were few replicated interaction effects across outcomes or samples. Table 11.6 shows the best examples of replication, assuming similarity in some cases between types of child variables (a high ADHD score and HIA problems, anxiety, and shy/withdrawn behavior) and types of macrovariables (low SES, African American ethnicity, bad neighborhood).

As we discussed in chapter 5, we distinguished between types of interaction effects: enhancing, suppressing, and nonlinear interaction effects.

Replicated interaction effects were only included in Table 11.6 if they were of the same type. Seventy-five percent of the interactions involved lack of guilt, 50% concerned HIA or ADHD, and none of the replicated interactions

TABLE 11.6
Replication of Interaction Effects Across Nine Outcomes (%)

| | | | | B = No | | B = Yes | |
Variable A	Variable B	Sample	Outcome	A = No	A = Yes	A = No	A = Yes
Lack of guilt	Shy/withdrawn	Y	ADHD score	14.1	58.1	30.4	46.2
Lack of guilt	Shy/withdrawn	M	Physical aggression	11.8	54.3	37.0	54.0
Lack of guilt	HIA problems	Y	Shy/withdrawn	16.8	39.7	39.5	36.8
Lack of guilt	HIA problems	Y	Covert behavior	13.7	46.0	52.6	57.9
Lack of guilt	High ADHD score	Y	Delinquency	18.8	57.4	38.7	42.6
Lack of guilt	High HIA score	O	Delinquency	24.8	54.1	52.9	61.2
Low achievement	Anxiety	M	Substance use	8.2	29.3	19.8	22.0
Low achievement	Shy/withdrawn	M	Conduct problems	14.6	39.2	36.3	37.3
Lack of guilt	Low SES	M	Substance use	8.2	23.6	28.8	22.0
Lack of guilt	African American	O	Sexual intercourse	10.9	42.1	61.5	63.4
HIA problems	Low SES	M	Physical aggression	18.5	55.4	34.6	52.6
HIA problems	Bad neighborhood (P)	M	Covert behavior	15.4	51.4	35.4	31.8

Note. Y = youngest sample; M = middle sample; O = oldest sample.

consisted of family interactional variables. As it happens, all of these replicated interaction effects were suppressing effects. For example, the presence of guilt feelings and not having HIA problems was associated with a particularly low probability of an adverse outcome such as delinquency. Perhaps the most interesting replicable interaction effects are between child and macrofactors. For example, the absence of HIA problems, combined with the joint absence of low SES (or bad neighborhood), was associated with a low likelihood of adverse outcomes, such as physical aggression or covert behavior.

In summary, we found only evidence for suppressing interaction effects. Two conclusions can be drawn. First, the absence of certain explanatory factors is associated with favorable outcomes over and above the contribution of the individual explanatory factors. Second, such interactive effects were not found for the presence of multiple explanatory factors, which tended to be independently associated with unfavorable outcomes in an additive manner. Third, we did not find replicated effects of interactions between child factors and parental childrearing practices. In other words, we failed to find that the joint impact of child factors and poor childrearing practices was larger or smaller than the impact of each separately. These unexpected results concur with findings reported by McCord (1994) in the Cambridge–Somerville Youth Study showing the absence of an interaction between early disruptive child behavior and maternal competence (which included disciplinary practices).

IDENTIFYING MULTIPROBLEM BOYS

So far the analyses in this chapter and the preceding chapters concerned associations between explanatory factors and one or more outcomes. It is clear from the relationships between the different outcomes that a proportion of boys show multiple problem behavior. As a rule, multiproblem boys have an early age at onset, show an increasing rate of offending over time, and are at risk for a career of chronic delinquency (Loeber, 1982). Therefore, we need to understand better (a) how many boys can be characterized as multiproblem boys, and (b) which explanatory factors can account for multiproblem boys. Along that line, we need to examine the degree that explanatory factors for multiproblem boys are quantitatively or qualitatively different from explanatory factors for less problematic boys.

To investigate these questions, each boy was scored according to the number of problems he possessed out of eight outcomes (delinquency, substance use, a high ADHD score, conduct problems, physical aggression, covert behavior, depressed mood, and shy/withdrawn behavior). Table 11.7 shows the number of boys with each score, from 0 to 8. When a boy was not known on any problem, his score on the remaining problems was scaled up appropriately. For

TABLE 11.7
Number of Boys with Different Problem Outcomes (%)

Number of Outcomes	Sample					
	Youngest		Middle		Oldest	
0	152	(30.2)	153	(30.1)	118	(23.3)
1	114	(22.7)	95	(18.7)	114	(22.5)
2	70	(13.9)	83	(16.3)	89	(17.6)
3	67	(13.3)	63	(12.4)	62	(12.3)
4	48	(9.5)	45	(8.9)	65	(12.8)
5	27	(5.4)	45	(8.9)	34	(6.7)
6	18	(3.6)	18	(3.5)	17	(3.4)
7	4	(.8)	4	(.8)	5	(1.0)
8	3	(.6)	2	(.4)	2	(.4)
4 or more	100	(19.9)	114	(22.4)	123	(24.3)

Note. Total percent varies due to rounding.

example, if a boy had four out of seven problems, this fraction (4/7) was multiplied by 8 and rounded up or down to the nearest integer to produce the boy's score. (In this case, (4/7) x 8 = 4.57, giving a score of 5.)

Table 11.7 shows that the number and percent of boys steadily decreased in each of the three samples with an increasing number of outcomes they displayed. We decided to identify the worst 20% to 25% of the boys in each sample—those with four or more problems out of eight—as the multiproblem boys. It can be seen that there were 100 (19.9%) of these boys in the youngest sample, 114 (22.4%) in the middle sample, and 123 (24.3%) in the oldest sample.

MULTIPROBLEM BOYS VERSUS DIFFERENT OUTCOMES

Table 11.8 shows the extent to which boys with each outcome were multiproblem boys. For example, 140 boys were classified as delinquents in the youngest sample and 69 (49.3%) of them were multiproblem boys, compared with only 31 of the 363 nondelinquents (8.5%), giving an odds ratio of 10.4. The odds ratios were highest for covert behavior (19.6, 19.4, and 22.4 for the youngest, middle, and oldest samples, respectively), a high ADHD score (12.7, 18.4, 16.3), conduct problems (25.2, 14.7, 14.2), physical aggression (16.1, 14.1, 10.4), and delinquency (10.4, 9.2, 7.8), showing that the multiproblem boys were especially characterized by these externalizing outcomes. Conversely, the multiproblem boys were less likely to be substance users (3.8, 5.8, 4.7) or to engage in internalizing behaviors: shy/withdrawn behavior (5.5, 6.6, 3.0) or depressed mood (4.1, 3.6, 4.5).

TABLE 11.8
Percent Multiproblem Boys with Different Outcomes

	Sample								
	Youngest			Middle			Oldest		
Outcome	%	(N)	OR	%	(N)	OR	%	(N)	OR
High ADHD score	53.5	(129)	12.7	64.8	(122)	18.4	67.5	(117)	16.3
Physical aggression	59.1	(115)	16.1	56.8	(146)	14.1	61.9	(113)	10.4
Covert behavior	59.2	(125)	19.6	64.1	(128)	19.4	70.5	(122)	22.4
Conduct problems	65.2	(112)	25.2	61.1	(126)	14.7	62.0	(137)	14.2
Delinquency	49.3	(140)	10.4	52.9	(140)	9.2	48.1	(185)	7.8
Substance use	41.2	(85)	3.8	53.9	(76)	5.8	48.4	(122)	4.7
Shy/withdrawn	44.1	(118)	5.5	47.1	(153)	6.6	39.6	(149)	3.0
Depressed mood	39.8	(118)	4.1	41.7	(115)	3.6	48.3	(116)	4.5

Note. The figures show the percentage of boys with each outcome who were multiproblem boys. OR = odds ratio.

EXPLANATORY VARIABLES FOR
MULTIPROBLEM BOYS

Analyses so far showed that several explanatory factors applied to most outcomes. However, it remains to be verified, that the same explanatory factors apply to those boys who score high on multiple problems.

Table 11.9 shows how far the multiproblem boys were predicted by explanatory variables (excluding explanatory variables such as depressed mood that were also outcomes). The best predictors in all these samples were lack of guilt (Odds Ratios = 6.1, 7.3, and 5.8 in the youngest, middle, and oldest samples, respectively) and HIA problems (5.7, 4.9, 5.8). Low achievement (according to parents, boys, and teachers), poor parent–boy communication, high parental stress, and a broken family were also strong predictors. Slightly less strongly (but still consistently across the three samples) were old for grade, poor supervision, boy not involved, unhappy parents, parent substance use problems, parent anxiety/depression, father behavior problems, low SES, and family on welfare. In addition, several explanatory factors in the middle and oldest samples were associated with multiproblem boys: anxiety, poor communication, physical punishment, low reinforcement, and parent disagreement about discipline. Finally, a few explanatory factors in the youngest and middle samples were associated with multiproblem boys: low achievement according to CAT scores, unemployed mother, and African American ethnicity.

REGRESSION ANALYSES FOR
MULTIPROBLEM BOYS

Because we know that several of the prior explanatory factors are correlated, we need to identify those explanatory factors that predict multiproblem boys when other explanatory factors are statistically controlled. Table 11.10 shows the results of hierarchical multiple regression analyses carried out to establish the most important independent predictors of multiproblem boys. As before, the child variables were entered first, then the family variables, and finally the macrovariables. (Table 11.9 also indicates that this was the order of importance of the categories of variables according to odds ratios.)

Lack of guilt and HIA problems proved to be the most important predictors in all three samples, followed by low achievement and anxiety (in two samples). The most important family predictors were poor parent–boy com

TABLE 11.9
Odds Ratios for Explanatory Variables for Multiproblem Boys

Variable	Sample		
	Youngest	Middle	Oldest
Child			
Lack of guilt	6.1****	7.3****	5.8****
Old for grade	1.8*	2.3****	1.6*
HIA problems	5.7****	4.9****	5.8****
Low achievement (PBT)	3.0****	3.7****	3.9****
Low achievement (CAT)	1.6*	2.1***	1.3
Low jobs/chores involvement	1.0	1.3	1.6*
Anxiety	1.6	3.0****	2.1***
Family			
Poor supervision	2.2***	2.4****	2.9****
Poor communication	—	4.4****	4.0****
Physical punishment	1.3	2.3****	2.3***
Low reinforcement	1.0	1.8**	2.0***
Boy not involved	1.7*	1.6*	1.9**
Disagree on discipline	—	2.4**	1.8*
Boy not close to mother	—	1.3	2.1**
Unhappy parents	2.7**	2.5**	2.0*
Parent antisocial attitude	2.3***	1.2	-1.1
High parental stress	2.0**	3.3****	3.0****
Parent substance use problems	2.6****	2.0**	1.6*
Parent anxiety/depression	2.7****	2.0**	2.4****
Father behavior problems	3.0****	1.5	2.3***
Macro			
Socioeconomic			
Low SES	2.0**	1.8**	1.7**
Family on welfare	2.4***	1.8**	1.6*
Poor housing	1.0	1.3	2.1***
Unemployed father	1.4	2.1*	-1.1
Unemployed mother	1.9*	1.7*	1.2
Poorly educated mother	1.9**	1.0	2.5****
Demographic			
African American	1.6*	1.5*	−1.2
Large family	1.7*	1.1	1.5*
Broken family	4.0****	2.7****	2.2***
Neighborhood			
Bad neighborhood (C)	1.8*	−1.1	1.1
Bad neighborhood (P)	2.5****	1.1	2.1***

Note. C = census, P = parent, B = boy, CAT = California Achievement Test, T = teacher. * $p <.05$. ** $p <.01$. *** $p <.001$. **** $p <.0001$. p values one-tailed based on chi-square with correction for continuity. No significant relationship: low organizational participation, few friends, low religiosity, young mother, small house, no set time home. —, Variable not measured in this sample. Variables not included: shy/withdrawn, depressed mood, and a high ADHD score.

TABLE 11.10
Hierarchical Multiple Regression Analyses for Multiproblem Boys

Variable	Multiple R	F Change	p
Youngest sample			
Child			
Lack of guilt	.352	65.01	.0001
HIA problems	.418	27.98	.0001
Low achievement (PBT)	.426	3.89	.025
Family			
Parent anxiety/depression	.457	8.61	.002
Unhappy parents	.473	4.83	.014
Parent antisocial attitude	.482	2.66	.052
Macro			
Bad neighborhood (P)	.500	5.81	.008
Middle Sample			
Child			
Lack of guilt	.410	89.20	.0001
HIA Problems	.455	21.87	.0001
Anxiety	.485	16.21	.0001
Low achievement (PBT)	.502	10.04	.0008
Family			
Poor communication	.527	15.54	.0001
High parental stress	.541	9.15	.001
Oldest Sample			
Child			
Lack of guilt	.358	65.28	.0001
HIA Problems	.419	25.52	.0001
Low achievement (PBT)	.440	9.94	.0009
Anxiety	.448	3.84	.025
Family			
Poor communication	.491	23.14	.0001
Parent anxiety/depression	.508	10.41	.0007
Physical punishment	.525	10.29	.0007
High parental stress	.533	5.41	.011
Macro			
Poorly educated mother	.540	4.32	.019

Note. p values one-tailed.

munication, parent anxiety/depression, and high parental stress (all in two samples). In addition, parent antisocial attitude contributed in the youngest sample only. With only two exceptions (bad neighborhood in the youngest sample and a poorly educated mother in the oldest sample), the macrofactors were not important predictors independently of the child and family factors.

In summary, in the multivariate analyses, three child characteristics—lack of guilt, HIA problems, and low academic achievement—independently predicted multiproblem boys in each of the samples. In contrast, family and macrofactors varied more across the three samples. For the youngest sample, parent characteristics (deviant behavior and attitudes, but not childrearing practices) contributed most, followed by bad neighborhood. For the middle sample, poor communication and high parental stress contributed most, but no neighborhood or other macrofactors. For the oldest sample, poor communication, physical punishment, and high parental stress contributed most, followed by poor education of the mother. Again, macrofactors including bad neighborhood did not enter in the equation.

Thus, the three multiple regressions showed consistency in terms of child behavior, but a shift from deviant parent behavior and attitude in the youngest sample (antisocial attitude, unhappy parents, parent anxiety/depression) to less than optimal childrearing practices (such as poor communication and physical punishment) in the older age groups. The second shift was from the presence of neighborhood effects in the youngest sample to the absence of such effects (or most other macroeffects) in the older two samples.

DETECTING INTERACTION EFFECTS FOR MULTIPROBLEM BOYS

A search was carried out for interaction effects among the independently important predictors in each sample. Only one interaction was statistically significant over and above the main effect. The combination of parent anxiety/depression and a poorly educated mother was associated with a high prevalence of multiproblem boys in the oldest sample (of boys with neither of these, 16.6% were multiproblem boys; of boys with parent anxiety/depression only, 26.3% were multiproblem boys; of boys with a poorly educated mother only, 24.7% were multi-problem boys; of boys with both a poorly educated mother and an anxious/depressed parent, 60.0% were multiproblem boys; LRCS = 3.77, $p = .052$; F change in regression = 4.15, $p = .042$). Thus, in the oldest sample, a poorly educated mother predicted multiproblem boys primarily when there was also parent anxiety/depression or, conversely, parent anxiety/depression predicted multiproblem boys primarily in the presence of a poorly educated mother.

EXPLANATORY VARIABLES
EXCLUDING MULTIPROBLEM BOYS

It remains to be seen whether explanatory factors associated with multiproblem boys are quantitatively or qualitatively the same as those for less problematic boys. To investigate this, the multiproblem boys were excluded from the analyses and the relationships between key explanatory variables and eight outcomes were examined for the remaining boys. The findings showed that the significant relationships generally were attenuated but did not disappear; decreases in odds ratios were usually marginal.

By far the largest decreases in odds ratios occurred for the relationships between HIA problems and a high ADHD score in the oldest sample (from 3.3 to 1.3) and between HIA problems and conduct problems in the youngest sample (from 4.0 to 1.2). These decreases probably occurred because most of the boys who had both HIA problems and a high ADHD score, or both HIA problems and conduct problems, were in the group of multiproblem boys.

Remarkably, for covert behavior in the oldest sample, the odds ratios generally increased after excluding the multiproblem boys (for nine predictors, with one unchanged and only four decreasing). The greatest increase was for African American ethnicity (from 1.1 to 3.2), suggesting that the overlap between African American ethnicity and covert behavior was greater among boys who were not in the multiproblem group.

Uniquely, the strength of the relationship between African American ethnicity and delinquency was always greater after excluding the multiproblem boys in all three samples (odds ratios = 1.9–2.3 in youngest sample, 2.5–2.7 in middle sample, and 2.3–3.9 in oldest sample). Again, this suggests that the overlap between African American ethnicity and delinquency was greater among boys who did not have multiple problems than among the multiproblem boys.

In summary, the results indicate that overall there were no qualitative differences in explanatory factors explaining multiproblem boys compared with boys with fewer problems.

RISK SCORES VERSUS
MULTIPROBLEM BOYS

To investigate the cumulative effect of risk factors on the prevalence of multiproblem boys, we scored all the boys according to their number of independent predictors identified in Table 11.10. For example, because there

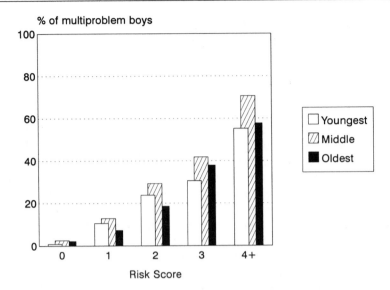

FIG. 11.1. Percentage of multiproblem boys as a function of increasing risk score.

were seven independent predictors of multiproblem boys in the youngest sample, we scored each boy from 0 to 7 according to how many of them he possessed. (As before, the scores of boys not known on one or more of these predictors were prorated accordingly.) Figure 11.1 shows the increasing prevalence of multiproblem boys with increasing risk scores. For example, of boys scoring four or more (with four or more risk factors), 55.2% were multiproblem boys in the youngest sample, 70.7% were multiproblem boys in the middle sample, and 57.7% were multiproblem boys in the oldest sample. The odds ratios corresponding to these discriminations were 7.3, 12.5, and 7.3, respectively.

CONCLUSIONS

In this chapter, we first examined the degree that the overlap among different outcomes could be interpreted as representing a general set of problem behaviors or whether the evidence favored more differentiated distinctions among problem behaviors. Next, we examined the extent that different outcomes shared the same explanatory factors and the extent to which each explanatory factor predicted several different outcomes. We then identified the multiproblem boys and investigated the explanatory factors that best predicted them. We closed with an examination of whether explanatory factors that accounted for multiproblem boys also applied to less problematic boys. We discuss the implications of the findings in the concluding chapter.

12

Summary and Conclusions

This chapter presents an overview of the major themes of this book in an effort to describe and explain juvenile delinquency, substance use, sexual intercourse, and mental health problems (covert behavior, physical aggression, conduct problems, attention deficit/hyperactivity, shy/withdrawn behavior, and depressed mood). The main aims of this volume were to address the following questions:

1. What is the prevalence and age of onset of delinquency, substance use, and early sexual behavior for three samples of boys at ages 7, 11, and 14? What is the prevalence of mental health problems for these ages? How strong are the relationships among these problem behaviors in each of the samples?

2. Which factors best explain individual differences among the boys in their manifestations of delinquency, substance use, early sexual behavior, and mental health problems? To what extent do explanatory factors vary with age? How accurately can boys with different outcomes be identified by risk scores based on hierarchical multiple regressions?

3. To what extent are explanatory factors associated with one outcome also associated with other outcomes? Are explanatory factors that are especially characteristic of a multiproblem group of boys (who display many different problem behaviors) different from explanatory factors associated with boys with few problems?

4. Do the results fit a general theory of juvenile problem behaviors or is a differentiated theory more applicable?

To address these questions, we first summarize the basic design of the study, and its limitations and strengths. We then consider the degree to which the findings support a general problem theory or whether the data fit better a differentiated problem theory. Under that heading, we review the: (a) interrelationships among problem behaviors, (b) age shifts in problem behavior and explanatory factors, and (c) specific and general explanatory factors.

Next, we summarize the explanatory factors that apply to multiproblem boys and compare them to boys with fewer problems. We then review the fit of our hierarchical model of individual and family and macroinfluences, and present a theoretical integration of the findings. We close with a discussion of the implications of the findings for interventions.

THE BASIC DESIGN AND RATIONALE OF THE PITTSBURGH YOUTH STUDY

Chapter 1 expressed the need for a new study on the course of antisocial behavior and factors affecting that course. Our rationale was that a new study was needed with an enriched sample of boys who were followed up frequently over time, preferably at half-yearly or yearly intervals. We also made the case that an accelerated longitudinal design with several samples of boys (we chose boys in Grades 1, 4, and 7) would be advantageous. With the help of the Pittsburgh Public School Board, we drew random samples from boys in these grades. By means of a screening procedure, we identified about 250 boys at highest risk in each of the three samples and then randomly selected 250 other boys in each grade. This led to the study of 503 boys in the first grade, 508 boys in the fourth grade, and 506 boys in seventh grade (called the youngest, middle, and oldest samples, respectively). Just over half of the boys were African American, with virtually all the remainder being White.

This book reports on the screening data wave and the first follow-up 6 months after that screening. A host of measurements were taken, detailed in chapter 3, most of them based on several informants, the boy, his parent—usually the mother—and his teacher. Measurements took place in several domains: child factors (e.g., low academic achievement, lack of guilt), family factors (e.g., parents' childrearing practices, deviant parent behavior, high parental stress), and macrofactors (including socioeconomic, demographic, and neighborhood factors). We tried to measure all constructs that were alleged to be important predictors or correlates of delinquency in the literature.

We made a deliberate attempt to select among all measured risk factors only those that we felt were reasonably independent of the outcomes, particularly delinquency (see chap. 5). For that reason we considered deviant behavior by peers as a correlate rather than an explanatory factor (see chap. 5). Thus, we attempted to minimize the likelihood of producing spuriously accurate predictions by introducing explanatory factors that were not conceptually independent of the outcome variables.

In the Methodological Appendix that follows this chapter, we explained the various reasons for executing most analyses with dichotomized data; we dichotomized the majority of the variables to differentiate the worst 25% of boys approximately. To check for the impact of dichotomization, we examined in bivariate analyses to what extent dichotomization produced different results from those obtained with continuous measures. We found that the correlations between the two types of results were extremely high. Also, we examined to what extent continuous explanatory variables produced similar results in a logistic regression compared with dichotomized ones. Again, the results were highly correlated, making us confident that the procedure that we followed with dichotomous variables was producing valid, replicable results.

LIMITATIONS AND STRENGTHS OF THE PRESENT BOOK

We wanted to stress both the limitations and strengths of the study. The study was limited to boys in inner city first, fourth, and seventh grades, with one follow-up a half-year later. The boys are representative of the grades in the Pittsburgh public schools from which they were drawn, but are not necessarily representative of boys in Pennsylvania or the United States, or of boys in rural areas. Although a large number of explanatory factors are considered in the study, the focus was on explanatory factors for delinquency rather than for mental health outcomes such as internalizing problems. The present volume did not pretend to address causal processes and certainly, given its basic cross-sectional design, could not address the cumulative impact of explanatory factors on later outcomes. However, this will be rectified in later longitudinal analyses. Further, we did not attempt to establish causality by altering or intervening in processes associated with child problem behaviors.

We also realize that the hierarchical multiple regression analyses that we used established the statistically optimal combination of explanatory factors and that results based on such analyses do not necessarily represent actual processes leading to child problem behavior. Although in our choice of possible explanatory factors we were guided by past research, it was impossible for us to adequately take account of genetic effects. (Biological factors and their interaction with psychosocial factors is the topic of a special project for the youngest sample co-directed by Adrian Raine.) Also, we attempted to collect data from multiple informants familiar with the boys.

However, given the large percentage of absent fathers, it was not practical to include them. Their exclusion meant that statistical power was lost for the analyses.

Against the limitations of the study, there are many strengths. It had a high participant cooperation rate during the study as well as at follow-up. The outcome measures were exceptionally varied and conceptually derived from different approaches to child problem behavior (psychology, psychiatry, criminology, and epidemiology): delinquency, substance use, sexual intercourse, covert behavior, physical aggression, conduct problems, attention deficit/hyperactivity, shy/withdrawn behavior, and depressed mood.

The availability of three grade samples allowed us to examine age differences in the prevalence and average score for the outcomes we had selected. Moreover, retrospective reports of the age of onset of delinquency, substance use, and sexual intercourse allowed us to construct age of onset curves for each of these outcomes. In the case of delinquency, we were able to validate the delinquency seriousness scale (based on boy's and parent's reports) against records of court referrals up to 6 years later. Thus, we were able to present new information about delinquency, substance use, sexual intercourse, and mental health problems in the three grade samples.

We considered a rich array of possible explanatory factors in the realms of individual, family, school, and neighborhood. Associations between independent and dependent measures were ascertained by means of bivariate statistics (odds ratios), hierarchical multiple regressions, and cumulative risk scores. Because most of the analyses ran parallel for each outcome, it was possible to compare the extent that explanatory factors associated with one outcome also applied to other outcomes (or were specific to a certain outcome). The study also allowed the identification of a group of multiproblem boys and a specification of those explanatory factors that best predicted for this group of boys. Perhaps most important, the availability of three large samples of boys of different grades permitted replication of results, as well as insights into possible trends in the development of problem behaviors and developmental shifts in explanatory factors. Moreover, the study made it possible to evaluate the utility of a general problem theory compared with a more differentiated problem theory.

A GENERAL PROBLEM THEORY VERSUS A DIFFERENTIATED PROBLEM THEORY

In the introduction, we referred to Jessor and Jessor's (1977) general problem theory. One of the main thrusts of this theory is that, because different juvenile problem behaviors are highly intercorrelated, they can be suitably subsumed under a general problem syndrome. The theory also postulates that explanatory factors that apply to one problem behavior also apply to other problem behaviors. A third characteristic of the theory is that explanatory factors for problem behavior are similar irrespective of the age at which the problem behavior emerged, or was measured.

We have great respect for Jessor and Jessor's theory and for the empirical support they have mustered for it (e.g., Donovan et al., 1988; Jessor & Jessor, 1977; Jessor et al., 1991). At the same time, we see serious limitations to the theory. First, it appears to be adevelopmental and does not take account of large differences in the age of onset and prevalence rates of problem behaviors as a function of age. In fact, empirical support for the theory was largely derived from studies of high school students and college freshmen and, therefore, data were not provided on problem behavior in the elementary school-age period nor on different ages of onset of problem behaviors. Second, the theory does not sufficiently explain why some juveniles develop one problem behavior and not another and why some juveniles develop multiple problem behaviors.

Because problem behavior theory focused mostly on externalizing problems and substance use, it was not tested on two other critical domains of juvenile problem behavior: attention deficit/hyperactivity and internalizing problems, such as shy/withdrawn behavior and depressed mood. An additional limitation concerned measurement: Studies were limited to information from the young people themselves about their problem behavior and about their reports of factors that were thought to influence their behavior. Whereas such a measurement strategy is defensible, autocorrelations between explanatory factors and outcomes are much more common as a result. Also, it is currently more accepted that multiple informants (such as juveniles and parents) are needed to improve the validity of the constructs.

We propose a differentiated problem theory with a developmental underpinning and test this by means of the following:

1. Interrelationships among problem behaviors. According to a general problem theory, we would expect different problem behaviors to be equally interrelated, whereas in a differentiated problem theory, the interrelationships among problems would vary, with some being similar but others being stronger or weaker.

2. Age shifts. A general problem theory puts little emphasis on age differences in the onset of various problem behaviors, variations in the prevalence of problem behaviors with age, and temporal sequences in the unfolding of different problems. In contrast, a differentiated problem theory attaches importance to such age shifts because, among other things, they

indicate optimal times for interventions. In a general problem theory, we would expect that explanatory factors for problem behavior at one age would also apply to other ages. In contrast, in a differentiated problem theory, we would expect that some explanatory factors would be similarly associated with problem behaviors across different ages, whereas other explanatory factors would be more associated with problem behaviors at certain age periods rather than others.

3. Specific and general explanatory factors. If a general problem theory applied, we would expect that explanatory factors associated with one problem also would apply to other problem behaviors. In contrast, in a differentiated problem theory, we would expect that certain sets of explanatory factors would be shared by different problem behaviors, whereas other explanatory factors would be specific to particular outcomes.

We now evaluate each of these above points against the findings presented in this book.

Interrelationships Among Problem Behaviors

We showed (particularly in chap. 11) that the outcomes we studied were interrelated but with variations in pattern. We interpret these findings to show a basic underlying structure of disruptive and delinquent behavior that cuts across different age groups. Early manifestations of externalizing problems (a high ADHD score, physical aggression, covert behavior, and conduct problems) were particularly highly interrelated. Thus, like Jessor (Jessor & Jessor, 1977; Jessor et al., 1991) and others (Martin et al., 1994), we found associations among different externalizing problems (with the understanding that a small part of the intercorrelations in the present study resulted from the few common elements among these outcomes).

However, we go beyond Jessor and Jessor's (1977) formulation by stressing the importance of variations among different domains of problems that are linked to externalizing behaviors. For example, we found that shy/withdrawn behavior, unlike depressed mood, was not related to substance use. We also found that the relationships among early manifestations of externalizing problems (a high ADHD score, physical aggression, covert behavior, and conduct problems) were stronger than between early and later externalizing problems (delinquency, substance use). We see attention-deficit/hyperactivity as a key element in boys' progression to diverse problem behaviors; it is associated with their progression to delinquency and substance use and with their vulnerability for internalizing problems (shy/withdrawn behavior and depressed mood). However, in line with other longitudinal studies (e.g., Farrington, Loeber, & Van Kammen,

1990; Loeber et al., 1995), we suggest that boys with ADHD only are not at high risk of developing serious delinquency or substance use. Instead, we conceptualize that ADHD leads to serious forms of externalizing problems only when it is associated with minor problem behaviors (such as physical fighting and covert behavior).

In addition, we see serious problem behavior of elementary school-age boys as involving several domains of maladaptation. First because of the presence of externalizing problems, and second because of comorbid internalizing problems. In that sense, early serious problem behaviors often involves a mixture of poor control over acting out behavior, socially distant and withdrawn behavior, and mood dysregulation.

Age Shifts

In a differentiated problem theory, we would expect several forms of age shifts: (a) in the manifestations of problem behaviors, (b) in the interrelationships among different problem behaviors, and (c) in the patterns of explanatory factors associated with the problem behaviors at different ages.

Age Shifts in Problem Behaviors

We found the following age trends in problem behaviors (see chap. 4 for details).

Delinquency.   For each boy, we computed a lifetime delinquency seriousness score (detailed in chap. 3) with four levels of seriousness: no delinquency, minor delinquency, moderate delinquency, and serious delinquency. Boys were assigned to the most serious level of delinquency that they had reached at the time of the first follow-up. The prevalence results (chap. 4) show that the percentage of nondelinquent boys decreased with age and that boys engaging in more serious behaviors increased with age—tripling from 8.8% in the youngest sample to 28.7% in the oldest sample.

Onset curves (Fig. 4.1 and 4.2 in chap. 4) show that, for the middle and oldest samples, the prevalence of delinquency greatly increased from ages 5 to 7 and accelerated between ages 7 and 10. The onset curve for moderate delinquency accelerated earlier than the onset curve for serious delinquency. Thus, there was a sequential pattern of onset, with less serious forms of delinquency occurring first and most serious forms of delinquency occurring last. These results were observed in both samples. In summary, the prime time for the emergence of minor and moderate forms of delinquency was in the elementary school-age period, whereas the middle school period was the most crucial time for the emergence of more serious forms of delinquent acts. Prevalence data were presented for all three samples showing that the lifetime prevalence of theft and vandalism increased substantially between ages 7 and 11. Between ages 11 and 14, the lifetime prevalence of violence and fraud increased substantially. Also, with age, the variety of delinquent acts greatly increased.

In addition, between middle childhood and adolescence, the frequency of delinquent acts increased considerably (we could not measure frequency for the youngest sample). When we studied the active delinquent boys, we found that, across all delinquent acts, those boys in the middle sample averaged 8.2 acts in the previous 6 months, compared with an average of 13.6 for the boys in the oldest sample. This constituted a relative increase of 65%. It has long been known that seriousness, frequency, and variety of offending are intercorrelated (e.g., Farrington, 1973). However, we found that the correlations were highest between seriousness and variety and between frequency and variety, but lower between seriousness and frequency.

We also found that a proportion of the youth committed both violence and theft. This percentage was clearly smallest for the youngest sample and greatest for the oldest sample (21.6%, 47.1%, and 62.7% in the three samples, respectively). Thus, versatility in offending increased with age. Conversely, specialized offending was more common among younger than among older boys.

Substance Use.   Substance use was classified in five categories (chap. 3): beer or wine, tobacco, hard liquor use, marijuana use, and other drug use. Prevalence data (chap. 4) showed that the percentage of boys not using any substance decreased from 84.4% in the youngest sample to 63% in the middle sample and to 25.9% in the oldest sample. Between ages 7 and 11, the percentage of boys having reached as the highest level in substance use the drinking of beer or wine more than doubled (9.3%–25.2%) and further increased to 32.5% at age 14. For all substances, we found that the percentage of boys using them gradually increased often by a factor of 3 when we compared the youngest to the oldest sample.

Age at onset as reported by the boys in the middle and oldest samples (Figs. 4.3 and 4.4 in chap. 4) showed that the onset of substance use gradually unfolded over time with beer or wine use coming first, liquor use coming next, and the onset of marijuana and other illegal drugs following slightly later (measured in the middle and oldest samples only). For both samples, we demonstrated that the degree of onset of substance use during the elementary school age period was already substantial, even when substances used without parental knowledge were included.

Also in these samples, we measured the frequency of substance use (chap. 4), which steadily increased between ages 11 and 14 (the exception was wine).

The largest increase was found for marijuana use, which for users increased from an average frequency of 40.7 per year in the middle sample to an average of 61.0 in the oldest sample. We found some indication that boys' escalation to more serious substance use was associated with a higher frequency of use of lower levels. In other words, high frequency use at one level of substance use was associated with a high probability of transition to substance use at a more serious level.

Disruptive Behavior Disorders.   We found that one in five of the boys suffered from a disruptive behavior disorder (chap. 4). Of these disorders, ADHD was most common, affecting 15.2% of the youngest sample, 10.5% of the middle sample, and 7.6% of the oldest sample. These results confirm other studies showing that the prevalence of this disorder decreases with age. However, what we know from other studies is that attention deficit accounts for most of the persistence in ADHD symptoms (Hart et al., 1995).

We also found a slight increase in oppositional defiant disorder with age—from 2.2% in the youngest sample to 4.8% in the middle sample and 5% in the oldest sample. Finally, we found an increase in the prevalence of conduct disorder with age—from 5.6% and 5.4% in the youngest and middle samples, respectively, to 8.3% in the oldest sample. Thus, we observed a gradual decrease in ADHD across the three age groups, but an increase, particularly in the elementary school-age period, in oppositional defiant disorder and an increase in conduct disorder between ages 7, 11, and 14.

Mental Health.   Turning to internalizing problems, we found that the average shy/withdrawn score increased with age, but that there was a substantial decrease in the average depressed mood and anxiety scores.

Sexual Intercourse.   Not surprisingly, the percentage of boys who had engaged in sexual intercourse in the oldest sample slowly increased between ages 6 and 9, after which it accelerated sharply (sexual intercourse was not measured in the two younger samples.) The prevalence of sexual intercourse was consistently higher for African American boys compared with White boys. However, once this difference in prevalence was taken into account, the number of times that boys had sexual intercourse, or the number of partners they had, did not differ between the two ethnic groups.

Age Trends in Interrelationships Among Problem Behaviors

We found that most often the interrelationships among problem behaviors did not vary materially with age. However, several exceptions should be noted.

The association between physical aggression and delinquency decreased across the different grade samples, which was also the case for the strength of association between substance use and delinquency. We interpret this as meaning that the comorbid association among different early forms of problem behavior is particularly high in elementary school-age boys. Between that period and adolescence, however, as we know from other research findings (Loeber, 1985, 1988), the associations between physical aggression and delinquency and between substance use and delinquency decreased with age largely because of the emergence of a group of less deviant or more normal delinquents, such as nonaggressive and not seriously substance-using delinquents. However, over time, a minority of juveniles become characterized by multiple serious problem behaviors. Longitudinal research is needed to demonstrate to what extent this group emerges from the young comorbid group discussed before.

Conclusion. A considerable number of boys in this inner city sample engaged in problem behaviors. Major age differences were observed between the samples. Different courses of problem behavior were also noted, with some behaviors decreasing with age (depressed mood, ADHD) and others increasing with age (shy/withdrawn behavior, oppositional behavior, conduct problems, serious delinquency, serious substance use, sexual intercourse). In addition, we found that different seriousness levels of delinquency and substance use each unfolded over time in an apparent orderly fashion. We considered the findings strong enough not to lump all of these behaviors together into a single problem behavior syndrome.

Shift in Explanatory Factors With Age.

The next criterion for evaluating a problem theory is the extent that explanatory factors were similar at different ages. We found that many explanatory factors, especially child factors, were associated with the same variety of outcomes at different ages.

However, for several explanatory factors (shy/withdrawn behavior, old for grade [reflecting low attainment], low achievement, and having few friends), the largest variety of associations was observed at a young age and there were fewer associations at an older age. All of these factors also emerged in multivariate analyses, showing that, they independently contributed to outcomes when other variables were taken into account, but only at a young age.

The same applied to several family factors, in that several forms of parent deviance—including parent substance use problems, father behavior problems, and, to a lesser extent, parent anxiety/depression—were more associated with a large variety of outcomes at a young age than at older ages. Remarkably, with the exception of the latter factor, all of these forms of family deviance independently contributed to multiple problem outcomes in multivariate analyses.

The same was true for unhappy parents. Only in the case of childrearing practices did we find trends for the strength of an association with a given outcome to increase across the grade samples. This was the case for physical punishment, which became increasingly related to physical aggression, particularly between late childhood and adolescence, and poor supervision, which became increasingly related to covert behavior with age.

Several macrofactors were associated with a higher variety of outcomes in the younger age group compared with the older age group. This applied to bad neighborhood (according to census information), unemployed mother, large family, and African American ethnicity. However, only unemployed mother emerged in the multivariate analyses.

Finally, opposite age effects were observed for a few explanatory factors. In the cases of HIA problems, poor supervision, physical punishment, and high parental stress, the association with multiple outcomes increased across the grade samples.

Thus, against a background of findings of explanatory factors being related to similar sets of outcomes across the three age groups, we found several instances of what we consider important age effects. The fact that several explanatory factors were associated with an increased diversity of problem behaviors over time indicates the importance of such factors over and above those factors with an apparently more consistent effect.

Specific and General Explanatory Factors

To what extent are explanatory factors that are associated with one outcome also associated with other outcomes? We calculated this by summarizing relevant tables from prior chapters across the different outcomes in terms of the percentage of significant odds ratios and the magnitudes of odds ratios (chap. 11). Using the percentage of significant odds ratios as a criterion, we found that our two measures of attention deficit/impulsivity and hyperactivity (a high ADHD score and HIA problems) were consistently related to multiple outcomes. This also applied to low achievement (which is often associated with attention problems) and lack of guilt. When the results were narrowed down to those resulting from hierarchical multiple regressions, the following variables independently contributed to multiple outcomes: a high ADHD score, HIA problems, and lack of guilt.

Of the family factors, only poor communication and poor supervision showed a high percentage of significant associations across multiple outcomes. However, in hierarchical multiple regression analyses, only poor communication survived. None of the macrofactors was consistently related to multiple outcomes, nor did these factors emerge consistently in the regression analyses.

In summary, several explanatory factors were consistently associated with multiple outcomes in each of the three samples. However, most explanatory factors, and particularly macrofactors, were not consistently related to all outcomes.

The magnitude of odds ratios is another criterion for examining possible differential effects of explanatory factors across different outcomes. For several explanatory factors, the magnitudes of odds ratios remained the same across outcomes (e.g., low achievement and HIA problems). In contrast, several child factors were more related to externalizing than other problem behaviors. These included lack of guilt, which was most strongly related to a high ADHD score, conduct problems, physical aggression, and delinquency. Also, several family factors were mostly related to externalizing problems. For instance, poor communication was especially strongly related to externalizing behaviors, including a high ADHD score, conduct problems, and covert behavior. Likewise, poor supervision was more related to externalizing problems than internalizing problems. In addition, high parental stress was most strongly related to early forms of externalizing problems (a high ADHD score, physical aggression, and covert behavior) and slightly less to delinquency. The results agree with findings reported by Conger, Patterson, and Ge (1995), showing that high parental stress affected adolescents' adjustment through parents' depressed mood and their poor disciplinary practices.

Several macrofactors, such as a broken family, low SES, bad neighborhood, and African American ethnicity, were more strongly related to externalizing rather than internalizing problems. In fact, African American ethnicity was specifically related to delinquency but not to other outcomes. Also, bad neighborhood was especially related to delinquency, physical aggression, and covert behavior. These associations, except for African American ethnicity, survived in multivariate analyses when child and family factors were also taken into account, but not for all samples. Thus, neighborhood characteristics, as perceived by the parents, independently contributed to the explanation of some forms of externalizing problem behaviors. It should be noted that bad neighborhood was less strongly associated with a high ADHD score, covert behavior, substance use, and depressed mood, and was not related to shy/withdrawn behavior.

A few explanatory factors were differentially associated with internalizing problems: Lack of guilt was more related to shy/withdrawn behavior than to depressed mood, whereas the opposite applied to physical punishment, which was related to depressed mood but not to shy/withdrawn behavior.

Another criterion to evaluate a general theory of problem behavior is to examine the degree that explanatory factors for pairs of problem behavior were interchangeable or not, suggesting similar forms of influences on several outcomes. The results show that explanatory factors for substance use were largely, but not fully, a subset of the risk factors for delinquency. Similarly, the explanatory factors for depressed mood (and shy/withdrawn behavior) were largely but not fully a subset of the explanatory factors for conduct problems, covert behavior (two of the three samples), physical aggression, and a high ADHD score.

However, explanatory factors for substance use were largely different from explanatory factors for physical aggression, covert behavior, and conduct problems. There was least overlap between explanatory factors for substance use and those associated with a high ADHD score. Finally, we found considerable overlap among the explanatory factors for the following pairs of outcomes: delinquency and conduct problems, delinquency and physical aggression, delinquency and covert behavior, and delinquency and a high ADHD score.

Conclusions Concerning a Differentiated Problem Theory

We presented three perspectives to evaluate a general problem theory: (a) the interrelationships among problem behaviors, (b) age shifts in problem behavior and explanatory factors, and (c) specific and general explanatory factors. In each instance, we presented data to show that, at a minimum, a general problem theory needs to be qualified to fit our results. In that sense, the formulation of a more differentiated problem theory appears appropriate and inevitable. The differentiated problem theory needs to predict both explanatory factors that apply to multiple outcomes and explanatory factors that are specific to certain outcomes. For example, awareness of explanatory factors that apply to multiple outcomes is potentially relevant for early interventions because the modification of explanatory factors that predict several outcomes will have a greater impact on child psychopathology and maladjustment—and hence greater cost-effectiveness—than the modification of explanatory factors that predict only a single outcome. Awareness of explanatory factors that apply to some but not other outcomes is important. It sharpens interventions to make them more specifically applicable to the outcome of particular concern.

MULTIPROBLEM BOYS

Clinicians, parole officers, and school psychologists rarely base their decisions on relationships between explanatory factors and outcomes. Instead, they attempt to establish which type of intervention can be best applied to which kinds of youth. They often are particularly concerned about multiproblem youth because of the complexities of the presenting problems and the risk these youth incur for poor outcomes in the long run. Some part of the professionals' decisions is influenced by what they know about factors that have shaped these youth in becoming multiproblem children. Certainly those professionals who are interested in devising preventive interventions want to know what are the most important factors that can explain the emergence of this group among all youth of a particular age group.

Chapter 11 investigated the extent that explanatory factors that applied to multiproblem boys also applied to boys with fewer problems. The results are summarized here. We saw that multiproblem boys were best predicted by sets of explanatory factors in the domains of child and family, and, to a much lesser extent, macrovariables. Among the child variables, the most powerful explanatory factors were lack of guilt, HIA problems, low achievement (based on parent, boy, and teacher ratings or, according to CAT score, youngest and middle samples), poor communication (middle and oldest samples), anxiety (middle and oldest samples), and, slightly less strongly, old for grade. Of these, the following survived in multivariate analyses: lack of guilt, and HIA problems (all three samples), followed by low achievement and anxiety (in two samples).

Of the family factors, univariate analyses showed that the following factors were associated with multiproblem boys: poor supervision, boy not involved in family activities, unhappy parents, parent substance use problems, parent anxiety/depression, and father behavior problems. In addition, several explanatory factors in the middle and oldest samples were associated with multiproblem boys: poor communication, physical punishment, low reinforcement, and parental disagreement about discipline. However, only the following family factors survived in the multivariate analyses: poor parent–boy communication, parent anxiety/depression, and high parental stress (all in two samples). In addition, parent antisocial attitude and bad neighborhood (parent rating) contributed in the youngest sample only.

Finally, only a few macrovariables were at a bivariate level associated with multiproblem boys: low SES, family on welfare, and African American ethnicity (two samples). With only two exceptions (bad neighborhood in the youngest sample and poorly educated mother in the oldest sample), the macrofactors were not important independently of the child and family factors. Remarkably, most of the factors that accounted for multiproblem boys also accounted for boys with fewer problems.

FROM EXPLANATION TO THEORY

At this juncture, we need to integrate the findings of explanatory factors reported for each outcome (chaps. 5–10) into a theoretical framework and ensure that such a framework can help us better grasp the emergence of multiproblem boys (chap. 11). We conceptualized (Fig. 1.2 in chap. 1) a hierarchical model of influences on outcomes, in which child factors contributed most directly, family factors through child factors, and macrofactors indirectly through family factors. Substantially, the results support this model, albeit with several exceptions. Poor parent–boy communication was an important predictor independently of child variables for the majority of outcomes. Therefore, the results suggest that, at least in this instance, family influences had a direct rather than an indirect impact on outcomes, warranting a slight modification in the model that we proposed.

Turning to macrofactors, the results confirm that macrovariables contributed little to the prediction of outcomes after controlling for child and family variables. This varied with different outcomes. For example, bad neighborhood (based on the parent rating) was an independent predictor of only one outcome (delinquency) in the youngest sample, one outcome (covert behavior) in the middle sample, and two outcomes (delinquency and physical aggression) in the oldest sample.

Overall, multiple regression analyses indicated a hierarchical model of influences, with individual factors having the largest impact, family factors the next largest, and macrofactors the least. However, there are a few caveats. The full model of individual, family, and macrofactors applied best to externalizing problems, whereas a partial model of individual and family factors (but not macrofactors) applied more to ADHD, substance use, and internalizing problems. Second, as shown in the Methodological Appendix, when blocks of variables were entered in the reverse order (i.e., macrovariables first, family variables next, and child variables last), similar results were found. This finding challenges conventional wisdom about how best to test different models to indentify the direction of influences between different groups of variables. Therefore, model testing proved of limited value in the present study.

We now elaborate on how we conceptualize that different factors operate within and between each of these domains. Starting with individual factors, we see three key elements as relevant for the development of problem behaviors: (a) poor impulse control, (b) attention problems, and (c) lack of guilt feelings. Each can lead to a diversity of problem behaviors independently of each other, and this is supported by the small number of interaction effects found in chapters 5 to 10.

We assume that poor impulse control and attention problems are measured by our constructs of HIA problems and high ADHD score, which measure impulsivity, overactivity, and attention problems. In Table 11.4, we saw that ADHD was related to all outcomes and that HIA was related to most outcomes. We see these findings as a fundamental indication that poor self-control and attentional problems are associated with externalizing problems (delinquency, conduct problems, covert behavior, and physical fighting), internalizing problems (shy/withdrawn behavior, depressed mood), and substance use.

We do not propose that juveniles have to display both impulsive problems and attention deficits. Factor analytic studies show that impulsive and hyperactive behaviors often appear in a single factor and attention problems in another factor (Hinshaw, 1987). *DSM–IV* has recognized a distinction between two subtypes of ADHD: a predominant overactive (and impulsive) type and a predominant attention deficit type (American Psychiatric Association, 1994). This distinction represents two etiologies of problem behavior. One etiology is dependent on the presence of persisting impulsive behavior that can result in many different forms of externalizing problems, including reckless behavior, aggression, theft, and so on. The other etiology is dependent on the presence of attention deficit. By itself, attention deficit does not necessarily lead to problem behaviors. However, like learning problems, it makes it less likely that juveniles will anticipate the consequences of their own actions, will readily learn from these consequences, or will learn from directions and sanctions applied by their caregivers or others in their social environment.

Maguin and Loeber (1996) showed that attention problems are probably of more importance than poor academic performance, at least for delinquency. In their meta-analysis, they found that the relationship between poor academic performance and delinquency became nonsignificant once attention problems were taken into account (or partialed out in statistical parlance).

A third etiology of problem behavior is based on the absence of internal inhibitions, of which we have stressed guilt feelings as the most important one measured in this study. Lack of guilt was most strongly associated with externalizing behaviors and associated with substance use and shy/withdrawn behavior but at a less strong level (see Table 11.3). We conceptualize normal development as consisting of a shift from external controls (mostly by adults) to internal controls as exemplified by guilt feelings and empathy with others. Juveniles' persistence in delinquency and other externalizing problems exemplifies disruption in the transition from external to internal controls.

Thus, disinhibiting and inhibiting factors on the individual child level should be seen as together explaining deviant outcomes. We see two ways in which our key individual elements interacted in producing problem behaviors. One idea is that the higher the number of deviant elements in boys, the higher the risk of an adverse outcome. This is shown by the hierarchical multiple regressions, which indicated that a high ADHD score and lack of guilt independently contributed to a majority of the outcomes. Thus, the joint presence of a high ADHD score and lack of guilt added to the prediction of diverse problem behaviors.

The other train of thought concerns the cumulative interaction between factors in which the joint presence of each explains more of the outcome over and above the risk associated with each factor by itself. We did not find any instances of cumulative interaction effects between a high ADHD score and lack of guilt. However, we found that the joint absence of ADHD (or HIA problems) and lack of guilt was associated with an unusually low likelihood of several problem behaviors (delinquency, covert behavior, and shy/withdrawn behavior) over and above the reduced risk associated with each factor by itself (although the results varied by sample; see Table 11.6).

A better understanding of the operation of individual factors can be reached by including constraining and facilitating factors in the family and neighborhood contexts. Like other researchers (e.g., Patterson, 1982; Rutter & Giller, 1983), we see the risk of serious problem behaviors in childhood and adolescence resulting from the convergence of individual risk factors (poor self-control, attention problems, and lack of moral inhibitions) and risk factors in the youth's social environment. Principal social influences lie in boys' parents, peers, and neighborhoods. Boys' interactions with others form the thousands of learning trials by which boys learn verbal and physical aggression. In these interchanges, others often become protagonists, leading to coercive cycles in which boys' minor aggressive acts can escalate to more serious aggressive acts (Patterson, 1982; Patterson, Reid, & Dishion, 1992). Along that line, we found that physical punishment by parents was particularly related to physical aggression in their children.

Not all externalizing problems can be explained by coercive interchanges. Particularly, the social interactional origins of boys' acquisition of covert or concealing behaviors are far less researched. Earlier we postulated that covert child problem behaviors result particularly from parental neglect, as manifested in poor supervision and poor communication (Loeber & Stouthamer-Loeber, 1986). In the present study, we found that poor supervision became increasingly strongly related to covert behavior with age. We also found that poor communication was related to all externalizing outcomes, but most strongly to covert behavior. Poor communication can be conceptualized as resulting from parents becoming disenchanted with their problem child, but poor communication can also represent a powerful origin of the problem behavior. First, poor communication occurs when parents neglect their children (i.e., have little involvement in their daily activities, including speaking with them). Second, poor communication inhibits the transfer from parent to child of socially acceptable standards of conduct. In addition, poor communication frustrates children's learning of prosocial problem solving because of inadequate spelling out and rehearsal by parents of alternatives to maladjusted juvenile behaviors. The latter also applies to internalizing problems, which we found to be especially related to poor parent–child communication.

The day-to-day interactions between parents and children should be seen against the backdrop of the presence of more enduring parent characteristics. We see the impact of parental deviant behavior and attitudes (e.g., parent substance use problems, father behavior problems, and, to a lesser extent, parent anxiety/depression) influencing day-to-day interactions such as supervision and communication, as well as contributing independently to problem behavior. The impact of parental deviancy was greatest with boys of a young age. Therefore, we conceptualize parental deviance as a relatively important factor for the emergence of early problem behavior in juveniles and of lesser import for the development of late-onset problems.

Finally, child individual and family factors operate in the context of macrofactors, particularly neighborhood factors. Poverty and living in crime-ridden and disadvantaged neighborhoods will affect children and parents. Although not detailed in the present study, we conceptualize neighborhood influences as forces that lead to juveniles' exposure to deviant activities by others, facilitating the onset and adoption of such behaviors by the juveniles. The macrofactors do not uniformly affect all different forms of juvenile problems, but are more relevant for externalizing than for internalizing problems. Specifically, we see juveniles' delinquency and other externalizing problems (covert behavior and physical aggression) as becoming more probable if they live in a bad neighborhood. In contrast, we see a bad neighborhood as less important for the etiology of ADHD, substance use, and internalizing problems (which can affect children irrespective of where they live).

These theoretical formulations are rather conventional in their emphasis on the explanation of diverse outcomes by means of a series of independent variables. An alternative and, in our opinion, more interesting approach is first to examine the best explanatory factors of an outcome (such as delinquency) and then determine what are the best predictors of these explanatory variables. This is an empirical method of identifying causal sequences. Thus, in a series of analyses, the best explanatory variable in one analysis became the dependent variable in the next set of analyses, for which the best explanatory variables were then found, and so on. We have given an example of such an iterative approach in the Methodological Appendix.

Specifically, we found that lack of guilt was the best predictor of delinquency in all three samples. We then investigated what were the best predictors of boys' lack of guilt out of all nonchild variables and found these were poor parental supervision and poor parent–child communication. Then we investigated what were the best predictors of poor supervision and communication out of the macrofactors (demographic, socioeconomic, and neighborhood). The most important variables predicting poor supervision were African American ethnicity (youngest sample) and poor housing (oldest sample), whereas the best explanatory variable for poor communication in the middle sample was a broken family. Surprisingly, a poorly educated mother contributed to poor supervision and communication in all three samples, and the same was true for an unemployed mother or father. Hence, the repeated regression analyses empirically indicate a hierarchical theory of delinquency, with macrovariables influencing family variables, family variables influencing child variables, and child variables influencing delinquency, was plausible (see also Farrington and Loeber, in press). We see much promise in carrying out similar analyses for outcomes other than delinquency, particularly when done with longitudinal data collected over the years.

IMPLICATIONS

Out of the wealth of findings, we wanted to stress some important implications for intervention. Although this book basically reported on cross-sectional analyses, we stress the developmental relevance of the results. The results show two major developmental themes: (a) the gradual unfolding of problem behaviors during preadolescence and adolescence, and (b) the concentration and shifts in explanatory factors with age.

With some liberty (and knowledge of findings in other studies), we stress the following recommendations for interventions:

1. Early manifestations of externalizing problems were more common in families characterized by parental deviant behavior. We also know from other studies that an early onset of problem behaviors is highly associated with later chronic offending (Farrington et al., 1990; Loeber, 1982). This does not mean that such a young generation of youth has to be doomed to continue in deviant behavior. The current findings indicate a need for early intervention, particularly by engaging parents or introducing alternative protective factors in the lives of these juveniles.

2. Interventions should deal with early problem behaviors in an attempt to prevent their escalation to serious levels. Particular candidates are physical fighting, covert behaviors, and chronic disobedience, which we assume (Loeber et al., 1993) are keystone behaviors in the development of more serious acts.

3. Interventions should deal with a subgroup of boys with externalizing problems who also are shy and withdrawn. Although we do not know the developmental ordering between these behaviors, we see social distancing as reflecting a disinclination to communicate, to test reality, and, possibly, to be receptive to feedback about one's behavior. This kind of socially withdrawn behavior may facilitate boys' commission of delinquent acts.

4. A proportion of boys with externalizing problems are likely to become depressed. The fact that depression in this group is often associated with attention-deficit and hyperactivity further reinforces the importance of depression in the development of multiple problems with age. Thus, the time has

come to realize that a proportion of antisocial youth is severely affected by internalizing problems as well.

5. Boys who show externalizing problems often also lack guilt feelings. In our opinion, this is not inherently so, but results from the fact that these boys have developed inadequate moral standards of conduct that normally inhibit problem behaviors. Therefore, interventions that do not enhance moral development are necessarily at a disadvantage compared with interventions that do.

6. Externalizing problems, unlike internalizing problems, were associated with neighborhood factors. Most of the externalizing problems we studied, and particularly physical aggression and delinquency, were more prevalent in the worse neighborhoods. Therefore, interventions for externalizing problems will need to take neighborhood context into account.

7. A proportion of boys with externalizing problems will engage in serious forms of substance use. Eventually, serious drug use and delinquency tend to become intertwined because drug dependence fuels the commission of crimes, or because drug dealing enhances the risk for violent victimization and the commission of violent acts (Van Kammen & Loeber, 1994).

8. Our findings highlighted the importance of explanatory factors that are relevant for multiple outcomes. Theoretically, interventions that modify such explanatory factors can be expected to have a broad impact on multiple outcomes. Examples of such general explanatory factors are lack of guilt, poor academic achievement, and attention-deficit and hyperactivity.

Many of the prior issues need to be studied better by means of further longitudinal analyses and systematic interventions. As to the former, boys in the youngest and oldest samples of the Pittsburgh Youth Study continue to be followed up, whereas boys in the middle sample have been followed up for a more limited time. Analyses of these longitudinal data, to be described in our next book, will further enrich our understanding of the origins of the multiple problem behaviors that are of great concern to society, the boys, their parents, and their teachers.

Methodological Appendix

Starting in chapter 5, we made certain methodological and strategic choices to carry out the analyses and present results that might be understandable for professionals with a nonstatistical background. However, for more methodologically inclined readers, we include here the justification for the choices we made. Our illustrations are based on analyses of delinquency.

The first choice was between using continuous and dichotomous independent and dependent variables. We discuss the general implications of our choice of dichotomization and then show the extent that the data are nonlinear. Next, we make comparisons between results based on continuous and dichotomized data. We then compare the results of ordinary least squares and logistic regressions with continuous or dichotomized data.

Other methodological topics covered in this appendix concern whether unweighted variables produced the same results as weighted variables, when corrected for the screening procedure we had applied at the outset of the study. We then briefly examine the need to repeat the analyses for each of the three samples or merge the data across the samples. Finally, we take some steps beyond the usual multivariate analyses. Normally such analyses identify the most powerful independent variables that can explain an outcome while statistically controlling for the presence of other independent variables. This assumes that all explanatory variables have simultaneous effects on the outcome variable. However, there may be sequential effects, such that one explanatory variable affects another explanatory variable, which in turn affects the outcome variable. To detect sequential effects, we establish what is the best predictor of delinquency, what explanatory variable is the best predictor of that predictor, and so on. As to model testing, we also show that results obtained in our hierarchical multiple regression analyses are similar to those obtained in hierarchical multiple regression analyses using the opposite order of entry of conceptual blocks of variables in the equation.

JUSTIFICATION FOR USING DICHOTOMOUS VARIABLES

In accordance with our risk factor approach to delinquency and other outcomes, we have generally used dichotomous variables. Readers might challenge us for the use of dichotomous rather than continuous variables because the latter are often seen as statistically more powerful than the former for variables whose true underlying distribution is normal (e.g., Cohen, 1983). In other words, common measures of association (such as the product–moment correlation) are generally higher with continuous variables and often have a maximum possible value below 1 for dichotomous variables (Farrington & Loeber, 1989).

There are several grounds to justify our choice of using dichotomous variables. A first set of rationales has to do with the nature of the variables being studied. Some variables are inherently dichotomous, such as boys' living in a household with either one or two biological parents or the family being on welfare or not. Second, many of the independent and dependent variables of interest are not normally distributed. Instead, their true distributions are often highly skewed. Dichotomization helps to isolate the boys who are worst affected and the relative importance of all variables can be addressed by direct comparison. In our experience, a one quarter–three quarter split is useful in identifying comparably deviant (but not too extreme) cases.

A second set of rationales for the choice of dichotomous variables has to do with the association between independent and dependent variables. As is discussed in the next section, we found that there are often nonlinear relationships between explanatory variables and delinquency so that the risk of delinquency increased greatly only in the worst category. Also, as already mentioned, dichotomization fits in with a risk factor approach to the study of delinquency and other forms of maladjustment, in that the cumulative effects of risk factors can easily be studied and communicated to readers.

Dichotomization allows the use of the odds ratio, which, unlike phi, is not sensitive to variations in the marginal distribution of the variables (e.g., the prevalence). Unless variables are truly measured on normally distributed interval scales, product–moment correlations are also affected by the marginal distributions. The odds ratio (Fleiss, 1981) expresses the likelihood that an outcome such as delinquency occurs as a function of a particular risk factor (see chap. 5).

Another reason for using odds ratios is that they are more easily understood than other measures of association (such as the Pearson product–moment correlation) and often convey a more realistic impression of the strength of the association. For example, an odds ratio of 2—doubling the risk of delinquency—might correspond to a correlation of about .12, which translates into 1.4% of the variance explained. The use of the percentage of variance explained gives a misleading impression of low predictability. It is not uncommon that researchers, clinicians, and policymakers discount such a small amount of explained variance, whereas they appropriately react more positively (and indeed more realistically) when they know that the risk has increased twofold (see also Rosenthal, 1983).

Another reason is that dichotomization makes it easier to study interactions between variables and different patterns of associations within subgroups of participants. For example, poor supervision may be more strongly related to delinquency in bad neighborhoods than in good neighborhoods. The study of such interaction effects is rather straightforward when variables are dichotomized, but is more difficult to calculate and communicate when continuous variables are used.

Also, perhaps most important, dichotomized constructs encourage a focus on individuals rather than on variables. The percentage of individuals affected is a highly meaningful statistic. Individual-based information may be more relevant for preventive interventions than variable-based information. Moreover, dichotomization makes it possible to study the cumulative impact of several risk factors or focus on those individuals who are affected by multiple risk factors. As mentioned in chapter 11, Magnusson and Bergman (1988) concluded that many of the results obtained in variable-oriented research were produced by a small minority of chronically antisocial people.

There are, of course, disadvantages to the use of dichotomous variables. They involve some loss of information. Strictly speaking, the use of these variables in multivariate analyses requires the use of logistic regression techniques. These have the severe disadvantage of loss of cases when there is a fair amount of missing data (e.g., because just over half of the boys had resident fathers, approaching half were missing on the single variable of unemployed father). Logistic regression techniques require listwise deletion of data, whereas ordinary least squares multiple regression can make full use of available data by pairwise deletion. Fortunately, multiple regression and logistic regression produce similar results with dichotomous data, at least in regard to the relative importance of predictors (e.g., Cleary & Angel, 1984). To minimize the problem of missing data in analyses, we primarily used multiple regression.

It is reasonable to inquire whether dichotomous analyses will lead to incorrect conclusions because of the loss of information, just as it is reasonable to inquire whether continuous analyses will lead to incorrect conclusions because of the violation of underlying assumptions (e.g., of normally distributed, linearly related variables). As is shown later, regression analyses using dichotomous data produce patterns of results that are highly similar to those based on continuously measured variables. Therefore, we considered that the advantages of dichotomization outweighed its disadvantages.

NONLINEAR RELATIONSHIPS

To what extent are many of the variables that we use nonlinearly distributed? As examples, we first consider the distribution of age within each sample and its association with delinquency and then the distribution of several other explanatory variables and their association with delinquency.

First, as to age, Table MA.1 shows that the percentage of boys who were delinquent increased with age within all three samples. For instance, when the samples were divided into age quartiles, in the youngest sample, 23.6% of the boys below age 7 were delinquent, compared with 26% of the boys between ages 7 and 7.4, 25.0% between ages 7.4 and 7.8, and rising to 37.4% of the boys over 7.8 years of age. For the middle and oldest samples, of the boys in the most extreme age category (over age 11, and 14.5, respectively), 44.9% and 48.4% had committed delinquent acts. In summary, the relationship between age and delinquency was not linear; delinquency increased in a positively accelerated fashion with age in each of the three samples.

This nonlinear relationship suggested that age, by itself, was not the important variable. What mattered was the identification of boys who were old for the school grade they were in (i.e., who were older than their classmates almost certainly because they had been held back for failing grades). The percentage of age-inappropriate boys increased up to the 7th grade, so that some of those

TABLE MA.1
Percentage of Delinquent Boys in Different Age Quartiles

Sample	Age (years)	% Delinquent
Youngest	−7.0	23.6
	7–7.4	26.0
	7.4–7.8	25.0
	7.8+	37.4
Middle	−10.2	16.7
	10.2–10.6	18.9
	10.6–11	29.9
	11+	44.9
Oldest	−13.25	27.6
	13.25–13.75	29.1
	13.75–14.5	40.3
	14.5+	48.4

TABLE MA.2
Percentage Delinquent Boys at Different Levels
of Selected Explanatory Variables (Oldest Sample)

Variable	Level of Explanatory Variable			
	Good	Good Average	Bad Average	Bad
Neighborhood (P)	31.1	33.1	31.3	48.4
Young mother (P)	34.2	24.2	35.0	50.4
Achievement (PBT)	16.8	32.5	40.8	54.9
HIA problems (PT)	12.4	33.0	43.6	55.9
Supervision (PB)	23.1	29.1	38.3	52.7

Note. B = boy; P = parent; T = teacher.

in the third quartile of this grade were age-inappropriate. The nonlinear relationship supports our notion of dichotomizing the age variable to isolate the boys who are old for their grade in each sample.

Does a nonlinear relationship apply to other explanatory variables? Table MA.2 shows the percentage of delinquents at different levels of some explanatory variables in the oldest sample. For example, 31.3% to 33.1% of the boys in either good, good average, or bad average neighborhoods were delinquent, compared with 48.4% in the bad neighborhoods. Similarly, the age of the mother at the boy's birth was nonlinearly related to delinquency. The mothers in the youngest quartile (age 19.4 or less) were associated with the highest prevalence of delinquent boys (50.4%), whereas the moderately old mothers (age's 23–26.7) were associated with the lowest prevalence. In contrast, achievement and HIA problems were more linearly related to delinquency.

Usually the percentage of delinquents increased sharply in the worst category, as is shown in the final example of parental supervision. Whereas 23.1% of the boys who received good supervision were delinquent, this percentage accelerated with increasingly poor supervision, resulting in 52.7% of the boys who were badly supervised becoming delinquent.

These results, which are quite typical, support our decision to dichotomize the independent variables between the bad average level and the bad level, thereby isolating the worst category on each of the explanatory variables as a risk factor (about 25% of the cases).

DO DICHOTOMOUS VARIABLES PRODUCE DIFFERENT RESULTS FROM CONTINUOUS VARIABLES?

It can be objected that our use of dichotomous variables decreases the power for detecting significant relationships between independent and dependent variables. For this reason, we compared the results obtained with dichotomous

and continuous variables. The relationships between the most important explanatory variables and the full four-point delinquency scale are shown in Table
MA.3, which can be compared with Table 5.6 in chapter 5, which uses
dichotomized explanatory variables and a dichotomized outcome.

Dichotomizing the outcome variables had little effect. For example, for
dichotomous explanatory variables in the oldest sample, the overall correlation
between dichotomous delinquency correlations and continuous (four-category)
delinquency correlations was .94. For continuous explanatory variables in the
oldest sample, the overall correlation between dichotomous delinquency correlations and continuous (four-category) delinquency correlations was .96.

Dichotomizing the explanatory variables had only slightly more effect. For
dichotomous delinquency in the oldest sample, the overall correlation between
dichotomous explanatory variable correlations and continuous explanatory variable correlations was .86. Similarly, for continuous (four-category) delinquency
in the oldest sample, the overall correlation between dichotomous explanatory
variable correlations and continuous explanatory variable correlations was .86.
All these overall correlations were based on 33 individual correlations relating
explanatory variables and delinquency (excluding seven explanatory variables,
which were only measured dichotomously).

It would be unrealistic to assume that the four-point delinquency scale was an
equal-interval or ratio scale, as is required by parametric statistics such as the
product–moment correlation. In any case, our interest is in the seriously delinquent
boys implying that delinquency should be dichotomized. Therefore, the only
realistic choice is between dichotomous and continuous explanatory variables. As
already noted, the results with these two types of variables were highly correlated
(.86). The average value of correlations was slightly greater with continuous
explanatory variables (.11 as opposed to .09 with dichotomous explanatory variables). However, we felt that, on balance, the advantages of dichotomous explanatory variables outweighed their disadvantages and that the high correlation between
the two approaches (.86) meant that they would produce similar results with regard
to the relative importance of explanatory variables.

The absolute size of correlations between dichotomous variables can be increased by using the tetrachoric correlation or RIOC. The tetrachoric correlation
essentially estimates what the product–moment correlation would have been if the
variables had not been dichotomized, on the assumption that they are truly normally
distributed, intervally scaled variables. The RIOC essentially corrects the value of
the phi correlation for its maximum possible value, because RIOC = phi/maximum
phi (Farrington & Loeber, 1989). The average value of tetrachoric correlations,
with dichotomous data was .15, whereas the average value of the RIOCs was .11.

Generally, absolute values of correlations were higher using the tetrachoric
correlations with dichotomous explanatory variables than using the product–moment correlation with continuous explanatory variables. However, we did not think

TABLE MA.3
Important Explanatory Variables % Versus Full Delinquency Scale

	Delinquency					
Variable	None	Minor	Moderate	Serious	Total	p
Youngest sample	(198)	(165)	(89)	(51)		
Old for grade	19.7	20.0	24.7	43.1	23.1	.003
Lack of guilt	10.4	21.6	29.3	54.2	21.9	.0001
HIA problems	10.6	17.6	20.2	33.3	16.9	.001
High ADHD score	11.1	33.3	39.3	33.3	25.6	.0001
Low achievement (PBT)	19.7	24.2	29.2	37.3	24.7	.046
Depressed mood	12.8	24.8	36.0	39.2	23.6	.0001
Poor supervision	17.3	25.0	29.8	38.8	24.3	.008
Physical punishment	13.4	19.4	22.5	28.0	18.5	.061
Low SES	20.6	32.1	29.2	42.0	28.1	.009
Family on welfare	37.3	55.4	60.2	68.8	50.5	.0001
African American	47.0	61.2	66.3	72.5	57.7	.0006
Broken family	49.2	67.7	66.7	83.7	61.9	.0001
Bad neighborhood (C)	18.1	32.1	34.1	50.0	28.7	.0001
Bad neighborhood (P)	17.9	26.1	34.8	43.1	26.1	.0004
Middle sample	(102)	(153)	(113)	(140)		
Old for grade	16.7	21.6	36.3	47.1	30.9	.0001
Lack of guilt	10.5	15.9	34.3	54.0	29.5	.0001
HIA problems	7.8	13.1	19.5	31.4	18.5	.0001
High ADHD score	11.8	15.7	28.3	38.6	24.0	.0001
Low achievement (PBT)	11.8	11.8	36.3	38.6	24.6	.0001
Depressed mood	7.8	17.1	34.5	30.7	22.8	.0001
Poor supervision	15.0	26.5	33.3	34.3	27.9	.005
Poor communication	9.8	23.7	23.6	37.1	24.6	.0001
Physical punishment	25.7	37.1	30.0	47.9	36.3	.002
Low SES	15.0	16.4	30.0	36.2	24.6	.0001
Family on welfare	26.6	36.6	47.1	59.1	43.2	.0001
African American	38.2	53.6	55.8	71.4	55.9	.0001
Broken family	44.4	52.3	66.1	77.5	60.8	.0001
Bad neighborhood (C)	21.1	22.2	24.5	33.8	25.8	.089
Bad neighborhood (P)	17.6	22.4	22.0	32.1	24.1	.051
Oldest sample	(89)	(98)	(134)	(185)		
Old for grade	28.1	29.6	40.3	53.5	40.9	.0001

Table MA.3 (continued)

Variable	None	Minor	Moderate	Serious	Total	p
			Delinquency			
Oldest Sample (cont.)						
Lack of guilt	3.4	18.7	23.9	40.4	24.9	.0001
HIA problems	1.1	13.3	20.1	28.1	18.4	.0001
High ADHD score	5.6	21.4	26.9	29.7	23.1	.0001
Low achievement (PBT)	13.5	11.2	25.4	36.2	24.5	.0001
Depressed mood	11.2	20.4	23.9	29.3	23.0	.009
Poor supervision	9.0	18.4	26.7	37.8	25.9	.0001
Poor communication	13.5	21.6	29.2	29.7	25.1	.017
Physical punishment	11.2	17.5	18.2	26.7	19.9	.019
Low SES	21.6	23.5	26.3	32.8	27.3	ns
Family on welfare	29.3	23.9	37.8	52.0	38.8	.0001
African American	44.9	55.1	50.7	69.7	57.5	.0002
Broken family	55.8	54.1	67.4	80.6	67.4	.0001
Bad neighborhood (C)	18.2	23.9	27.2	39.7	29.4	.001
Bad neighborhood (P)	12.4	14.4	30.3	33.9	25.3	.0001

Note. p based on 4 x 2 chi-square (two-tailed). PBT = parent, boy, teacher measure; P = parent measure; C = census measure. Poor communication was not measured in the youngest sample.

that it was necessary to use tetrachoric correlations, because they are less familiar to readers than phi correlations and because they assume true underlying normal distributions, whereas the true underlying distributions may be skewed. The overall correlation between tetrachoric and phi correlations was .999 and between RIOC and phi correlations was .988. Hence, the relative importance of explanatory variables would clearly be the same using all these methods.

Finally, it should be noted that, in any given analysis, results obtained with phi correlations are similar to results obtained with odds ratios. The phi correlation is mathematically related to the logarithm of the odds ratio. If the cell entries in a 2 x 2 table are a, b, c, d, the asymptotic standard error (ASE) of the logarithm of the odds ratio (LOR) is: ASE = Square Root $(1/a + 1/b + 1/c + 1/d)$ (Agresti, 1990, p. 54). Hence, (LOR/ASE) squared is distributed as Z squared. However, Z squared = chi squared = N x phi squared. Hence, asymptotically, phi = LOR x (a constant). In agreement with this mathematical relationship, the overall correlation between phi and LOR in the oldest sample (for relationships between 40 explanatory variables and delinquency) was .998. Therefore, conclusions about the relative importance of explanatory variables is almost identical whether based on phi correlations or odds ratios. We have used odds ratios because they give a more realistic impression of strength of effect, as explained before.

ARE THE RESULTS SIMILAR WITH CONTINUOUS EXPLANATORY VARIABLES AND LOGISTIC REGRESSION?

We have argued that our results, obtained with multiple regression of dichotomous variables, would be similar if continuous explanatory variables were used or if logistic regression were used. Table MA.4 presents an empirical test of this for the oldest sample.

Eleven variables were identified as independently important in the multiple regression of dichotomous variables (Table 5.8 in chap. 5). Eight of these were also identified as independently important in the multiple regression of continuous explanatory variables and eight were also identified as independently important in the logistic regression of dichotomous variables. Lack of guilt, old for grade, HIA problems, poor supervision, physical punishment, a young mother, and bad neighborhood were identified as independently important variables in all three analyses. These included six of the seven most significant variables in the original multiple regression of dichotomous variables (all except depressed mood, which appeared in the logistic regression but not in the multiple regression of continuous variables).

Overall, we conclude that our multiple regression of dichotomous variables identified the most important explanatory variables. Interestingly, the multiple regression of dichotomous variables identified more independently important variables than the other two methods (11 as opposed to 9). Where there are marked differences in the results obtained in the three analyses, they are often understandable. For example, a young mother was more important as a dichotomous variable than as a continuous variable because of the nonlinear relationship between the age of the mother and delinquency (Table MA.2). Being a teenage mother at the time of the boy's birth was a risk factor, but the age of the mother was not linearly related to delinquency. Therefore, we considered the dichotomous result to be more valid and meaningful.

DO UNWEIGHTED VARIABLES PRODUCE THE SAME RESULTS AS WEIGHTED VARIABLES?

Because our three samples were selected on the basis of a screening procedure (see chap. 2), the prevalence rates presented in chapter 4 were weighted to obtain estimates for the original population. The question arises of whether

TABLE MA.4

Comparison of Regression Methods for Delinquency (Oldest Sample)

Variable	Dichotomous Multiple Regression			Continuous Multiple Regression			Dichotomous Logistics Regression		
	Order	F change	p	Order	F change	p	Order	F change	p
Child									
Lack of guilt	1	34.48	.0001	1	51.32	.0001	1	31.05	.0001
Old for grade	2	11.30	.0004	2	5.80	.008	2	9.87	.0009
Depressed mood	3	4.82	.014	3	4.91	.014	4	4.17	.021
HIA problems	4	2.60	.054				3	6.35	.006
Low achievement (PBT)	5	2.12	.073						
Low religiosity				4	2.41	.061			
Family									
Poor supervision	6	6.41	.006	5	4.61	.016	6	2.22	.068
Physical punishment	7	4.78	.015	6	2.21	.069	5	3.58	.029
Macro									
Young mother	8	8.10	.002	9	1.98	.080	7	10.50	.0006
Bad neighborhood (C)	9	6.67	.005	8	2.56	.055			
Nonbiological parent	10	2.60	.054	7	4.78	.015			
Bad neighborhood (P)	11	2.02	.078				9	2.53	.056
African American							8	5.36	.010

we also needed to weight both the independent and dependent variables for the correlational analyses. To answer this, we computed the overall correlation among the correlations based on weighted and unweighted data in the manner described earlier. (The continuous variables were used in this analysis.) The overall correlation over 33 explanatory variables came to .996 in the oldest sample, indicating that, to a high degree the results based on unweighted variables were exactly the same as those based on weighted variables.

ARE THE EXPLANATORY FACTORS FOR DELINQUENCY THE SAME AT EACH AGE?

We wanted to examine the extent that, on average, the explanatory factors for delinquency were similar or different in the three grade samples representing distinct age groups. If the results were similar, this would justify merging the data across the three samples. However, if the results did not correspond highly, the implication is that the three samples should be analyzed separately.

To investigate this, we first correlated each explanatory factor with delinquency in each sample (using phi correlations for dichotomous variables). To ascertain whether each sample essentially had the same results, we calculated an overall correlation by correlating the correlations in one sample with the correlations in another. For example, the overall correlation between the middle and oldest samples was based on 40 pairs of observations (individual correlations between explanatory variables and delinquency). A caveat here is that the measurement of variables was sometimes slightly different for the younger boys than for the older boys (see chap. 3).

The overall correlation was .67 between the youngest and middle samples, .67 between the middle and oldest samples, and .61 between the youngest and oldest samples. Thus, the strength of the explanatory factors for delinquency were largely, but not fully, the same across the different samples, and tended to be stable with age, at least for the age period considered here. Also, the mean correlation (over 37 explanatory variables, excluding 3 not measured in the youngest sample) was similar in all three samples, but far from reaching unity. Therefore, we consider that the results are sufficiently distinct to warrant reporting results for each sample separately. There are two additional advantages of this strategy. It allows us to replicate results and examine age-related shifts across the three grade samples.

THE LOGIC OF THE SEQUENCE OF OUR MULTIVARIATE ANALYSES

Multivariate analyses often lead to the identification of several explanatory variables that are associated with an outcome while other explanatory variables are statistically controlled. Usually multivariate analyses stop there. The implicit assumption is that all explanatory variables have simultaneous effects on delinquency. However, it is quite reasonable to ask this question: What are the best explanatory factors that predict the explanatory factors identified as the best predictors of delinquency in a multivariate analysis? This assumes sequential effects of some explanatory factors on other explanatory factors or indirect effects on delinquency. Multivariate analyses can be repeated several times in an iterative fashion, each time addressing this question with a different explanatory variable. We give an example with delinquency as the initial outcome to be explained.

We found (Table 5.6 in chap. 5) that the child variable of lack of guilt was the best predictor of delinquency in all three samples. Several theories of delinquency suggest that lack of guilt arises from low internal inhibitions or controls, which in turn develop as a result of poor external controls, such as poor parenting (e.g., social learning theory; Patterson, 1982; self-control theory; Gottfredson & Hirschi, 1990). For that reason, we then investigated what were the best predictor for boys' lack of guilt out of all nonchild variables. This, as is shown, was poor parental supervision in two samples and poor parent–child communication in the other sample. Then we investigated what were the best predictors of poor supervision/communication out of the macrofactors (demographic, socioeconomic, and neighborhood). Thus, in a series of analyses, the best explanatory variable in one analysis became the dependent variable in the next set of analyses, for which the best explanatory variables were then found, and so on.

The detailed results of these analyses are shown in Tables MA.5 and MA.6. The most powerful variables for explaining boys' lack of guilt were poor supervision (in the youngest and oldest samples) and poor communication (middle sample and, less strongly, in the oldest sample), whereas physical punishment and unhappy parents also contributed in both samples. Bad neighborhood was associated with lack of guilt in the youngest and middle samples but more strongly in the youngest sample. Broken family was a contributor to the equation in all three samples. Of the socioeconomic variables, an unemployed father was associated for the oldest sample only. Interestingly, high parental stress was the second best explanatory factor for lack of guilt, but only in the oldest sample. In conclusion, lack of guilt was most strongly associated with poor parenting (supervision, communication, and physical punishment).

TABLE MA.5
Multiple Regression for Lack of Guilt

Variable	Multiple R	F change	p
Youngest sample			
Poor supervision	.229	13.23	.0002
Bad neighborhood (C)	.273	5.65	.009
Broken family	.290	2.53	.057
Physical punishment	.306	2.52	.057
Unhappy parents	.323	2.71	.051
Middle sample			
Poor communication	.230	14.91	.0001
Broken family	.299	10.66	.0006
Unhappy parents	.359	11.91	.0003
Physical punishment	.376	3.91	.025
Bad neighborhood (C)	.385	2.10	.074
Oldest sample			
Poor supervision	.205	10.59	.0007
High parental stress	.260	6.68	.005
Broken family	.302	6.14	.007
Unemployed father	.318	2.73	.050
Poor communication	.329	1.81	.090

TABLE MA.6
Multiple Regression for Poor Supervision/Communication

Variable	Multiple R	F change	p
Youngest sample			
African American	.192	9.58	.001
Unemployed father	.215	2.39	.062
Poorly educated mother	.230	1.77	.093
Middle sample			
Broken family	.150	6.50	.006
Unemployed father	.193	4.30	.020
Poorly educated mother	.210	1.95	.082
Oldest sample			
Poor housing	.196	17.03	.0001
Broken family	.232	6.96	.004
Unemployed mother	.254	4.93	.014
Bad neighborhood (C)	.268	3.26	.036
Poorly educated mother	.276	1.96	.08

We then investigated the best predictors of poor supervision and communication, excluding parent and child variables from our analyses. The most important variables predicting poor supervision were African-American ethnicity (youngest sample) and poor housing (oldest sample), whereas the best explanatory variable for poor communication in the middle sample was a broken family. Surprisingly, a poorly educated mother contributed to poor supervision and communication in all three samples and the same was true for an unemployed mother or father. However, the best explanatory factors for these family variables were not consistently in only one of our conceptual categories (demographic, socioeconomic, neighborhood).

Hence, our repeated regression analyses empirically indicates that a sequential theory of delinquency was needed, with macrovariables influencing family variables, family variables influencing child variables, and child variables influencing delinquency. In turn, this sequential theory of delinquency implied hierarchical regression analyses.

Cohen and Cohen (1983) argued that hierarchical multiple regression analysis should be carried out in the reverse order to the one we have used, (i.e., with the most distal variables entering the equation first and the most proximal last). Two main arguments are advanced in favor of this ordering. One is that hierarchical multiple regression measures direct effects of variables entered last (independently of variables already in the equation) and both direct and indirect effects of variables entered first (because all other variables are not in the equation). Entering variables in the reverse order makes it possible to measure direct effects of proximal variables and direct and indirect effects of distal variables.

The second argument is that successive hierarchical regression analyses can indicate indirect effects of more distal variables. For example, if variable A had a significant weighting (β-value) by itself in an equation predicting delinquency but a nonsignificant weighting in an equation along with other variables, this might indicate that variable A had an indirect effect on delinquency that was mediated through those other variables. Unfortunately, an alternative hypothesis is that the significant weighting of variable A disappeared because it was intercorrelated with one of the other variables (i.e., both were essentially measuring the same underlying construct). Gordon (1968) showed how the weighting of any variable depended on the number of other similar variables in a multiple regression analysis. This is one of the reasons that we have focused on F changes in stepwise regression rather than β-values.

As an exercise, we investigated the effect of carrying out the hierarchical regression analysis in the reverse order with delinquency. Table MA.7 shows the results. For example, in the youngest sample, three macrovariables (unemployed father, bad neighborhood–parent, poorly educated mother) independently predicted delinquency. Similarly, three family variables (poor

TABLE MA.7
Alternative Hierarchical Multiple Regression Analyses for Delinquency

Variable	β-values		
	M or F or C	M + F	M + F + C
Youngest sample			
Macro			
Unemployed father	.135	.136	.141
Bad neighborhood (P)	.128	.150	.107
Poorly educated mother	.114	—	
Family			
Poor supervision	.129	—	
Parent substance use problems	.118	.103	—
Unhappy parents	.113	.121	.137
Child			
Lack of guilt	.249		.226
Depressed mood	.184		.198
Old for grade	.081		—
Middle Sample			
Macro			
Unemployed father	.181	.153	.126
Broken family	.150	—	
African American	.102	.160	.097
Family			
Poor communication	.127	.153	—
Parent anxiety/depression	.120	.128	—
Physical punishment	.118	—	
Disagree on discipline	.118	—	
Child			
Lack of guilt	.258		.235
Low achievement (CAT)	.133		.116
Old for grade	.107		.116
High ADHD score	.083		.101
Oldest sample			
Macro			
Broken family	.154	.152	.106
Young mother	.130	.119	.125
Bad neighborhood (P)	.117	.125	.107
Bad neighborhood (C)	.098	—	
Family			
Poor supervision	.212	.180	.123
Physical punishment	.130	.090	—

TABLE MA.7 (continued)

Variable	β - values		
	M or F or C	M + F	M + F + C
Child			
Lack of guilt	.237		.217
Old for grade	.137		.088
Depressed mood	.107		.100
HIA problems	.098		—

Note. M = macro; F = family; C = child

supervision, parent substance problems, unhappy parents) independently predicted delinquency. When these six macro's and family variables were then included in the equation, four of them were independent predictors (all except poorly educated mother and poor supervision). There was no marked decrease in the weightings (β-values) of the four significant variables. This either means that there are no indirect effects or that reductions in β-values indicating indirect effects are counteracted by increases in β-values consequential on the use of fewer indicator variables in a conceptual block. The weightings were generally lower when all six variables were included in the equation (unemployed father, .117 as opposed to .136; bad neighborhood, .119 as opposed to .150; unhappy parents, .109 as opposed to .121; parent substance use problems, unchanged at .103).

When the three significant child variables were added to the equation, only five out of seven variables had significant β-values. The weighting of bad neighborhood decreased markedly (from .150 to .107), but other weightings did not. More important, the results shown in Table MA.7 are similar to those obtained with the hierarchical multiple regression carried out in the reverse order (see Table 5.8 in chap.5). The four most important variables were still lack of guilt, depressed mood, unemployed father, and unhappy parents. The only difference was that bad neighborhood was the fifth most important variable in Table MA.7, but the sixth in Table 5.8.

Similar results were obtained with the middle and oldest samples. For the middle sample, the six most important variables in both analyses were lack of guilt, low achievement (CAT), old for grade, high ADHD score, unemployed father, and African-American ethnicity. For the oldest sample, six of the seven variables in Table MA.7 were significant in Table 5.8. The only difference was that physical punishment was only significant in Table 5.8 (its *p* value in Table MA.7 was .063), whereas broken family was only significant in Table MA.7 (its *p* value in Table 5.8 was .054). Essentially, the two methods of carrying out hierarchical multiple regression analysis produced much the same results.

References

Abikoff, H., & Klein, R.G. (1992). Attention-deficit hyperactivity and conduct disorder: Comorbidity and implications for treatment. *Journal of Consulting and Clinical Psychology, 60,* 881–892.

Achenbach, T. M. (1978). The child behavior profile: I. Boys aged 6–11. *Journal of Consulting and Clinical Psychology, 46,* 478–488.

Achenbach, T. M. (1985). *Assessment and taxonomy of child and adolescent psychopathology.* Beverly Hills: Sage.

Achenbach, T. M., Conners, C. K., Quay, H. C., Verhulst, F. C., & Howell, C. T. (1989). Replication of empirically derived syndromes as a basis for taxonomy of child/adolescent psycho-pathology. *Journal of Abnormal Child Psychology, 17,* 299–320.

Achenbach, T. M., & Edelbrock, C. S. (1979). The child behavior profile: II. Boys aged 12–16 and girls aged 6–11 and 12–16. *Journal of Consulting and Clinical Psychology, 47,* 223–233.

Achenbach, T. M., & Edelbrock, C. S. (1983). *Manual for the Child Behavior Checklist and Revised Child Behavior Profile.* Burlington, VT: University of Vermont, Department of Psychiatry.

Achenbach, T. M., & Edelbrock, C. S. (1987). *Manual for the Youth Self-Report and Profile.* Burlington, VT: University of Vermont, Department of Psychiatry.

Agresti, A. (1990). *Categorical data analysis.* New York: Wiley.

Alexander, C. S., Somerfield, M. R., Ensminger, M. E., Johnson, K. E., & Kim, Y. J. (1993). Consistency of adolescents' self-report of sexual behavior in a longitudinal study. *Journal of Youth and Adolescence, 2,* 455–472.

Alterman, A. I., & Tarter, R. E. (1986). An examination of selected typologies. Hyperactivity, familial, and antisocial alcoholism. In M. Galanter (Ed.), *Recent developments in alcohol* (Vol. 4, pp. 169–189). New York: Plenum.

Amdur, R. L. (1989). Testing causal models of delinquency: A methodological critique. *Criminal Justice and Behavior, 16,* 35–62.

American Psychiatric Association. (1982). *Diagnostic and statistical manual of mental disorders* (3rd ed. DSM–III) Washington, DC: American Psychiatric Association.

American Psychiatric Association. (1987). *Diagnostic and statistical manual of mental disorders* (3rd ed. rev. DSM–III–R). Washington, DC: American Psychiatric Association.

American Psychiatric Association. (1994). *Diagnostic and statistical manual of mental disorders* (4th ed. DSM–IV). Washington, DC: American Psychiatric Association.

Anastopoulos, A. D., Guevremont, D. C., Shelton, T. L., & DuPaul, G. J. (1992). Parenting stress among families of children with attention deficit hyperactivity disorder. *Journal of Abnormal Child Psychology, 20*, 503–520.

Anderson, J. C., Williams, S., McGee, R., & Silva, P. A. (1987). DSM–III disorders in preadolescent children: Prevalence in a large sample from the general population. *Archives of General Psychiatry, 44*, 69–76.

Angold, A., Erkanli, A., Loeber, R., Costello, E. J., Van Kammen, W., & Stouthamer–Loeber, M. (1996). Disappearing depression in a population of boys. *Journal of Emotional and Behavioral Disorders. 4*, 95–104.

Asher, S. R., & Coie, J. D. (1990). *Peer rejection in childhood*. Cambridge, England: Cambridge University Press.

August, G. J., & Stewart, M. A. (1982). Is there a syndrome of pure hyperactivity? *British Journal of Psychiatry, 140*, 305–311.

Barkley, R. A. (1990). *Attention deficit hyperactivity disorder: A handbook for diagnosis and treatment*. New York: Guilford.

Barnes, H., & Olson, D. H. (1982). Parent adolescent communication. In D. H. Olson, H.McCubbin, H. Barnes, A. Larsen, M. Muxen, & W. Wilson (Eds.), *Family inventories* (pp. 55–57). St Paul, MN: University of Minnesota Press.

Baumeister, R. F., Stillwell, A. M., & Heatherton, T. F. (1994). Guilt: An interpersonal approach. *Psychological Bulletin, 115*, 243–267.

Beardslee, W. R., Bemporad, J., Keller, M. B., & Klerman, G. L. (1983). Children of parents with major affective disorder: A review. *American Journal of Psychiatry, 140*, 825–832.

Bell, R. Q. (1953). Convergence: An accelerated longitudinal approach. *Child Development, 24*, 145–152.

Bell, R. Q. (1954). An experimental test of the accelerated longitudinal approach. *Child Development, 25*, 281–286.

Belson, W. A. (1975). *Juvenile theft: The causal factors*. London: Harper & Row.

Biederman, J., Munir, K., & Knee, D. (1987). Conduct and oppositional disorder in clinically referred children with attention deficit disorder: A controlled family study. *Journal of the American Academy of Child and Adolescent Psychiatry, 26*, 724–727.

Biederman, J., Newcorn, J., & Sprich, S. (1991). Comorbidity of attention-deficit hyperactivity disorder with conduct, depressive, anxiety, and other disorders. *American Journal of Psychiatry, 148*, 564–577.

Biglan, A., Metzler, C. W., Wirt, R., Ary, D., Noell, J., Ochs, L., French, C., & Hood, D. (1990). Social and behavioral factors associated with high–risk sexual behavior among adolescents. *Journal of Behavioral Medicine, 15*, 245–261.

Bird, H. R., Canino, G., Rubio-Stipec, M., Gould, M. S., Ribera, J., Sesman, M., Woodbury, M., Huertas-Goldman, S., Pagan, A., Sanchez-Lacay, A., & Moscoso, M. (1988). Estimates of the prevalence of childhood maladjustment in a community survey in Puerto Rico. *Archives of General Psychiatry, 45*, 1120–1126.

Blouin, A. G., Conners, C.K., Seidel, W. T., & Blouin, J. (1989). The independence of hyperactivity from conduct disorder: Methodological considerations. *Canadian Journal of Psychiatry, 34*, 279–282.

Blumstein, A., Cohen, J., Roth, J. A., & Visher, C. A. (Eds.). (1986). *Criminal careers and "career criminals."* Washington, DC: National Academy of Sciences.

References   287

Boyle, M.A., Offord, D.R., Racine, Y.A., Szatmari, P., Fleming, J.E., & Links, P.S. (1992). Predicting substance use in late adolescence: Results from the Ontario Child Health Study Follow-up. *American Journal of Psychiatry, 146*, 761–767.

Britton, J. (1835). *Chronological history and graphic illustrations of Christian architecture in England.* London: M. A. Nattali.

Bronfenbrenner, U. (1979). *The ecology of human development. Experiments by nature and design.* Cambridge, MA: Harvard University Press.

Brook, J. S., Balka, E. B., Abernathy, T., & Hamburg, B. A. (1994). Sequence of sexual behavior and its relationship to other problem behaviors in African American and Puerto Rican adolescents. *Journal of Genetic Psychology, 155*, 107–114.

Brook, J. S., Whiteman, M., & Cohen, P. (1995). Stage of drug use, aggression, and theft/vandalism. In H. B. Kaplan (Ed.), *Drugs, crime, and other deviant adaptations: Longitudinal studies* (pp. 83–96). New York: Plenum.

Brunswick, A. F. (1984). Health consequences of drug use: A longitudinal study of urban Black youth. In S. A. Mednick, M. Harway, & K. M. Finello (Eds.), *Handbook of longitudinal research: Volume 2. Teenage and adult cohorts* (pp. 290–314). New York: Praeger.

Brunswick, A. F., & Boyle, J. M. (1979). Patterns of drug involvement: Developmental and secular influences on age at initiation. *Youth and Society, 11*, 139–162.

Bukstein, O. G., Brent, D. A., & Kaminer, Y. (1989). Comorbidity of substance abuse and other psychiatric disorders in adolescents. *American Journal of Psychiatry, 146*, 1131–1141.

Burns, G. J. (1991). Mental health services used by adolescents in the 1970s and 1980s. *Journal of the American Academy of Child and Adolescent Psychiatry, 30*, 144–150.

Bursik, R. J., & Webb, J. (1982). Community change and patterns of delinquency. *American Journal of Sociology, 88*, 24–42.

Cairns, R. B., & Cairns, B. D. (1994). *Lifelines and risks: Pathways of youth in our time.* Cambridge, England: University of Cambridge Press.

Cantwell, D. P., & Baker, L. (1992). Attention-deficit disorder with and without hyperactivity—A review and comparison of matched groups. *Journal of the American Academy of Child and Adolescent Psychiatry, 31*, 432–438.

Capaldi, D.M. (1991). Co-occurrence of conduct problems and depressive symptoms in early adolescent boys: I. Familial factors and general adjustment at Grade 6. *Development and Psychopathology, 3*, 277–300.

Capaldi, D. M. (1992). The co-occurrence of conduct problems and depressive symptoms in early adolescent boys: II. A 2-year follow-up at Grade 8. *Development and Psychopathology, 4*, 125–144.

Capaldi, D., & Patterson, G.R. (1987). An approach to the problem of recruitment and retention rates for longitudinal research. *Behavioral Assessment, 9*, 169–177.

Capaldi, D. M., & Patterson, G. R. (1994). Interrelated influences of contextual factors on antisocial behavior in childhood and adolescence for males. In D. C. Fowles, P. Sutker, & S. H. Goodman (Eds.), *Progress in experimental personality & psychopathology research* (pp. 165–198). New York: Springer.

Caron, C., & Rutter, M. (1991). Comorbidity in child psychopathology: Concepts, issues and research strategies. *Journal of Child Psychology and Psychiatry, 32*, 1063–1080.

Caspi, A., Moffitt, T. E., Newman, D. J., & Silva, P. A. (1996). Behavioral observations at age 3 years predict adult psychiatric disorders. *Archives of General Psychiatry, 53*, 1033–1039.

Clark, J. P., & Wenninger, E. P. (1962). Socio-economic class and area as correlates of illegal behavior among juveniles. *American Sociological Review, 27,* 826–834.

Clark, S. D., Zabin, L. S., & Hardy, J. B. (1984). Sex, contraception and parenthood: Experience and attitudes among urban Black young men. *Family Planning Perspectives, 16,* 77–82.

Cleary, P. D., & Angel, R. (1984). The analysis of relationships involving dichotomous dependent variables. *Journal of Health and Social Behavior, 25,* 334–348.

Cloward, R. A., & Ohlin, L. E. (1960). *Delinquency and opportunity.* New York: The Free Press.

Cochran, J. K., Wood, P. B., & Arneklev, B. J. (1994). Is the religiosity–delinquency relationship spurious? A test of arousal and social control theories. *Journal of Research in Crime and Delinquency, 31,* 92–123.

Cohen, A. K. (1955). *Delinquent boys: The subculture of the gang.* Glencoe, IL: The Free Press.

Cohen, J. (1983). The cost of dichotomization. *Applied Psychological Measurement, 7,* 249–253.

Cohen, J., Cohen, P. (1983). *Applied multiple regression/correlation analysis for the behavioral sciences* (2nd ed.). Hillsdale, NJ: Lawrence Erlbaum Associates.

Cohen, P., & Brook, J. (1987). Family factors related to the persistence of psychopathology in childhood and adolescence. *Psychiatry, 50,* 332–345.

Cohen, P., Cohen, J., Kasen, S., Velez, C. N., Hartmark, C., Johnson, J., Rogas, M., Brook, J., & Strenning, E. L. (1993). An epidemiological study of disorders in late childhood and adolescence: I. Age- and gender-specific prevalence. *Journal of Child Psychology and Psychiatry, 34,* 851–867.

Coie, J. D., Lochman, J. E., Terry, R., & Hyman, C. (1992). Predicting early adolescent disorder from childhood aggression and peer rejection. *Journal of Consulting and Clinical Psychology, 60,* 783–792.

Collins, J. J. (1981). Alcohol careers and criminal careers. In J. J. Collins (Ed.), *Drinking and crime.* New York: Guildford.

Conger, R. D., Patterson, G. R., & Ge, X. (1995). It takes two to replicate: A mediational model for the impact of parents' stress on adolescent adjustment. *Child Development, 66,* 80–97.

Costa, F. M., Jessor, R., Donovan, J. E., & Fortenberry, J. D. (1995). Early initiation of sexual intercourse: The influence of psychosocial unconventionality. *Journal of Research on Adolescence, 5,* 93–121.

Costello, A., Edelbrock, C., Kalas, R., Kessler, R., & Klaric, S. H. (1982). *The Diagnostic Interview Schedule for Children, Parent Version (rev.).* Worcester, MA: University of Massachusetts Medical Center.

Costello, E. J., & Angold, A. (1988). Scales to assess child and adolescent depression: Checklists, screens and nets. *Journal of the American Academy of Child and Adolescent Psychiatry, 27,* 726–737.

Costello, E. J., Edelbrock, C., & Costello, A. J. (1985). The validity of the NIMH Diagnostic Interview Schedule for Children (DISC): A comparison between pediatric and psychiatric referrals. *Journal of Abnormal Child Psychology, 13,* 579–595.

Cronbach, L. J. (1951). Coefficient alpha and the internal structure of tests. *Psychometrika, 16,* 297–334.

CTB/McGraw–Hill. (1979). *California Achievement Tests, Technical Bulletin 1, Forms C and D.* Monterey, CA: McGraw–Hill.

CTB/McGraw–Hill. (1980). *California Achievement Tests, Technical Bulletin 2, Forms C and D.* Monterey, CA: McGraw–Hill.

Dishion, T. J., French, D. C., & Patterson, G. R. (1995). The development and ecology of antisocial behavior. In D. Cicchetti & D. Cohen (Eds.), *Manual of developmental psychopathology* (pp. 421–471). New York: Cambridge University Press.

Devine, D., Long, P., & Forehand, R. (1993). A prospective study of adolescent sexual activity: Description, correlates, and predictors. *Advances in Behavioral Research and Theory, 15,* 185–209.

Dishion, T. J., & Loeber, R. (1985). Adolescent marijuana and alcohol use: The role of parents and peers revisited. *American Journal of Drug and Alcohol Abuse, 11*, 11–26.

Dodge, K. A., Coie, J. D., & Brakke, N. P. (1982). Behavior patterns of socially rejected and neglected preadolescents: The roles of social approach and aggression. *Journal of Abnormal Child Psychology, 10*, 349–410.

Donovan, J. E., Jessor, R., & Costa, F. M. (1988). Syndrome of problem behavior in adolescence: A replication. *Journal of Consulting and Clinical Psychology, 56*, 762–765.

Douglas, J. W. B., Ross, J. M., Hammond, W. A., & Mulligan, D. G. (1966). Delinquency and social class. *British Journal of Criminology, 6*, 294–302.

Edelbrock, C., & Achenbach, T. (1984). The teacher version of the Child Behavior Profile: I. Boys aged six through eleven. *Journal of Consulting and Clinical Psychology, 52*, 207–217.

Ellickson, P. L., Hays, R. D., & Bell, R. M. (1992). Stepping through the drug use sequence: Longitudinal scalogram analysis of initiation and regular drug use. *Journal of Abnormal Psychology, 101*, 441–451.

Elliott, D. S. (1994). Longitudinal research in criminology: Promise and practice. In E.G.M. Weitekamp & H. Kerner (Eds.), *Cross-national longitudinal research on human development and criminal behavior*. Dordrecht, Netherlands: Kluwer.

Elliott, D. S., Huizinga, D., & Ageton, S. S. (1985). *Explaining delinquency and drug use*. Beverly Hills, CA: Sage.

Elliott, D. S., Huizinga, D., & Menard, S. (1989). *Multiple problem youth*. New York: Springer-Verlag.

Ensminger, M. E., Kellam, S. G., & Rubin, B. R. (1983). School and family origins of delinquency: Comparisons by sex. In K. T. Van Dusen & S. A. Mednick (Eds.), *Prospective studies on crime and delinquency* (pp. 73–98). Boston: Kluwer-Nijhoff.

Erhardt, D., & Hinshaw, S. P. (1994). Initial sociometric impressions of attention–deficit hyperactivity disorder and comparison boys: Predictions from social behaviors and from nonverbal variables. *Journal of Consulting and Clinical Psychology, 62*, 833–842.

Eron, L. D., & Huesmann, L. R. (1990). The stability of aggressive behavior—even unto the third generation. In M. Lewis & S. M. Miller (Eds.), *Handbook of developmental psychopathology* (pp. 147–156). New York: Plenum.

Eron, L. D., Huesmann, L. R., Dubow, E., Romanoff, R., & Yarmel, P. W. (1987). Aggression and its correlates. In D. H. Crowell, I. M. Evans, & C. R. O'Donnell (Eds.), *Childhood aggression and violence* (pp. 249–262). New York: Plenum.

Evans, T. D., Cullen, F. T., Dunaway, R. G., & Burton, V. S. (1995). Religion and crime reexamined: The impact of religion, secular controls, and social ecology on adult criminality. *Criminology, 33*, 195–224.

Faraone, S. V., Biederman, J., Keenan, K., & Tsuang, M. T. (1991). Separation of *DSM–III* attention deficit disorder and conduct disorder: Evidence from a family–genetic study of American child psychiatric patients. *Biological Medicine, 21*, 109–121.

Farrington, D. P. (1973). Self-reports of deviant behavior: Predictive and reliable? *Journal of Criminal Law & Criminology, 64*, 99–110.

Farrington, D. P. (1979). Longitudinal research on crime and delinquency. In N. Morris & M. Tonry (Eds.), *Crime and justice* (Vol. 1, pp. 289–348). Chicago: University of Chicago Press.

Farrington, D. P. (1988). Advancing knowledge about delinquency and crime: The need for a coordinated program of longitudinal research. *Behavioral Sciences and the Law, 6*, 307–331.

Farrington, D. P. (1990). Age, period, cohort and offending. In D. M. Gottfredson & R. V. Clarke (Eds.), *Policy and theory in criminal justice* (pp. 51–75). Aldershot: Avebury.

Farrington, D. P. (1991). Childhood aggression and adult violence: Early precursors and later life outcomes. In D. J. Pepler & K. H. Rubin (Eds.), *The development and treatment of childhood aggression* (pp. 5–29). Hillsdale, NJ: Lawrence Erlbaum Associates.

Farrington, D. P. (1992a). Criminal career research in the United Kingdom. *British Journal of Criminology, 32*, 521–536.

Farrington, D. P. (1992b). Juvenile delinquency. In J. C. Coleman (Ed.), *The school years* (2nd ed., pp. 123–163). London: Routledge.

Farrington, D. P. (1994). Interactions between individual and contextual factors in the development of offending. In R. K. Silbereisen & E. Todt (Eds.), *Adolescence in context* (pp. 366–389). New York: Springer-Verlag.

Farrington, D. P. (1995). The development of offending and antisocial behaviour from childhood: Key findings from the Cambridge Study in Delinquent Development. *Journal of Child Psychology and Psychiatry, 36,* 929–964.

Farrington, D. P., Gallagher, B., Morley, L., St. Ledger, R. J., & West, D. J. (1988). A 24-year follow-up of men from vulnerable backgrounds. In R. L. Jenkins (Ed.), *The abandonment of delinquent behavior* (pp. 155–173). New York: Praeger.

Farrington, D. P., Gallagher, B., Morley, L., St. Ledger, R., & West, D. J. (1990). Minimizing attrition in longitudinal research: Methods of tracing and securing cooperation in a 24-year follow-up study. In L. Bergman, & D. Magnusson (Eds.), *Data quality in longitudinal research* (pp. 122–147). Cambridge, England: Cambridge University Press.

Farrington, D. P., & Loeber, R. (1989). Relative improvement over chance (RIOC) and phi as measures of predictive efficiency and strength of association in 2 x 2 tables. *Journal of Quantitative Criminology, 5,* 201–213.

Farrington, D. P. & Loeber, R. (in press). Transatlantic replicability of risk factors in the development of delinquency. In P. Cohen, C. Slomkowski, & L. N. Robins (Eds.), *Where and When: The influence of history and geography on aspects of psychopathology.* Mahwah, NJ: Lawrence Erlbaum Associates.

Farrington, D. P., Loeber, R., Elliott, D. S., Hawkins, J. D., Kandel, D. B., Klein, M. W., McCord, J., Rowe, D. C., & Tremblay, R. E. (1990). Advancing knowledge about the onset of delinquency and crime. In B. B. Lahey & A. E. Kazdin (Eds.), *Advances in clinical child psychology* (Vol. 13, pp. 283–342). New York: Plenum.

Farrington, D. P., Loeber, R., Stouthamer-Loeber, M., van Kammen, W. B., & Schmidt, L. (1996). Self-reported delinquency and a combined delinquency seriousness scale based on boys, mothers, and teachers: Concurrent and predicitve validity for African-Americans and caucasians. *Criminology, 34,* 501–525.

Farrington, D. P., Loeber, R., & Van Kammen, W. B. (1990). Long-term criminal outcomes of hyperactivity–impulsivity–attention deficit and conduct problems in childhood. In L. N. Robins & M. Rutter (Eds.), *Straight and devious pathways from childhood to adulthood* (pp. 62–81). New York: Cambridge University Press.

Farrington, D. P., Ohlin, L. E., & Wilson, J. Q. (1986). *Understanding and controlling crime: Toward a new research strategy.* New York: Springer-Verlag.

Farrington, D. P., & Tarling, R. (Eds.). (1985). *Prediction in criminology.* Albany, NY: State University of New York Press.

Farrington, D. P., & West, D. J. (1990). The Cambridge study in delinquent development: A long term follow-up of 411 males. In H. J. Kerner & G. Kaiser (Eds.), *Criminality: Personality, behavior and life history* (pp. 115–138). Berlin: Springer-Verlag.

Feehan, M. (1993). *The continuity of mental health disorders from age 15 to age 18 years.* Unpublished doctoral dissertation, University of Otago, Dunedin, New Zealand.

Ferdinand, R. F., & Verhulst, F. C. (1994). The prediction of poor outcome in young adults: Comparison of the young adult self-report, the General Health Questionnaire and the Symptom Checklist. *ACTA Psychiatrica Scandinavica*, *89*, 405–410.

Fergusson, D. M. (1993). Conduct problems and attention deficit behavior in middle childhood and cannabis use by age 15. *Australian & New Zealand Journal of Psychiatry*, *27*, 673–682.

Fergusson, D. M., Horwood, L. J., & Lynskey, M. (1994). The childhoods of multiple problem adolescents: A 15 year longitudinal study. *Journal of Child Psychology and Psychiatry*, *35*, 1123–1140.

Fischer, M., Barkley, R. A., Fletcher, K., & Smallish, L. (1993). The adolescent outcome of hyperactive children: Predictors of psychiatric, academic, social and emotional adjustment. *Journal of the American Academy of Child and Adolescent Psychiatry*, *32*, 324–332.

Fleiss, J. L. (1981). *Statistical methods for rates and proportions* (2nd ed.). New York: Wiley.

Forehand, R., Wierson, M., Frame, C., Kempton, T., & Armistead, L. (1991). Juvenile delinquency entry and persistence: Do attention problems contribute to conduct problems? *Journal of Behavioral Theory and Experimental Psychiatry*, *22*, 261–264.

Frey, J. H. (1983). *Survey research by telephone*. Beverly Hills, CA: Sage.

Frick, P. J., Lahey, B. B., Kamphaus, R. W., Loeber, R., Christ, M. A. G., Hart, E. L., & Tannenbaum, L. E. (1991). Academic underachievement and the disruptive behavior disorders. *Journal of Consulting and Clinical Psychology*, *59*, 289–294.

Frick, P. J., Lahey, B. B., Loeber, R., Tannenbaum, L., Van Horn, Y., Christ, M. A. G., Hart, E. A., & Hanson, K. (1993). Oppositional defiant disorder and conduct disorder: A meta-analytic review of factor analyses and cross-validation in a clinic sample. *Clinical Psychology Review*, *13*, 319–340.

Gilmore, M. R., Hawkins, J. D., Catalano, R. F., Day, E. E., Moore, M., & Abbott, R. (1991). The structure of problem behavior in preadolescence. *Journal of Consulting and Clinical Psychology*, *59*, 499–506.

Gittelman, R., Mannuzza, S., Shenker, R., & Bonagura, N. (1985). Hyperactive boys almost grown up. *Archives of General Psychiatry*, *42*, 937–947.

Glueck, S., & Glueck, E. (1943). *Criminal careers in retrospect*. New York: The Commonwealth Fund.

Glueck, S., & Glueck, E. T. (1950). *Unravelling juvenile delinquency*. Cambridge, MA: Harvard University Press.

Glueck, S., & Glueck, E. T. (1968). *Delinquents and non-delinquents in perspective*. Cambridge, MA: Harvard University Press.

Gold, M., & Reimer, D. J. (1975). Changing patterns of delinquent behavior among Americans 13 to 16 years old: 1967–1972. *Crime and Delinquency Literature*, *7*, 483–517.

Gordon, R. A. (1968). Issues in multiple regression. *American Journal of Sociology*, *73*, 592–616.

Gottfredson, D. C., McNeil, R. J., & Gottfredson, G. D. (1991). Social area influences on delinquency—A multilevel analysis. *Journal of Research in Crime and Delinquency*, *28*, 197–226.

Gottfredson, M., & Hirschi, T. (1990). *A general theory of crime*. Stanford, CA: Stanford University Press.

Hare, R. D., Hart, S. D., & Harpur, T. J. (1991). Psychopathy and the DSM–IV criteria for antisocial personality disorder. *Journal of Abnormal Psychology*, *100*, 391–398.

Harris, L., & Associates. (1986). *Children's needs and public responsibility in the Pittsburgh area: A survey of local attitudes about the problems and prospects of American children*. Unpublished manuscript.

Hart, E. L., Lahey, B. B., Loeber, R., Applegate, B., & Frick, P. J. (1995). Developmental change in attention–deficit hyperactivity disorder in boys: A four-year longitudinal study. *Journal of Abnormal Child Psychology*, *23*, 729–749.

Hechtman, L., Weiss, G., Perlman, T., & Amsel, R. (1984). Hyperactives as young adults—initial predictors of adult outcome. *Journal of the American Academy of Child Psychiatry, 23,* 250–260.

Henry, B., Feehan, M., McGee, R., Stanton, W., Moffitt, T. E., & Silva, P. (1993). The importance of conduct problems and depressive symptoms in predicting adolescent substance use. *Journal of Abnormal Child Psychology, 21,* 469–480.

Hindelang, M. J., Hirschi, T., & Weis, J. G. (1981). *Measuring delinquency.* Beverly Hills, CA: Sage.

Hinshaw, S. P. (1987). On the distinction between attentional deficit/hyperactivity and conduct problems/aggression in child psychopathology. *Psychological Bulletin, 101,* 443–463.

Hinshaw, S. P., Lahey, B. B., & Hart, E. L. (1993). Issues of taxonomy and comorbidity in the development of conduct disorder. *Development and Psychopathology, 5,* 31–49.

Hoffman, M. S. (Ed.). (1991). *The world almanac and book of facts, 1992.* New York: Pharos.

Hollingshead, A. B. (1975). *Four factor index of social status.* New Haven, CT: Unpublished manuscript.

Holmes, S. J., & Robins, L. N. (1987). The influence of childhood disciplinary experience on the development of alcoholism and depression. *Journal of Child Psychology and Psychiatry, 28,* 399–416.

Holtzman, D., Lowry, R., Kann, L., Collins, J. L., Kolbe, L. J. (1994). Change in HIV-related information sources, instruction, knowledge, and behaviors among U.S. high school students, 1989 and 1990. *American Journal of Public Health, 84,* 389–393.

Huessy, H. R., & Howell, D. C. (1985). Relationship between adult and childhood behavior disorders. *Psychiatric Journal of the University of Ottawa, 10,* 114–119.

Huizinga, D. (1995). Developmental sequences in delinquency. In L. Crockett & N. Crowder (Eds.), *Pathways through adolescence: Individual development in context* (pp. 15–34). Hillsdale, NJ: Lawrence Erlbaum Associates.

Huizinga, D., Loeber, R., & Thornberry, T. (1993). Longitudinal study of delinquency, drug use, sexual activity, and pregnancy among children and youth in three cities. *Public Health Reports: Journal of the U.S. Public Health Service, 108* (Suppl. 1), 90–96.

Jensen, P.S., Shervette, R. E., Xenakis, S. N., & Richters, J. (1993). Anxiety and depression disorders in attention deficit disorder with hyperactivity: New findings. *American Journal of Psychiatry, 150,* 1203–1209.

Jessor, R., Donovan, J. E., & Costa, F. M. (1991). *Beyond adolescence: Problem behavior and young adult development.* Cambridge, England: Cambridge University Press.

Jessor, R., & Jessor, S. L. (1977). *Problem behavior and psychosocial development.* New York: Academic Press.

Johnston, L. D., O'Malley, P. M., & Bachman, J. G. (1993). *National survey results on drug use from Monitoring the Future Study, 1975–1992.* Rockville, MD: National Institute on Drug Abuse.

Justice, B., Justice, R., & Kraft, I. A. (1974). Early warning signs of violence: Is a triad enough? *American Journal of Psychiatry, 131,* 457–459.

Kandel, D. B. (1975). Stages in adolescent involvement in patterns of drug use. *Science, 190,* 912–914.

Kandel, D. B., Yamaguchi, K., & Chen, K. (1992). Stages of progression in drug involvement from adolescence to adulthood: Further evidence of the gateway theory. *Journal of Studies on Alcohol, 53,* 447–457.

Kaplan, H. B. (1980). *Deviant behavior in defense of self.* New York: Academic Press.

Kellam, S. G., Brown, C. H., Rubin, B. R., & Ensminger, M. E. (1983). Paths leading to teenage psychiatric symptoms and substance use: Developmental epidemiological studies in Woodlawn. In S. B. Guze, F. J. Earls, & J. E. Barrett (Eds.), *Childhood psychopathology and development* (pp. 17–51). New York: Raven.

Kellam, S. G., Ensminger, M. E., & Simon, M. B. (1980). Mental health in first grade and teenage drug, alcohol and cigarette use. *Drug and Alcohol Dependency, 5*, 273–304.

Kellam, S. G., Rebok, G. W., Mayer, L. S., Ialongo, N., & Kalodner, C. R. (1994). Depressive symptoms over first grade and their response to a developmental epidemiologically based preventive trial aimed at improving achievement. *Development and Psychopathology, 6*, 463–481.

Kellam, S. G., Werthamer-Larsson, L., Dolan, L. J., Brown, C. H., Mayer, L. S., Rebok, G. W., Anthony, J. C., Laudolff, J., & Edelson, G. (1991). Developmental epidemiologically based preventive trials: Baseline modeling of early target behaviors and depressed symptoms. *American Journal of Community Psychology, 19*, 563–584.

Klinteberg, B. A., Andersson, T., Magnusson, D., & Stattin, H. (1993). Hyperactive behavior in childhood as related to subsequent alcohol problems & violent offending—A longitudinal study of male subjects. *Personality and Individual Differences, 15*, 381–388.

Kolko, D. J. (1993). Conduct disorder and attention deficit disorder with hyperactivity in child inpatients: Comparisons on home and hospital measures. *Journal of Emotional and Behavioral Disorders, 1*, 75–86.

Kolvin, I., Miller, F. J. W., Fleeting, M., & Kolvin, P. A. (1988). Social and parenting factors affecting criminal-offense rates: Findings from the Newcastle 1000 Family Study (1947–1980). *British Journal of Psychiatry, 152*, 80–90.

Kolvin, I., Miller, F. J. W., Scott, D. McI., Gatzanis, S. R. M., & Fleeting, M. (1990). *Continuities of deprivation? The Newcastle 1000 Family Study.* Brookfield: Avebury.

Kovacs, M., Paulauskas, S., Gatsonis, C., & Richards, C. (1988). Depressive disorders in childhood. *Journal of Affective Disorders, 15*, 205–217.

Lahey, B. B., Loeber, R., Hart, E. L., Frick, P. J., Applegate, B., Zhang, Q., Green, S. M., & Russo, M. (1995). Four-year longitudinal study of conduct disorder: Patterns and predictors of persistence. *Journal of Abnormal Psychology, 104*, 83–93.

Lahey, B. B., Pelham, W. E., Schaughency, E. A., Atkins, M. S., Murphy, H. A., Hynd, G. W., Russo, M., Hartdagen, S., & Lorys-Vernon, A. (1989). Dimensions and types of attention deficit disorder. *Journal of the American Academy of Child and Adolescent Psychiatry, 27*, 330–335.

Lahey, B. B., Schaughency, E. A., Hynd, G. W., Carlson, C. L., & Nieves, N. (1987). Attention deficit disorder with and without hyperactivity: Comparison of behavioral characteristics of clinic-referred children. *Journal of the American Academy of Child and Adolescent Psychiatry, 26*, 718–723.

Le Blanc, M. (1994). Family, school, delinquency and criminality: The predictive power of an elaborated social control theory for males. *Criminal Behavior and Mental Health, 4*, 101–117.

Le Blanc, M., & Fréchette, M. (1989). *Male criminal activity from childhood through youth.* New York: Springer–Verlag.

Levine, R. (1988, November). In search of Eden: City stress index. *Psychology Today*, pp. 53–58.

Lewinsohn, P. M., Roberts, R. E., Seeley, J. R., Rhode, P., Gotlib, I. H., & Hops, H. (1994). Adolescent psychopathology: II. Psychosocial risk factors for depression. *Journal of Abnormal Psychology, 103*, 302–315.

Lewis, D. O., Shanok, S. S., Grant, M., & Ritvo, E. (1983). Homicidally aggressive young children: Neuropsychiatric and experimental correlates. *American Journal of Psychiatry, 140,* 148–153.

Loeber, R. (1982). The stability of antisocial and delinquent child behavior. *Child Development, 53,* 1431–1446.

Loeber, R. (1985). Patterns and development of antisocial child behavior. In G. J. Whitehurst (Ed.), *Annals of child development* (Vol. 2, pp. 77–116). Greenwich, CT: JAI Press.

Loeber, R. (1988). Natural histories of conduct problems, delinquency, and associated substance use. In B. B. Lahey & A. E. Kazdin (Eds.), *Advances in clinical child psychology* (Vol. 11, pp. 73–124). New York: Plenum.

Loeber, R., Brinthaupt, V. P., & Green, S. M. (1990). Attention deficits, impulsivity, and hyperactivity with or without conduct problems: Relationship to delinquency and unique contextual factors. In R. J. McMahon & R. DeV. Peters (Eds.), *Behavior disorders of adolescence: Research, intervention, and policy in clinical and school settings* (pp. 39–61). New York: Plenum.

Loeber, R., DeLamatre, M., Keenan, K., & Zhang, Q. (in press). A prospective replication of developmental pathways in distruptive and delinquent behavior. In R. Cairns (Ed.). *The individual as a focus in developmental research.* Thousand Oaks, CA: Sage.

Loeber, R., & Dishion, T. J. (1983). Early predictors of male delinquency: A review. *Psychological Bulletin, 94,* 68–99.

Loeber, R., Green, S. M., Keenan, K., & Lahey, B. B. (1995). Which boys will fare worse? Early predictors of the onset of conduct disorder in a six-year longitudinal study. *Journal of the American Academy of Child and Adolescent Psychiatry, 34,* 499–509.

Loeber, R., Green, S. M., & Lahey, B. B. (1990). Mental health professionals' perception of the utility of children, mothers, and teachers as informants on childhood psychopathology. *Journal of Clinical Child Psychology, 19,* 136–143.

Loeber, R., Green, S. M., Lahey, B. B., Christ, M. A. G., & Frick, P. J. (1992). Developmental sequences in the age of onset of disruptive child behaviors. *Journal of Child and Family Studies, 1,* 21–41.

Loeber, R., Green, S. M., Lahey, B. B., & Stouthamer-Loeber, M. (1989). Optimal informants on childhood disruptive behaviors. *Development and Psychopathology, 1,* 317–337.

Loeber, R., & Hay, D. F. (1994). Developmental approaches to aggression and conduct problems. In M. L. Rutter & D. H. Hay (Eds.), *Development through life: A handbook for clinicians* (pp. 488–515). Oxford: Blackwell.

Loeber, R., & Keenan, K. (1994). The interaction between conduct disorder and its comorbid conditions: Effects of age and gender. *Clinical Psychology Review, 14,* 497–523.

Loeber, R., Keenan, K. & Zhang, Q. (1997). Boys' experimentation and persistence in developmental pathways toward serious delinquency. *Journal of Child and Family Studies, 6,* 321–357.

Loeber, R., & Le Blanc, M. (1990). Toward a developmental criminology. In M. Tonry & N. Morris (Eds.), *Crime and Justice* (Vol. 12, pp. 375–473). Chicago: University of Chicago Press.

Loeber, R., Russo, M. F., Stouthamer-Loeber, M., & Lahey, B. B. (1994). Internalizing problems and their relation to the development of disruptive behaviors in adolescence. *Journal of Research on Adolescence, 4,* 615–637.

Loeber, R., & Schmaling, K. (1985a). Empirical evidence for overt and covert patterns of antisocial conduct problems. *Journal of Abnormal Child Psychology, 13,* 337–352.

Loeber, R., & Schmaling, K. (1985b). The utility of differentiating between mixed and pure forms of antisocial child behavior. *Journal of Abnormal Child Psychology, 13,* 315–336.

Loeber, R., & Snyder, H. N. (1990). Rate of offending in juvenile careers: Findings of constancy and change in lambda. *Criminology, 28,* 97–109.

Loeber, R., & Stouthamer-Loeber, M. (1986). Family factors as correlates and predictors of juvenile conduct problems and delinquency. In N. Morris & M. Tonry (Eds.), *Crime and justice* (Vol. 7, pp. 29–149). Chicago: University of Chicago Press.

Loeber, R., & Stouthamer-Loeber, M. (1987). Prediction. In H. C. Quay (Ed.), *Handbook of juvenile delinquency* (pp. 325 383). New York: Wiley.

Loeber, R., & Stouthamer-Loeber, M. (in press). The development of juvenile aggression and violence: Some common misconceptions and controversies. *American Psychologist.*

Loeber, R., Stouthamer-Loeber, M., & Green, S. M. (1991). Age at onset of problem behavior in boys, and later disruptive and delinquent behaviours. *Criminal Behavior and Mental Health, 1,* 229–246.

Loeber, R., Stouthamer-Loeber, M., Van Kammen, W. B., & Farrington, D. P. (1989). Development of a new measure of self-reported antisocial behavior for young children: Prevalence and reliability. In M. Klein (Ed.), *Cross-national research in self-reported crime and delinquency* (pp. 203–225). Dordrecht, Netherlands: Kluwer-Nijhoff.

Loeber, R., Tremblay, R. E., Gagnon, C., & Charlebois, P. (1989). Continuity and desistance in disruptive boys' early fighting in school. *Development and Psychopathology, 1,* 39–50.

Loeber, R., Wung, P., Keenan, K., Giroux, B., Stouthamer-Loeber, M., & Van Kammen, W. B. (1993). Developmental pathways in disruptive child behavior. *Development and Psychopathology, 5,* 101–132.

Maddahian, E. (1985). Single and multiple patterns of adolescent substance use: Longitudinal comparisons of four ethnic groups. *Journal of Drug Education, 15,* 311–326.

Magnusson, D. (1988). *Individual development from an interactional perspective: A longitudinal study.* Hillsdale, NJ: Lawrence Erlbaum Associates.

Magnusson, D., & Bergman, L. R. (1988). Individual and variable based approaches to longitudinal research on early risk factors. In M. Rutter (Ed.), *Studies of psychosocial risk* (pp. 45–61). Cambridge, England: Cambridge University Press.

Maguin, E. (1994). *Manual for retrieving juvenile court data from the Allegheny County Juvenile Court files.* Unpublished manuscript. Western Psychiatric Institute and Clinic, University of Pittsburgh, Pittsburgh, PA.

Maguin, E., & Loeber, R. (1996). Academic performance and delinquency. In M. Tonry (Ed.), *Crime and justice* (Vol. 20, pp. 145–264). Chicago: University of Chicago Press.

Mannuzza, S., Klein, R., Konig, P. H., & Giampino, T. (1989). Hyperactive boys almost grown up: IV. Criminality and its relationship to psychiatric status. *Archives of General Psychiatry, 46,* 1073–1079.

Mannuzza, S., Klein, R.G., Bessler, A., Malloy, P., & LaPadula, M. (1993). Adult outcome of hyperactive boys: Educational achievement, occupational rank, and psychiatric status. *Archives of General Psychiatry, 46,* 1073–1079.

Martin, C. S., Earleywine, M., Blackson, T. C., Vanyukov, M. M., Moss, H. B., & Tarter, R. E. (1994). Aggressivity, inattention, hyperactivity, and impulsivity in boys at high and low risk for substance abuse. *Journal of Abnormal Child Psychology, 22,* 177–204.

Masten, A. S. (1988). Toward a developmental psychopathology of early adolescence. In M. D. Levine & E. R. McAnarney (Eds.), *Early adolescent transitions* (pp. 261–278). Lexington, MA: Heath.

McCord, J. (1979). Some child-rearing antecedents of criminal behavior in adult men. *Journal of Personality and Social Psychology, 37,* 1477–1486.

McCord, J. (1982). A longitudinal view of the relationship between paternal absence and crime. In J. Gunn & D. P. Farrington (Eds.), *Abnormal offenders, delinquency and the criminal justice system* (pp. 113–128). London: Wiley.

McCord, J. (1991). Family relationships, juvenile delinquency, and adult criminality. *Criminology, 29*, 397–417.

McCord, J. (1994). Family socialization and antisocial behavior: Searching for causal relationships in longitudinal research. In E. G. M. Weitekamp & H–J. Kerner (Eds.), *Cross-national longitudinal research on human development and criminal behavior* (pp. 177–188). Dordrecht, Netherlands: Kluwer.

McCord, J., & Ensminger, M. E. (in press). Multiple risks and comorbidity in an African-American population. *Criminal Behavior and Mental Health.*

McGee, R., Williams, S., & Silva, P. A. (1985). Factor structure and correlations of ratings of inattention, hyperactivity, and antisocial behavior in a large sample of 9-year-old children from the general population. *Journal of Consulting and Clinical Psychology, 53*, 480–489.

Messer, S. C., Angold, A., Loeber, R., Costello, E. J., Van Kammen, W. B., & Stouthamer-Loeber, M. (1995). The development of a short questionnaire for use in epidemiological studies of depression in children and adolescents: Factor composition and structure across development. *International Journal of Methods in Psychiatric Research, 5*, 251–262.

Miller, B. C., & Dyk, P. A. H. (1993). Sexuality. In P. H. Tolan & B. H. Cohler (Eds.), *Handbook of clinical research & practice with adolescents* (pp. 95–123). New York: Wiley.

Miller, B. C., McCoy, J. K., Olson, T. D., & Wallace, C. M. (1986). Parental control attempts in relation to adolescent sexual attitudes and behavior. *Journal of Marriage and the Family, 48*, 503–512.

Moffitt, T. E. (1993). "Life-course-persistent" and "adolescent-limited" antisocial behavior: A developmental taxonomy. *Psychological Review, 100*, 674–701.

Moffitt, T. E., Silva, P. A., Lynam, D. R., & Henry, B. (1994). Self–reported delinquency at age 18: New Zealand's Dunedin Multidisciplinary Health and Developmental Study. In J. Junger-Tas, G. J. Terlouw, & M. W. Klein (Eds.), *Delinquent behavior among young people in the Western world. First results of the international self–report delinquency study* (pp. 354–369). Amsterdam: Kugler.

Moos, R. H., & Moos, B. S. (1975). Evaluating correctional and community settings. In R. H. Moos (Ed.), *Families* (pp. 263–286). New York: Wiley.

Morash, M., & Rucker, L. (1989). An exploratory study of the connection of mother's age at childbearing to her children's delinquency in four data sets. *Crime and Delinquency, 35*, 45–93.

Mott, F. L., & Haurin, R. J. (1988). Linkages between sexual activity and alcohol and drug use among American adolescents. *Family Planning Perspectives, 20*, 128–136.

National Center for Juvenile Justice (1994). *Juvenile court statistics, 1991.* Pittsburgh, PA: National Center for Juvenile Justice.

Nottelmann, E. D., & Jensen, P. S. (1995). Comorbidity of disorders in children and adolescents: Developmental perspectives. In T. H. Ollendick & R. J. Prinz (Eds.), *Advances in clinical child psychology* (Vol. 17, pp. 109–155). New York: Plenum.

Nye, F. I., & Short, J. F. (1957). Scaling delinquent behavior. *American Sociological Review, 22*, 326–331.

Nylander, I. (1979). A 20-year prospective follow-up study of 2, 164 cases at the child guidance clinics in Stockholm. *Acta Paediatrica Scandinavica, 68*, 1–45.

O'Donnell, J. A., & Clayton, R. R. (1979). Determinants of early marijuana use. In G. M. Besdner & A. S. Friedman (Eds.), *Youth drug abuse* (pp. 63–104). Lexington, MA: Lexington Books.

Offord, D. R., Alder, R. J., & Boyle, M. H. (1986). Prevalence and sociodemographic correlates of conduct disorder. *American Journal of Social Psychiatry, 4,* 272–278.

Offord, D. R., Sullivan, K., Allen, N., & Abrams, N. (1979). Delinquency and hyperactivity. *Journal of Nervous and Mental Disease, 167,* 734–741.

Olweus, D. (1979). Stability of aggressive reaction patterns in males: A review. *Psychological Bulletin, 86,* 822–857.

Osgood, D. W., Johnston, L. D., O'Malley, P. M., & Bachman, J. G. (1988). The generality of deviance in late adolescence and early adulthood. *American Sociological Review, 53,* 81–93.

Ouston, J. (1984). Delinquency, family background and educational attainment. *British Journal of Criminology, 24,* 2–26.

Parker, J. G., & Asher, S. R. (1987). Peer relations and later personal adjustment: Are low-accepted children at risk? *Psychological Bulletin, 102,* 357–389.

Patterson, G. R. (1982). *A social learning approach: Vol. 3. Coercive family process.* Eugene, OR: Castalia.

Patterson, G. R., & Forgatch, M. S. (1990). Initiation and maintenance of processes disrupting single-mother families. In G. R. Patterson (Ed.), *Depression and aggression in family interaction* (pp. 209–246). Hillsdale, NJ: Lawrence Erlbaum Associates.

Patterson, G. R., Reid, J. B., & Dishion, T. J. (1992). *Antisocial boys: A social interactional approach* (Vol. 4). Eugene, OR: Castalia.

Patterson, G. R., & Stouthamer-Loeber, M. (1984). The correlation of family management practices and delinquency. *Child Development, 55,* 1299–1307.

Paykel, E. S. (1971). Classification of depressed patients: A cluster analysis derived grouping. *British Journal of Psychiatry, 118,* 275–288.

Peterson, P. L., Hawkins, J. D., Abbott, R. D., & Catalano, R. F. (1994). Disentangling the effects of parental drinking, family management and parental alcohol norms on current drinking by black and white adolescents. *Journal of Research on Adolescence, 4,* 203–227.

Pittsburgh Public Schools. (1986). *Membership report as of September 22, 1986.* Unpublished document.

Pittsburgh Public Schools. (1987). *Membership report as of September 22, 1987.* Unpublished document.

Pliszka, S.R. (1992). Comorbidity of attention-deficit hyperactivity disorder and overanxious disorder. *Journal of the American Academy of Child and Adolescent Psychiatry, 31,* 197–203.

Puig-Antich, J. (1982). Major depression and conduct disorder in prepuberty. *Journal of the American Academy of Child Psychiatry, 21,* 118–128.

Puig–Antich, J., Goetz, D., Davies, M., Kaplan, T., Davies, J., Ostrow, L., Asnis, L., Twomey, J., Iyengar, S., & Ryan, N. D. (1989). A controlled family history study of prepubertal major depressive disorder. *Archives of General Psychiatry, 46,* 406–420.

Pulkkinen, L. (1988). Delinquent development: Theoretical and empirical considerations. In M. Rutter (Ed.), *Studies of psychosocial risk* (pp. 184–199). Cambridge, England: Cambridge University Press.

Pulkkinen, L., & Hurme, H. (1984). Aggression as a predictor of weak self–control. In L. Pulkkinen & P. Lytinen (Eds.), *Human action and personality* (pp. 172–189). Jyvaskyla, Finland: University of Jyvaskyla.

Pulkkinen, L., & Pitkanen, T. (1993). Continuities in aggressive behavior from childhood to adulthood. *Aggressive Behavior, 19,* 249–263.

Radke-Yarrow, M., Campbell, J. D., & Burton, R. V. (1968). *Childrearing: An inquiry into research and methods.* San Francisco: Jossey–Bass.

Reid, W. J., & Crisafulli, A. (1990). Marital discord and child behavior problems: A meta-analysis. *Journal of Abnormal Child Psychology, 18*, 105–117.

Reinherz, H. Z., Giaconia, R. M., Pakiz, B., Silverman, A. B., Frost, A. K., & Lefkowitz, E. S. (1993). Psychosocial risks for major depression in late adolescence—A longitudinal community study. *Journal of the American Academy of Child and Adolescent Psychiatry, 32*, 1155–1163.

Reiss, A. J. (1986). Co-offending influences on criminal careers. In A. Blumstein, J. Cohen, J. A. Roth, & C. A. Visher (Eds.), *Criminal careers and career criminals* (pp. 121–160). Washington, DC: National Academy Press.

Reiss, A. J., & Farrington, D. P. (1991). Advancing knowledge about co-offending: Results from a prospective longitudinal survey of London males. *Journal of Criminal Law and Criminology, 82*, 360–395.

Rey, J. M. (1994). Comorbidity between disruptive disorders and depression in referred adolescents. *Australian and New Zealand Journal of Psychiatry, 28*, 106–113.

Richman, N., Stevenson, J., & Graham, P. J. (1982). *Preschool to school: A behavioural study*. London: Academic Press.

Robins, L. N. (1966). *Deviant children grown up*. Baltimore: Williams & Wilkins.

Robins, L. N. (1979). Sturdy childhood predictors of adult outcomes: Replications from longitudinal studies. In J. E. Barrett, R. M. Rose, & G. L. Klerman (Eds.), *Stress and mental disorder* (pp. 219–235). New York: Raven.

Robins, L. (1986). Changes in conduct disorder over time. In D. C. Farren & J. D. McKinney (Eds.), *Risk in Intellectual and Psychosocial Development* (pp. 227–259). New York: Academic Press.

Robins, L. N., Darvish, H. S., & Murphy, G. E. (1970). The long-term outcome for adolescent drug users: A follow-up study of 76 users and 146 nonusers. In J. Zubin & A. M. Freedman (Eds.), *The psychopathy of adolescence* (pp. 628–684). New York: Grune & Stratton.

Robins, L. N., & Ratcliff, K. S. (1979). Risk factors in the continuation of childhood antisocial behavior into adulthood. *International Journal of Mental Health, 7*, 96–116.

Robins, L. N., & Wish, E. (1977). Childhood deviance as a developmental process: A study of 223 urban black men from birth to 18. *Social Forces, 56*, 448–473.

Rosenthal, R. (1983). Assessing the statistical and social importance of psychotherapy. *Journal of Consulting and Clinical Psychology, 51*, 4–13.

Roff, J. D., & Wirt, R. D. (1984). Childhood aggression and social adjustment as antecedents of delinquency. *Journal of Abnormal Child Psychology, 12*, 111–126.

Russo, M. F., & Beidel, D. C. (1994). Comorbidity of childhood anxiety & externalizing disorders: Prevalence, associated characteristics, and validation issues. *Clinical Psychology Review, 14*, 199–221.

Rutter, M. (1978). Family, area and school influences in the genesis of conduct disorders. In L. A. Hersov, M. Berger, & D. Shaffer (Eds.), *Aggression and antisocial behavior in childhood and adolescence* (pp. 95–113). Oxford: Pergamon.

Rutter, M. (1981a). The city and the child. *American Journal of Orthopsychiatry, 51*, 610–625.

Rutter, M. (1981b). Isle of Wight and Inner London studies. In S. A. Mednick & A. E. Baert (Eds.), *Prospective longitudinal research* (pp. 122–131). Oxford: Oxford University Press.

Rutter, M., Cox, A., Tupling, C., Berger, M., & Yule, W. (1975a). Attainment and adjustment in two geographical areas: I. The prevalence of psychiatric disorder. *British Journal of Psychiatry, 126*, 493–509.

Rutter, M., & Giller, H. (1983). *Juvenile delinquency: Trends and perspectives*. Harmondsworth: Penguin.

Rutter, M., Tizard, J., & Whitmore, K. (1970). *Education, health and behavior*. New York: Wiley.

Rutter, M., Yule, B., Quinton, D., Rowlands, O., Yule, W., & Berger, M. (1975b). Attainment and adjustment in two geographical areas: III. Some factors accounting for area differences. *British Journal of Psychiatry, 126,* 520–533.

Sampson, R. J., & Laub, J. H. (1993). *Crime in the making: Pathways and turning points through life.* Cambridge, MA: Harvard University Press.

Satterfield, J. H. (1987). The hyperactive child syndrome: A precursor of adult psychopathy? In R. D. Hare & D. Schalling (Eds.), *Psychopathic behavior: Approaches to research* (pp. 329–346). New York: Wiley.

Schachar, R., Rutter, M., & Smith, A. (1981). The characteristics of situationally and pervasively hyperactive children: Implications for syndrome definition. *Journal of Child Psychology and Psychiatry, 22,* 375–392.

Serbin, L. A., Moskowitz, D. S., Schwartzman, A. E., & Ledingham, J. E. (1991). Aggressive, withdrawn, and aggressive/withdrawn children in adolescence: Into the next generation. In D. J. Pepler & K. H. Rubin (Eds.), *The development and treatment of childhood aggression* (pp. 55–70). Hillsdale, NJ: Lawrence Erlbaum Associates.

Shannon, L. W. (1988). *Criminal career continuity: Its social context.* New York: Human Sciences Press.

Sharply, C. F., & Cross, D. G. (1982). A psychometric evaluation of the Spanier Dyadic Adjustment Scale. *Journal of Marriage and the Family, 49,* 739–741.

Shaw, C. R., & McKay, H. D. (1969). *Juvenile delinquency and urban areas.* Chicago: University of Chicago Press.

Simcha-Fagan, O., Gersten, J. C., & Langner, T. S. (1986). Early precursors and concurrent correlates of patterns of illicit drug use in adolescence. *Journal of Drug Issues, 16,* 7–28.

Simcha–Fagan, O., & Schwartz, J. E. (1986). Neighborhood and delinquency: An assessment of contextual effects. *Criminology, 24,* 667–703.

Skinner, H. A., Steinhauer, P. D., & Santa–Barbara, J. (1983). The family assessment measure. *Canadian Journal of Community Mental Health, 2,* 91–105.

Spanier, G. B. (1976). Measuring dyadic adjustment: New scales for assessing the quality of marriage and similar dyads. *Journal of Marriage and the Family, 38,* 15–28.

Stoolmiller, M. (1994). Antisocial behavior, delinquent peer association, and unsupervised wandering for boys: Growth and change from childhood to early adolescence. *Multivariate Behavioral Research, 29,* 263–288.

Stouthamer-Loeber, M. (1991). Young children's verbal misrepresentations of reality. In K. J. Rotenberg (Ed.), *Children's interpersonal trust: Sensitivity to lying, deception, and promise violation* (pp. 20–42). New York: Springer-Verlag.

Stouthamer-Loeber, M., Loeber, R., & Thomas, C. (1992). Caretakers seeking help for boys with disruptive and delinquent child behavior. *Comprehensive Mental Health Care, 2,* 159–178.

Stouthamer-Loeber, M., & Van Kammen, W. B. (1995). *Data collection and management: A practical guide.* Newbury Park, CA: Sage.

Stouthamer-Loeber, M., Van Kammen, W. B., & Loeber, R. (1992). The nuts and bolts of implementing large-scale longitudinal studies. *Violence and Victims, 7,* 63–78.

Stouthamer-Loeber, M., & Wei, E. (in press). The precursors of young fatherhood and its effect on the delinquency career of teenage males. *Journal of Adolescent Health.*

Thornberry, T. P., & Farnworth, M. (1982). Social correlates of criminal involvement: Further evidence on the relationship between social status and criminal behavior. *American Sociological Review, 47,* 505–518.

Thornberry, T., Huizinga, D., & Loeber, R. (1995). The prevention of serious delinquency and violence: Implications from the Program of Research on the Causes and Correlates of Delinquency. In J. Howell, B. Krisberg, D. Hawkins, & J. D. Wilson (Eds.), *Sourcebook on serious, violent and chronic juvenile offenders* (pp. 213–327). Thousand Oaks, CA: Sage.

Thornberry, T., Lizotte, A. J., Krohn, M. D., Farnworth, M., & Jang, S. J. (1994). Delinquent peers, beliefs, and delinquent behavior: A longitudinal test of interaction theory. *Criminology, 32*, 601–637.

Tildesley, E. A., Hops, H., Ary, D., & Andrews, J. A. (1995). Multitrait-multimethod model of adolescent deviance, drug use, academic, and sexual behaviors. *Journal of Psychopathology and Behavioral Assessment, 17*, 85–215.

Tonry, M., Ohlin, L. E., & Farrington, D. P. (1991). *Human Development and Criminal Behavior.* New York: Springer-Verlag.

Tracy, P. E., Wolfgang, M. E., & Figlio, R. M. (1985). *Delinquency in two birth cohorts.* Washington, DC: National Institute of Juvenile Justice and Delinquency Prevention.

Tracy, P. E., Wolfgang, M. E., & Figlio, R. M. (1990). *Delinquency careers in two birth cohorts.* New York: Plenum.

Trasler, G.B. (1962). *The explanation of criminality.* London: Routledge & Kegan Paul.

Tremblay, R. E., Massé, B., Perron, D., Le Blanc, M., Schwartzmann, A. E., & Ledingham, J. E. (1992). Early disruptive behavior, poor school achievement, delinquent behavior, and delinquent personality: Longitudinal analyses. *Journal of Consulting and Clinical Psychology, 60*, 64–72.

Tremblay, R.E., Vitaro, F., Bertrand, L., Le Blanc, M., Beauchesne, H., Boileau, H., & David, L. (1992). Parent and child training to prevent early onset of delinquency: The Montreal longitudinal-experimental study. In J. McCord & R. Tremblay (Eds.), *Preventing antisocial behavior* (pp. 117–138). New York: Guilford.

Udry, J.R. (1988). Biological predispositions and social control in adolescent sexual behavior. *American Sociological Review, 53*, 709–722.

U.S. Department of Commerce. (1990). *Census of population and housing.* Washington, DC: U.S. Department of Commerce, Bureau of the Census.

Van Kammen, W. B., & Loeber, R. (1994). Are fluctuations in delinquent activities related to the onset and offset of juvenile illegal drug use and drug dealing? *Journal of Drug Issues, 24*, 9–24.

Van Kammen, W., Loeber, R., & Stouthamer-Loeber, M. (1991). Substance use and its relationship to conduct problems and delinquency in young boys. *Journal of Youth and Adolescence, 20*, 399–414.

Velez, C. N., Johnson, J., & Cohen, P. (1989). A longitudinal analysis of selected risk factors for childhood psychopathology. *Journal of the American Academy of Child and Adolescent Psychiatry, 28*, 861–864.

Wadsworth, M. (1979). *Roots of delinquency: Infancy, adolescence and crime.* London: Martin Robertson.

Wadsworth, M. E. J. (1991). *The imprint of time.* Oxford: Oxford University Press.

Wechsler, H., & Thum, D. (1973). Teen-age drinking, drug use, and social correlates. *Quarterly Journal of Studies on Alcohol, 34*, 1220–1227.

Weinrott, M. (1975). *Manual for retrieval of juvenile court data.* Unpublished manuscript, Evaluation Research Group, Eugene, OR.

Weiss, G., & Hechtman, L. T. (1986). *Hyperactive children grown up.* New York: Guilford.

Werner, E. E., & Smith R. S. (1982). *Vulnerable but invincible.* New York: McGraw-Hill.

Werner, E. E., & Smith, R. S. (1992). *Overcoming the Odds.* Ithaca, NJ: Cornell University Press.

West, D.J. (1982). *Delinquency: Its roots, careers and prospects.* London: Heinemann.

West, D. J., & Farrington, D. P. (1973). *Who becomes delinquent?* London: Heinemann.

West, D. J., & Farrington, D. P. (1977). *The delinquent way of life.* London: Heinemann.

White, H. R. (1988). Longitudinal patterns of cocaine use among adolescents. *American Journal of Drug and Alcohol Abuse, 14,* 1–15.

White, H. R. (1990). The drug use-delinquency connection in adolescence. In R. Weisheit (Ed.), *Drugs, crime and the criminal justice system* (pp. 215–256). Cincinnati, OH: Anderson.

White, H. R., & Labouvie, E. W. (1994). Generality versus specificity of problem behavior: Psychological and functional differences. *Journal of Drug Issues, 24,* 55–74.

Wiggins, J. S. (1973). *Personality and prediction: Principles of personality assessment.* Reading, MA: Addison Wesley.

Wikström, P.-O. (1990). Age and crime in a Stockholm cohort. *Journal of Quantitative Criminology, 6,* 61–84.

Wilens, T. E., Biederman, J., Spencer, T. J., & Frances, R. J. (1994). Comorbidity of attention deficit hyperactivity and psychoactive substance use disorders. *Hospital and Community Psychiatry, 45,* 421–423, 435.

Williams, C., & Bybee, J. (1994). What do children feel guilty about? Developmental and gender differences. *Developmental Psychology, 30,* 617–623.

Wolfgang, M., Figlio, R. M., Tracy, P. E., & Singer, S. I. (1985). *The National Survey of Crime Severity.* Washington, DC: U.S. Government Printing Office.

Wolfgang, M. E., Thornberry, T. P., & Figlio, R. M. (1987). *From boy to man, from delinquency to crime.* Chicago: University of Chicago Press.

Yamaguchi, K., & Kandel, D. B. (1984). Patterns of drug use from adolescence to young adulthood: II. Sequences of progression. *American Journal of Public Health, 74,* 668–672.

Zeitlin, H. (1986). *The natural history of psychiatric disorder in children.* Oxford: Oxford University Press.

Zelnik, M., & Shah, F. K. (1983). First intercourse among young Americans. *Family Planning Perspectives, 15,* 64–70.

Author Index

A

Abbott, R. D. 5, 12, *297, 291*
Abernathy, T., 92, *287*
Abikoff, H., 166, *285*
Abrams, N., 166, *297*
Achenbach, T. M., 3, 6, 40, 42, 201, *285, 289*
Adler, R. J., 92, *297*
Ageton, S. S., 10, 40, *289*
Agresti, A., 276, *285*
Alexander, C. S., 87, *285*
Allen, N., 166, *297*
Alterman, A. I., 148, *285*
Amdur, R. L., 10, 106, *285*
American Psychiatric Association, 1, 7, 44, 88, 107, 165, 264, *285, 286*
Amsel, R., 148, 166, *292*
Anastopoulos, A. D., 183, *286*
Anderson, J. C., 91, 201, *286*
Andersson, T., 13, 148, 199, *293*
Andrews, J. A., 5, *300*
Angel, R., 271, *288*
Angold, A., 44, 92, 206, 215, *286, 288, 296*
Anthony, J. C., 201, 202, *293*
Applegate, B., 3, 92, 257, *291, 293*
Armistead, L., 166, *291*
Arneklev, B. J., 124, *288*
Ary, D., 5, 162, *286, 300*
Asher, S. R., 188, *286, 297*
Asnis, L., 201, *297*
Atkins, M. S., 183, *293*
August, G. J., *286*

B

Bachman, J. G., 5, 7, 91, *292, 297*
Baker, L., 166, *287*
Balka, E. B., 92, *287*
Barkley, R. A., 183, 239, *286, 291*
Barnes, H., 46, *286*
Baumeister, R. F., 107, *286*
Beardslee, W. R., 202, *286*
Beauchesne, H., 14, *300*
Beidel, D. C., 201, *298*
Bell, R. M., 3, 91, *289*
Bell, R. Q., 14, 20, *286*
Belson, W. A., 4, 93, *286*
Bemporad, J., 202, *286*
Berger, M., 127, 128, *298, 299*
Bergman, L. R., 271, *295*
Bertrand, L., 14, *300*
Bessler, A., 87, 166, *295*
Biederman, J., 148, 182, 183, 201, 221, *286, 289, 301*
Biglan, A., 162, *286*
Bird, H. R., 91, *286*
Blackson, T. C., 254, *295*
Blouin, A. G., 124, *286*
Blouin, J., 124, *286*
Blumstein, A., 2, *286*
Boileau, H. 14, *300*
Bonagura, N., 123, 148, *291*
Boyle, J. M., 148, *287*
Boyle, M. A., 134, 148, *287*
Boyle, M. H., 92, *297*

303

Subject Index

A

Academic achievement
  association to outcomes, 230
  attention-deficit hyperactivity, 169, 170,
      178, 179, 181
    hierarchical multiple regression analy-
        ses, 173, 174
    interaction effects, 176, 177
  conduct problems, 171, 172
    hierarchical multiple regression analy-
        ses, 173, 175
    interaction effects, 176, 177
  construct, 62
  covert behavior, 190, 191
  depressed mood, 202, 204, 205, 214
  delinquency, 109, 110, 114, 115, 123
  multiproblem boys, 243, 244, 245, 246
  physical aggression, 188, 189
  scores and school selection, 28
  sexual intercourse, 156, 157, 162
  shy/withdrawn behavior, 209, 210
  substance use, 138, 139
    hierarchical multiple regression analy-
        ses, 142, 143
    interaction effects detection, 144, 145
    study comparisons, 148
Address, update in data collection, 34
ADHD, see Attention-Deficit Hyperactivity Dis-
    order
Adult behavior, emulation and parental/society
    concerns, 1–2

African Americans, see also Caucasians; Ethnic-
    ity
  delinquency, 230
    hierarchical multiple regression, 115, 116
    risk factors, 110, 111
    seriousness and predictions of Juvenile
        Court petitions, 102–103
  depressed mood, 205, 206
  multiproblem boys, 243, 244
  physical aggression, 188, 189
  sexual intercourse
    age shift, 257
    comparative studies, 161
    hierarchical multiple regression analy-
        ses, 159, 160
    interaction effects, 160
    prevalence and delinquency, 155, 156
    risk factor, 162
    versus caucasians, 151–152
  study participants reports, 28, 32, 36, 68
Age
  delinquency
    at onset, 54, 78–80, 90
    depressed mood, 203
    parents at birth of participant and risk,
        110, 111, 115, 116
    seriousness classification, 77, 78, 99
    shifts, 255–256, 279
    substance use in comparison studies,
        147–148
  depressed mood and shy/withdrawn behav-
      ior, 215–216

309

Y

Young parents construct, parents reports, 69
Youth Risk Behavior Survey-1990, study comparison with Pittsburgh Youth study, 92
Youth Self-Report (YSR)

administration during assessment, 40, 43, 44, 45
competence construct, 62
delinquency construct, 53
psychopathology and conduct behavior construct, 60
YSR, *see* Youth Self-Report